YES, YOUR PARENTS
ARE CRAZY!

Michael J. Bradley, Ed.D.

Cartoons by Randy Glasbergen

HARBOR PRESS

GIG HARBOR, WA

Library of Congress Cataloging-in-Publication Data

Bradley, Michael J., 1951–
Yes, your parents are crazy! a teen survival guide / Michael J. Bradley.
p. cm.
Summary: Discusses the difficulties of being a teenager in today's society and provides insights on how to survive adolescence and stay connected with one's parents.
Includes bibliographical references and index.
ISBN 13: 978-0-936197-48-7
Teenagers—United States. 2. Parent and teenager—United States. 3. Adolescence.
[1. Teenagers. 2. Parent and teenager. 3. Adolescence.] I. Title.

HQ796.B6862 2004
305.235—dc22

2003056689

YES, YOUR PARENTS ARE CRAZY!
A Teen Survival Guide

Text copyright © 2004 by Michael J. Bradley
Cartoons copyright © 1996, 1997, 1998, 2000, 2002, 2003 by Randy Glasbergen

All rights reserved. No part of this book may be reproduced in any form by any means without permission in writing from the publisher.

Printed in the United States of America
10 9 8 7

Harbor Press, Inc.
P.O. Box 1656
Gig Harbor, WA 98335

HARBOR PRESS and the nautilus shell design are registered trademarks of Harbor Press, Inc.

To Hajime Kondo and Steve McWilliams
Though now they smile from another place,
their love still warms us here.

Visit Michael J. Bradley, Ed.D., on the Internet at
www.docmikebradley.com

Contents

Foreword

Being a teenager can be hard sometimes. Not long ago, I struggled with the same problems you do and felt the same things you feel. I was that nice, kind of nerdy, average kid who sits next to you in school. I wanted to be cool and to fit in, but I never really felt good about myself—how I looked, how I dressed—all the stuff that seems really important to you. Now I understand that my clothes and my "look" are just the "wrapping," what's on the *outside*. What really counts is what's *inside* of me—who I am, what I believe in. When I changed my look for *American Idol*, it felt strange at first, but then I realized that I'm still the same person on the *inside*. And I'm still the same person I was back in high school; I just have a different wrapping now.

Believe me, I know how hard it is to be comfortable with yourself when you're a teenager. When I was about 17, I finally decided that it was just too much work to try to be what other kids thought was acceptable, and I decided to be who I am—nothing more, nothing less. That's when everything changed. I was finally able to focus on what's important to *me*. I still wasn't the coolest kid in school, but it gave me the confidence to open up to more people and become more outgoing. The more comfortable I was with myself, the more comfortable other people were with me. For the first time, I felt really good about *myself*.

So much of what helped me get through those tough times came from good adults around me. Yes, parents can be annoying, even "crazy," and yes, teachers can be boring. But the truth is that those annoying, boring adults can help you a lot, if you can somehow learn how to talk and listen to each other—I mean *really* talk, and *really* listen. I was cut by *American Idol* twice before I made it to the finals, but I never quit chasing my dream. I kept on going. I didn't learn how to do that from some high school football jock. I learned that from good adults (including my mom), as well as good friends, who encouraged me to believe in myself. I also learned that from the special-needs kids I taught for eight years, and from their parents. Although I was the "teacher," the parents and the kids taught me so much about character and determination and compassion. Most of all, they taught me the importance of having faith in yourself in spite of the challenges you face.

This book is awesome. It will help you discover how to believe in yourself and see how easy it is to feel comfortable with who you really are, not who others think you should be. It's amazing how many times I saw myself and my friends in so many of Dr. Bradley's stories. I think you'll recognize yourself in some of them, too.

I know your parents might seem "crazy" to you sometimes, but the good ones can really help you through this confusing time in your life. Though they might make lots of mistakes along the way, your parents are trying as hard as they can to bring out the best in you. Try to be patient and open-minded. If you are, you might find your "crazy" self feeling a little closer to your "crazy" parents. Then, both of you won't feel quite so crazy anymore. That, I think, is the best thing of all.

CLAY AIKEN
Raleigh, NC

Before You Begin...

The world is far more difficult and confusing today than it was when your parents were young. When they were teenagers, knives didn't usually kill and no one had semiautomatic weapons. Marijuana was not laced with PCP, and crack cocaine—the most addictive of all drugs—was not being used. Sex could lead to pregnancy, but not AIDS. And most parents didn't pressure their kids to be absolutely the best at everything—school, sports, music, you name it.

But in spite of the massive challenges you face, now is the time for you to begin the process of figuring out *who you are* and who you want to become. This means that you need to experiment with different ideas and experiences, without being *told* what to think and how to feel. Throughout this book, Dr. Bradley will encourage you to explore all of your options as you search for the path you want to travel in life. And he'll provide you with lots of company for the journey, as he shares dozens of stories of teens, just like you, who are trying to make sense of the world and its problems—things like divorce, blended families, and rejection by other kids at school.

Also, after you read this book, I think you'll be surprised at how much better you'll understand your parents and their behavior. There are lots of good adults around who are on your side. Finding an adult who will listen—parent, teacher, counselor, coach—is often the most important step to solving whatever problems you face. When someone is in serious trouble, you or a friend, telling an adult you trust can be the most important thing you do.

Your friends also make a tremendous difference in your life. I once received a telephone call from a 15-year-old patient of mine who was concerned about a friend with an eating disorder. She and five other friends were very worried about this girl, who had gone from 130 to 85 pounds and vomited "secretly" after lunch each day. After

I suggested that the girls do an intervention, they dragged their friend into the guidance counselor's office and she called the girl's mother. As a result, the anorectic girl was taken to an eating disorders specialist and later—much later—thanked her friends for saving her life. In Dr. Bradley's book, you'll read many stories like this one that will illustrate how good friends can make a big difference when you need them the most.

Surrounding yourself with good adults and good friends will get you through even the most difficult times. The most important message for you to take away from this excellent book is that you *will* be able to cope with all of the ups and downs in life if you don't try to go it alone.

Clarice J. Kestenbaum, M.D.
Past President of the American Academy of Child and Adolescent Psychiatry

Acknowledgments

First, to all of those who shaped my thoughts, and so, shaped this book, the best I can do is to say thank you. Thanks to Bonnie Arena, Pete Bradley, Tony Chunn, Joe Ducette, Mattie Gershenfeld, Barry Kayes, Terry Longren, Father Michael McCarthy, Father John Riley, Chuck Schrader, Ginny Smith-Harvey, Gene Stivers, and Pat Williams.

Second, an incredibly inadequate thank you to that incredible team at Harbor Press. To Harry Lynn, publisher and iron will of this work. His unflagging determination through the darkest of days is an inspiration to us all. To Debby Young, editor and seamstress of this work. Her amazing magic weaves the thoughts of this author into polished threads of gold. To Peg Booth, publicist and promoter of this work: A woman who taught me to refuse to believe in rejection. And to Sandy McWilliams, publicity director and spiritual voice of this project. Her passionate wisdom makes the impossible probable.

Finally, thanks to the folks to whom I owe debts I can never repay. First, to my daughter Sarah, who is my joy: Thank you for all that adult understanding when your five-year-old face fell a thousand times after hearing me say I had no time to play. Without you, our family would be without life.

To my son Ross, who is my courage: Thanks for taking care of my family when I could not. I cannot tell you how much I love and admire who you are. Without you, our family would be without laughter.

And to my wife Cindy, who is my vision. Any good that ever springs from my life is all from you. Without you, our family would not be. You are the best person I will ever know. With all my love, I thank you.

Introduction

I could only sit and shake my head at Gerald's incredible predicament. I had to find a way to respond to this confused and upset 15-year-old boy so he wouldn't quit talking. Only last week, Gerald had finally begun to open up to me after two months of sessions, and I didn't want to blow it. To buy thinking time, I exhaled loudly and said, "OK, Gerald, tell me the story once again, so I get all the parts straight."

As he started retelling the tale, I sat back and reviewed my picture of Gerald: 8th grade honor student, 10th grade truant; 8th grade Abercrombie & Fitch, 10th grade skater baggies; 8th grade DARE group leader, 10th grade drug probation; 8th grade Dad's golfing buddy, 10th grade "orphan" ("I disowned my parents"); 8th grade smiles, 10th grade "thousand-yard-stare"; 8th grade church choir, 10th grade religion-hater; 8th grade naive and happy, 10th grade cynical and miserable; 8th grade perfect kid, 10th grade gangster. Simple, right? Gerald just changed. But it wasn't that simple at all. Adolescence is anything but simple. Gerald made this point clear as I continued to listen to his story.

> ". . . then Roger grabs me and says, 'Dude, I can't take the rap on this. I'm on serious probation. They'll put me away this time. You owe me, man. You have to say you did it, or at least don't tell them that I did.'" Gerald paused here and began staring out the office window as if he was seeing the scene he was describing. "Just then we hear sirens, and they're getting louder. Kids were running everywhere, bailing from the party through doors and windows. I freaked and pinned Roger against the wall. I screamed at him. I asked what was up with him, since he knew Kara was already messed up, and that she had a problem with

pills, and that he was supposed to be her friend, so how could he have given her all those Xanax (powerful tranquilizer pills).

"Roger started to cry. He was messed up, too. But then he zapped me. He told me that I had scored pills for Kara a couple of months before."

Gerald slowly shook his head at himself. "And that's true. He said I was just as guilty for her as he was, and that the cops would go lighter on me than him, and that he had taken the rap for me at school with a pipe they found in my locker. That was true too. It hit me right there what a screw-up I am.

"I couldn't think, you know? Like, in slow motion, I watch Roger take his bag of pills and push them into my hand. Then he bolts. I was frozen there, trying to think what I should do. I look back into the bedroom and see Kara's still lying there not moving, and now she's turning blue. Some kid knocks me down trying to get past me, and the pills fly all over. He stops, and looks at them, looks at me, and he screams, 'You f'ng bastard, you f'ng bastard.' I start to pick up the pills to run and ditch them, but then I think I can't leave Kara like that since she's maybe dying. Everything is still like, in slow motion. I go into the bedroom and try and get Kara breathing by slapping and shaking her.

"The next thing I know I'm on my back, seeing stars, and looking up at this huge cop. He's saying, 'Are these your pills, son? These are yours, right? You wanna tell me where you got them, son?' And standing behind him is the kid who ran me over in the hall. He's crying, and screaming, and pokin' his finger at me sayin', 'That's him! That's the kid who killed Kara!' The cop, he keeps askin' me questions, but the only thing I can hear is that he keeps calling me 'son,' you know?"

Gerald paused here and turned his gaze back to me. He had been very animated as he talked, very different from his usual slouched-back, half-closed-eyes, I-really-don't-give-a-damn pose. But suddenly, that gunfighter sneer of his that he called "Mr. Tude" (for attitude) reappeared. "I know what I did then was stupid," he grinned, "but I just can't stop myself. 'Mr. Tude,' you know? I sat up and rubbed my head where the cop had hit me, and I said . . ."

I interrupted Gerald. "Let me guess. I think I saw this in a Clint Eastwood movie. You said 'I'm not your son,' right?"

"Close," Gerald corrected. "I said 'I ain't your f'ng son.' Funny, huh?" The Clint Eastwood sneer evaporated as Gerald listened to his own words. Mr. Tude disappeared with a sigh, never to return.

"Anyway, the cops knew Kara was alive and on the way to the hospital. But they tell me she's probably dead by now, and that I better tell them where I got the pills, so things would go easier on me. But if Kara was dead, then I wanted . . . didn't care what happened to me, so I kept sayin' that the pills were mine, and that I'd never say where I got them. Why get anybody else in trouble if my life is over, right?

"Later, at the police station, a nice cop tells me that Kara was probably gonna' be OK, and now did I want to tell him about the pills; that if I cooperated maybe I could avoid goin' to 'juvey' (juvenile prison), that all he wanted from me was a name. I just stared at him while a thousand pictures flashed through my head: like Roger in handcuffs, knowin' I turned him in; Kara in the hospital with her parents there crying; that kid saying I killed her. Then I pictured my friends' faces if I ratted out Roger. I saw my own parents' faces, hearing that I'd almost killed a kid. And Roger's parents' faces if they thought he'd almost killed a kid. Last, I pictured your face when you told me last week how, like, impressed you were that I'd been straight for two months, and I thought of how you'd look if you heard I'd almost killed a kid with drugs."

Gerald stopped talking here and stared at the carpet between his boots. He always made me crazy when he did this, leaving me hanging in the middle of a story. But he wasn't just playing with me for fun this time.

"So?" I finally asked.

"So?" he mimicked, "What would you have done?"

When I tried to wave off his question as unimportant, Gerald raised his eyes to lock on mine: "I really need to know this. If I'm supposed to trust you, I need to know who you are, what you think is right, and what kind of kid you were. So, what-would-you-have-done?"

Now a thousand pictures started rushing through my head about the impossible dilemmas that confront teenagers today. Like having to make life-altering decisions about issues that are very complicated, even for adults, such as sex, drugs, and violence. And you have to do this when you're too young to handle this stuff well. I pictured Gerald possibly going away to prison. I imagined him coming out of jail, cold and tough, locked and loaded for revenge against the world.

As if in a chess game I started to think of how my possible answers to his question might play out, and that I had to invent a good answer to keep my connection with him. Then, in his eyes, I saw what he was really looking for: Truth. Simple, straight-up honesty from an adult.

"Gerald," I sighed, "I hate to tell you this, since I don't want to lose your respect, and then you might stop talking to me. But the answer to your question is that I would have ratted Roger out, and then I would have told everyone that I did it because it was the 'right' thing to do. The ugly truth is that I'd rat him out only because I was scared, not 'right.' In your place, I'd never have worried about anyone but myself. I have to tell you that, even now, as an adult, while I don't agree with your view of things, I am in awe of how you struggle with these tough decisions." Then I waited for the shoe to drop.

After 10 seconds of staring hard at me with those half-closed eyes, Gerald slowly smiled. "OK," he said, "I don't care if you narc'd somebody out when you were a kid. I just don't want you to BS me now. Adults hardly ever tell the truth, you know. It's hard to find one who does. I need to know that you'll tell me the truth, even if you think it'll make you look bad. Adults don't do that, you know. They're kinda' crazy that way."

As he slowly shook his head, I knew that Gerald was picturing his parents, who had flat-out lied to him about some weed he had found stashed in their bedroom two years ago. Instead of owning up, they had used the same lame excuse every teen uses when he gets caught with something. They said they were "holding it for a friend." Sure.

Gerald recalled that scene as the beginning of the end of his closeness with his parents, and the start of his "crazy" years. As he painfully related that conversation, you could almost hear the shattering of his loving connection with his parents, a bond that might have helped him avoid so much pain through his teen years.

Gerald was right and yet wrong about adults. They are frequently less than honest with their kids, but for many reasons aside from not wanting to look bad. Often, they lie for your own good, or so they believe. Like to protect you from something you're not ready to know, or so they assume. Or perhaps to avoid something that would make you stop loving them, or so they fear. Sometimes, they'll even lie by pretending that they're something better than they are, in the hope that you'll become something better than they are. Or so they wish.

Of course, none of this works. What works best for parents is what works best for kids: being honest. Parents usually know this, but they continue to do these strange sorts of things that can make tough teen/parent relationships even tougher. They often do the worst of things with the best of intentions. That's because, like I said to Gerald after he told his story, "Yes, your parents are crazy!"

Which brings me to the first goal of this book: *understanding your crazy parents.* Throughout this book, while we're talking about your own struggles with the "craziness" of adolescence, we'll also be talking about your struggles with those rapidly aging, often confused, occasionally terrified, and strangely dressed folks who now mostly stand off to the side of your life (except when they get in your face, from time to time): Hello, Mom and Dad. We have to talk about them because, as it turns out, your adolescent "craziness" is contagious: You can make your parents crazy, as well. And yet, having parents who stay sane turns out to be a great help to you in surviving these years.

Your parents can get nuts in lots of different ways. Some become too controlling and strict. Others become too laid back and let kids do whatever. Still others just seem overwhelmed, helpless, and confused, and they whine and nag a lot. Many go back and forth between these styles (these parents might be the most confusing of all). But you can survive this "parent craziness" *if it is caused by your parents' love for you.* Almost always, that is the case. Before you read on, you need to ask yourself if that's true for your parents. And think about your answer right up front, because your answer changes everything.

Some crazy parents are controlling, or permissive, or nagging because they really don't love their kids. These parents are too involved in themselves to care much about their kids. These are truly scary folks, like abusers or addicts. Luckily, they are also rare folks. The fact is that most parents *do love their children.* Sometimes clumsily, often stupidly, but always with the best intentions. Most controlling, permissive, and nagging parents become that way because they think it will help their kids. So before you proceed, take a minute and ask yourself this question: Are my parents nuts because they love me, or because they don't care about me? If you choose Door Number Two, be sure that it's not your anger talking. Often, we get confused and feel that people who make us mad do so because they don't love us. The weird thing is that the folks who can make you the maddest are often the ones who love you the most. They are also the ones who show up to cover your back when you're up against a wall. Parents are almost always those kinds of people, the ones who make you miserable, yet who would take a bullet for you without thinking. Try to hold onto that thought as we criticize and joke about parents. Remember that what's in their heart is what truly counts. This thought can make all the difference in helping you to hold onto them as you crash through the million changes going on in your world.

Each of these changes you're going through is like an earthquake. Your "quakes" (changes) rattle everything around you, especially your parents. Sometimes, these tremors can cause mountains (like family traditions) to collapse, phone towers (like child/parent communication) to fall, and safety structures (like loving parent connections) to fail. Far too often, the fallout from adolescence can make your family look like "The Big One" just hit. *But it doesn't have to be that way.*

You can help make your family adolescence-proof, just as we can make buildings earthquake-proof. With a little work, you and your parents can make your relationships strong enough to absorb these shocks without cracking a single foundation, without losing any love. Just as with buildings, we do this by making families *flexible,* helping them learn to *adjust* to teenage changes, instead of going to war over them.

Nobody really wins a war, you know. One side just loses more than the other. Everybody loses—and usually they all lose a lot. But *adolescence does not have to become a war within your family.* I promise you that you really can grow and change and become a young adult with very few family fireworks.

Speaking of fireworks, the second goal of this book is *figuring out who you are*—what you believe in and what you stand for, so you can build a happy ending to your own story and maybe Gerald's, as well. When you think about it, in one very important way, Gerald is just like you and your friends: He has suddenly been thrown into an incredibly complex and dangerous world at a time when he doesn't know who he is or how he's supposed to live, a world in which adults don't seem to have many answers for themselves, let alone for him. Gerald could be the poster boy for today's adolescents.

When I sat down to write this book, I couldn't get Gerald's face and words out of my head: "*Adults hardly ever tell the truth . . . they're kinda' crazy that way.*" I remembered how close I came to lying to him that day, and that made me realize how I'd never have read a book like this, written by an adult, when I was a teenager. I didn't trust many grown-ups, either. I can remember quite clearly the times when they hit me for hitting, cursed at me for cursing, and insulted me for being insulting. I can remember adults telling me I shouldn't do things that they did themselves, like drink. I remember too few grown-ups who taught kids with tolerance, love, and respect. I can so clearly remember feeling alone, and trying to figure out who I was in a world that I thought was dangerous and scary.

I hope you come from a world with better adults around you, because you live in a world that's 10 times scarier and 20 times more dangerous than my world (and your parents') was, which makes figuring out who you are that much harder. *But figuring out who you are is your number-one job right now,* because the more you discover about yourself, *the better life gets for you*. You'll feel more sane, accomplish more goals, do fewer crazy things, get along better with people (especially your parents), worry less, and become *happy* with your life (yes, this is possible). Shrinks call getting to know yourself *identity development,* or *identity consolidation*. I call it growing up.

But growing up does not mean just getting older. As you can tell by looking at the adult world around you, a lot of adults are not grown-ups. Growing up is really about becoming in charge of yourself and making sense out of your life. Doing this requires that you first figure out who you are, the second goal this book is going to help you to accomplish.

And here's the third: giving you some "down and dirty" suggestions for how to handle life in the adolescent lane. These tips are what most kids read these books for: to get some ideas about how to survive your teen years, and maybe even to have some fun while you're surviving. But a lot of kids have told me that the "down and dirty" suggestion books often don't help because each teen and each teen's world are so different that it's impossible to come up with one suggestion that works for all. That's why the first two goals of this book (understanding your parents and understanding yourself) are really the most important. They give you the tools you need to build your own solutions to your own problems. And your own solutions will work best of all.

We're going to hit those three goals by looking at adolescence in three parts. In Part One, you'll learn about how your brain and your body work. I think you're going to be amazed by this part. For example, we just recently discovered that your brain is going through huge growth changes that can sometimes cause you to think weird thoughts, act on some weird impulses, feel very confused, and occasionally worry about going crazy. These physical changes are why, so often, you honestly have no answer when somebody asks why you said or did some strange thing. Part One might help you to not feel so weirded out about yourself.

In Part Two, we'll look at the world you live in and see how it may be affecting you. In case you haven't noticed, it's an over-the-edge, hypocritical, and dangerous place. In many ways, *we adults* tell you that drugs, sex, and rock 'n roll (violence) are cool to do, and then we go crazy if you do it. This second part of the book will help you begin to see who you are, apart from this toxic world we handed to you, and will help you develop your own values that can keep you sane and alive.

Part Three is about the issues you have to deal with every day. Here, we'll take a look at the million and one concerns that confront you, and give you some ideas that might help you to figure them out. These ideas aren't mine; they're coming from good friends of yours, who you're about to meet.

This book is really like talking with a hundred Geralds. It is a collection of actual conversations with other kids coping with adolescence. All of the stories you'll read here are true. They are case notes from my files of working with teenagers (although I've hidden their identities, for privacy). For years, I've been writing down these special stories about teens and their families, stories that moved me—sometimes to astonishment, often to laughter, occasionally to tears, but always to some understanding. These stories taught me all I know about adolescence. They might help you, as well.

But, before we start, I need you to promise me something: that you will read this book through from the beginning. If you do what I always did, and skip ahead to the end, you'll miss out on the parts that can help you the most. Although the specific suggestions in the book are helpful, what is much more helpful is that you first learn about who you are, so that you can come up with your *own* strategies to live your own life. As I already said, and you already know, those are the best answers of all.

A word of caution: Learning about ourselves is not always easy. This book may cause you to think a lot (that's always good), feel a lot (that can be good and bad), and maybe even become a little overwhelmed at times (always bad). If you find that you're getting stressed out, PUT THE BOOK DOWN. Find an adult you trust and respect, maybe a teacher, a counselor, or a parent (stop smirking), and tell that person what you're feeling. Rotten feelings are just like rotten foods: They can only hurt you if you keep them inside. So, if you're feeling really bad, go throw up on an adult (emotionally, that is). Even though they're often crazy, grown-ups can actually be helpful at times.

And finally, two apologies: First, I worry that the way this book is written may get you mad at times. Writing a book that attempts to tell a large group of people about themselves is really an arrogant thing to do. You'll find that some of the things you'll read here *do not* reflect who you are. That's because you are unique, different in so many ways from everyone around you. Please be patient, and understand that this book tries to look at the most common issues of adolescence in a way that I think will help the greatest number of kids. I apologize if anything I say offends you.

You might also find that the wording of this book is sometimes off-putting. That's because there is no "one" teenage language. How kids talk varies a lot by region and by age. Philly kids speak very differently from LA kids. Twelve-year-olds speak very differently from 16-year-olds. Writing this book for all teenagers is like trying to write one book for all Europeans. Attempting to find one type of wording that works for everyone in a group as diverse as teenagers is very hard. But please try to see past the wording into the truths that these stories might offer to you.

So what did Gerald end up doing? I can't tell you—yet, because Gerald's journey was the same one you have to make: taking a long, hard look at both the world and at yourself before you make life-altering decisions. So, if you're ready, strap yourself in and turn the page to Part One, where we'll take a look at what's going on in your brain and your body. It's really quite amazing. And as Elysa discovered, your hands might even start to talk to you.

YOU RIGHT NOW

It's The Best of Times and It's The Worst of Times

"And these are supposed to be the best years of my life? I really, really hope not."
—Ariella, age 14

"Do you think that you can learn stuff about people by watching their hands?" Elysa asked. Put off by this question that seemed unrelated to what we had been discussing, I fumbled some vague answer to get us back to talking about her parents' upcoming divorce. But, luckily, she continued. "I think that when people talk, sometimes their hands show what's really true, and . . ." she paused and then gave up her thought, like adolescents do when they sense that adults aren't really listening. "Forget it," she sighed. "It's stupid."

I had forgotten, once again, what word detours are all about in teenaged conversations. Elysa was trying to do something much more important than talking about the divorce. She was trying to learn about herself.

"Please," I apologized, "I'm sorry. Please finish your thought."

She looked up hesitantly, and then began to speak again. "Well, I watch people's hands when they talk. Sometimes, you'll see things in their hands that they hide from their words, you know? My father's hands are guilty now. He says he's leaving mom so they'll both be happier, but his hands are flying all over, like he's a little kid about to get caught. I think he's been cheating on her for a long time. Mom's hands are, like, locked together all the time. That means she's really freaked and furious, although she puts on this show of saying that she's really OK with my dad's decision to leave. It's crazy."

After a minute, I asked, "What do your hands say about you, Elysa?"

She smiled sadly and studied her palms. "They stopped talking awhile ago. It's weird. Since, like, 8th grade, I feel like I have no idea what I really think, what I really feel, what I really believe in—things like that, you know? It's like I lost myself." She held up her hands to me. "These could belong to anybody. There's nothing there that makes them me. I guess I have no idea who I am." She dropped her eyes, and lowered her hands, along with her voice. "I guess that scares me a lot more than the divorce. How do you learn who you are?"

Welcome to the time in your life when your "talking" hands can become quiet, unsure of who you are, how to be, and what to say. A time when, in case you haven't noticed, you're changing—*a lot.* Like on a theme park ride, you find yourself hurtling with breakneck speed through monster change after monster change. And yet, when you think about it, most of what you seem to notice is that you're bored—*a lot.* It's very weird. It's called adolescence.

Like on a theme park ride, you find yourself hurtling with break-neck speed through monster change after monster change.

Adults actually don't remember very much about this time in their own lives, although they think they do. When people get older, they sometimes romanticize their teen years as being a kind of wonderful age of freedom, excitement, and lack of responsibility. In my work with parents of teenagers, I often have to jog their memories a bit to help them recall what it was really like. Remembering helps them not act so crazy with you. When they remember the real deal, they usually stop smiling, and they usually start becoming a lot more sympathetic.

Parents can be like those guys who tell you how great it was being in the Army, when it really wasn't. Sometimes, adults remember only the good parts of being a teen, which often were very few. And sometimes, they even exaggerate those times as they keep sharing the tales over and over, like that fish story that grows with each telling.

The truth is that, at times, adolescence can be very tough. As a teen, you're caught between the two very different worlds of "childhood" and "adultville," with two very different types of rules and expectations imposed on you from the outside. In addition, you have two very different people inside of you struggling for control: you the child, and you the adult. This all happens at a time when the world around you seems to scream "sex, drugs, and rock 'n roll (violence) are *sooo* cool." And your parents suddenly seem so absolutely useless to you that feelings of being alone and isolated seem permanent, as if this is how it will be for the rest of your life. You're attempting to survive all of this at a time when you're going through jumbo changes in every conceivable way.

Your body is developing, your emotions are bubbling, your hormones are rushing, your intellect is expanding, and, last but not least, your brain is going through an incredible growth spurt that can literally change who you are from one day to the next. But, believe it or not, there's a wonderful upside to this time of your life, as well.

As a teenager, you'll see yourself finally beginning to make that last great leap toward adulthood, and that can be pretty exciting. Think for a minute: Aren't you impressed by how much you've grown in only a year, and in so many ways? Suddenly, your brain sees things in much deeper ways. Amazingly, your athletic skills have leapt to new levels. Mysteriously, your tastes in music have expanded in new directions. Incredibly, your life has become much more involved as you begin to understand *and care about* things like art, philosophy, or justice, ideas that held little meaning for you up to now.

You're growing up. Can't you sometimes feel the excitement of all these new possibilities rushing through your veins, both good and, at the same time, scary? What Charles Dickens wrote to begin his adventure novel *A Tale of Two Cities* could well apply to your own adventure of adolescence: "It was the best of times. It was the worst of times." Part One of this book will help you to maximize those best of times and minimize those worst of times by showing you what kind of creatures we are when we're adolescents. You'll see how your brain and your body are growing, and what this growth does to affect your thinking, and then your life. Knowing how these things work can give you much more power and control over your decisions, and so over your entire world.

Perhaps most importantly, knowing about your body and your brain can help you get along better with those large people downstairs in the living room, whom you've come to suspect are frequently mentally unstable: *your parents.* Like it or not, they get whacked by each and every change your brain and body go through, and they often get whacked even harder than you. How?

Ever play "crack the whip"? You know, that game where you line up and hold hands with a bunch of other kids, who then swing around like a whip, trying to shake off the last kid in line? Your folks are often like that last poor kid on the line, desperately hanging on for dear life as you whip through the huge changes of adolescence. They're desperately hanging on to their *relationship* with you, a connection they can feel is straining and creaking, a bond that feels like it might break apart at any moment. This is high-fear time for Mom and Dad. To them, it feels like you're sort of dying. And the fact is, *you are sort of dying.*

Not that long ago, you were a sweet, agreeable child. You used to think that your folks were great. You laughed at their jokes and were very impressed by how smart and athletic they were. Amazingly, you did almost everything they told you to do without a fight. You were really easy to parent.

But almost overnight everything changed. You might not think your folks are so cool anymore. They seem to have lost their comic timing, along with their throwing arms and their brain power. And now you seem to resist doing almost everything they tell you to do. You seem so much harder to parent.

What happened is that the old you, the little kid who just did whatever she was told without thinking much about it, died. A new you, a big kid who thinks for herself, and who often gets mad whenever someone (such as a parent) tells her what to do, has taken her place. You should celebrate these changes because they prove that you are growing up, fast becoming a unique person with your own identity, apart from your parents. That's very exciting for you, and a cause for celebration.

You should celebrate these changes because they prove that you are growing up, fast becoming a unique person with your own identity, apart from your parents.

This is also cause for a funeral for your parents. Your parents might mourn these same changes because they prove that their easy-to-love little boy has left forever, never to return. That's very sad for them. In fact, some parents become so sad that they start to resent their often-angry teenager, who seems to have "body-snatched" their small child.

In Chapter 6, we'll talk more about this sadness that your folks can feel about your growing up. For now, understand that these brain and body changes we're about to discuss can sometimes be as hard on your parents as they are on you. Weird, but true. So, as you read Part One, try to understand how these shocking, amazing changes can amaze and shock your parents, and make it harder for them to feel connected to you.

And now, if you're ready, read on to see how that incredible head of yours works. Or, as Ryan discovered, why it sometimes doesn't work. You won't even have to be shrunk for this *Fantastic Voyage*.

YOUR BRAIN

Here's Your Brain . . . Here's Your Brain on Adolescence . . .

"There are two things that you absolutely, positively have to know about being a teenager. The first is, uh . . . um . . . uh . . . what was I just saying?" —*Kyle, age 12*

Ryan was completely mortified. He wouldn't even look at me. He started talking to a painting on my wall. "I don't want them [his parents] in here, OK? I know they're supposed to come in so we can talk about this, but I can't do that. Don't ask me, all right? JUST DON'T ASK ME!"

"OK. It's OK, Ryan," I soothed. I'd rarely before seen 14-year-old eyes look so ashamed. As an honor student, an athlete, and a Straight-Edger (someone who doesn't do drugs), Ryan was pretty bad at playing the part of a drug dealer. Unfortunately, this was his latest role at school—and it wasn't for the play.

As he calmed a bit, tears slowly found him. "I can't even tell you about it. I'm so freaked. I can't even tell *me* about it. People keep asking me why I didn't think about what I was doing, about how I could have killed somebody. The cop asked if I knew I could be charged with a felony (a very serious crime). I didn't think about any of that stuff. It's not like I just blew off all those things. I just wasn't thinking at all, sort of. I have no idea what the hell I was doing, or

> why I did it. How can I know I won't do this again?" Ryan paused to reflect a moment. "You know what?" he asked. "I must be psychotic. Isn't that what you call people who do things and then can't say why?" After another pause, he added the capper: "The only good thing about them making me come here is that I probably would have killed myself this afternoon. I'd rather die than go back to school tomorrow, even if they let me go back. Can't you see, this is not who I am, or at least not who I was. God, how do I face everybody tomorrow? How do I face myself? HOW COULD I HAVE DONE THIS? I'M 14, FOR GOD'S SAKE! I'M PRETTY MUCH AN ADULT! I SHOULD KNOW BETTER! WHAT'S WRONG WITH MY HEAD?"
>
> Ryan was referred to me by his school for a drug-risk assessment. They wanted me to decide whether he was so heavily involved in drugs that he might be a danger to himself or to other kids. That morning, he had swiped a handful of his dad's Valium (a powerful antianxiety drug) and was dosing his friends at school. He got caught after one friend, who had assured him that he knew how many pills to take to get "safely" high, passed out and split his head open falling down.

Ryan was not psychotic, just misinformed. Like you, he was operating under a bunch of bad assumptions about being a teenager that can make you feel like you are nuts. Like you, he was given this misinformation by adults, who are usually as misinformed as you are about you. Take your head, for instance.

Ryan's first mistake was believing what his biology textbook told him. Based on what he'd read, he thought that his brain was the same as an adult's. Ryan's text, like most books on human development, stated that our brains are almost fully developed (about 95 percent) by age six. Researchers came to this conclusion by measuring the size of kids' brains. In these studies, it was assumed that the brain grew uniformly, which means that all the critical parts (which have different functions) were almost completely developed by age six. That assumption led to the popular thinking that the first five years of your life would determine how you would turn out, and that for you to change after age six would be very difficult. In other words, if your early years were positive, stimulating, and loving, you would be cool; and, if those years were bad, well, watch out!

This belief caused most of us to focus our attention on those first six years of children's lives, trying to help kids to feel good about themselves, and develop their skills and abilities. It got pretty weird, with some parents giving two-year-old kids violin and gymnastics lessons, thinking that for children to become really good at something, they had to start very young and practice all their lives. Up until very recently, those years after age six were not considered nearly as critical. The importance of teenage years, in particular, was terribly neglected.

All throughout this parenting "revolution," a lot of folks kept noticing some very amazing things that didn't fit that "all-by-age-six" thinking. Like basketball coaches who were astonished to watch 14-year-old kids who never played basketball become starters after only one year of practice. Like music teachers who had rooms full of very accomplished 15-year-old violin players whose only early exposure to the violin was at age two, when they tried to eat one. And psychologists, like me, who thought we were geniuses after counseling 12-year-olds who turned around a lifetime of bad behavior in only eight months. This old assumption about uniform brain development was very powerful, but do you know what can happen whenever you ass-u-me (assume) something? Well, that's what happened here.

The good news is that the adolescent brain is capable of astounding feats of learning and growing.

As it turns out, another phase of brain development is at least as critical as those early years: *adolescence*. This is a time when the *most* important parts of your head do *most* of their growing, when your brain is open to all kinds of new learning (both good and bad), and when you are capable of building amazing skills with incredible speed. This fact presents you with some good and bad news.

The good news is that the adolescent brain is capable of astounding feats of learning and growing. That is why your head seems to be in nonstop motion. Want to play music like Dave Matthews? Sign up for lessons. Your brain is now more open to learning new music skills, faster than Dave's. Think being a United Nations interpreter might be a cool job? Sign up for French. An adult's capability to learn a language is nothing in comparison to yours. Tired of being

"I CAN'T GO TO THE MOVIES WITH YOU, ELENORE. I'M STILL GROUNDED FOR SOMETHING I DID IN 1937!"

an average student? Sign up for tutoring. You can rewire your brain to make that "worst-to-first" jump in grades more easily than your dad could. The proof is in some revolutionary brain pictures I'll tell you about in a minute.

But, as Ryan found out, there's also a downside to being Super-Teen. All of those miraculous brain changes can also cause some pretty weird thoughts and impulses. Ideas and actions that can leave you staring into a mirror, wondering whether you are truly nuts, while your red-faced dad stands behind you waiting for an explanation of your latest strange behavior. Like when you parked his now-impounded truck sideways across handicapped, new-mother, and fire-zone spaces at the mall. And you have no idea why.

I know why. It's right there, in those brain pictures.

YOUR BRAIN UNDER CONSTRUCTION

A few years ago, some researchers who questioned the "all-by-age-six" brain thinking started taking thousands of MRIs (magnetic resonance imagings) of kids' brains, to see how they developed throughout childhood. They were curious to see whether any changes occurred in the physical structure of your brain that might relate to how you behave and change as you become a teen. What they found knocked their socks off: *The most advanced parts of the brain begin a wild growth spurt at the beginning of adolescence (around age eleven), and this growth spurt doesn't finish up until the end (around age 20).* The implications of this are tremendous, and they can go a long way to helping you understand yourself.

The most critical changing brain part is called the *pre-frontal cortex* (AKA *frontal lobe*, or *gray matter*). The pre-frontal cortex is what largely distinguishes us from lower life forms such as hamsters, or halibut, or Homer Simpson. This part of the brain handles sophisticated tasks, such as planning *("I cannot believe I didn't allow enough time for my project!")*, organization *("Dad, I sort of lost my coat again . . .")*, and predicting—and caring about—outcomes of actions *("I still can't believe how ticked off the principal got when I pointed out his hairpiece!")*.

Predicting and then caring about the outcomes of actions (consequences) is one of the key failings of the adolescent brain that is likely due to that incomplete gray matter. These failings can occur in the most disciplined of settings (such as with Catholic altar boys, at very solemn religious services) and with the most brilliant of students (such as future psychologists and high-school principals):

> "Father Ryder was a very plump priest who was very unlucky in having once made a very small gaseous noise while genuflecting (bowing on one knee) during Mass. Not loud enough for anyone to hear, mind you, except for his two altar boys: me and Billy Banawicz. Being in Catholic school in 1965, and thus being terrified most of the time, I wouldn't even have thought of publicly embarrassing Father Ryder with this. But my altar partner, Billy, was occasionally willing to die for the sake of a good joke. Having witnessed Father Ryder's emission, Billy was now pretty much a maniac with a deadly weapon. At first, he did nothing other than share the tale with the other altar boys. We knew, however, that this was all too easy. Something big had to be coming.
>
> "That following week, Billy and I (along with four other inmates) were assigned to serve the rarely seen High Mass, a two-hour,

late-night affair so formal and solemn that it looked like a wedding and an execution rolled into one ceremony. Another aspect was that all the school nuns (our teachers who beat us up regularly for the most minor offenses) were all lined up in the front rows, just mere feet from our neurologically challenged brains. Not a lot was tolerated by the good sisters. Laughing while on the altar, for example, was a capital offense. As proof that God loves to mess with people, Father Ryder was picked to say this High Mass, a service that required endless genuflections on the part of the priest.

"All was well until we got almost to the end. Then I noticed Billy's eyes had gotten 'bulgier.' Billy was a kid who strangely resembled the Peanuts' Charlie Brown: a big round face, little hair, and bulgy eyes. I had previously learned that the 'bulgier' his eyes got, the harder Billy was working to desperately restrain some suicidal prank. Billy's eyes were at record bulge levels that night.

"The noises started inaudibly, and then grew slowly louder, each one perfectly timed with every down stroke of Father Ryder's repeated genuflections: 'phfft'; 'fssst'; 'fffrrrt.' Hoping I was hallucinating from the incense, I twisted my eyes to see Billy's mouth. To my horror, I was not tripping: Billy was making fart noises in time to Father Ryder's knee bends: 'brrt'; 'brrt', 'bblllaapppp.' This was funny enough to get us killed.

"I mentally mumbled a desperate prayer for God (or whoever was willing) to strike Billy dead. As if in retaliation, Billy immediately went on a roll: 'brp, brp, brp,' a pause for effect, then a loud flapper: 'BBLLLLLLFFFFFFTTTTTPPPP.' Attempting to not laugh that night was the hardest single effort of my life. The mix of intense fear and sublime comedy was overwhelming. The pain I felt in my shoulder blades is hard to describe. I was reasonably sure that one of the nuns had stabbed me with a crucifix, until I saw Howie Semanchuck's shoulders twisting in laugh-avoiding pain, as well. A friend in the audience later said that our shoulders were all heaving as if we were overcome by the awesome sadness of the High Mass. We were not sad. We were hysterical. We were hand grenades ready to explode. With Father Ryder's final genuflection, Billy loudly pulled our pins:

"'BBBBBRRRRRRAAAAAAAAAAPPPPPPPPPFFFFF-SSSSTTTT.'

"Five psychotic altar boys stunned the congregation by rolling about the altar in choking convulsions. Ten silently raging, homocidal nuns coldly wrote down six boys' names, and crossed one out in red."

—From the personal journal of Dr. Michael Bradley

That red-lined, ex-altar boy Billy (who survived to become a high-school principal, of all things) had just suffered a pre-frontal failure so typical of these kinds of situations, in which parents stare at kids as if they are quite insane, and ask that worst-of-all bad question: "WHY?" It was difficult for Billy to explain why making fart noises seemed to be a good idea while he was six feet away from extremely religious and sometimes violent people (the nuns), during their most solemn ceremony. He could have more safely danced through a Ku Klux Klan march, screaming, "White people SUCK!" These kinds of adolescent pre-frontal failures might best be described as *actions with no plans*.

Before a military unit decides to go somewhere dangerous, it is required to have a plan, to consider and plan for all the possible consequences of what it is about to do. If the planners decide that the benefits of the action are outweighed by the risks, they'll cancel the action: "Nope—not worth the casualties we might incur." End of action.

...in the adolescent head, the subject of consequences sometimes never comes up.

But Billy's brain, like that of many adolescents, didn't stop to think about whether his action was worth the possible consequences. In fact, in the adolescent head, the subject of consequences sometimes never comes up. That's how Billy, or you, end up staring blankly back at exploding parents who think you are being defiant when you truthfully say, "I have no idea why I made those fart noises. It seemed funny at the time." Billy (AKA Principal Banawicz) now daily faces the supremely ironic task of helping adolescents cope with the very same problems with gray matter that nearly cost him his life at age 13. I hear he's a very understanding principal.

This gray matter (your new brain growth) also coordinates the activities of many other areas of the brain to do very important tasks. Such as learning complex skills (like driving a car), regulating your emotions (like ignoring that driver who's challenging you to a fight), and reigning in crazy impulses (like wondering if Mom's SUV can do a wheelie). One famous researcher went so far as to call the frontal lobe (your developing brain region) "the seat of civilization." Mishel found out why when she was 13 and chatting in the cafeteria, just before she got suspended for the first time in her life.

> Mishel couldn't believe her own story. "Josie does this stuff all the time. Why did it get to me that day? I was just sitting there at lunch, feeling fine, telling Paul my opinion of *A Catcher in the Rye* when Josie butts in, like she always does, and tells me I'm, like, 'soooo stupid.' I tell her she mistook me for someone who cares what *she* thinks, and she says, 'Oh yeah, like any real person cares what a pot-head like you has to say.' This is everyday trash talk for Josie. She does this all the time. But that day, without even thinking about it, I, like, suddenly realize I'm punching the crap out of her. I've never, ever, had a real fight in my whole life. Everybody keeps asking me why I did that." Mishel slowly shook her head. "The truth is, I have no idea why I did that."

Both Mishel and Ryan had experienced the downside of having such a wondrous, expanding, potential-laden brain: Sometimes it just misfires. Sometimes it allows strange impulses to overpower its capability to make good decisions. Believe it or not, the cause of your impulsive behavior—your brain's growth spurt and rewiring—is scientific news. Not too long ago, if Mishel or Ryan had been dragged into a shrink's office, a psychologist like me might have interpreted their behaviors as a symptom of an underlying problem, perhaps indicating a deeply buried mental conflict, or a need to rebel. You know, like maybe Mom and Dad yelled too much, or maybe they took away their binkies too soon. The more mundane truth is that these occasional episodes of apparent madness are pretty normal, and they're often just bloopers from that new brain wiring that has to straighten itself out.

> "Maybe my [rap] music is getting to me," Jimmy mused. "I've never disrespected my mom like that. What I said to my own mother is so bad I can't even tell you what I said. Nothing personal, but I don't really care what you think. But I care a whole lot what my mother thinks. I never use that kind of language, anywhere. Well, almost

never, but I'd never think of using it on my mother. It just kind of jumped out of me in the middle of our argument. I had no idea that I was going to say something like that. If I did, I would have walked away first." Jimmy sat quietly for a minute, and then in a low voice he shared his silent thought: "In my whole life, I don't think I'll ever forget her face when I called her a [the profanity]. That was the first time I've ever seen her cry, except at a dumb movie, or when Grandmom died. I can't stop thinking about her face looking so hurt. Now, I don't even want to talk with her. She thinks I'm still mad at her, 'cause I won't apologize. I'm really just too ashamed to sit in the same room with her, and I can't even tell her that."

What happened to Ryan, Mishel, and Jimmy happens every day to bunches of kids. Most adolescents at some time or other have these weird impulses jump out of them, before they have a chance to stop and think. What happened to Ryan, Mishel, and Jimmy *almost* happens every day to bunches of adults. They get many of the same urges as you do to say and do outrageous things. The difference is that most adults are more able to keep themselves from punching out the Josies of the world (as Mishel did) by channeling their instant-attack urges through the fully formed, pre-frontal cortex of their adult brains. The gray matter there is able to coordinate a bunch of other brain areas, to help them make better decisions. What the brain does is call for a committee meeting—*inside your head.*

Most adolescents at some time or other have these weird impulses jump out of them, before they have a chance to stop and think.

If a grown-up Mishel got that impulse from her brain Anger Center to smack Josie, her fully formed frontal cortex would first check in with the Forecaster Section of her brain. The Forecaster Section would say, "You know, if we break Josie's ignorant nose, the likely outcomes will be as follows: (1) our nose will also hurt, (2) we'll get suspended, (3) we'll get grounded from Friday's sleep-over, and (4) we'll have to go see Dr. Bradley again. Therefore, we here in the Forecaster Section recommend not punching Josie out." But then the Anger Center might start to whine, "Yeah, well, maybe bad stuff will happen, but we're so ticked off we don't care. We have to do something!" At that point, the frontal cortex could consult the Creative Planning Department of her brain, which would calmly suggest, "It might be better to be sarcastic than violent. Why not zap Josie back with words instead of fists, so we won't get in trouble?" "What do you think, Anger Center?" your gray matter would ask, "Would sarcastic get it done?" "Oh, all right," the Anger Center would sigh, "as long as it's a really good cut."

If Mishel's frontal cortex were sufficiently developed, she could have resisted the urge to physically attack Josie. Instead, she might have simply continued talking to Paul (loud enough for Josie to hear) and said, "As I was explaining, I think the book is really about rude, immature kids who try to improve their miserable lives by constantly interrupting conversations to put other kids down."

Sound like too much work to do quickly while watching Josie smirk? Amazingly, it's not. A fully developed frontal cortex can do all of that in a nanosecond, without having to actually think out all of those thoughts—kind of like a reflex—if you've practiced thinking like that a number of times. That's because the more you repeat a certain action, the more it becomes etched into your brain—quite literally. Researchers have discovered that the more you repeat a behavior, the more the brain strengthens the circuits that produce that behavior, by insulating (and preserving) those particular brain "wires." They call this process *hard-wiring*, which means that once you get that wiring in place, you pretty much have it forever.

Remember how hard it was to first learn how to ride a bike, at age 6? Remember how, at age 14, you hadn't ridden for years, yet you got right on a bike and rode great? That's an example of how hard-wiring works in your brain. The problem in adolescence is that your gray matter (where your higher-level abilities live) is not yet fully developed (or hard-wired). So, it's often difficult for you to control an impulse, have good organization/planning skills, or think through a difficult situation. And this dilemma is even more of a challenge because the world around you is more dangerous than ever before.

You're trying to navigate a world saturated with sex, drugs, and rock 'n roll (violence), while your adolescent brain is struggling to develop the complex skills it needs to cope with these things. And this is a challenge that has never before confronted teenagers to the extreme extent that it does today. The truly embarrassing fact is that *adults* have created a world that is dripping with sex, drugs, and rock 'n roll like it never has before. You read that right: Adults have done this, and yet they act as if you're the ones who are nuts. You could well argue that adults are truly the crazy ones, and you'd be right. But you'd also be wrong.

SEX, DRUGS, AND ROCK 'N ROLL
You're Just Reacting to the World Around You

A myth has grown that says that teens themselves are the reason that they get into more trouble these days with sex, drugs, and rock 'n roll (violence) than ever before. The belief is that kids today are so much less moral, hard working, and responsible than today's adults were as teens. This is stupid and dangerous thinking, and it's simply not true. What is true is that you are just reacting to the world around you (your teen culture) exactly as every other generation of adolescents has done from the dawn of time. But the real irony is that your teen world is mostly a reflection of the adult world, which is also dripping with sex, drugs, and rock 'n roll. So adults who criticize you for doing exactly what they're doing seem crazy to you. This doesn't help you to listen and think about what they're saying. In fact, this double standard can sometimes make you lean further toward doing those very things you're told *not* to do. Look, for example, at the adult world's obsession with sex. (It's actually pretty hard to miss.)

What is true is that you are just reacting to the world around you (your teen culture) exactly as every other generation of adolescents has done from the dawn of time.

Our Sex-Obsessed World

Adults can appear to have a sex problem. Sometimes, it looks like they can't think about much else. The world they've created around you is just saturated with sex. Think I'm kidding? In a recent two-year period, TV shows increased general references to sex by *74 percent—in the family hour viewing times.* Over a four-year period ending in 2003, specific references to intercourse increased by *100 percent.* Given the amount of TV sex talk that existed before, increasing it by this much could not have been easy to do.

The same thing has occurred in music, movies, video games, and even advertising. Have you noticed that whenever you see an ad trying to sell you something, it almost always has some kind of sexual reference? In other words, the world pounds sex at you 24/7, telling you that this stuff is cool, and fun, and mature, and that if you're not doing it, then you're not cool, or fun, or mature.

The results are predictable. Although the numbers have fallen a bit recently, about 50 percent of teenagers are sexually active. Kids are also having sex at earlier and earlier ages, although not always voluntarily. Sexual assault against girls is off the charts. We'll talk more about sex in later chapters, but, for now, understand that this cultural obsession with sex did not come from you. It comes from the *adults* who produce these shows, write this music, design these ads, and model these behaviors. And what you're seeing is not the reality of healthy sex, but a twisted, unhealthy, and sometimes violence-laden version of what should be an expression of love. Sometimes, it seems that adults love this stuff. And yet, it's also adults who act shocked, appalled, and judgmental when the latest statistics about teen sex are published. Kids like Ashley pay with their pain for this sex obsession.

> "It hadn't been a great 13th birthday for me. My boyfriend took me home for a "private party," and it wasn't much of a surprise. He stole a bottle [of liquor] from his dad and got pretty drunk. We were watching a music video, one where the girl gets, like, raped, but she really enjoys it? Then he started grabbin' at me to have sex, and trying to make me drink, too. When I said no, he wouldn't stop. He, like, got crazy, sayin' I was teasing him, and he wasn't takin' this anymore, and that he 'had rights.' When he pinned me down, I just froze at first, and then I remembered a sex class we had at school, sayin' we should fight, so I did. I screamed as loud as I could, and scratched his face."
>
> My stomach was knotted as Ashley told her story. She was narrating this horror too calmly. "That, like, made him sort of wake up. First, he just stared at me with his crazy eyes. Then, slowly, he got off me. He sat on the edge of the bed and started to cry, sayin' he was so sorry, that he didn't know what happened to him. I told him it was

> OK, that I understood. I said that because I just wanted to get out of there, but also because I thought that maybe I did lead him on, you know? But this next part you won't believe: HE TRIED IT AGAIN!" Ashley's pain finally caught up with her story.
>
> "I had to freakin' fight him off all over again," she sobbed. "And I thought he really loved me. I ran out of his house half dressed, and sneaked into my house so no one would see me. I was so scared I threw up. I showered for an hour, and cried all night, but soft, so my mom wouldn't hear. The worst part was, the next day in school, I heard that he was bragging to his friends about how he got me. Then, one of his friends came up to me, laughing and looking back at his 'boys,' and he asked me for a . . . a date." Ashley cried long and hard for a while, and then quieted. "My friend Lisa has it right. She says boys say there's only two types of girls: sluts and prudes. But boys, they're just cool, no matter what they do." After crying for a while, Ashley looked up at me and asked, "Is that true, about the two types of girls?"

I had no idea where to begin to respond to Ashley. Our sex-crazed culture has painted a target on her back, and jerks are lining up in record numbers to take their shots: *One in five adolescent girls is sexually assaulted by a "boyfriend." One in four women in this nation can expect to be sexually assaulted in her lifetime.* These are outrageous and scary numbers.

Later, we'll talk about what you can do if this ever happens to you. For now, understand that Ashley and her boyfriend aren't the only ones responsible for what happened on that night. Ashley knew she was being dumb, and "Mr. Wonderful" knew he was being dumber. But a lot of that stupidity belongs to adults who use sex to sell everything in this world, who buy everything that uses sex as a sales pitch, and who stand around and act as if that's all OK. The world tells you that this over-the-edge emphasis on sex is OK and normal, just when your brain is having a tough time making hard decisions about a lot of things, including sex. In other words, the world tells you that casual sex is fine, and the world tells you that casual sex is not fine. This double standard can make you crazy.

Many teenagers say that this mess is the fault of adults, like their parents. After all, parents let this happen to the world, right?

What a mom said:

"I didn't ask for this 24/7 sex culture. It just happened around me. I do what I can, but often I feel helpless, and scared, and overwhelmed, like there's nothing I can do to help my kids make smarter decisions about sex. It is true that a lot of adults make lousy decisions about sex, and I guess that gets confusing for kids. After all, we get bombarded by the same nonsense as the kids, and I guess that affects some grown-ups, as well.

"But not all parents are crazy. I think most of us try to do the right things most of the time. Do you know how kids get mad when adults say that *all* kids are bad, just because a few do bad things? Well, that's how I feel when my kid says all adults are hypocrites, because a few act out with sex. And, geeezz, whenever I try to talk to my son about sex, he covers his ears, rolls his eyes, and whines, 'GAAAWWWDD, Mom, I know all that stuff. Leave it alone, OK?'

"So just what are parents supposed to do?"

That's a good question. If you were *your* parent, what would you say to you about sex? How would you parent your own teen? Would you lay down the law and get tough, with restrictions, or would you sit back and let your kid do whatever she wanted? And if you decide that you'd be a lot more strict with your own kid than your parents are with you, what does that say about what you're doing now? Why is it OK for you to do something, but not for your kid?

You need to think about this, because this kind of confusion about sex happens with other things that can hurt you, as well. Like drugs.

The Adult Drug Culture

Just as with sex, adults can look pretty crazy when they tell you not to do drugs or alcohol. These are curious words, since they come from the most heavily drug-involved adult population in our history. Again, just as with sex, many adults in this culture are heavily into drugs and alcohol, with booze being the drug of choice among adults. As we'll discuss later on, alcohol *is* a drug, and in fact is one of the most dangerous ones out there. Most adults drink, and many adults drink a whole lot, all the time. We have pushers (bars) everywhere, and we have addicts (alcoholics) everywhere. Yet, still we spend many millions of dollars on advertising—TV, magazines, newspapers, race cars, you name it—to create new addicts who will do this very legal, very dangerous drug. And the booze pushers' ads are doing a first-rate job. How effective are they? Hold onto your D.A.R.E. tee shirt.

Among American adults last year, every "druggie loser" who died as a result of illegal drug use was buried along with *15* "good citizens" who quite legally drank themselves literally to death. Approximately 12 million to 14 million adults are currently alcohol dependent (addicted), with another 8 million to 10 million adults using so much that their lives and health are seriously hurting. This means that the teenagers in more than *one out of every four families* in America are trying to cope with the monstrous fallout of adult addiction in their families. So the next time a grown-up goes on about how today's kids have a drug problem, you might quietly point out that the most common drug problem of today's teens is *trying to survive the addictions of adults.* And they're forced to do this at the same time that their brains are being rewired. Kinda' makes you think, doesn't it?

These numbers make adults look really nuts when they confront you about *your* use of drugs, particularly certain drugs. They get upset if you use their drug of choice, alcohol, but they go berserk if you smoke weed. Marijuana is another drug that can be very dangerous (oh, yes, it can—I'll show you later), but, physically, it's *less dangerous than alcohol.* Yet most adults would prefer to see you drunk on booze than stoned on weed. This double standard can make kids shake their heads in bewilderment and mutter, "Yes, my parents *are* crazy." But I'm afraid that teenagers aren't doing so great on the alcohol front, either.

Last year, the Partnership for a Drug Free America took a survey and found out that more than one-half of 7th through 12th graders said they drink. One in 5 students admitted to drinking weekly, and about 1 in 10 announced that they binge drink (at least five shots in a row) monthly. Every year, about 45,000 kids get badly broken bodies from booze-related accidents, and annually, we get to bury thousands of kids who drink "very well," and then drive very badly. We lose more of you to alcohol than to all of the other drugs *combined.* If these numbers sound like a gruesome body count from some terrible war, you're getting the idea. Booze is the big killer. But your generation is also finding other unique (stupid) ways of hurting (if not killing) yourselves with chemicals. And you're setting impressive records.

Last year, almost half of your peers used *cannabis* (marijuana, weed). Speed (methamphetamine) and cocaine/crack use tied at grabbing about 10 percent of teenagers, and heroin got into the bloodstream of 4 percent of your buddies. And while use of ecstasy (E) has dropped a bit from a frightening 12 percent, that slack was more than taken up by the 20 percent of adolescents that did inhalants (glue, whippets). In later chapters, we'll talk more about the dangers of each of these chemicals (yes, ecstasy is dangerous); but, for now, aren't you at least a little weirded out by the sheer size of these numbers? No? How about if I told you that, every year, kids start to use at younger and younger ages? Still no? Well, let me add two more facts: The first is that we now know that the younger a person starts to use drugs (including alcohol), the greater the odds that he'll become addicted. This gets scary when you consider that inhalant use among 8th graders increased by *14 percent* last year.

...we now know that the younger a person starts to use drugs (including alcohol), the greater the odds that he'll become addicted.

The second fact is one we already talked about. Young teenage brains go through a huge growth spurt, where they can learn or hard-wire new behaviors (habits, skills, attitudes) for the rest of their lives. Should that hard-wiring be about music, or marijuana? Carpentry, or cocaine? As Lester discovered, these are tough questions that are often hard to see, and often easy to ignore.

This kid clearly thought I was stupid. We had argued for an hour about the seriousness of this 14-year-old selling his grandmother's tranquilizers to other kids at school. Now he was getting mad. "I'll say this just one more time," Lester sighed wearily. "Junior high kids are old enough to decide for themselves if they want to do pills or not. I just made a couple of bucks. What's so wrong with that? They'd have just gotten pills somewhere else."

I sat for a minute, and then tried a different approach. "Lester," I asked, "what would you do if some kid sold pills to your little [10-year-old] brother?"

Without a pause, Lester narrowed his eyes and took the bait. "I'd kill him," he yelled! "Nobody does that to my family. Nobody, you understand? We ain't havin' no junkies in my family, you understand?"

"No, Lester, I don't," I quickly shot back. "Man, I *know* you sold pills to your little brother."

Lester's eyes went wild as he rose up to get in my face, but he froze as he began to understand. I kept talking. "That was somebody's little brother you sold to—somebody's son, right? Maybe a step-brother you never knew? Perhaps a cousin? How about your neighbor's kid, whose mom helped out your family when your mom was sick? How about you? Is dope OK for you? Just where do you draw your line? Who's in, and who's out? Who counts, and who gets to play junkie roulette? No, Lester, I don't understand. Explain it to me."

Lester stared angrily for a bit, then slowly sat back down and hung his head. After a minute, he spoke again, but this time quietly: "You know, I've thought about what you said, on my own, but I keep pushing it out of my head. It gets real complicated, you know?"

Lester was right. It gets really complicated. Even adults with fully developed brains often have a terrible time sorting these questions out. So how did we get to this ridiculous point, where we force 14-year-olds with brain challenges to confront life-threatening decisions like these? Look to the adult world for the answer.

Many, many adults have lost control of things like drug use in their own lives. If you label alcohol as a dangerous drug (it is), then the adult culture can be labeled a drug culture, because, by comparison, *adults do a lot more drugs than kids*. Somewhere along the line, the wheels fell off of our adult world, a force that so powerfully shapes your life. And then many adults turn around and talk about how horrible kids are these days, as if they are blameless. This can make *you* crazy.

I worry a lot about how adults look to the adolescents they're supposed to be teaching. Hypocrisy is not a great way to grow respect in teenagers. It *is* a great way to grow adolescent anger, though, and resentment makes sex, drugs and rock 'n roll (violence) look more attractive. But I'm not the only adult who worries about this.

What a dad said:

"Well, I don't do any drugs, and I work hard to try to keep kids off drugs, although the kids have no idea that's what I'm doing. I coach a small baseball team of 10-year-olds. The coach (me) stinks, the team

> stinks, and we have a great time. Last year, we won one game, and from the yelling and screaming, you'd have thought that we won the World Series. Everybody plays the same amount of time on my team, good players, bad players, whatever. I love those guys, and they love each other. You never hear a bad word from a good player towards a bad player who just messed up. Only encouragement. It sounds silly, but I think that helps kids stay away from drugs, you know? Maybe they learn that it's OK to mess up in baseball, that it's only a game. That what counts is how well you care about others, not how well you field grounders. That kind of strength shows in your heart, not in your arm. I believe that these kinds of lessons make kids stronger and able to see past the drugs, to understand what's really important in life.
>
> "You know what kills me? Dads showing up at games with beer on their breath. That happens more times than you can imagine. I can see my kids looking at them, hearing their slurred words, seeing them get crazy over some call, screaming insults. It's horrible. I feel like they look back at me wondering if most adults do this stuff, or if most adults are like me. I think they're trying to figure out how the world really works."

Adults like those drunk parents can really make adults like that coach go a little crazy. That coach is a little too strict with his own kids, so he seems a little crazy to them sometimes—but he has no idea what else to do to keep them safe. What would *you* do? Yes, your parents are crazy, but part of that is because the adult world is also crazy.

While we're on the subject of the crazy adult world, there is one more set of problems that are blamed on you that you didn't create. You didn't think your generation created rock 'n roll, did you?

Teen Violence: The Big Lie

Everyone knows that adolescents today are much more violent than adults were when they were teens, right? Every time you turn around, there's another school shooting, right? And kids today are nothing but a bunch of homicidal maniacs roaming the streets, right? And society needs protection from you, with things like school metal detectors, guard dogs, and cops with automatic weapons, right?

WRONG! Ready for a flash? Your generation of teenagers is the *least* violent in recent history, at least in most ways. And yet, in one way, we've never seen killers quite as deadly as you. Confused? Let's straighten it out with a pop quiz.

Pick A or B: Whose was the most murderous teen generation?
A. Yours (gangsta' rap, school shootings, guns everywhere)
B. Your parents' (peace, love, flower power)

ANSWER: B

The F.B.I. says that your Dad's peers killed *twice* as many citizens as your "gangster" generation (so much for flower power).

True or False: School violence today is out of control.

ANSWER: False

Your generation of teenagers is the least violent in recent history, at least in most ways.

The only out-of-control aspect of school violence is this out-of-control school violence myth that we can't seem to kill. The fact is that serious school violence has gone down anywhere from 25 percent to 40 percent over the past 10 years. But don't feel left out. There is one category of violence that your generation is likely to rule for a long, long time: *suicide.*

Suicide: The Deadliest Epidemic

Kids are killing themselves in epidemic numbers. When The Centers for Disease Control last asked, *2 in every 10 kids* admitted that they had either attempted suicide, or had a serious plan to off themselves. This represents a *400 percent* increase since your parents were crazed adolescents. Suicide is the teen violence that this country should be worried about, not school shootings. High-school massacres are just like plane crashes: horrors when they do happen, but horrors that hardly ever happen. We'll talk more about suicide later on, but, for now, understand that teenage self-murder has recently grown from a rare act of total hopelessness to a bizarre game often played by angry, self-centered, and attention-seeking kamikazes willing to die to make some useless point that no one remembers anyhow. Some kids call this stupid. And they know what they're talking about.

The circle of 16-year-old friends silently shuffled into my office and sat down. I was thinking of how these guys always reminded me of watching some very noisy TV show, with the mute button on. Their appearance was as loud as could be: orange sneakers, green and purple hair, neon-yellow shirts, piercings everywhere—you know the picture. But their silence was that of a graveyard. Finally, one huge kid with a small voice spoke up: "It's been three months now, and we still can't get back what we had. Remember?" he asked the group. "Remember Friday nights?"

The group started to move a bit. Another kid smiled, "Yeah, remember when Redner set up the surprise for his sister's surprise party?" A third grinned and jumped in, "And we switched off the electricity, and we lined up at all the windows with those *Scream* masks and flashlights on our faces?" The fourth chuckled, "No lie, Dr. B., those girls screamed for an hour, nonstop. I think Deanna peed herself." The group tried to build this funny memory into a laugh, but their pain crashed down on them once again. After a minute, the big kid asked no one in particular a question he regretted almost immediately, "What's Deanna up to these days?" The kid next to him shifted uneasily, and began retying his Jordans for the third time as he spoke. "Well, she's, you know, like, hangin' in, I guess. She's been in the psych hospital two times now, and she's, like, stoned out on medicine or something.' Or maybe it ain't the pills; maybe it's, like, having your own brother, you know, do what Redner did."

"JUST SAY IT, OK?" the big kid yelled. "SAY HE SHOT HIMSELF, OK? HE DID SHOOT HIMSELF, REMEMBER? I REMEMBER, AND I'LL NEVER FORGIVE HIM. BIG MAN, RIGHT? TOUGH GUY, RIGHT? WRONG! HE DIDN'T GIVE A CRAP ABOUT US, OR EVEN HIS OWN FAMILY. HE PUNKED OUT, MAN. HE WAS NOTHIN' BUT AN F'NG PUNK COWARD. I HATE HIM FOR WHAT HE DID TO EVERYBODY. ALL HE CARED ABOUT WAS HIMSELF, PUTTING ON A BIG, SICK SHOW (suiciding), JUST TO GET BACK AT HIS PARENTS! HE WAS, LIKE, MY HERO, AND NOW HE AIN'T NOTHIN' BUT STUPID!" The big kid quieted down but kept muttering, "Stupid—just stupid—nothin' but stupid. . . ."

Stupid happens to be a great suicide word. It very accurately describes how that act looks to the survivors, the real victims who are left behind to clean up the mess and try to move on with their shattered lives. Movies and TV shows like to make suicide look like a kind of sweet, sad, romantic adventure, like Romeo and Juliet. These movies also do this with war. But the realities of war and suicide are not romantic. They're just dark, gut-wrenching, bloody, and foul-smelling failures of humanity. Like the big kid said about suicide, ". . . just stupid—nothin' but stupid. . . ."

Kids are more violent in other ways, as well. It shows in your love lives, of all places. For example, did you know that, in a recent national survey, 3 of every 10 girls said that it was OK for a boy to slap a girlfriend who disrespected him by simply *talking* to another boy? And another violence game rapidly rising in popularity is slipping drugs into girls' drinks, to take sexual advantage of them (by the way, rape is not sexy; it's a violent assault). Some guys really know how to talk to girls, don't they?

So how did these forms of violence become so popular in your adolescent culture? The adult culture pounds this junk into your head until it starts to seem normal. That "family hour" TV-viewing study we talked about earlier revealed another startling statistic: In two recent years, we increased violent references in these "family" shows by *60 percent.* Once again, as with the sexual references, packing in this many violent themes could not have been easy to do. Imagine what's going on in the non-family-hour shows. Does watching one violent movie make kids act out with suicide or murder? No. But does watching that stuff almost nonstop for years and years affect some kids? Yes, it does. In two ways: First, some kids who are always "ready-to-go" (inclined towards aggression) can be influenced, by crazy movies, to do crazy things. By the way, these kids tend to be teens who do not have adults in their lives who they respect and admire.

Growing up in a culture that loves violence can make kids not really see the violence for what it is, even when it's whispering right in their ears.

But second, and more importantly, the bystander kids (the ones who never pull the trigger, but who know the ones who might) *often are lulled into doing nothing to stop the insanity*. Growing up in a culture that loves violence can make kids not really see the violence for what it is, *even when it's whispering right in their ears.* When the U.S. Secret Service studied school shootings, it found that, in almost all of the cases, *"bystander" kids had been told by the shooters that they were going to do these insane things.* And when we investigate teen suicides, we usually find that these kids also had told bystanders about their plans, often on the Net.

Why do so many of these bystander kids do nothing? Perhaps because, just like you, they've been raised in a world so saturated with make-believe violence that the real thing sort of blends into the fantasy junk, and it becomes hard to see it for what it is: crazy!

When we ask friends of suiciders why they didn't tell adults about the suicider's repeated threats, we usually get the same answer as we get from the friends of the school shooters: *"Kids say this stuff all the time. We never thought he'd do it."*

Here again, as with drugs and sex, the world *makes* you crazy. It puts you in a culture dripping with suggestions to act out with drugs, sex, and rock 'n roll (violence), at the very time that your brain is just beginning to learn how to make complex decisions, and how to control your impulses. You do not make the movies, music, games, and commercials that sell with sex, drugs, and violence. You are just bombarded by them. Yet, how often have you heard adults yacking about how immoral teens are today? The unspoken truth is that the bad stuff your generation does is just what grown-ups would have done in your place, had they grown up in your world, bombarded by the same nonsense that rains on your brain.

But that means it's all hopeless, right? Bad brain + Bad culture = Bad Kid, right? Wrong! Your incredible expanding brain has a magical, mysterious, and miraculous built-in defense system that can not only protect you from the ravages of your toxic culture, but that can also help you to have a wonderful life. *That defense system is learning who you are.*

THE IDENTITY ANTIDOTE
Your Brain's Defense Against Insanity

Why do so many kids do just great in this crazy world they live in? There are many pieces to that puzzle, but a huge part is that kids who do well almost always are kids who *know who they are.* They know a lot about what they believe in, what values are important to them, and what their good and not-so-good parts are. Above all, they feel some comfort (or acceptance) with those things. You could say that they're cool with themselves.

When you have this sense of who you are, we call this *identity consolidation*, which means that the different aspects of a person fall together into one picture that makes sense to her. But, as simple as this might sound, identity consolidation occurs only toward the end of a very long teenage journey called *identity development*. This is an epic adventure that will take you to many strange, wondrous, and occasionally scary places, where you will learn about your true self—not the person others want you to be, but the real adult person inside of you, who's impatiently waiting to burst out of the shell of your adolescence.

You can feel him in there, can't you? Haven't you often sensed that you're evolving, changing, becoming something, some person who no one really knows yet, even you? Don't you sometimes drift off into weird, brooding moments, times when you think so deeply and powerfully that you can't even find words to explain where you were in your head? And, at times, wouldn't you give anything to stop feeling like no one really understands you, including you?

These are all symptoms of "adolescent flu," also known as the teenage search for identity. As difficult as these aches and pains can be, understand that they are just part of nature's plan for you to become *you*. Just like that butterfly fighting to get out of her cocoon, your own restless agitation and conflict are really just the visible parts of your fight to become yourself. The more you can accept these feelings and behaviors as being normal, the less scary the process will be as you fight your way out of your own adolescent cocoon into adulthood. It isn't always an easy journey, but developing your identity is the way your brain defends you against the insanity in the world.

Three things about this journey make it different from any other you may experience: Identity development is the one voyage (1) that you *must take*, (2) that you *must take alone*, and (3) that you *must take as it comes*.

Identity Development: One Journey You Must Take

Write this down on your backpack somewhere, so you'll see it every day: *MY NUMBER-ONE, NON-NEGOTIABLE, TOP PRIORITY IS FIGURING OUT WHO I AM.*

Identity development is your ultimate goal right now, because of those brain changes that are rolling through your head as you're reading this book. Remember, as that most critical part of your brain grows (the pre-frontal cortex), you get to decide what is wired into it. And what is wired into it can stick for the rest of your life. You want to be very sure that what you put in reflects who you are, and who you want to become. It's just like with cars: Factory installed options always work best. Rewiring later can be very hard to do, whether in your car or in your head.

Have you ever read any of those books or seen movies in which the heroes or heroines go on an adventure and discover that they are really on a quest to discover who they are? You know, works such as *Lord of the Rings*, *The Catcher in the Rye*, and the *Harry Potter* and *Star Wars* series? Well, here you are: Frodo, Holden, Harry, or Leia, ready to embark on a journey to who-knows-where, at the end of which you will become who-knows-who.

Developing your identity means trying on a million different hats of ideas and values, to see which ones fit you.

Your identity-development voyage requires that you do things like thinking, exploring, thinking, talking, writing, thinking, vegging, working and, uh, oh yeah, thinking. Developing your identity means trying on a million different hats of ideas and values, to see which ones fit you. It means talking to a million different people, to see which ones say and do things that make sense to you. It means doing a million different things, to see which ones feel like they might be you, and ruling out those things that are not a good fit. Often, it means wasting time, at least in the view of the adults around you. Too many grown-ups have forgotten how incredibly productive wasted time can be.

"My dad is really weirded out by my helping Mr. Connor," Brianne sighed, "but I like to spend time working with him. It flies by so fast I always forget what time it is. He's this artist-sculptor who lives in a barn where he does his work. He's, like, 200 years old now, so he can't get around like when he was young, so I do a lot of moving and getting stuff for him. Last week, we went to the junkyard, and together we picked out all sorts of weird stuff that we put together in a sculpture that they're gonna' put in my school lobby. Isn't that cool? It was amazing. He showed me how the junk people throw away tells things about their lives, their hopes, their fears, and their dreams. He says this is what art is all about: Telling about people, about life. In all the art classes I've had at school, no one ever taught me that before, at least not so I got it."

Brianne's bright face turned dark. "My dad, he says this is a stupid waste of time, that I should be studying chemistry or joining cheering again. I told him how I'm not flunking anymore since I work with Mr. Connor, that he always pushes me to do my schoolwork and stuff. Mr. Connor even showed me how he uses chemistry to change the color of metals in his artwork. That's the first time chemistry made any sense to me."

"Did you tell your dad about that?" I asked, hoping she'd say no, so she'd still have a card to play with Dad.

"Uh-huh," she nodded sadly, "in the same talk where I told my dad I wanted to be an artist, like Mr. Connor. He started laughing at me and asked real sarcastically if I also wanted to live in a crummy shack like Mr. Connor. My dad really doesn't get it. He really doesn't know who I am. Now I wish he had found out that I used to smoke weed all the time, so I could tell him how I haven't hardly smoked since I started to hang out with Mr. Connor in that "crummy shack."

Brianne's dad made the common adult mistake of thinking that chemistry had to be more important than art for his daughter. He thought that pursuing a "useful" subject that had no meaning for her was more important than chasing after some "stupid" dream she loved. He didn't understand the critical neurological importance of having teenagers like Brianne "waste time" with silly dreams.

When you chase after something you love, you do wonderful things for your brain. First, just like with exercising muscles, you actually strengthen your brain by using it as you explore, learn, and think about whatever you're doing. Your brain works on the same "use it or lose it" principle as your body. Those MRIs of teenage brains showed that the new brain growth in your pre-frontal cortex withers and dies off if it is not used (scientists call this *pruning*). The more you experience life by pursuing things that interest you, the more wiring you put in place for keeps, and the more you learn about who you are.

Second, keeping your brain actively engaged in doing things you enjoy keeps you much safer.

Pop quiz time again.

Which one of the following most reduces adolescent drug abuse, pregnancy, and suicide?

A. The D.A.R.E. program
B. Antidepressant medications
C. The new Eminem CD
D. The school chess club

ANSWER: D—sort of.

Research shows that kids who are involved in after-school activities (jobs, clubs, sports, community service) have far fewer instances of self-destructive behaviors than those who just slack. Additionally, involved kids also get better grades and report feeling much better about themselves (which, incidentally, is why employers and colleges love seeing that stuff on your application). This makes sense when you consider Brianne's experience.

She had gotten heavy into marijuana, largely because she was so bored. She was so bored because life had no meaning for her. Life had no meaning because she had not yet started her voyage of discovering who she was. All she was doing before she discovered that she loved art was slacking and smoking. But luckily for Brianne, her brain was still open to *distractions*, those things that take us down strange new roads to see what's there, and that might tell us something about ourselves. Which brings us to the next requirement on your journey of discovering who you are and how you want to live your life.

Your identity must originate only from you.

Identity Development: One Journey You Must Take Alone

Your identity must originate only from you. It is not what others think you should be, or what others want you to be. And it cannot be what others need you to be, not even if those "others" are your loving parents, or your best friends. Even being a perfect kid provides no shortcuts. Ironically, being perfect can add painful years to your journey. If your goal is to become what *others* see as perfect, then you will find yourself doing things to please others instead of becoming you. As Francine learned the hard way, the name of this identity game is to be real, not perfect. Perfect is never real.

Francine was not at all what I expected. Her mother's phone message said that her daughter was an extremely gifted, 27-year-old graduate student who had unexpectedly appeared back at home after "running away" from a famous university. She was just one year shy of finishing her doctoral program in economics, after putting in six long years of very hard work. Mom said that her daughter needed "a little motivational talk" to finish her studies, since a very high-paying job was waiting for her. According to Mom, "Francine would be stupid to give all of this up."

This daughter who needed "a little motivational talk" walked in, collapsed on my sofa, and sobbed hard for 15 minutes, without a pause. Finally, she spoke with the exhausted voice of someone who was drowning in an ocean current that she couldn't even see, let alone navigate.

"I've tried so hard, but I can't go on. My parents keep telling me to just tough it out. I feel like I'll die if I have to go back there [to her school]. Don't tell them this, but twice I came very close to killing myself with pills last semester. I don't know what's wrong with me. I'm letting everyone down. They were all so proud when I first got accepted. Back then, my father was interviewed in the newspaper, and he bragged and bragged about me getting that scholarship to school. He was so proud. Now he's so disappointed in me. . . ." Francine could only cry again as waves of guilt washed over her. "I'm so ashamed," she wept. "My parents sacrificed all their lives for me. In high school and college I never let them down—not even once. I never did one thing wrong. I was the perfect daughter. Now look at what I'm doing to them."

Francine spoke about her agonizing struggle to stay in a school she disliked, studying a subject she hated, and preparing for a lifetime of work in a field she despised. "I used to get nauseous just walking into the building. The only parts I enjoyed were teaching college students and interviewing poor single mothers for some research we were doing. I loved the teaching, and I loved helping those struggling women when I could, even though that was not part of my job.

Those were the only times I ever felt alive in the last six years—and maybe in my entire life."

When I asked Francine whether she ever considered switching her field of study, she just stared at me as if she was finally hearing her own lost voice talking to her, a voice she had been ignoring. She was also ignoring my question: "I knew in my first semester that I hated economics. But everyone kept telling me how much money I could make in that field. I didn't know what else to do, so I stayed." She paused and studied her tissue awhile, and then looked up and zeroed in on her real pain: "You know, I'm not a real person. When you asked about me switching my program, I thought, 'To what? I don't even know who I am. How am I supposed to know what I should do with my life?' I'm like a hologram. I'm an illusion of a person. Life passes right through me. I have no substance, no sense of myself." She paused and shook her head in amazement. "My god, how did I end up like this?"

Ever been caught in a rip current at the beach? That's where the water rushes out so fast that you can't swim fast enough to get back to shore. If you keep swimming hard, straight toward the beach, you get nowhere, and, eventually, you just drown from exhaustion. You'll never reach the shore.

Kids like Francine, who don't know who they are, can be caught in rip currents of other peoples' expectations of them. They swim so hard trying to meet these goals that they eventually drop from exhaustion. That's because, no matter how many people you please, there's always somebody else setting new expectations and demands for you. You never get to feel OK about yourself, because you're always working to please them, and not you. Always pleasing others is another place where you'll never reach the shore.

If you ever are caught in a rip of seawater, the first thing to do is to do nothing. Take a timeout, roll over on your back, float, and relax a bit. Yes, you'll lose some ground, but that's OK. Calming yourself down is well worth the loss. Next, think about what *you* want to do, and not what the onlookers are yelling at you to do. If swimming frantically against a relentless current gets you nowhere but crazy and exhausted, that's a message that you're in the wrong place, doing the wrong thing. So do something different. Try swimming *at your own pace* and *sideways* to the beach. You won't end up exactly where you planned, but slowly you'll get out of the craziness of that rip current and into calmer waters. You can then decide where you want to land. And you'll always reach the shore.

If you ever are caught in a rip current of others' expectations while you're trying to make a decision, the strategy is exactly the same. Call a timeout and "float" for a bit. Put aside what everyone else tells you is right for you, and try to find out what *you* think is right for you. Try to find that voice of your own identity, and when you find it, learn to listen to it above all others. That internal "who-you-are" voice can do some amazing things—things that would have helped Francine avoid all that pain.

First, as I said, knowing who you are is your best defense against insanity. Had Francine been more able to stand up to the expectations of her family, by knowing and being who she was, she would not have ended up clutching handfuls of lethal pills.

Second, as Francine was finally learning, identity is also your best offense to becoming happy in life. Had Francine been able to recognize and trust her own voice telling her to dump economics and chase her love of teaching or helping others, she would have found meaning for her life. That is gold you can get only by learning and becoming who you are. But as this next tip about identity development makes clear, this journey is not without potholes. Ironically, *those potholes are critical to the process of wiring identity into your brain.*

Identity Development: One Journey You Must Take As It Comes

Try not to become too frustrated or upset that you're so distracted these days. These feelings are just your brain's way of handling your search for identity. But, at times, they create a very bumpy roller-coaster ride, and, often, you just have to hold on tight and go where the car takes you. Right now, your frontal wiring is wildly expanding, growing in 500 directions at once. It wants to try everything and see everything firsthand. It wants to challenge old ideas, open closed doors, and look beyond all the fences in your life. This is all as it should be at this time of your life, because this is how you will discover you.

This also means that you're going to screw up sometimes. Many of those explorations, distractions, and detours will turn out to be stupid, pointless, and embarrassing experiences, *which will be at least as important to you as your successes.* How can this be true? It's true because, win or lose, each of your experiences becomes part of who you are, of your identity. If you did great on some adventure, that's wonderful. You now know about something you love, something that you should pursue. If the adventure turns out to be a disaster, that's at least as wonderful, because you now know about something you hate, something that you should avoid in your life. *Learning who* you are not *is at least as important as learning who* you are. Ask Thomas.

Learning who you are not is at least as important as learning who you are.

Thomas seemed strangely calm for being where he was at the moment. Caught taking his father's car, without permission, on a midnight joyride to the beach left him facing all sorts of problems with judges, cops, and parents. But he didn't whine about how unfair everyone was being. Instead, as happens a lot in my work with teenagers, he stunned me with a piece of wisdom you'd think could only come from someone much older than 15: "I have no idea why I did pull that stunt . . . well, that's actually not true. I had always wondered what it would be like to just, you know, take off wild and free," here he mimicked a song, "'runnin' from the law.' I've never done anything like that before, but the songs all make it sound so cool."

Thomas laughed softly and shook his head. "It's not so cool, at least not for me. I was just scared the whole time, and felt really, really bad for how scared I knew my parents would be when they found I was gone. But as weird as this sounds, I'm not totally sorry that this happened. I learned something real important: That gangster stuff is not me. It's just not who I am. I know that now, and that's OK. I guess I just went nuts. My dad called this a brain fart."

With the going-nuts stuff, try to not take these brain farts too hard. These occasional impulsive blips are not horrible moral failings or character flaws. They are mostly just wiring problems and identity searches. If you can stay cool, and think things through, you can learn from your mistakes in ways that can help your brain to develop to make you stronger and smarter. In my own life, I've learned much more from my screw-ups than from my successes. Big mistakes can become even bigger opportunities to mature, to learn about yourself, if you can be straight up with yourself about what you did. If you stubbornly refuse to look at your screw-ups, they can become self-destructive, life-threatening habits—*parts of your identity.* Remember, the things you do repeatedly in your adolescence can be etched in stone in your brain, and stay with you for the rest of your life. If those things are skills like language, learning, and lacrosse, the sky is the limit for where you could go. If those things are wastes like slacking, smoking, or selfishness, you know where a lifetime of those will take you.

So the choice is really yours. The problem is that you might not see that yet, because *believing that you are capable of changing for the better can be hard to accept,* even for adults. And sometimes, your brain, your world, and even your loving parents can conspire to make you feel and think that life is always going to be this hard. Then, like a lot of your friends, you can tragically sell yourself terribly short.

We're not going let that happen to you. Keep reading. But part of the solution to all of this craziness, believe it or not, is dealing with the craziness *of your parents.*

I'm sure you're very familiar with that wide-eyed, open-mouthed, slightly drooling parent who stands there astonished, angry, or perhaps even frightened by whatever weird thing you just said or did. Keep in mind that, while you're trying to handle all of this craziness, one or two adults (parents), who got used to having you do whatever they said without question, are now completely at a loss as to what to do or say. They try all sorts of things, like yelling, threatening, or begging, to get you to be their little kid again. They might lecture, nag, leave newspaper clippings in your backpack, or have Uncle Leonard stop by for an "unplanned" visit. You know, just to see how you are, shoot some hoops, get a Slurpee®, ask you if you're doing drugs—you know, just a normal visit from Uncle Leonard, who never once asked you to shoot hoops in his life. It can get pretty weird, watching your parents get pretty weird. But remember, they're watching you get pretty weird at times, as well, and it scares them to death. Please be kind to the animals (parents). They're people, much like you, who now also have to go through a lot of changes, much like you. Change is hard for everybody, especially when the changes are as challenging and exciting as somebody growing up.

But beyond kindness, there's another reason you might want to be kind to the animals (parents). As much as they can make you crazy, *they can also help keep you sane.*

THE CONNECTION ANTIDOTE: Your Brain's Other Defense Against Insanity

Remember when I said that one huge part of staying sane in adolescence (and in life) is learning who you are? Well, would you care to guess what the other part is? Believe it or not, it's *staying connected to your parents.*

The research I told you about earlier that studied happy, successful teens also found that kids who had good relationships with their parents almost always did great as adults. This is another topic we'll get into later; but for now, note that your developing brain develops much better when you talk to Mom and Dad.

That doesn't mean anybody should be up anybody else's rear end. It does mean that you and your folks should work hard at maintaining a loving, respect-based relationship. That doesn't mean you happily do everything they tell you to do. It does mean that you guys find ways of working out differences without resorting to threats or rage. That doesn't mean that you never get mad. It does mean that you learn that it's OK to be mad at people you love, as long as you can *say* the anger instead of *becoming* it. And that you *can* care about their feelings, even if you disagree with their position.

If those things sound like how your family is now, congratulations. That's probably why things are going well for you. If those things sound like a fairy tale, you have some work to do, but that's OK. We're going to help you make it better. You will find that some of the "talking-with-parent" tips that kids offer to you in this book will be so powerful that you will leave your folks stuttering and stammering in amazement.

Speaking of stuttering, stammering, and amazed parents, it's time to cut to the chase, and get to the topic that gets your parents really stuttering, stammering, and amazed: your body.

YOUR BODY

Morphing from a Child into an Adult

"When I look around at my 7th grade class, most of the girls look like they work at Hooters and most of the boys look like they work at not falling out of their chairs. What's going on?" —Matthew, age 13

By now, you've probably had about all of the health/sex education lectures you can stand, so we'll keep this chapter short and embarrassing. Most parents tell me that when they try to sit down with their kids to have The Talk (about sex), their kids groan, roll their eyes, and sigh loudly. That's certainly what happens when I try to talk with my own kids. But when I talk with kids who are not my own (which, by the way, happens to be a whole lot easier), it seems that many of them have slept through those health/sex education lectures.

Often, you don't know exactly what is happening to your bodies, you get freaked by some of the changes, and you don't feel comfortable asking anyone about them. This is due to the Jerk Factor, something depicted well in one of my son's favorite Gary Larsen ("The Far Side") cartoons. The cartoon shows God at a workbench, building the world. Behind him are containers of ingredients labeled *Whales*, *Trees*, and so on. God is pictured emptying a container labeled *Jerks* onto the earth, while he says, ". . . and just to make things interesting. . . ."

Jerks really can "make things interesting" about lots of stuff, particularly sex, by intimidating you into not asking questions. They can make you shut up, for fear of being laughed at, called "gay" (a whole other subject we'll get into later), or just appearing stupid. Kids are scared to be seen as not knowing something that the jerks will say they "knew for years." In reality, the jerks usually know less than you do. That's because being ignorant is a requirement for being a jerk. But it's not a smart way to be. You need to know as much as you can about everything, to help you make better decisions, and to figure out who you are (which, as you now know, is the whole point of adolescence). So, in the event that you slept through your first-period health class, here's the crash course on what's going on with your body, starting with the physical changes. At the end of this book, I list a few other books that go into much more detail about puberty, which you should consider reading, as well.

THE TEENAGE BODY
Remember Your Power Rangers?

It's almost something out of a sci-fi movie when you really think about it: Childrens' bodies "morphing" into young-adult physiques, all within a few years. And the changes don't always happen gracefully or easily. They're usually accompanied by the sounds of grunting (you), groaning (your parents), and the tearing of clothes (the result of out-sizing or out-styling).

Remember that Monday morning when you tried to put on the pants you wore a week earlier? The waist still fit, but the two pant legs were suddenly two inches too short. The mirror told your astonished eyes that your legs *were* two inches longer, but the rest of you looked the same. Do you also recall that recent night when adolescence snuck in, causing *all* of your extremities to suddenly extend one-half inch? The following morning, on the way to breakfast, you smacked into every doorjamb, wall, and breakable item, causing your parents to shake their heads in amazement. There is an earthly explanation for all of this.

Teen changes usually start with something called "the growth spurt," a time when you stretch very quickly to 98 percent of your full adult height. For girls, the teen growth spurt usually starts around age 10 and runs for two to three years (and sometimes a lot less). During this time, females typically will shoot up seven inches or so, and some tower over the boys for a bit, because the guys don't start this wild growing until about age 12. While this difference can make both the taller girls and the shorter boys feel a little strange, it only lasts for a short while. The boys then more than compensate for the height disadvantage by tacking on about nine inches during their two to three years of morphing. Keep in mind that these numbers are all just averages, so your own experience may be very different. Don't get worried if you start this stuff later or earlier.

Teen changes usually start with something called "the growth spurt," a time when you stretch very quickly to 98 percent of your full adult height.

The weird part is that this growth hits different body parts at different times. Your legs finish growing six to nine months before the rest of you, with your shoulders and chest bringing up the rear, so to speak, and finishing up at the end of the growth cycle. This strange sequence can make you start to get nervous about how your body sometimes looks a little uneven. Mark's nervousness made his 13-year-old social life a little uneven.

> "My mom thinks that I'm afraid of water now, just because I won't go to pool parties and to the beach. She's all worried that I'm, like, water phobic or something. I can't tell her the truth. It's really embarrassing. I can't tell you, either."
>
> Having once been a 13-year-old male in the summertime, I took a wild guess: "Mark, is this about your body? Are you feeling weird about how you look?" Mark went off like a shaken can of Pepsi: "Just look at me," he whined. "My legs are chicken-skinny, I've got absolutely no chest at all, and my arms are way too long. I'm like a freak all of a sudden. My mother can't even find shirts that fit me. If one fits my neck, then the sleeves are like a foot short. My brother calls me 'Cheetah' [Tarzan's monkey]. He makes jokes about the backs of my hands dragging on the ground. It's humiliating. I can only go to places where I can wear sweats, so nobody sees my body. Then I can act like I look like everybody else."

"AT YOUR AGE, TOMMY, A BOY'S BODY GOES THROUGH CHANGES THAT ARE NOT ALWAYS EASY TO UNDERSTAND."

If you're avoiding water to avoid revealing your body, RELAX! First, understand that most of us look pretty much the same at that age. You probably *do* look like everybody else, even if you don't feel like it. And second, know that time is on your side. If you just stay cool, your body will work all of this out within a year. If you get nuts about these changes, you'll waste a lot of time worrying about nothing, and you can create a lifetime of painfully obsessing on your appearance.

Remember, now is when you begin wiring lifelong habits into that expanding brain of yours (see Chapter 1). No previous generation of teens has ever worried so painfully about how they look, with too many kids literally "dying" to look a certain way, starving themselves to death to look "attractive." While girls still dominate this tragic club, boys are increasingly becoming victims of this insanity, as well, something that we didn't see a generation ago. Eating disorders are yet another huge problem the adult world has stuck you with, a very bad situation we'll discuss later.

This growth spurt is accompanied by other changes that vary by sex, and that can cause you a lot of needless worry, and even pain. Although boys typically grow leaner and more muscular, with widening shoulders and thicker necks, girls begin to get rounder, with developing breasts and a kind of "padding" building up on their hips. This padding is a *normal and healthy development, genetically programmed into girls,* to prepare their bodies for eventually having children. In the old days (40 years ago), this padding was even considered *attractive.* But, recently, our culture has decided that we know better than Mother Nature how we human beings are supposed to look. Kids are pounded with these messages so much (from TV, movies, and advertising) that the information actually creates changes in our values about the changes in our bodies (like female hip padding). What used to look attractive now looks unattractive. Just who was this committee who made this decision without consulting Mother Nature?

We inflict this stupidity on boys as well as girls, convincing them that the way they naturally and healthfully look can't be OK. Boys are told that their arms and chests are supposed to look like those GI Joes they used to drag around (I used to be in the Army, and I knew only one guy out of hundreds who looked anything like that). And if their bellies aren't six-pack buff, then they must be wimps.

And the girls? What dolls do we stick in front of them as ideal body images? Do many women actually look like that? It's really quite arrogant when you think about it. We actually think we're smarter than nature about what is good for kids like Heather. It turns out that Mother Nature really hates being disrespected.

"I don't do drugs, you know? And when their stupid pee test comes back, they'll see I don't do drugs. Why don't they believe me?"

I did not want to answer that question. At 13, Heather sure looked "heroin chic," with sunken eyes, a pasty complexion, and way-too-thin arms. "Well," I offered, "passing out in math class a few times may have raised some eyebrows, don't you think?" Heather just stared out the window for a while, like she knew I was going to say that. I guessed that she wanted me to just ask straight up, so I did. "What is it, Heather? What's going on?"

"This," she finally answered, pointing to her hips. "THIS is what's going ON. And it won't come OFF, no matter what I do."

"Are you starving yourself, Heather? Is that what's causing you to faint?"

She just nodded glumly. "I think so." She paused and sighed. "Sometimes, I won't eat for two or three days, and the only things that get thinner are my arms and face. I could starve to death, and I'd die with these fat, nasty hips. I'm truly disgusting."

Heather was close to being right about starving to death. She really could hurt herself trying to look a certain way that *our culture* tells her is the only way to be attractive. But Mother Nature has her own ideas about how our bodies are supposed to look, and she doesn't care what we think. She always wins these contests. She'll even play dirty. As she did with Heather, she'll shut you down (make you pass out) before she'll allow those concentration-camp, boy-skinny hips that you see on those sort-of-human models in those ridiculous magazines (that adults sell). Nature has this silly idea that we should be healthy and happy as we are, instead of killing ourselves trying to become something that we were never physically designed to be. Apparently, Mother Nature doesn't subscribe to *Cosmopolitan.*

As we speak, 10 million American females and 1 million males are fighting for their very lives against eating disorders.

How out-of-hand has this appearance thing gotten? Pretty much over the edge. Later, we'll talk more about eating disorders, but, for now, know that these dangerous diseases are at an all-time high for both boys and girls. As we speak, 10 million American females and 1 million males are fighting for their very lives against eating disorders. Even more scary, last year, *20 percent* of this nation's college women reported becoming bulimic (intentionally vomiting their food) at times, trying to beat Mother Nature in a game they can't win. And these numbers only reflect the actual diseases. They don't include the tens of millions of kids who do crazy crash diets, or who painfully worry over each mouthful of food they consume. That's nuts! So try to coexist with these body changes, and not uselessly fight them. You have to stay cool about changing, since right now your life is about nothing *but* changes. Like what else, you ask? Like PUBERTY, I answer.

PUBERTY: Where We Separate the Men from the Boys, the Women from the Girls, and the Boys from the Girls

There are two parts to the puberty experience. The first is the physical/hormonal part, which deals with the visible body changes that occur as you become a sexual creature. The second aspect of puberty is the emotional/psychological part. And because the second part is a lot more overwhelming than the first, let's start with the first part.

Physical/Hormonal Puberty: Where Gym Showers Get Tense

The first clue that physical puberty is hitting you might be when Roger (the jerk sitting next to you in homeroom) very loudly and leeringly inquires, "Jeeeeezzzz, who stinks?" This is when you learn that critical skill of publicly yet secretly sniffing your armpits to see if you are the pungent answer to Roger's question. In puberty, we start to sweat a lot more. And we start to stink a lot more. A new bunch of sweat glands (called *apocrine glands*) develop at the onset of puberty; all this sweat mingles with skin bacteria to the point of getting Roger to pretend to gag. And no, ladies, the boys are not the big, walking apocrine glands you like to joke about. Females actually have many more apocrine glands than males; however, girls usually address these odiferous problems a lot faster and a lot better than boys (it's the showers and deodorant that make the difference).

What's really happening here is a biochemical hormone hurricane. First, an alarm clock in your brain goes off (yes, there really is such a thing) and yells at your pituitary gland, "YO, YOU! WAKE UP! TIME FOR PUBERTY! AND GET YOUR CRASH HELMET ON!" Your pituitary gland (by way of a chemical it releases) starts to shake other parts of you awake that had been just hanging out until now, making them release the parentally feared "hormones." For boys, the main hormone is testosterone, which comes from the adrenal glands (located near your kidneys) and the testes.

Girls' hormonal marching orders come from their ovaries, which produce estrogen and progesterone. These hormones, in turn, set off the next round of changes, which usually occur in a specific order. In addition to the padding we mentioned before, breast development usually begins first, followed by the appearance of pubic and underarm hair. Then menstruation (periods) starts, although usually irregularly at first.

For boys, the testes enlarge, the penis grows, and pubic and underarm hair starts to appear. About a year later, sperm becomes present in semen. Facial hair arrives last, along with oily skin and hair. By the way, this means you guys need to shower and shampoo a lot more, unless you don't mind getting those "EEEWWW" looks from girls. Most boys don't need to shave much until the end of adolescence, but then that delightful ritual becomes a daily chore, as well (don't those dumb beards suddenly make sense?). It sure takes a lot of work to become a sex symbol, doesn't it? And you thought just brushing your teeth every morning was a huge hassle.

And about everybody who's anybody gets some acne at some point during puberty. For most kids, the major zit attacks start to disappear along with your senior year.

So isn't growing up just grand? *Weeellllll*, yes. It can be a hassle, but, yes, it is also quite exciting when you think about it. Keep the big picture in mind as you live through these changes: Here, at last, is your final transition into adulthood. If you become obsessed with minor aggravating details, like pimples or padding, you'll miss this big adventure and have absolutely no fun. Take a step back from the temporary annoyances, and try to remember how amazing it is that you are actually growing up. You'll be a teen only once, so try to lighten up a bit. This can also be a wonderful time in your life.

That about finishes your abbreviated, crash course on the physical changes, although there are a few twists and turns that you should know about. The first is that many kids go through these changes on very different schedules. Although boys usually start puberty a couple of years after girls, there is lots of variability in this rule. Don't get freaked if you are changing earlier or later than the other kids in the locker room. The jerks in the gym shower might be very annoying if you are an early or late bloomer, but if you can just stay calm, the change gets around to almost everyone by about age 15 (if your growth spurt has not happened by then, it's time to see your doctor).

The second twist is that many girls are now beginning sexual growth (with breast development) at very early ages, sometimes even as young as seven. This growth is happening so frequently these days that it is not considered to be a disorder. We don't understand exactly why this is happening, but we do know that there are no bad physical effects associated with starting the change early. So if that has happened to you, don't worry about it.

EMOTIONAL/PSYCHOLOGICAL PUBERTY: Where the Rest of Your Life Gets Tense

Getting the equipment in place (physical puberty) is easy. The internal change, emotional/psychological puberty, is where it becomes really interesting. The same hormones that are reshaping your body can reshape your emotions, as well, and often make you feel like you just got run over by a garbage truck. Almost overnight, your entire view of the world, and of yourself, can seem very, very different, and, at first, very, very weird.

The same hormones that are reshaping your body can reshape your emotions, as well, and often make you feel like you just got run over by a garbage truck.

Suddenly, you see the world around you through this new lens of sexual awareness that can sometimes cause you to withdraw too much from your life. Innocent hugs with good people might start to make you uneasy. So you stop hugging good people. Innocent songs you used to hum now seem filled with sexual references you never noticed before. So you stop singing songs you love. Innocent wrestling games might cause an unintended sexual arousal that makes you want to disappear from the confusion, or embarrassment, or shame. So you stop playing games you like. Sometimes you can't stop thinking that some adult couple you know and used to be comfortable chatting with (like your parents?) does *"it"* (has sex). That very weird and unwanted thought can make you stammer midsentence as you chat with them. So you stop talking with people important to you. For a while, you can even worry that there might be something wrong with you, because you seem to think about little else except sex.

How do I know these things? I know because they happened to me. They happen to everyone: your parents, teachers, and every other kid you know. Ask Jake.

> Jake talked too fast and too loud, like a kid about to be sentenced for some terrible crime. "Man, there's no way I can talk with my Dad about this [sex] stuff. It all just goes around in a circle, you know? The more I talk, the weirder it gets. I can't talk to anyone about it. I fake it with my friends. We all, like, get tense if anybody asks a real question

or anything, and real fast we turn the talk into jokes and stuff. And you have to be careful that you joke just right, you know, or they'll think you're gay or something, and then they'll do you in. That happens to lots of kids who don't play the game right. There's always some nasty kid just waiting to pounce on you when you say the wrong word, or whatever. I can't even tell you what I think about [sex], because I think you'll think I'm like, crazy or something. I think that I am crazy. It seems like every time I turn around, there's something putting sex thoughts back in my head, you know, from music videos, and CDs, and magazines, and everything. Those videos are the worst!"

When Jake finally stopped talking, to catch his breath, he pointed at me. "How did you keep from going crazy from this stuff when you were a kid?"

His question made me laugh out loud. "Jake, you probably won't believe this, but as you were talking, you made me remember my friends' 1963 version of your music videos. It was the Sears catalog." Jake stared at me like I was crazy. "The catalog underwear ads were pretty much our only source of sex education, and those pictures were 10 times more tame than what you see watching a 'family hour' TV show today. The stranger-than-fiction part of this was that on catalog day, our mothers would race us to the mailboxes, to tear out the catalog pages with the women's underwear ads before we could get our little hormonal brains insane with stimulation. We always hoped that at least one of us would be faster than his mom. Even in those 'Brady Bunch' days, we thought we were all sex-crazed maniacs. I can't imagine being a teen and having to deal with the nonstop pounding you guys get on sex."

I share Jake's story for two reasons: First, to remind me to share that Sears catalog story with other parents. Those silly-but-true stories help us adults begin to understand the incredible differences between our teen years and yours. Parents really do come from a very different world. And trying to deal with these differences, and the fact that your world is nothing like the world they grew up in, can make your parents crazy—and, often, a little scared.

What a mom said:

"I try my best to give my kids a normal, healthy attitude about sex, but I feel like my influence is just a blip on the screen compared to

> TV, the Net, radio, and their friends. Of course, I want them to be open with me, but they're getting so much information, so fast, that I'm shocked by some of the questions, and I just don't know how to react. Sometimes, I'm speechless, and I wish I knew what to say or do. How do you explain certain sexual acts to a 13-year-old, when *you* didn't even know about them until you were in college? I want to be there for my kids, but I just can't get used to how quickly they're growing up—way before they're ready to handle all of the information they're getting. I worry all the time that they're going to get hurt."

Some parents, like this mom, get crazy trying to find a way to raise healthy kids in this insane world. Other adults like to run on about how immoral teens are these days, and how much more upstanding and righteous they were when they were kids. They're crazy, too, just in a different way. They don't realize (or don't want to admit) that the difference was the world around them. They did less sex and drugs *only because the culture around us wasn't so crazy back then*. If they had been bombarded, as you are, with these things, they'd have behaved exactly the same way. We all are pretty much the same when we're teenagers: nuts, and searching for answers to questions we can't ask, and sometimes don't even know we have.

> *We all are pretty much the same when we're teenagers: nuts, and searching for answers to questions we can't ask, and sometimes don't even know we have.*

Which brings me to the second reason I'm telling you about Jake. I can't recall any other kid who had the nerve or the insight to say that much about sex after meeting me only twice. He was actually able to put some words to his confusion, and he told me that he felt a lot better after just saying what he felt. He said just knowing that this is what everyone goes through helped him calm down. When we keep stuff like this bottled up inside ourselves, it kind of grows and grows, causing us to keep to ourselves way too much. So take a lesson from Jake: Try to talk this stuff out with an adult you respect and trust, like a parent, or teacher, or counselor. Keep in mind that they, too, were all overwhelmed by sex when they were teens. If you ask them to think back and remember, *really* remember what those days were *really* like, they'll understand. Maybe then they'll also realize how much tougher things are for you guys on this subject of sex, and perhaps they won't act so "*gay*" about it. Which brings me to another "committee" question: Who was the committee who decided that "gay" equals "bad"?

THIS IS REALLY GAY

Before we jump into the subject of sexual orientation (and my hate mail starts arriving) you need to read my small-print disclaimer:

> The section you are about to read examines the topic of sexual orientation strictly from a scientific and psychological perspective. This is not intended to supercede your own religious and/or moral beliefs. I encourage you to use this information as a scientific basis over which to impose your own religious views.

You have a big sex problem. Your teen culture has somehow decided that people who are sexually different are sick, perverse, and dangerous whackos who should be feared, ridiculed, and persecuted. These are kids who are called "gay," but who actually have a variety of sexual differences. This group includes teenagers who might be *gay* (male homosexual), *lesbian* (female homosexual), *bisexual* (males or females attracted to both sexes), or *transgendered* (boys or girls who feel trapped in the wrong-sex body). We might more accurately call this group GLBT (for *G*ay, *L*esbian, *B*isexual and *T*ransgendered kids), but we'll just use the term *gay* for now.

As a result of your culture's bigotry against GLBT people, the word *gay* has now been elected as the worst possible teen descriptor for anything bad or hated. ("Man, that math test was really gay"; "I hate Mindy. She's so mean—she's really gay.") How many kids *don't* say this?

Why is it a problem? Two reasons: First, talking like this says you approve of bigotry and hatred, two things our world has plenty of already. Don't think so? OK, what is the "label" *you've* been given—how are you identified? Are you the "black" kid, the "jock," the "cheerleader"? Perhaps you're the "smart" one, or the "white" one. How would it feel to hear your 20 African-American friends constantly say, "Man, that Osama bin Laden, he's, like, really 'white,' you know?" And if you think this "gay-bash" talk doesn't happen that much, think again.

In a recent National School Climate Survey, gay (GLBT) high-school kids reported that the year had not been pleasant. Ninety-one percent were present when "gay" was used as a put-down by their friends; 84 percent had been verbally harassed for being "gay"; 41 percent had been pushed or shoved for being "gay." And just for being sexually different, 21 percent of these students were *assaulted* (punched, kicked, or injured with a weapon).

Kids will be kids, right? Well, let's take a look at how the "responsible" adults were doing. Twenty-four percent of the surveyed kids heard antigay remarks *from the teachers,* and *82 percent watched the teachers do nothing when they heard others talk this trash.* This dangerous ignorance has become so common in our culture that we don't even see it for what it is.

The second reason this prejudicial language is a problem is that of those 20 friends you're hanging out with, laughing and telling gay jokes, at least one or two of those kids are laughing outside but crying inside *because they are gay.* That's the statistical fact. But which ones? Could it be your best friend who stuck with you when Ashley decided you weren't cool enough to make it onto her "cool kids" list (wasn't Ashley really "white" for hurting you like that?)? Maybe it's Susan, who pulled your butt out of the fire when she helped you pass math last semester (and that nasty math teacher, he was, like, really, really "white," you know?). Or how about that football player you didn't even know, who jumped in and took your back when the gangsters were getting ready to rearrange your front?

> Tom winced as if I had just drilled his tooth without numbing it. He repeated my question as if to point out its stupidity: "Have I ever thought of coming out of the closet [announce that he's gay] to my friends? Only all of the time! Don't you think that I'm in agony living secretly as a homosexual? But do you have any idea what it's like to be 17 years old and gay? I don't know where you grew up, but I'm not kidding when I say that, if word got out about me, there's a good chance I'd be dead before my senior prom. I play football, and nobody messes with me now. The team protects its own, you know what I'm sayin'?

> But, man, if the kids ever knew I was gay, I'd be hunted down like a mad dog by the skinheads, and no one would lift a freakin' finger to help. No one would even call 911. Just another dead fag, right?"
>
> Tom paused to collect himself. He took a deep breath and then he quietly continued. "That's not the worst part, you know? I could, like, handle the skins, I think. I'd be scared, but you know what? Those red-suspender posers are not what worry me. They couldn't scare me enough to make me live like this. The thing that would make me really want to die is the look I know I'd see on my friends' faces when I told them who I really am." This tough boy's eyes began to mist. "We're really tight, you know? We're like brothers. Most of us come from bad times and bad homes. We're all the family most of us got." Tom got up and walked to my pictures of my wife and kids. "So when you ask me that question, you think about whether you'd ever say anything that would make you lose your family. And not just lose them, like in a car wreck, but have them walk away from you, like you were some dangerous, sicko pervert or something. So tell me, Doc, what would you do?"

Think of Tom before you start to tell gay jokes the next time. Think of your best friend, or your little sister, because the psychological fact is that a sexual difference is not a disease or a defect: *It's a difference*, one that can happen to anyone. The Homer Simpsons of the world have this belief that, if something is different, then it's automatically sick and weird, and should automatically be hated and feared. It's embarrassing to admit this, but the Homer types largely control our society's view of sexual differences. They say bizarre things, like gays are dangerous sexual predators who might molest our kids. And that being different sexually means that you are messed up morally. The fact is that gays are just people, like you and me. Most are good, moral, and caring people (just like straight folks), who happen to be different sexually. A few could be dangerous sexual predators, *just as with straight people*. The Homers also like to say that gays are "recruited" by other gays (they aren't), or that they "choose" to be gay (they don't), so they can "choose" to be straight (they can't). Kids don't decide to be gay or straight, any more than they choose to be short or tall.

Kids don't decide to be gay or straight, any more than they choose to be short or tall.

The scientific evidence strongly suggests (and will likely very soon prove) that sexual orientation is determined by brain structure, which most likely results from genetic differences. Knowing this, how can we justify persecuting gay kids? Even if you believe that sexual differences result from some dysfunction (and there is no scientific evidence to support that), why is it OK to hurt these teens?

If it's OK to tell harmful gay jokes, then racial, ethnic, and religious hatred must also be cool, right? And if it's OK to hate, harass, and hurt people, just because they're different from us, then that good ol' boy Osama had every right to kill three thousand Americans, just because we're Americans, right? No? Well, then, where do we draw the line? Once we decide that it's OK to hate someone because he's different, we become a dangerous weapon that kills much more stupidly and effectively than any terrorist could ever dream. Taking that first small step down that ignorant road of prejudice makes all of the next steps possible, particularly for the crazies among us who hunt for reasons to hunt for humans. That journey starts with "innocently" calling things, or behaviors, or people we hate "gay," and can end with great kids being beaten to death because they're different. Think about it. Think about Tom the next time the gay bashing starts. Think about Ryan.

"I never knew what being really scared really meant. I do now. Ever since I started the [Gay/Straight Alliance] club at school, I got pretty much what I expected. You know, the taunts, and slurs, and stuff. Sometimes it got nasty, but that, like, comes with the turf, you know?" Ryan's voice got much smaller. "But I never expected what happened on Friday night." As he paused to collect himself, Ryan's stitched and puffy eyes reminded me of those of a combat survivor: small, fearful, flitting around the room as if waiting for an unseen shell to go off. "They grabbed me at the dance. In the parking lot, somebody pulled a pillow case over my head, and pulled me down. All I remember is being kicked a lot, and thinking that if I just lay still and don't scream, they'll stop. They didn't. I guess I passed out for a while, and then I, like, woke up somewhere else. It was in a field or something. I remember hearing crickets that seemed really, really loud, even though the bag was still over my head. My arms and legs wouldn't move. Later, I found out I was tied up. I guess I was moaning or something, because this one voice kept whispering, 'Shut-up, fag. You're a dead f'ng fag now.' I smelled beer. It had been poured all over me.

"This sounds weird, but I still didn't think I was going to die. I was pretty sure these were kids from my school, so there was no way they would kill me, right? Then a car pulls up, and the crickets stopped. The whisperer starts screaming, 'Did you get it? Did you actually f'ng get it?' Then he yells, 'ALL RIGHT!' I hear car doors open and close, and lots of feet and murmurs—like an argument was starting. The voices got quiet, and 'Whisperer' starts laughing, real crazy. I feel this hard thing pressed against my ear, and 'Whisperer' screams, 'DIE, FAG,' and cocks the gun. Then I knew I was actually going to die." Ryan's purple, swollen face contorted into sobs, "I started crying and begging them to not kill me. I swore I'd never tell on them. I promised to leave school and town if they'd let me live. 'Whisperer' just laughs crazy again, and then he pulls the trigger."

Ryan cried hard for 10 minutes. Finally, he quieted, trying to cover his face from a shame that belonged to many, but not to him. "Later, I found that I had wet my pants from being so scared. The cops keep asking me if the gun was real, and if it was loaded. How the hell would I know? Maybe it was, and it didn't work. Or maybe it wasn't, and this was a sick joke. DOES THAT MAKE A GOD-DAMN DIFFERENCE?"

When he composed himself again, Ryan looked quizzically at me with those tortured eyes full of pain, both physical and emotional. "You know what the last cop asked me? He asked if I had tried to rape anybody at the dance. He didn't say 'meet,' or 'hook up.' He said 'rape.' Why would he ask that? If *you* got beat up, would he ask *you* that?" Ryan knew the answer to his own question.

—Notes from an interview with a hate-crime
assault victim. The attackers were never identified.

The hatred that Tom and Ryan must deal with 24/7 is an amazing thing, because of its intensity, and where it comes from. Much of that hatred comes from a fear of *ourselves*, a fear that can arise during the normal process of developing sexually. This process, which I'm about to explain, is called "resolving" or "fixing" your sexual orientation in place. If kids don't stay calm during this phase, they can sometimes transform their fear of themselves into the seething hatred that infected the kids who attacked Ryan. Like his "Whisperer" proved so terrifyingly well, the only "different" people we need to fear are those who need to hate.

A late, great cartoonist named Walt Kelly said it best when he paraphrased an American war hero's words: "I have met the enemy, and he is *us*!"

How Sexual Orientation Gets Resolved

Just when you think that sex issues can't get any tougher, they do. One of the reasons that we hate gays so much is that, when we're young, many, or most, of us can have very confusing sexual thoughts and feelings that can make us uncertain of our own sexual orientation. So we hate them because they remind us of something uncomfortable about ourselves. For example, sometimes we might do things like fantasize about being the opposite sex, and wonder what that might be like. Sound weird? It's actually very common, normal, and harmless, and it has nothing to do with making you gay or straight.

Another cause for confusion (and sometimes fear and hate) is that, as you develop sexually in adolescence, your initial sexual feelings can be kind of vague, with sort-of attractions to both males and females. That's because, during adolescence, you develop the ability to feel and understand things on a much deeper level, and your emotions become much stronger and more intense than when you were younger. These feelings make your relationships much stronger, both with friends you have who are boys, friends you have who are girls, and adult friends. The new, powerful sex urges you feel get mixed up with the new, powerful relationships you now have with kids and adults whom you like and admire. Because your brain is new to all of this, sometimes the wiring gets a little scrambled, and you have a confusing sexual attraction mixed in with your emotional attachment to certain people, whether they're the same or opposite sex, kids or adults.

DON'T BE FREAKED OUT BY THESE THINGS. These experiences are very common, and they do not mean that you'll be gay or straight. It's best to not act on these confusing urges, because they just go away after a while, as your true sexual orientation emerges. Then you'll be left with the "real" and valuable parts of these relationships, which you will see were not really sexual after all. Just bad wiring that straightens out in a bit (see Chapter 1).

But these things can freak some people out if they're not prepared, and they can be terrified that this means they might be sexually different. Too many take this fear, fan it into anger, and then blast it at those brave people who are courageous enough to be honest about their sexual orientation. A good offense is the best defense, right? If we put down gays long enough, loudly enough, or violently enough, then no one would ever suspect that we suspect that we might be homosexual, right?

Anyone who feels secure about himself feels no need to hate others.

The fact is that the "macho" guy who *talks* the most trash about hating gays is very often the same "macho" guy who *worries* the most about being gay, or of even just being called gay. Anyone who feels secure about himself feels no need to hate others. Think about that: *If you're OK with you, putting down other people is no fun at all.*

In Part Three of this book, we'll talk more about your "what to do when . . ." questions about sex. For now, just understand that growing up is anything but simple when it comes to sex issues. And the weirdness can be affecting some other folks even more than you. Like who? Like . . .

YOUR PARENTS: The Only Folks More Weirded Out by You Than You

The single greatest shake-up of your relationship with Mom and Dad happens when you become a sexual creature. Just as your own life changes so drastically as you develop sexually, so does your relationship with your parents. The rules of how they relate to you suddenly get put under a microscope. Overnight, old ways can become wrong ways, and sometimes, infuriating ways.

With girls, Dad may suddenly find that the old, friendly "pat-on-the-rear" is now most unwelcome. After that first verbal beating from his daughter ("DON'T YOU *EVER* PAT MY BUTT AGAIN IN FRONT OF MY FRIENDS! OR ANY OTHER TIME!"), Dad might slowly and sadly withdraw completely from a daughter he loves so much, thinking that she doesn't want him around anymore.

Boys have been known to flip out on moms who think it's "so cute" that Junior hates it when Mom walks into the bathroom unannounced while he's in the tub. She might even laugh with Junior's sister about his newfound modesty. Major bad idea. The resulting explosion from Junior can wound Mom terribly, causing her to see Junior as some abusive monster to be avoided.

For both boys and girls, things that used to be fun ways of connecting with parents (like parent-forced hugs, rear-end pattings, and hair messings) suddenly become horrendously embarrassing violations of personal space. It's a really hard time, because both sides of this issue have a point. Your parents might argue that all that cutesy stuff was great by you yesterday, so why are you snapping out on them today? In response, you could argue that it's unlikely Dad would show his affection for other adults by making fart noises on their hairy male arms, or by patting their female butts. In other words, you feel like an adult now, and those old child games feel so stupid all of a sudden.

Here's the problem: How can you stay connected without baby-noise games? How can your relationship with your parents evolve to handle these huge changes in you?

> "Things are, like, cold at home. I don't know what's happened. It's not like we had a big fight or anything." At 13, Becky seemed bewildered and sad beyond her years. "Mom looks like someone died or something, and my dad acts all hurt. I don't get it. All I did was to ask them to stop talking to me like a little girl. I didn't tell them to stop talking."

Parents have this, like, learning disability. It's another part of their craziness. They're very bad with numbers when it comes to remembering their kid's age. They can't seem to get it in their heads that their child is growing up. They try to stay hip, to see their teenager as a human being on the edge of becoming an adult, but they keep underestimating how old she really is. They make kids nuts when they do this, but it really is not intended to hurt. It's just that they usually love their kid so much that they can't stand the thought that she will very soon be leaving.

So, since they're crazy, parents will sometimes try to pretend away things that remind them that their time with their child is running out. Things like sexual development. For this one, huge change symbolizes, more than any other, that a child is growing up, and is, in fact, no longer really a *child*. She is now a *young woman*.

Because the old "child" rules no longer apply, too many parents sadly withdraw from kids in the face of their sexual development because they don't know how to stay connected. Don't let this happen with your parents. Try to reach out to them. Let them know that you still want to be connected with them, but in new ways that work better for you. As silly as this may sound, you have to educate them about what you want from them. They might be backing off, sadly and quietly confused about where and how to talk with you.

Suggest specific activities, like coffee-shop dates or after-dinner walks, or late-night chats. We'll talk a lot more about this later on, but, for now, understand that both your parents and you have to reach out to each other to renegotiate your relationship, since you're not a little kid anymore. Things can get crazy in a family when people stop talking to each other. Things mostly work out fine if parents and teens just stay connected—*particularly* through the crazy times.

Speaking of crazy times, we're now ready to talk about the inner "morphing" of adolescence: your psychological development. If you thought that your outward physical changes were something, wait until you see what's happening to your inward self. The next chapter will explain why your parents are again staring at you in wide-eyed, open-mouthed amazement: They're watching you race through huge changes that flash by like turnpike mile markers on your sprint toward adulthood. Welcome to Chapter 3: the wild, wacky, and wonderful world of intellectual, moral, social, and emotional teen growth.

By the way, are you housebroken yet? The only reason I ask is that, according to Ronnie, you're really a monkey becoming an elephant (turn the page).

YOUR PSYCHOLOGICAL DEVELOPMENT

It's like... a Disney Movie?

"I change so much, so fast, that I'm like a character on a TV show: 'Tune in next week to see who Devon will be.'"—Devon, age 15

Ronnie wracked his 14-year-old brain to find a way to explain his experience of being a teenager. And when he found one, he hated it because it reminded him of how he was so young—and yet, so old?

"Remember the first Aladdin movie? I haven't seen it in years, you know—I don't watch that stuff now. I'm not a little kid, you know." Looking flustered, Ronnie paused and asked a question he really didn't want answered: "Why am I telling you I'm not a little kid, if I'm sure I'm not? Maybe I'm not really sure. Adults don't have to say they're not little kids, do they?" He blinked, and then switched channels again: "I hate it when my head goes in circles like this. That's why I never answer questions from adults about myself, you know? They keep asking what I mean because I confuse them. And the more I explain, the more confused I keep getting. So I end up telling them, 'Forget it.' But that gets them really mad, like you're disrespecting them. So it's better to just shut up in the beginning."

Ronnie sighed and shook his head as if to shake out the loose, distracting parts of what he was trying to say. "Anyway," he continued,

> "remember that scene where the Genie is transforming Abu [Aladdin's monkey] into a dozen different things [a horse, a car, an elephant], to carry Aladdin to meet the princess? Abu keeps, like, popping from being one creature to another, except he keeps parts of the old creatures mixed in with the new ones? Fourteen is like that, I think. I don't know." He changed channels again: "Does everyone question themselves all the time, like I do?" Leaving no space for an answer, Ronnie sped on, "How do you know when you're really sure about something or. . . ."

I wrote down Ronnie's description of adolescence for two reasons: First, what he said made so much sense, but second, the *way* he spoke described it even better. Having a mind that seems to fly all over the place, jumping from one thought to the next, is pretty normal for teenagers. And his comparison of teenage development with Abu (Aladdin's monkey) was a great metaphor. Being an adolescent is very much like being that monkey who pops out a horse's head, then camel legs, then a '57 Chevy front end, and then an elephant trunk. But then, finally, for Abu and the adolescent, all the parts come together in one wonderful package.

Having a mind that seems to fly all over the place, jumping from one thought to the next, is pretty normal for teenagers.

Remember how your physical development happens in bursts (see Chapter 2), with some unpleasant and uneven phases, until it all smoothes out? Your psychological (non-body) self evolves exactly the same way, except, instead of *looking* strange to yourself, you can *feel* strange inside of yourself. So much so that, at times, you might worry that you have no idea who you are anymore. Although that might feel bad, it's actually part of the plan. Sometimes, growth is hard work. But this is work that's well worth the effort, because this is the time of your life when you must begin to find out who you truly are. Yet, at first in adolescence, who you are can seem to be constantly changing. It can feel a little crazy. You can end up talking like Ronnie, sounding a little crazy to yourself. (And you can make your parents crazy, too, trying to figure out what's going on with you, as you try to figure out what's going on with you.)

But you're not crazy—you're just traveling on four incredibly important journeys *all at the same time*. At fantastic speeds, you're growing intellectually, morally, socially, and last but by no means least, emotionally. Yet, just like traveling around the world, each of these four journeys ultimately brings you home to yourself, to who you are—to your identity. Kinda' makes your head swim, doesn't it?

IDENTITY: DON'T LEAVE HOME WITHOUT IT!

Forget geometry if you have to, drop AP history if you want, give up basketball, even miss out on the prom if you must, but do not, under any circumstances, miss out on developing your identity in adolescence. It's the most precious thing you can take with you into adulthood. Remember, in Chapter 1, we spoke of how identity formation is your brain's defense against the insanity in the world, and how learning who you are is like a journey? In this chapter, which describes your development (growth), you'll see that your identity voyage is actually four separate development journeys wrapped up into one huge adventure of you searching for your identity. But what exactly is identity?

Alena was embarrassed from the moment she walked in the door. At 15, she wore the leftover pieces of all the different styles she had experimented with in the past few years. Goth, boarder, punk, preppie—she seemed to have at least one leftover piercing, wristband, tattoo, or shirt from each era. "This was all really a big mistake," she apologized. "I shouldn't be here. There's nothing wrong with me. You should be seeing some other kid who really does need a doctor. I'm, like, taking up someone's space."

After she sat and picked at her black nail polish a bit, she looked up again. "My mom, like, overreacted that night when I said I needed to talk to a counselor. Like I told her, there's nothing wrong, really. I'm not, like, gonna' kill myself or anything. She doesn't believe me. She's sure I'm a rape victim, or am pregnant or something." Alena looked up, half smiled and sighed, "I'm not any of those things."

"Well," I asked, "Then what things are you? Can you tell me a little about yourself?" Watching her head slump back down, I knew that I had blundered into the thing she was trying to say to her mom that night.

She sat silently for many minutes before speaking, but you could feel her worry growing in the silence. "No," she said quietly, "I can't tell you about myself. I don't know what to say. Whenever I think of something, I immediately realize that it's not me. It's just like a wrapper around me, you know?"

When I told her I wasn't sure I understood, she sighed again. "How can I explain something to you that I can't explain to me!" she snapped. Irritated, she held up her tattooed arm to me. "Look," she said. "See this 'tat [tattoo]? It's punk. That's a wrapper. That's not me. That's not who I am. For years, I've been doing wrappers instead of finding out who I am inside, you know? Now do you understand?" Her eyes seemed to be begging me to say I understood.

But before I could answer, Alena exhaled loudly in frustration. "Forget it. This is stupid, pointless crap. I told you this was a waste of time. I don't even know what I'm saying." But, suddenly, she found the idea she was searching for. She spoke slowly. "Is this about what my teacher calls 'finding your identity'? Exactly what is identity?"

Identity is what and who you *are.* Identity is the sum all of the things that make you *you*: your morals and music, your weaknesses and wisdom, your looks and likes, your hopes and heritage—the assembled parts of you. Identity development is much like putting together a fascinating jigsaw puzzle of yourself.

Picture the world as a giant box of puzzle pieces. As you race through adolescence, you see a billion different things (pieces) that you must look at, try on, and then decide if they fit. The puzzle parts of identity include everything that makes up the world: values, vulgarities, beliefs, boxing, politics, piercings, rugby, religion . . . the list is just as endless as the "must-answer" questions that keep you up at night: "Am I a good person?" "Am I a good dancer?" "Should I do dishes?" "Should I do drugs?" "Why can't I be cool?" "Why can't I be cool with not being cool?" and so on, and so on. . . . As I said in Chapter 1, the hard part is that each of these "must-answer" questions must be answered *by you.* No one else can tell you who you are. No book, no friend, no religion, no shrink, no philosophy, no parent—NO ONE BUT YOU, because answering these questions is only done by living, seeing, questioning, and reflecting. There are no short cuts. Trust me on this, I've looked. You have to do this yourself.

"I'VE GOTTA BE ME . . . BUT I CAN'T HELP THINKING SOMEONE ELSE WOULD BE MORE QUALIFIED!"

If this sounds like a lot of work, it is. But the rewards are incredible, because when you form your identity (shrinks call this *identity consolidation*), wonderful things begin to happen for you, in a million different ways. It might even make you smile.

I hardly recognized Timothy, but I couldn't figure out why. Physically, he looked pretty much the same as when I had last seen him at age 15. But, three years later, something was very different. "I'm back home on spring break [from college]," he explained, "and, for some reason, I had this strong urge to see you." He startled both of us with a booming laugh. "I'm laughing because, do you remember when I couldn't say things like," he deepened his voice here for effect, "'I HAD THIS STRONG URGE TO SEE YOU,' because I was always so scared people would think I was talking about sex or something?" He laughed at his old self again, causing me to flash back to Tim three years prior: uncertain, anxious, timid—constantly obsessed with what everyone else was thinking about him, too fearful to do anything that might make him stand out and possibly be ridiculed. And, as I used to point out to him, he never, ever, seemed to smile.

"Things are mostly good with me," he continued. "I don't know where to begin. I've discovered I love art—sculpting, actually. I have no idea how I'll make a living at it, but you know what? I really don't care. I'm just following my dream for now. I know that I'll make it work out somehow. You know what else? I don't even care about the weird looks I get from other people when I tell them what I'm doing. I spent last summer fixing bombed-out, inner-city houses for poor families, and loved that, too. Some neighborhood drug dealers used to make fun of us. We'd blow kisses and flash peace signs. They didn't know what to do with that. Can you believe that was me? And remember how I'd only chase hot girls who'd make me look good? Hold onto your clipboard: I'm in heavy love with a girl who isn't a 'Baywatch Babe.' She's just, like, a real person, you know?"

"Tim," I asked, "If you could summarize what's changed about you, how would you say it?"

His smile left for the moment, but in its place was a relaxed, thoughtful look, as he searched himself. "I don't know," he shrugged. "I think it's like I suddenly stopped apologizing to everybody for everything I was not, you know? I used to always worry about all the things I wasn't, like cool, or athletic, or brilliant. Then I started to see who I was: what I like, what I believe, what kind of person I am. And you know something? I'm not so bad. I guess I'm getting comfortable with who I am. If others don't like it," he shrugged again, "well, that just sucks for them."

Watching his smile return, it hit me what was so very different about him: Tim was smiling.

The first step to getting your smile back (the one you used to have before you started adolescence) is discovering who you are.

Identity consolidation can do that. It can make you smile, which is what happens when you finally stop worrying so much. You stop worrying so much because you can start to be yourself, instead of constantly trying to become something else that others might like better. The first step to getting your smile back (the one you used to have before you started adolescence) is discovering who you are. When I asked him, Tim had one last message to share with you about your own search for identity:

> "If I had to do it [adolescence] all over again, I'd try and not worry so much, you know? Your head just goes 24/7, thinking that you're so messed up. I wish there was some way I could tell kids to not worry so much, that all that stuff going through their heads is just part of how we figure out who we are, that they'll be OK, that they'll survive."
>
> "And maybe even smile again?" I asked.
>
> "Yeah," he nodded, "If I could, anybody can."

With Tim's wise words echoing in your head, it's time to talk about those four identity-building growth adventures that have taken over your life: intellectual, moral, social, and emotional. The first, intellectual growth, will help explain my teenage son's amazed stares as he tries to figure out how his brilliant father suddenly got so stupid in the past year.

YOUR INTELLECTUAL JOURNEY: Night Vision for Your Brain

Buying computers makes me crazy. It seems that every time I'm driving home with my latest Star-Wars, killer-fast computer, feeling all smug about how cutting edge it is, I pass a billboard that's showing off a newer model that makes mine look like yesterday's Chicken McNuggets.

Raising teenagers makes me crazy, too. It seems that every time I'm driving home with my son, we pass a billboard that he reacts to in a way that tells me he's just burst onto another intellectual level that makes my old mental picture of him look like yesterday's . . . well, you know. In this way, computers and kids are the same: They both grow new capabilities with astonishing speed that's hard to keep up with.

This is what's happening right now, to the computer in your head: your brain. With each month that passes, you develop higher and higher powers of mental functioning that can create some pretty spectacular thinking. And that thinking can create some pretty spectacular conflicts.

That spectacular thinking involves a bunch of new skills that began emerging, along with your growth spurt. These are new powers that make you as different from a younger kid as your computer is different from a calculator. Like that calculator, kids up to about age 10 can think only in very simple ways. For example, not that long ago, you saw a concept like justice in very black-and-white terms. Some person was either innocent or guilty, some action either good or bad, some belief either right or wrong.

Now, all of a sudden, you're seeing everything in much more complex ways. Things that used to be black or white have become much more involved, often with many maddening shades of gray that can make your head hurt. Like Melissa's did when she discovered that "simple justice" isn't so simple once your intellect grows in adolescence.

> "When I was a little girl [at age 8], I hated my father for leaving my mother. It seemed so unfair, like there was no justice. So I wouldn't go to see him, I wouldn't take his phone calls, and I used to rip up all the cards and things he'd send to me. Now [at age 13], I'm starting to see things I never noticed before. Like how my mother always tears him down, how she exaggerates and lies about what a creep he is, and how she acts like I don't love her if I say anything good about my dad, or even if I just keep quiet when she's yelling about him. I'm also realizing how he did keep trying to see me all these years, even though I was so horrible to him all the time, and how he never, ever, said even one mean thing to me about my mother. Now, I don't know what to believe. I still think he's a creep for leaving, but maybe he had some good reasons . . . and maybe I hurt him really bad. . . ." Melissa's voice trailed off into tears.
>
> After a minute, she continued, but in a very small voice: "Now I think that maybe I've been a creep, too. And I see my mom as a semi-creep. It's so hard to know what's right. Justice used to be so simple. But I guess it wasn't ever really simple. It was just that I saw things like a little kid back then. I guess *I* was what used to be simple."

Melissa had stumbled into the most powerful aspect to adolescent intellectual growth: *It makes you go back and reevaluate everything you once thought was true.* Remember when you found out there was no Santa Claus? Adolescent mental growth is like the Santa scandal, a hundred times over. In other words, all things that you were told were true suddenly become questionable in the bright light of your new powers of intellect. Your new brain can perform miraculous new functions that can punch holes in many of your old beliefs about the world, beliefs that often were Santa-Claus-type explanations that adults just handed you. Back then, you were naive enough to accept them without question. Your new skills make you very different now.

Now you can see that, at times, Mom, Dad, teachers, coaches, and political and religious leaders all can be wrong in their views, that they can make mistakes, that they don't have all the answers.

Your new brain skills include seeing new possibilities, creating hypotheses (other possible explanations of things), predicting outcomes, and doing critical thinking on complex levels that not only allow, but *compel,* you to analyze the world *on your own*, and not just accept others' opinions as fact. Now you can see that, at times, Mom, Dad, teachers, coaches, and political and religious leaders all can be wrong in their views, that they can make mistakes, that they don't have all the answers. But, then again, you can see that neither do you. This can make you mad. This can make you crazy. This can make your parents crazy.

I noted to Michelle that today she was a very different 13-year-old from the one who sat in my office last week and emotionally gutted her very ill mother. She smiled weakly and offered an even weaker explanation that she clearly didn't buy herself: "That's 'cause the dumb, dying bitch ain't here today." Shocked at the venom in her own words, she kept talking, but kept getting more upset with the depth of her own rage. "Look, I'm sorry, OK? But I've had it with the smiley-face, look-on-the-bright-side, God-opens-doors crap. My mother's dying, and nobody's gonna' stop that, OK? How can they [her parents] keep pretending everything's cool? They can keep fooling themselves and my sister if they want, but they better shut up with that around me, 'cause I deal with life straight up, you know? I can't stand hearing them talk like that, and every time they don't talk straight, I'll get so nasty that they'll finally leave me alone. It's the only way they learn. If they can't be mature, then I don't want to hear a damn thing from them."

I let her sit and replay her own words for a bit. In her eyes, you could see a thousand thoughts that she didn't want to say out loud. Finally, as gently as I could, I asked, "So how should they talk about this with you, Michelle? How should they talk about something that scary? Maybe you're right. Maybe their way isn't so good. But what exactly is the 'right' way for your folks to talk about your mom's cancer, so that you won't get mad?"

I paused, feeling my own stomach get tight, and then spoke even more softly: "Or is it that maybe you just don't want to hear about it at all, since it's just too awful? Michelle, are there any words that can make this OK?"

Michelle started to get up to leave, muttering that this was "all just too f'ng stupid." Then she grabbed a smiley-face squish toy from my table, whirled, and fired it at the wall, smashing the glass in a picture frame. She spun back around to glare at me, hands on her hips as if daring me to respond. At first, her fierce eyes locked coldly on mine, but, ever so slowly, they rimmed and filled with tears. "I'M NOT GOING TO CRY!" she yelled. "I'M NOT F'NG CRYING. THAT'S WHAT YOU WANT, RIGHT? WELL TOO F'NG BAD! TOO F'NG. . . ." As her sobs made a liar out of her, she tried to hold on to her anger, to avoid feeling her pain: "There," she choked, "Happy? Now I'm an f'ng mess just like them. That's what you wanted, right? So, now that you won, you tell me, 'doctor-knows-every-f'ng-thing': What is the RIGHT f'ng way to talk about this? WELL?" she demanded, as she folded her arms like a teacher, "I'M WAITING."

To my surprise, I found old, leftover tears from my own old losses in my own older eyes. I could see that Michelle's face was softening as she saw them, too. "Michelle," I sighed, "I have no idea what the right way is. I don't think there is a right way, and I've been through this a few times in my own life. But I do think that a wrong way is to just shut up and be angry all the time. Maybe your folks don't have the answers, but maybe nobody else does, either: You, me, or . . .," I nodded toward the now glass-encrusted toy she had hurled at my wall, ". . . or even poor Smiley." Looking at poor Smiley seemed to drain the rage out of Michelle. With a sob-chuckle, she spoke, but gently now: "Sorry about Smiley. I'll fix your diploma thing."

I pretended to be horrified: "Geezzz, out of 15 dumb plaques, you had to zero in on my diploma?" Michelle actually smiled for a tenth of a second, but then she had something important to say.

"You know, it's really, really hard, the first time your parents don't know what to do about something. You suddenly see that they're just people. Like that song says, "just a slob like one of us." I get mad at them for being so stupid, but I know I'm at least as stupid. And I hate myself for hating them, when they're just doing the best they can. I feel like I'm fighting all the time, outside with my parents, and inside with my own head. It just makes you mad, you know?"

Mad, and perhaps crazy? Or at least so it looks to parents, until they realize just how hard it can be to be a teenager whose intellectual growth just knocked Mom and Dad down a few rankings in the smart league. But the truth is that Mom and Dad are not getting a lot dumber, *you're just getting a lot smarter, and more able to successfully challenge their thinking*. And if you are typical, you might look for every opportunity to point this out to them. Michelle was a great example of how your new, spectacular thinking can lead to your new, spectacular conflicts, *both outside and inside of yourself*. Both types of fights (inner and outer) result from the simple, natural, and irresistible act of thinking for yourself. But strife is not always bad. Sometimes it's part of nature's plan for you. Conflict, both outward and inward, is one of the most important ways that you discover your identity.

In the end, the conflicts help you discover what you believe, and who you are.

You find who you are in the strangest places. Some, like writing, reading, or rapping, are calm and peaceful. Some, like hiking, hang gliding, or hanging out, are active and fun. But many identity-building experiences are loud and sometimes scary, like arguments with your parents about religion, fights with your best friends about drugs, and yelling matches with that infuriating kid in your mirror who still won't do her homework. As you engage the world, and yourself, you're forced to take stands, to have opinions that often conflict with others' or even with your own. But it's OK. In the end, the conflicts help you discover what you believe, and who you are.

THE OUTSIDE CONFLICTS: Sometimes You Have to Fight the Powers That Be

Be brutally honest. Haven't you just recently noticed how incredibly dumb grown-ups can be at times? Suddenly, it seems they've started saying things that make you want to scream because they're not true (in your mind), or they're obvious (at least to you), or because they're just pointless (to your life, anyway). It's like some "dumb-down" virus has been infecting the brain of every adult authority figure around you: Police, principals, presidents, and parents all seem to have this bug. What disease caused them to become so newly stupid? It's called TEENUS KNOWALLUS, and guess what? That virus is not in the adult heads, it's in yours. It works like this:

As your intellectual know-how increases, you get smarter. And, as you get smarter, authority figures around you get dumber, or at least they seem to. What's changing is not them, but your *view* of them. As you grow to see them more as equals, you also feel free to disagree with them more as chumps. If the disagreement concerns their vanilla versus your mucho-mocha-mango ice cream, that's not too big a deal. But if the disagreement concerns their saving your soul versus your spending eternity in hell, that's a very big deal. Brandon would rather have fought about the ice cream.

> "If my [born-again-Christian] parents lived in the Middle East and were forced to be Muslims or something, they'd know how I feel. I don't mean to hurt them, but I think their religion is just dumb. Now that I'm 15, I think I should be able to decide what I believe. They think God actually talks to them through their Bible and their minister. I think their Bible was just written by regular people, just like anybody. Who says God told them what to write? How do they know that? And I think their minister is a jerk. He yells, and screams, and disrespects people, and says everyone who doesn't believe what he believes is going to Hell. So God will send all the Jews, Buddhists, Muslims, and everybody else to Hell? I don't think so. I THINK THAT'S STUPID. AND I THINK THAT ANYBODY WHO CAN THINK THAT WAY IS STUPID." Brandon's anger faded, along with his yelling, leaving only the pain behind his words.

> "My mom and dad and I used to be really close, you know? But that was when I went to church with them and believed what they believe. Now, I realize I never really believed, you know? I was just doing what I was told, like cleaning up my room. I didn't think my room needed to be clean, I was just following orders." With a sigh he continued, "I still love them, even though they think I don't, or that I can't if I don't belong to their religion. I don't mean to put them down, but what am I supposed to do? I truly believe that their religion is stupid. Am I supposed to lie? Would that make their God happy if I pretend to believe in a bunch of crap I can't accept? Wouldn't that really be disrespecting them if I went to their church and lied about what I believe? How can I make a choice between loving my parents and telling the truth?"
>
> For a minute, Brandon's brain searched for another argument to (bolster) his point. When he found it, he immediately saw how it would make sense only to him, and not to his folks, but he shared it anyway: "Jesus' parents were Jewish, right? Did Mary and Joseph accuse him of not loving them because he didn't believe what they did? Didn't Jesus have to follow what his head told him was right for him? Shouldn't I?"

I had no slick answers for Brandon. There really aren't any easy solutions to these kinds of adolescent binds. He was caught between a rock and a hard place, between wanting to be connected with his parents and, at the same time, wanting to be connected with himself, with his identity. But his new skills of intellect were colliding with the old beliefs of his parents, and their relationship was caught in the crossfire. Sometimes, ignorance *is* bliss. Sometimes, intelligence *is* painful.

The answer here is easy, right? Brandon's parents are too controlling, right? And they should let him make up his own mind about religion, right? Sure, that could be right, I guess. But what about Brandon's parents' position? What if they truly, truly believe that Brandon will spend eternity in the fires of Hell if he leaves their faith? Maybe that sounds dumb to you, but what if that's what they hold as *their* truth? Can you honestly say that, if you were in their position, you'd just sit back and watch your kid lose his eternal soul? What kind of parents would, or could, do that? It's very easy to say that, no matter the issue, be it religion, sex, drugs, curfew, whatever, parents should just let teenagers decide. But what would you do if you were sure that letting your 15-year-old child do what she wanted might hurt her terribly, perhaps even kill her? Which is the act of greater parental love: Letting go, or fighting with your kid?

So, what's the answer? *First, to understand the question.* The fact is that, often, there is no one truth to guide these sorts of issues. Too many times, kids and parents fight endlessly about who is "right" and who is "wrong," as if there actually is a "right" position. A position that, somehow properly spoken, will magically convince the other side to say something like, "Oh, yes, Brandon dear, you're right. How could we have been so stupid? Thank you, our 15-year-old son, for showing us how dumb our life-long, strongly held religious beliefs are. Oh wise teen, please enlighten us about all the other mysteries of life." Not very likely, don't you think?

The fact is that good people (like you and your parents) can, *in good faith,* believe opposite things that conflict. The trick is to keep the conflict *on the issue,* and not let it spread to *destroy the relationship*. In other words, *listen to the opposing side's position, and acknowledge that their belief is right to them, especially if you disagree.* This is how we can all be different in this world, and yet get along. But many of the adults in your life may not know this trick.

The trick is to keep the conflict on the issue, and not let it spread to destroy the relationship.

The crazy culture that crazy adults have set up around you loves aggression. You can see it in sports and debates. Athletic competition no longer means a friendly, respect-based contest. Sports have become warlike exercises to prove who's the "winner," who's the "loser," and who gets to taunt whom about being worthless.

In our debates, we also like to taunt people, not for losing a game, but for having beliefs. We attack them as individuals because we disagree with their views. This cultural stupidity has also infected families, causing parents and teens to call each other names because they disagree on something like religion. Sports, debates, and family relationships are too often more about power and control (winning and losing) than about learning and respect.

If Brandon and his folks could separate their disagreement from their relationship, they might do a whole lot better. If they could remember that good, loving people can hold views very different from their own, they might stop yelling and start listening. Doing this allows very good things to happen that can't happen when folks are in each other's faces.

First, when we shut up and listen, we start to hear things that might cause us to learn, and to change our beliefs in ways that make even more sense to us. Second, when we shut up and listen, we stop infuriating the other side. This helps them to calm down, be more reasonable, and be more likely to listen and learn from us.

Third, and most important to families, shutting up and listening tells the other side that you love and care about them, even if you strongly disagree with their position. This is an absolutely essential quality to have in your family, because these new intellectual powers of yours will lead to many of these conflicts in which there are no "right" answers. Without tolerance to differences, we are doomed to fight forever, in our families as well as in our world. And, sometimes, even within ourselves.

THE INSIDE CONFLICTS: Like a . . . Lizard?

Another common aspect to growing intellectually (that your health class never mentioned) is sometimes feeling like you have multiple personalities. As your skills grow, you'll find yourself asking the same questions over and over again, and getting new answers each time. That's because, as time progresses, so do your intellectual skills, allowing you to see new, better answers to these same questions. The problem is that the older answers become part of what others see as being "you." So when you're always updating your answers, you may start to remind yourself of your old pet chameleon: *becoming a different person in different settings.*

Look at Brandon, for example. When he's young, he thinks his parents' religion is good, and he participates. So the folks at church "know" him as the kid who is religious. Then, his brain expands, and he decides that the religion makes no sense to him. But he still goes, not wanting to upset his parents, pretending to be something he's not, and feeling like he's two different people.

Then, at school, he starts to hang with kids who mock his parents' faith. At first, he thinks that's funny, because he no longer "believes," and he laughs. So the kids at school "know" him as the kid who hates religion. Then, his brain expands again, and he realizes that there was also a lot of good stuff at his church. But he still laughs, not wanting to upset his friends, again pretending to be something he's not, and now feeling like he's three different people. Know that feeling? It's called *conflict.* But this time, the fight is inside of you.

This conflict cycle can repeat itself many times, in many settings, causing you to develop two, three, or more "personalities": one for home (the quiet kid with parents); another for school (the cooperative kid with teachers); perhaps a third for one set of "nerdy" friends (the smart kid); and even a fourth for a wilder group of friends (the daredevil).

This is not multiple-personality disease—it's teenage normalcy. You're not nuts, you're just crazy, pretending to be people who you *are not,* in order to eventually figure out who you *are.* As Brandon lives and thinks and conflicts with himself and his world, he'll gradually decide which parts of those "personalities" are truly his. Conflict like this is one of Mother Nature's tools, to help you in your adolescent sprint toward that ultimate goal of learning who you are, of forming your identity. Mother Nature knows she can keep you alive—and even happy.

Speaking of happy, there's another journey that is required of all humans before they're granted that wonderful gift of happiness and joy in their lives. It's called morality.

YOUR MORAL JOURNEY: Where Your Heart Learns to See

"Hey, Doc, if you don't want me coming to your office anymore in uniform, just say the word. I think I maybe freaked out those people in your waiting room. I tried doing my Barney imitation for the little girl, but her mom doesn't know comic genius when she sees it."

Stan was a 17-year-old walking contradiction. He was extremely bright. His morals were not. His words were polite. His "uniform" was not. Rolled jeans, hobnail boots, white tee shirt, red suspenders, Nordic tattoos, and no hair. Stan was a skinhead: a racist, Jew-hating, and homosexual-harassing thug. He had quit seeing me a year before, when he had decided that I was unfairly biased against the principles of the skins. The real deal was that he himself was beginning to question the beliefs of these crazies who had become his family, and he wasn't ready to face that. But now, he was a big thug with a bigger problem: Out of nowhere, he was suddenly developing morals and beliefs that were locked in mortal combat with the years of insane poison he had been fed by the "brotherhood."

His easy manner was too easy today. "What's up, Stan?" I asked. "Barney is probably a bad omen?"

His silly smile vanished as he leaned forward. "I'm in deep poopy, Doc. I narc'd on Rommel. He's probably gonna' have me taken out." Rommel was the 22-year-old maniac leader of his skin clan. "He knows it was me who turned him in, 'cause I told him." If this were coming from any other kid, I'd have found it hard to believe. But Stan had this strange policy of being deadly honest, whether screaming racial slurs at a huge black man, or confronting his huge white leader. In a bizarre way, Stan was highly moral in fully honoring his obligation to the hate principles of the skinheads. If he thought something was right (no matter how horrific it was), he'd do it 110 percent, and offer no apologies. But things were coming apart for him now. What he had thought was right, wasn't.

"The first problem was when Rommel beat up this little Spanish [Hispanic] kid half his size. Our rules say you only bait same- or bigger-sized targets who can defend themselves if they have the guts. That way, it's a test of manhood, of whose beliefs are virtuous: 'The Viking Way.'" Stan used to say that last phrase loud, with pride. Now, I could see it sounded lame to him. "The breaker was when he picked up a 13-year-old female 'recruit' who had run away from home. He was having sex with her. That's another rule we have. We honor the white woman. . . ." Here, his words apparently sounded so nuts to him he couldn't finish his sentence. "Anyway, I told him she had to go back home. When he refused, we got into a fight. I won—bad idea. Then I told him she goes back or I call the cops. She didn't, so I did. Rommel's out on bail today, probably looking for me—and likely not in 'The Viking Way.'"

Looking lost and sad, Stan stared through the window, as if searching for someone he once loved. "You know, after my father split, the skins became my family. They protected my mother and me from the black and Russian gangs. I couldn't go back to school until the skins took me in." His voice got louder, as if in an argument with himself. "And I truly believe what they stand for. They have a code; they stand for something; they have principles. . . ." Stan's head sank into his hands as he realized that he didn't believe this anymore. "No, they don't," he sighed, "and I've known it for a long time. I used to be able to ignore stupid things they say and do that are just wrong, but I can't anymore. It's like I got allergic to the skins. The more I see them, the more I see them as cowards, who make up morals to justify their insanity. I just can't do it anymore."

Stan talked a bit about how he had come to now see morality as a complex thing, and how terrifyingly simple the brutal skinhead "philosophy" was. "Simple thinking is very dangerous," he noted. Then he quietly laughed at his dark joke: "Now, it might kill me."

Stan is a dramatic example of adolescent moral development, but he's really not all that different from you, or from many of the kids you might hang out with. Like Stan, we can all be stupidly and viciously cruel at times, particularly when we're young. The odds are that, at some point in your life, you've laughed or at least stood silent while watching some poor kid being bullied or shunned. When you were younger, you may have thought that cruel treatment of a "loser" kid was funny, that he deserved what he got for being, you know, a loser. Then, something happened inside of you that made harassment seem stupid and wrong, to the point where now you might even stick up for the victim.

The odds are that, at some point in your life, you've laughed or at least stood silent while watching some poor kid being bullied or shunned.

What happened was that the explosion of growth in your intellect set off a secondary shock in that part of your brain that houses your morals. Watch out now: You might actually have a conscience.

ADOLESCENT MORAL DEVELOPMENT

Intellectually understanding what's going on in the world (your intellectual development) is the easy half of becoming truly aware. The other half, your moral development, is much harder, and yet much more important. Moral development has to do with *understanding*, *caring*, and *taking action* about the right and wrong aspects of all those new, more powerful insights you're having (courtesy of your new, more powerful brain).

Think of your intellectual growth as being a night-vision scope: It helps you see a lot that you couldn't see before. Your moral growth is really *caring* about what you're suddenly seeing, trying to push back against the evil you can now see in the darkness. Really, truly caring about things is one sure sign that you're growing up.

Ironically, you may look a lot less moral to others at the same time you are becoming truly moral for the first time in your life. That's because, as you grow morally, you start to question, test, and abandon some of the moral beliefs hammered into you by others. Your parents might be looking rather pale and crazy these days as they watch you move away from values they hold dear to their own hearts. And you likely find that the number of principles that guide your life has decreased dramatically. That's because you've been tossing a lot of your old rules overboard. But fewer rules does not mean worse rules.

This is how you come to be truly moral. True morality is having a code (morals and values) that is truly yours, with principles that you live, whether or not anyone else is watching, because *you* believe in them as being right. True morality is not believing something just because others want you to believe.

Defining your true values is work that involves lots of thinking, observing, worrying, and sometimes even fighting. It was enough to make Troy's head hurt.

> "Evan was doing his usual thing at the party; you know, spitting game at [attempting to seduce] some young chick. I started getting madder and madder, thinking about Patrice, and all the other girls he's jumped. I couldn't get Patrice's face out of my head, when she was crying about how Evan said he would love her forever, how her life was over, and how she just wanted to die." Troy had told me earlier about how Evan "got Patrice pregnant" and then dumped her, claiming the baby could not be his, when he knew it was. "I used to think Evan was so cool, getting all these girls, you know? But when I saw him forcing vodka down this 8th-grader's throat, I went nuts. So right there, in front of everybody, I knocked the bottle out of his hand, and words started jumping out of me from nowhere. I was screaming that he was nothing but a lying punk, that he just uses people and throws them away."
>
> Troy rubbed a huge purple knot on his forehead as he grinned sheepishly. "I didn't actually call him a 'lying punk.' I used some

other words." He paused, and, in his head, replayed his words to Evan. "Imagine that," he chuckled. "Troy Flaherty has got ethics, or at least he's got one."

"Watch out," I warned. "This ethics stuff is addicting. You start out having one, and before you know it, you're doing ethics all the time. And not just socially—you might find yourself being ethical all alone. That's when you know you've got a problem."

"Yeah," Troy agreed, pointing to the lump where Evan had punched his head, "tell me about it. Another symptom is when you get ethics hangovers, like this one."

Troy began this particular moral journey as a young boy, being told by his parents that tricking girls into having sex was wrong. So that became his belief. Then, he met Evan, who convinced him that tricking girls into bed was harmless fun. So *that* became his belief. Then his intellect soared, and Troy could suddenly see Evan's belief for what it really was: self-serving garbage. This left Troy with his final position, that coerced sex is wrong.

He now had a *value*—a belief about the "rightness" or "wrongness" of something. This last belief (or value) was for real and forever, *because it was truly his,* based upon his own thought, observation, and experience. Like granite, this value will probably stand up to any other influence that he may encounter throughout the rest of his life.

Values become magical pieces of gold that we can carry with us forever. Magical, because, first, they can help guide us through this crazy, crazy world. Values act much like roadmaps to help us get to where we want to go in life, and avoid deadly detours with things that can hurt us, like sex, drugs, and rock 'n roll (violence). Values can keep us safe and sane. Second, a value can help us form other values. For example, if it's wrong to coerce sex, then maybe other forms of manipulation are wrong? Hmmm . . .

Values become magical pieces of gold that we can carry with us forever.

Third, having values (or morals) helps us to see and understand the world much more clearly, so we're much more able to sort the substantial from the stupid, the good from the ghastly, and the nice from the nasty.

Finally, and most importantly, values become the center of our identity. Incidentally, they're also a great sleep aid, helping us answer that maddening, sleep-shattering 3:00 A.M. question, "WHO AM I?" Our values make up much of who we are. They set us apart, endear us to others who love us, and define us as us. True morals (the ones we painstakingly develop on our own) are key pieces of the puzzle that we ultimately put together to form ourselves—our identity. And you know how important that is.

As you saw with Troy, much of this moral development occurs by watching good *and* bad people, and thinking about what they believe. You don't need to spend a lot of time with bad people to learn about the dark side of "the force"—you can learn a lot from them from a safe distance. But when you find someone you really admire, who you think really has it all together, you might want to hang out with that person as much as you can, and pick her (or his) brain about how she (or he) sees the world. Doing this can save you lots of time in developing your moral self. We call these walking shortcuts "models," or even "heroes." If you have two or three good ones in your whole life, you're very, very lucky. Don't let any of them slip away. You'll need models to help you achieve the end game of adolescent moral development, a hard-to-define quality known as character.

MODELS: GOOD FOR CHARACTER, BAD FOR PROMS

When I suggest that you hang out with models, I am referring to those people with great character, not to those characters with great teeth. As Mike found out, great teeth can occasionally indicate a total *lack* of character.

> Michael was devastated. He looked as if his whole 17-year-old world had collapsed around him. "I can't eat, and I hardly slept in a week," he sighed. "My friends keep telling me to just get over it, but I can't. I don't know if it's because I'm so hurt, or so ashamed, or so mad. I really, really liked Linda, and she said that she really, really liked me. I guess my mistake was to date a gorgeous girl. She's a model, you know. Really stunning. Perfect teeth, you know what I mean? She told me that I was so different from the usual types she dated: the 'big, cool football players.' Linda kept comparing me to

that one type of guy: big, cool, football player. She said she liked that I was so different: 'Kinda' nerdy and sincere,' she'd say.

"I used all my money for her school's junior prom. She said she couldn't afford to go, so I paid for her dress, the tickets—everything. Then, on prom morning, she calls to tell me she has the flu. She sounded awful. Really sick. I offered to spend the evening with her, but she said she just needed to sleep, so please don't even call her. That morning, in biology class, my teacher, Father McCarthy, asks if I'd be willing to escort a girl he knew from Linda's school to the same prom. He said she couldn't get a date because she was not the most attractive girl in the world. He had heard me telling other kids about Linda being sick. I already had a tux and all, so I said sure. I didn't call Linda to tell her, since she was so sick.

"That night, at Linda's school prom, I'm hanging out with another friend who was there, when he looks over my shoulder and turns white. He says, "Man, don't look now, but it looks like somebody made an amazing recovery from the flu." I turn, and there's Linda: out in the middle of the dance floor, draped all over, you guessed it, a 'big, cool football player.' And wearing the dress I paid for. If that wasn't enough, when she sees me staring, she starts to act scared: shaking, crying, pointing at me, and whispering some stuff to the football player and his herd. Then he and the other football monsters come over, wanting to fight me for 'talking trash about his girlfriend.'

"I didn't know whether to laugh, cry, or run, so I sort of did all three. I escaped alive, but humiliated in front of my friends. They act nice, but I know they're laughing their asses off behind my back. How can someone act so sweet and be that cold? How can I ever trust a girl again? How can people do whatever they want, without giving a damn about what happens to someone else?"

—Notes of what Dr. Bradley would have said if he had seen a shrink when he got crushed by Linda in 1969. Not that I'm still mad, but that happens to be her real name.

So what is character? That's a tough question. Like that Supreme Court Justice once said about pornography, it is hard to define, but I know it when I see it. Character might be best defined as the *strength* behind a value that helps you stand up for something you believe in, even though at times it might make your life hard. Values are like *thoughts*; character is like the *courage* behind the thoughts that gives us the guts to take action. Shrinks say that character is made of action qualities such as wisdom, courage, love, justice, humility, gratitude, and hope. Not a bad list. Not an easy list.

Values are like thoughts; character is like the courage behind the thoughts that gives us the guts to take action.

I know character when I see it, in the quiet dignity of parents, folks who are very important models for adolescents. And, unlike Paul, I can also see the gaping holes it leaves when it's missing in the adults around a teen.

Paul's shirt read: *"GIVE A MAN A FISH, AND HE EATS FOR A DAY. TEACH A MAN TO FISH . . . AND HE'LL SIT IN A BOAT AND DRINK BEER ALL DAY."* I didn't realize the shirt was more truth than humor for Paul.

"My dad split last year. I still see him some weekends. He's OK, except when I steal weed from his stash. Then he goes nutso on me, like he used to do when he lived with us." Studying Paul's 15-year-old face, I found no phoniness, no malice. With open, honest eyes, he answered all of my questions straight up, whether about his own out-of-control marijuana habit, or about his own out-of-control family.

"My father only gets crazy now when he's been drinking all day. He calls that 'going fishing.' That's when he beats me up, or at least tries to. I think he's afraid I could take him now. Mom's cool. She pretty much leaves us alone. She doesn't like my weed habit, but she just shuts up. I think she smokes up sometimes, too. She did weird us out on Christmas Eve, moving her latest boyfriend in without asking us [her children]. He was a drunk, too. We knew he'd be history in two weeks, so we just blew it off."

With a sinking feeling, I capped my pen, put down my clipboard, and said, "Paul, who do you look up to in your life? Who do you see as an adult who you'd like to emulate, to copy?"

Paul looked puzzled at my question. "You mean, an adult who doesn't do crazy stuff? You mean, an adult who's, like, a grown-up?"

"Exactly," I answered. "What adult do you know in your family who is a grown-up, who has a set of values, who says what he means and means what he says, who doesn't snap out—things like that."

Paul shook his head as his answer. "Well, how about in your extended family? Uncles, aunts, cousins?"

He continued to slowly shake his head as he sorted out the adult family faces in his brain. "Nobody, I think. . . . Nope," he concluded, "Nobody."

"Anybody at all?" I pleaded. "Coaches, teachers, neighbors—maybe one of those cops who busted you?"

Paul laughed, but he stopped shaking his head. "You know, this sounds nuts, but there was this one cop who was, like, nice to me. He wasn't in my face, like the others. He just talked quietly about other kids he knew who were as heavy into weed as I am, and how he was worried about it. He really seemed to care about me, without getting all judgmental. He made me think—a little, anyway." Paul paused, and then accidentally blurted out his thought: "I wondered what I would be like if he was my father. I wonder if I'd be high all day." He suddenly looked embarrassed, and then shifted gears with an uncertain grin. "You're playin' with me, right? This values stuff is just a load of crap, right? I mean, nobody actually believes in that junk, do they? I'm not stupid. I watch the news. It's every man for himself out there. Politicians, preachers, businessmen—you don't see a whole lot of values with them, right? It's grab all you can, dude. Just party 'til you die, and leave a good-looking corpse. There—there's my 'values.'" He laughed a hollow laugh that somehow didn't sound like laughter. His eyes weren't laughing at all.

I wondered if that cop he mentioned would be willing to spend some time with Paul. Sounded like the man had character.

Discussing character with Paul was like talking respect with Eminem. Neither one knows, or even has the ability to know, what you're talking about. Which made me very sad for Paul, since character might be the one thing that could eventually save his life. And that life-saving character does not have to be his own—it could come from any "grown-up" Paul might come to admire, respect, and want to copy. It could even belong to a cop. Sometimes, the character within others can inspire moral growth within ourselves, by making us want to be like them.

Character also can get you into lots of trouble. It's made firefighters rush into burning buildings to save people they didn't even know, because they believed it was the right thing to do. It's made teenagers rush into bullying situations to protect people they didn't even know, because they believed it was the right thing to do. Some of the most powerful character moments I've ever seen have to do with kids doing very hard things, all alone. These might be the toughest of character fights, because there is no crowd to applaud the bravery, no fans to recognize the good deed. Except for that most-important, one-person audience: the kids themselves. They've taught me that, contrary to what your world says, what *we* think of us is much more important than what *others* think of us. But this kind of thinking requires some heavy dues. Building character was expensive for two kids I know.

Thirteen-year-old Monica refused to go to a party where a "loser" girl was being intentionally excluded, and instead chose to hang out with the excluded girl that night. The reward for Monica's good deed was to be mocked and cut from the "cool kids" list.

Jaelin, struggling terribly with 10th-grade chemistry, turned down a chance to cheat on a chemistry test. For his show of character, he got an F on a final, where the cheaters got As. Two chumps, right? Could doing the right thing be worth it? I asked them.

> "I don't know," Monica wondered, as she slumped in the chair. "I don't know if it was worth it or not. To be honest, I really don't like Elissa [the excluded girl] all that much. We don't have a lot in common, you know? And she's sooo shy. And I was never 'Miss Popularity' to begin with, so I guess this cost me a lot." She sighed, but then sat up straight with a powerful thought: "You know what I just thought of? In a few years, I'll never see those jerk kids again, but I have a feeling I'll always remember what I did with Elissa. So I guess I did the right thing." After a pause she added, "This is very hard, doing the right thing—it's not like you get a medal or something. Sometimes, all you get is grief."

Jaelin was a lot more positive than Monica about his character decision: He was positive that he was dumber than sand.

> "That had to be the stupidest thing I ever did. Man, everybody cheated on that test." He started pounding the arm of the sofa as he yelled,

"THE FREAKIN' PRESIDENT OF THE FREAKIN' HONOR SOCIETY CHEATED ON THAT FREAKIN' TEST. AND THEN THEY ALL STRUTTED AROUND, FLASHIN' THEIR As AT ME, AND LAUGHING. I JUST WANNA' SCREAM. WHAT AN ASS_ _ _ _ I AM."

Jaelin buried his face on that same sofa arm and mumbled, "Damned if you do and damned if you don't." When I asked what he meant, he slowly sat back up, looking very tired. "It's like this," he sighed. "In the first semester, those same kids stole the answer sheet for the midterm exam. I was smart enough to buy a copy then, and I cheated my way to an A. My parents were so proud, 'cause they knew how hard chemistry was for me. But the more they told me how proud they were, the worse I felt. It got so bad, I stopped shaving." To my puzzled look, Jaelin explained, "I couldn't stand seeing my own face in the mirror to shave. At first, I was cool with cheating, but then, I was, like, so sorry I had done it. It ate me up inside. I still feel bad about it. See? Damned if you do and damned if you don't. My parents aren't so proud of me now, and this time I didn't cheat. So what's the freakin' point of trying?"

After a minute, I posed a question I hoped I wouldn't regret: "Jaelin, which is worse for you, the embarrassed F or the guilty A? Academic failure with a moral success, or academic success with a moral failure?"

Jaelin thought, and shook his head. "Got a coin?" he sighed. "I'm miserable either way." He picked up the candy dish, studied it awhile, and then finally took a stand: "I guess I'll pick Door Number One [the honest F]. It's my dad. I just asked myself what he would say if he knew about my choices. I know he'd prefer the straight-up F. He always says that he can handle anything I do if I'm straight up with things. He says that's how we'll stay close forever."

He put down the candy, and then climbed up another moral level: "I'm wrong. It's not about my dad anymore. Now it's all about me. I want to be straight up with me, you know? I couldn't look in the mirror before, because I wasn't being me, understand? Man, I hate failing chemistry. But I will not let chemistry or the smart-ass president of the freakin' Honor Society change who I am. I'm not goin' there anymore. Maybe an F student is who I am, but at least I know who I am. I think that's more important than my grades."

Jaelin grinned broadly across the coffee table at me. "So there we go, Doc! My moral crisis is all resolved. I'm all set to make righteous decisions the rest of my life—unless, of course, the geometry answer sheet comes on the market for less than 25 bucks."

In these situations that confronted Monica and Jaelin, it's one thing to sit and talk about what we *would* do if we were faced with these challenges. That's "talkin' the talk"—the morals part. It's an important first step, but it's only half of the moral-development game. The second half, character, is what we build when we go on the line ourselves and have to fight our way through these tough situations, weighing out the moral option versus the sellout one. That's "walkin' the walk." You have to pay your dues. I'm afraid there simply is no other way to get it done.

Speaking of paying dues, the time has come to move on to the next phase of your development, where the stakes get really high. You might be willing to struggle a lot for your moral growth, but that's nothing compared to the price you're willing to pay for success in this next adventure.

YOUR SOCIAL JOURNEY: Where Friends Aren't Everything; They're the Only Thing

Question: How many teenagers does it take to screw in a light bulb?

Answer: Ten—one to turn the bulb, and nine to mock her clothes, her hair, her weight. . . .

Did I mention that being a teen can be tough? I hope so, because most adults report that their adolescent years were the hardest of all. And nowhere are they harder than in the social aspect of your development. The short version of what happens is that Mom and Dad get replaced almost overnight as the controlling power of your life. Their opinions on things like clothes, hair, and music, which *actually mattered to you* not that long ago, have become irrelevant. One Independence Day, you suddenly realized that they have no idea at all about what's cool and what's not. But just as you were about to assume control of your own life, a new gang moved into town to seize power over your world. Sometimes, these people can be wonderfully supportive and fun. Sometimes, they can bring terrible pain. So would you like to start with the good news or the bad news?

THE BAD NEWS ABOUT YOUR SOCIAL DEVELOPMENT: The Dark Side of "The Force"

As intrusive as your parents were in controlling your life, these new gangsters can be much worse. They not only scrutinize everything you do, but they might lay out strict rules of behavior that cover everything, from speech, to music, to attitudes, to dress code. Should you dare to defy them, they can make your life quite uncomfortable. And, for a few years, you can become nearly addicted to them, constantly seeking their guidance and approval, fitfully fretting that the "approval committee" (just who is that, anyway?) might reject you some terrible night, branding the adolescent label of death across your forehead for all to see: "BEWARE: UNCOOL KID."

As intrusive as your parents were in controlling your life, these new gangsters can be much worse.

Who would dare to treat you like this? What horrible people could possibly have so much power over your life? Why, your peers, of course! Meghan's crowd must have been looking in mirrors when they said that they saw terrorists.

> Meghan smiled bravely through the tears she tried hard not to have in her eyes. When her furious blinking finally couldn't hold back the pain, she had no choice but to let it flow. "It's really no big deal," she softly wept. "I have no idea why everyone's making such a big deal over this. So I cut myself, OK? Lots of kids do that, you know. I don't mean to be mean, but I really don't need a doctor. I'll be fine."
>
> I had no choice but to hammer her to see if she needed a hospital. "Meghan, I'm really sorry," I apologized. "I know you like to handle things on your own. Like you, I'm real lousy at letting people into my business. But I've got to get into yours." I pointed toward her bandaged leg. "Something must have hurt you terribly to have a cut make a 15-year-old girl feel better. What's going on?"
>
> Meghan wouldn't respond, but she wasn't being defiant. You could see it in her face. She was just trying to keep her feelings inside to not be a bother to anybody. She felt so worthless that her pain didn't even warrant sharing with others. She wasn't mad; she was sad. And scared. But I had to press on. So again I apologized for intruding.

"Meghan, your mom says that the only thing she knows that happened to you recently is that you got cut out from a big party at school, and that all of a sudden you're getting cranked [harassing phone calls] all the time. She said that. . . ." A choked sob jumped out of Meghan, and then she cried hard for 10 long minutes. I started to apologize for the third time, but she cut me off while wiping her nose and made us both laugh.

"Stop apologizing already! It's OK! Are you feeling self-hate or something?"

"No," I said, "At least I don't think so. You've just seen the first of my many annoying nervous behaviors."

Meghan seemed pleased to learn that even psychologists can be insecure, like her. She decided to share. "That party was the party of the year for my class. I'm not a cool kid, but at least I have two good friends . . ." she paused to correct herself, and filled up again, "I had two good friends who were sort-of-cool." Meghan hung her head awhile. As I watched her, I could feel that whatever happened had wounded her so badly that the cut on her leg was just a small picture of the huge hurt inside. Again, bravely, she gathered herself to continue. "Everyone thought it would be funny to prank a loser. Naturally, I got picked. Everybody was in on it, including my two 'good' friends.

"The girl having the party told me the location was changed. It was real dark when I showed up at the new address and rang the bell. These foreign people—I think they were Middle Eastern—who didn't speak much English answered the door wearing these pajama-robe things. As I'm trying to explain myself, a bright light goes on behind me. All the kids were in cars, videotaping me and laughing hysterically. They screeched off screaming what a f'ng loser I was, that I should party with those terrorists. I could see one of my 'good' friends there, laughing with the rest.

"I walked around in the dark crying for a few hours, and then called my dad to pick me up. I felt so ashamed that I wasn't going to tell him what happened, but he knew. The kids had been crank-calling my house, telling my parents what a 'f'ng terrorist loser' I was, and how they should get a new daughter who's a real American, and stuff. I know, because my parents forgot to erase the tape. They didn't want me to hear it, but I did."

She stopped crying, but her sadness seemed even heavier. "I can't go to school now. All the kids kept showing the 'Meghan-the-terrorist' videotape for days. I can't walk down the hall without somebody laughing at me. The worst part was my two friends. They look kind of sorry now, but I think they're afraid to say anything, or be seen with 'the f'ng terrorist loser.'"

Meghan paused, and then asked me that question I've asked myself a thousand times in 30 years of counseling teenagers: "Why do kids do this stuff? It's not just me. I know I dress a little weird, and my views on things may be different—but I've seen this stuff done to other uncool kids who just get picked at random. How do kids switch from being sweet to you at three o'clock to stabbing you at nine? What *is* that?"

I don't know exactly what that is, but it is one cruel part of the most powerful aspect of your world right now: your social development. "Friends" (some of whom can be very unfriendly) become all-powerful to you, particularly in the middle-school years. It would be funny if it weren't so painful for so many. Here's this group of rebels (teenagers), pushing hard against conformity (parents' rules), yet they end up establishing new sets of rules that they must conform to or be forever banished as "uncool."

If you didn't make the cool list, you know exactly what I'm talking about. If you did, and you're shaking your head in disagreement, how about trying a little experiment? If you're a skateboarder, try showing up at the park in a nice, plaid, button-down shirt and some Dockers. Maybe get that preppy haircut you make fun of. Say that you just joined the Future Investment Bankers Club at school. And wear an *NSYNC jacket. That'll work, right?

Are you kind of preppie? For the next country club dance, perhaps those black baggies with the crotch on the floor, 10 pounds of bike chains, and pins would nicely complement the huge gangsta' sweat. Don't forget the black Yankees cap, sideways: *S'up, Mister Latham-dude? MMM-MMM! Yo bitch be hot too-nite! MMM-MMM-MMM, what be da' dilly-o, momma?* Think you'll be elected "most-likely-to-succeed" at the Harvest Ball?

The power of these teenage rules can go a lot deeper than just regulating clothing styles. These systems have mysterious ways of picking out "loser" kids (based on some unknown formula) and segregating them as if they had an incurable communicable disease: *Loseritus.* This is probably done to help the rest of us not have to feel so bad about ourselves. The weird thing is that it doesn't really work. Michael learned this the hard way on that day when he ditched Mason.

> "I was a brand-new, first-day freshman at a huge high school, and I was used to getting picked on a lot through grade school. I was definitely not a cool kid. I was desperate to try and fit in and find some friends this time. There I was, lost in the lunchroom, in a sea of faces I didn't know, and everyone else seemed to be making friends fast. Then this nice kid walks up to me and says, 'Hi! I'm Matt Mason. You look a little lost. Want to get some lunch?' What luck! I had made a friend by lunchtime. Matt went off to get the food, while I looked for seats. My relief suddenly turned to dread as a faceless voice whispered behind me, like a spy passing information.
>
> "'Are you crazy?' the voice hissed. 'Don't you know who that is? That's Mason, the most hated kid at St. Stephen's [grade school]. If you're seen with him, you're dead.' 'What's wrong with him?' I asked the faceless voice as I watched Matt smile and nod to me from the food line. 'What's wrong with him?' the voice mocked, 'What's wrong with him? Look at him! Everything's wrong with him. Man, you do what you want, but you better come sit with us if you know what's good for you. I won't be asking again.'
>
> "I was panicked. All I could do was picture being tortured for four more years. I knew there was nothing wrong with Mason. And I knew that made no difference. I turned to face the voice and said, 'OK. Where are you guys sitting?' The voice smiled, slapped my back, and said, 'Good choice, man. That was a close call. I'm your goddamn guardian angel.'
>
> "Mason had watched the whole dirty exchange. His face told me that he knew exactly what was happening, from a hundred feet away. To this day, I can't forget his sad eyes. He went on to be isolated and harassed through four years of high school by those vicious voices like my 'angel,' and by those cowardly listeners like me. In 11th grade, I tried apologizing to him, but he just angrily waved me off. The damage was too long done.

> "Of the many profound regrets of my life, abandoning Mason that day in the lunchroom ranks up high among my worst. I wish I could find him to apologize. I wish I could do that day all over again. I wish I'd had the courage to do better."
>
> —From the personal journal of Dr. Michael Bradley

This dark side of adolescent social development gets its power from the tidal wave of new emotions (like feeling vulnerable and needing approval) that surges over you in adolescence (we'll discuss these shortly). Now it seems you must turn more to your peers for approval, and less to your parents.

Mom and Dad seem to have lost that magical ability to solve your problems. They try, but somehow, when they tell you that you look fine, or that you're wonderful, it just sounds lame—nice, but lame. Yet, not that long ago, it seemed that they could make the monsters disappear. Without warning, that life-or-death power was suddenly transferred to your peer group. Sometimes, only the approving nods of the cool kids can help you feel better these days.

And friends are different, too. Not that long ago, they were just kids to do stuff with. If you saw them, that was OK, and if not, that was OK, too. But now, friends become critical lifelines to help you make it through. If they accept you, you survive another day. If not, it can feel like you won't survive the day.

These social pressures vary a lot by age and by sex. For boys, the dark side of these relationships is fairly simple and direct. Males will get in each others' faces more and tell it like it is. They'll tend to be more physically aggressive, but more verbally honest. Occasionally, they'll even beat the crap out of each other as a way of "resolving" conflicts. Girls wish they had it so good.

Sometimes, only the approving nods of the cool kids can help you feel better these days.

The female dark side can be secretive, plotting, and much more emotionally painful. They'll conspire against each other, setting up complex social rankings (who's better than whom) that go through more changes than Michael Jackson. Sometimes, they'll smile sweetly at one another, and then stick a verbal knife into their "friend's" gut for no apparent reason, other than to perhaps climb another rung closer to the "queen," the coolest girl who seems to be in charge of the group. Some girls, like Lindsay, will put endless amounts of time into maneuvering to be inches closer to the cooler kids—literally. Boys like Josh have no idea what this is all about. They think it's bizarre.

> "Mom and I were working on the diagram of who would get to sleep next to who at my sleepover party. It was really hard, you know, 'cause Renee and Kate are fighting now, and Kate thinks that Susan sided with Marie about what Tim said. But Lorna likes Kate. And if I don't have Lorna sleep next to Susan, Susan will flip out and convince Lorna to not come, and then no one will come except the losers, and then I'll never get invited to Lorna's or Marie's parties. But Lorna will be insulted if I don't put Marie next to her, 'cause she's the next coolest kid, you know?
>
> "Anyway, as Mom and I were working on the chart, Josh [Lindsay's twin brother] 'slithered' in from his sleepover and was hangin' in the 'fridge getting something to eat, and my mom whispers, 'Watch this.' Then she called to him: 'HEY JOSH, tell us: Who slept next to who at your sleepover?' For a minute, Josh stared at us like we were crazy. 'I have no idea,' he said. 'Who cares? And what kind of a weirdo question is that, anyway?' I think the question made him mad. Then he walked away, shaking his head, eating cold pizza, and mumbling 'women are truly bizarre.' I guess boys don't think about stuff like that."

Boys and girls usually *are* different in this social stuff, although there are many exceptions. (If you're one of those exceptions, that's OK. It just makes you unique.) Many boys hate long phone calls ("Hey! Yup. Naa. Later!"), while some girls can do three hours without missing a beat. Girls tend to be much more aware of group issues, often banding together in crowds to get things done. More boys are loners, and dislike large groupings, preferring instead to hang out with just a couple of friends. Girls tend to be more open, sharing their thoughts and feelings more easily. Boys tend to choose root canal over choosing to share their deeper thoughts and feelings.

However, both sexes see the greatest power of social development occurring in the middle-school years. This is where you are most controlled and judged by your peer group in dumb appearance things like clothes and hair, and in important emotional things like peer acceptance. Later on, we'll talk about peer pressure and how to handle these situations, but, for now, know that the worst of social development stuff for boys and girls usually happens in middle-school years.

Which means that time is on your side. As one survivor of a really bad middle-school bullying experience put it, "You just gotta' outlast the bastards." And on that note, allow me to pass along one important piece of information about those bastards you are trying to outlast. That old rap about how bullies (physical or social) are just kids who feel insecure can make you feel even worse, since often bullies don't look very insecure. When I was told that in my bully-dodging days, I didn't believe it for a minute. My jerks looked so cool, and swaggering, and popular, that I couldn't see any downside to being the jerk, and I saw a whole lot of downside to being the victim. Some of the bullied kids I work with tell me that they do see jerks as messed up kids, and that this does ease the pain a bit. Others tell me that today's bullies look just as I remember them: cool, and swaggering, and popular. This view is backed up by research showing that many bullies feel just great about themselves, and are popular with other kids. So if your bully seems cool and popular, he might be those things—but just for now. Because research also shows that this changes as kids get into high school. The jerks, whether insecure or not, all start to look like, well, *jerks.*

So whether your jerks are insecure or on top of the world, remember that secret to surviving the "dark side" of your social development: *Outlast the bastards.*

THE GOOD NEWS ABOUT YOUR SOCIAL DEVELOPMENT: Using the Good Side of "The Force" in the Face of the Bad

Brittany was really unhappy. Her parents had told me that this very successful 13-year-old girl was resisting going to school, getting lots of head- and stomach aches on school mornings, and asking to be transferred to a new school—to any new school. Yet her grades were good, and she seemed to be very popular. Brittany confirmed that this was all true, especially the part about hating her school even though she was doing so well. "The morning 'tag' reading was always making me crazy, but the snub with Laura pushed me over the edge." When she saw my puzzled look, Brittany explained. "The 'tag' thing is where girls walk up behind you and reach into your clothes to read the tags to see if you bought the 'right' clothes at the 'right' stores. If your tag is 'right,' they walk away without saying anything. If it's wrong, they'll announce how dumb or cheap your clothes are. It's insane. My parents aren't rich, and we buy stuff at discount stores where they cut the tags or mark them. So I get laughed at a lot. But I could live with that.

"Then I started getting threatened with being voted out of the cool crowd unless I stopped talking to my friend Laura. She's not a 'cool' kid, but I like her better than any of my 'cool' friends, you know? But I'm scared of getting dropped by the cool kids. What would my life be like then?"

Brittany took some deep breaths like some bully had just entered the room, and she was getting ready to fight or run. "Last week, Susan comes up to me while I'm talking to Laura. Right in front of Laura she says to me, 'Yooouuu talk to heeerrr? She's such a looossseeer.' Brittany lowered her head. "I was, like, paralyzed. Laura's eyes filled up, and then she says, 'It's OK, Brit; you go with Susan. It's all right,' and she meant it. As hurt as Laura was, she was still, like, worried for me." Brittany's voice got very small. "I walked away with Susan. But that was wrong, and I'm so ashamed I can't even talk to Laura now. I don't want to go back to that school. Those kids are nasty and hateful." She hesitated a moment, and then added, "And now, I guess, so am I."

Before I could respond, Brittany grew up a lot sitting right there on my couch. "But I'm not doing this anymore, and I'm also not running. That's my school, and it's Laura's school, and we can talk to whoever we want, and if they don't like it, well, screw them. Then I guess I'll just have to be uncool." She thought for a minute, and then added a most important truth, "I know I'll pay a lot for breaking the 'cool rules,' and I guess there will be times I'll really regret this. But not doing what I want, what I think is right, is a lot worse than getting cut out, you know?

Again, before I could respond, she added, "Thanks, Doctor Bradley. I feel a whole lot better. I'm really glad my parents made me talk with you. You're really good."

I hadn't said two words.

Brittany had the answers to her social-development dilemma inside of her when she walked in my door. But, more importantly, she was also learning many other lessons that had taken her far down the path of the good side of social development. She had come to see the almost irresistible and nasty power of our need for social acceptance. She had experienced first hand how we can sacrifice way too much of ourselves, just to get the approval of even stupid people that we sometimes don't even like. She had felt the pain of betraying her own values out of fear. She had crystallized what her true belief was regarding how friends should be treated, and what the word "friend" means. And, finally, she felt the pride of being herself, of being true to her belief, of becoming who she is regardless of who's watching and judging.

Here lies the good news about your social journey. Brittany learned all of this great stuff about herself from her social development, from dealing with herself as she dealt with other people. As you go through these social changes, you will learn important things about yourself that go a long way to forming your identity. This aspect of your growth can only occur in social settings. You can't sit alone and get it done. On our own, we can fool ourselves a lot about who we are and how we *think* we'd respond to a certain situation. It's only when we're really out there in the social game, dealing with other people, that we can see ourselves more clearly, for better and for worse.

She had experienced first hand how we can sacrifice way too much of ourselves, just to get the approval of even stupid people that we sometimes don't even like.

You have to get in the batter's box. You can't hide out in the dugout. In our social interactions with people, we learn about all of those nice-sounding, easy-to-talk, hard-to-walk values like compassion, loyalty, sharing, and courage, as they pop up in the ten thousand puzzles that your social journey will present to you. Later on, in the Part Three "what-to-do-when" chapters, we'll talk about some strategies for handling particular social situations.

Now the time has arrived to plunge headfirst into that most befuddling adolescent growth journey that you could argue is also the most critical and complex journey of all. For the other aspects of your being (intellectual, moral, and social) *control and are controlled by* this one final part. Which is very strange, since this final part is the one that can make you feel crazier or happier than all the others combined. It's where you live. Say hello to your emotional development.

YOUR EMOTIONAL JOURNEY: Beware the Emotion Haters

People are prejudiced in a strange way against emotional things. Often, they think that intellect is better than emotion, that reason is more accurate than feelings, and that science is more useful than art. They like to think that our intellectual skills are our salvation, that these can solve all the ills of the world. They're put off by displays of emotion. And they like to pretend that ultimately we are logical (not emotional) creatures.

What a crock! If you ask physicists or engineers (those highly unemotional types) why they pursue their rational (or intellectual) work, in the end, they admit that it makes them *feel* good to create order out of chaos, to find understanding in confusion. In other words, *our intellectual skills serve our emotional needs.* Science could be considered a mood-altering activity. Yet our culture largely disrespects and distrusts emotion.

You can see this prejudice in many places. Until very recently, women were thought to be incapable of handling important or difficult jobs (like being a pilot or a president) because they were "too emotional" (many still believe this, just less openly). Men are thought to be weak if they become, God forbid, *emotional.* Hurt or frightened children (especially boys) are told to "stop crying," as if they are being bad for showing their feelings.

Now, you are a target of this very same prejudice, because if you are any one thing in adolescence, it is *emotional.* Think for a minute. Haven't you recently noticed how powerfully you seem to feel things now, and how quickly your moods can change? How often have you been bopping along, feeling just great, and then, out of nowhere, you have this unexplained wave of anger or frustration surge over you to the point where you snarl horribly at your mom and have no idea why? Have you been in love yet? Gee, I hope not. It didn't do much for Trevor.

"God, I'm so sick," Trevor moaned. "I can't eat, I hardly sleep, and school—forget school. I'm cutting classes, 'cause I can't stand to see Carolyn talking to her new boyfriend. I feel like I'll go insane. My friends are all mad, 'cause they think I don't like them anymore, and I don't care. I can't get her face out of my head." This 15-year-old was absolutely miserable. "Coach got on me today. He told me to go check my locker for my brain, since I don't bring it to practice anymore. He asked me if I'm doin' drugs. He wasn't joking about that part." Trevor laughed an empty laugh. "My dad's a big help. He makes fun of me, sayin' it's no big deal, that it's just puppy love, and that I should get over it. What is puppy love, anyway?"

"Trevor," I sighed, "puppy love is what some adults call the love you feel for Carolyn. These are adults who have forgotten how deeply and overwhelmingly you can fall in love when you're an adolescent, and how much it can tear you up when it goes south. They've lost their memories of their emotional selves as teens. They think that, because you are young, you can't really hurt. I'm sorry you got zapped so bad. Sometimes life just really sucks, you know?"

Trevor nodded sadly. He looked like someone had ripped his heart out. Someone had.

Trevor's dad was trying to be helpful because he remembered that he loved his son. But he was being dumb because he forgot how powerful his emotions were when he was a teen. He was showing a prejudice against teenage emotion, a bigotry against adolescent feelings. He was doing that worst of all parent offenses that can make you want to go berserk: *talking down to his kid.* That's where parents tell you things like what you're feeling is wrong (feelings can't be right or wrong—they just are). Or they'll tell you that you're not feeling something that you do feel ("Oh, you don't really hate school.") Maybe the worst is discounting or tearing down your feelings ("LOVE? You can't be in love. You don't even know what love is.")

As with so many dumb things that crazy parents do, they do those prejudicial things mostly out of caring, thinking that they can erase painful, destructive, or scary thoughts from your brain by judging, mocking, or dismissing them. I know that's nuts, but that's how parents think sometimes.

But often, parents will show other aspects of bigotry against emotions: fear and anger. They might lash out at you because your new, intense levels of feelings can be frightening or hurtful to them. Later on in the book, we'll talk about how to handle this if it happens to you, but, for now, let's look at the three reasons why your emotions can rise and fall faster than a boy band.

ADOLESCENT MOOD SWINGS: A Roller Coaster Should Be So Scary

There are three motors driving your mood-swing ride. The first is your bubbling brain (see Chapter 1). That part of your brain that is just now developing (the pre-frontal cortex) is the primary culprit. When it is fully in place, your new wiring will help you to not be so prone to these unexplained high-highs and low-lows that you feel. The pre-frontal cortex grabs onto these emotional surges rushing through your brain and calms them down a bit, so that your mood stays more consistent from one moment to the next. Plus, as your brain grows, you develop the ability and the inclination to feel and care much more deeply about things. Minor interests can become powerful passions that consume you, causing your moods to shift like changing ocean tides.

> "I'm here because my parents think that I'm nuts," David explained. "Just because I'm 13 doesn't mean I'm wrong for what I believe in. Animal rights are really, really important to me. It makes me so angry to think of how animals are tortured in this country that I get mad and fight with my parents a lot about how they contribute to this problem. We'll be out together and having a good time until my mom orders veal at the restaurant, and then I'll go off on her. She calls that my mood swings. I call it my conviction. But I admit that lots of times I get a lot more emotional than even I think I should."

The second motor driving your moods has to do with your brand-new, overnight Fed-Exed hormones. While these likely do not directly cause mood fluctuations (as we used to think), they do contribute in other ways that add a lot of power to your emotional mood swings. Hormones can make boys feel more aggressive and challenging, and transform female crushes into Romeo and Juliet obsessions.

The third factor playing with your head is that crazy world around you. It literally bombards you with suggestions that can influence your mood, particularly when you are an adolescent. When I was a teen, whenever the local radio station played "Born to Be Wild" (by Steppenwolf), you'd suddenly hear the screech of teenager-driven, spinning tires all over town. Today, you are blasted with 10 times the acting-out suggestions than your parents were. It seems that, everywhere you look, you see nothing but examples of people allowing their self-centered emotions to control their behavior.

Feeling harassed? *Go taunt somebody.* Feeling taunted? *Go beat somebody.* Feeling beaten? *Go harass somebody.* These stupid circles go on forever. Yet that's what our culture seems to tell you to do when you feel bad.

When you combine these three adolescent ingredients of your brain, your hormones, and your culture, you can sometimes get a powerful potion that can do much more than just swing your moods. It can painfully distort two internal pictures of you that largely form your identity: your self-concept and your self-esteem.

SELF-CONCEPT AND SELF-ESTEEM: How You View Yourself and How You Value Yourself

If you were offered for sale in a catalogue, self-concept would be the product description that you would write. It would list all of your features as you see them, such as intelligence, abilities, religious beliefs, number of friends, values, skin color, food preferences, and so on. These things are important.

More important, beneath your description would be a price that you would set as estimating your worth. That price tag is your self-esteem (or self-worth). This is the value that you place upon yourself, not the value others place upon you. *How you value yourself is perhaps the most powerful force inside of you.* And, for better or for worse, your adolescent self-esteem can literally take control of the steering wheel of your mind, driving you to good or bad places, not just for now, *but for the rest of your life.* The problem is that as a teen you're more inclined to feel worse about yourself just at the time when you need to feel better.

How you value yourself is perhaps the most powerful force inside of you.

SELF-ESTEEM IN TEENAGERS: Picture Four-Engine Planes Flying on One Engine

Just before kids start adolescence, they usually feel OK about who they are (have good self-esteem). But the flip side of the new physical strength of adolescence is a new emotional weakness where kids (particularly girls) start to anguish over every aspect of themselves, seeing only glaring defects and few good points. Already feeling vulnerable, young teens then smash into middle school, where the motto is "NO IMPERFECTION IS TOO SMALL TO BE MOCKED," and the mocking can reach new levels of cruelty. In case you haven't noticed, teenagers can be brutal with each other, which can be bad, since other kids' opinions have become so critical to you. Taunting works like pouring acid into the open wounds of self-doubt. It causes painful scars that can harden into poor self-esteem. To understand how powerful these scars are, you have to climb inside some heads to see how this works.

Two friends who love to swim (and swim equally well) stand side by side, looking at the notice for swim-team tryouts. Kid Number One feels excitement and thinks, "Cool. I'm a decent swimmer, as good as most kids. Even if I don't make the team, at least I'll know I tried to make some school team. I know I'm not big or fast enough for football. And my parents will be proud that I took a shot, win or lose. This will be fun. I'm going!"

Kid Number Two feels fear and thinks, "Oh, no! I'm not any good at anything. There's no way I could do this, even though I can swim as good as most kids. I know I'll screw up. I'd like to be on some school team, but I'm not big or fast enough for football. Even if I made the swim team, I'd never be able to win an event. Then even my parents would know I'm a loser. No way I'm going!"

These are two very similar teenagers. Both know that they are decent swimmers (a self-concept). Both kids have a dream of joining some school team (a self-concept). Both kids know that they are not football players (a self-concept). But only one kid has a chance of making the dream come true. The other has no chance at all. The difference between these kids is only how they *value* themselves (self-esteem). Kid Number One feels OK about himself (has good self-esteem). This allows him to try things, even knowing that he might fail. Failing to him is not the end of the world. He feels OK taking positive risks (as opposed to negative risks like doing crazy, dangerous things). He understands that trying and failing at something is only the first step towards success. He will keep trying until he gets what he wants.

Kid Number Two feels lousy about himself (has poor self-esteem). This prevents him from trying anything he might fail. He is terrified about taking positive risks (such as striving for achievement). He may never know success, because he thinks that trying and failing at something would be too painful and scary for him to endure. Can poor self-esteem (a phrase that many people like to mock) really affect our teen lives in ways that control our adult lives? Ask Rialta.

"I guess I was just lucky to get good grades without trying until I hit 10th grade. I liked being seen as smart, but that was just a game. I'm not really smart—I'm dumb. I'm really not good at anything. Everyone keeps asking what's changed to make me quit trying, but the truth is that I'm the same—I never, ever, tried to study.

"Rialta," I pointed out, "You must be smart to get good grades up to now with no studying. Doesn't that fact make you want to try studying?" She shifted uneasily in her chair, as if I had suddenly made her think about jumping off of a scary diving board when she didn't know if she could swim. She was picturing all those scary "diving boards" she was avoiding in her life.

"How would I know," she snapped impatiently. "It doesn't matter since I'm just a stupid kid now, all right? Why can't you all leave me alone?" Rialta glared at me because she was smart enough to know what I was about to say. And when I opened my mouth, she cut me off angrily: "I KNOW, OK? I KNOW!" She sighed and got quieter. "I know that I'm afraid. I get scared every time I think about doing something that maybe I can't do, like studying and getting good grades. So I only do dumb, easy things I'm sure I can do. I even pick friends who I know won't ever be better than me."

She paused to stare at her hands. "Once in a while, when I try to open a book, my hands shake, my stomach gets in a knot, and my brain gets all twisted up." Now her voice was small and flat. "It's better to not try and fail than to try and fail, you know? That way, when I fail, my friends and parents think that I'm just lazy instead of stupid. Isn't that better than really trying and failing?" When I didn't answer, she answered herself. "No, it's not. Wimping out all the time sucks. It makes you feel lousy inside. I don't really know if I'm smart or not, but I do know that I'm too afraid to find out. I'm a scared loser. Everything about me is wrong. I haven't even got the guts to try."

For a quiet moment, I worked hard not to tell Rialta something "Disney," like, "Of course you can succeed!" Then I explained how she was not cowardly, just a victim of poor self-esteem, and that what she said about avoiding even healthy risks made a lot of sense, given how she felt. She looked a little relieved, but stunned by her next thought. "You know what I've been doing this past week? Making a list in my head of the boys I know that I could make marry me and take care of me. I can't picture ever taking care of myself." Amazed at herself, she stared again at her hands. "I listed them according to who I hated the least. There is no one on that list that I really like. So I'm willing to spend my life with someone I don't even like? Just because I don't think I can make it on my own?" She shuddered at her thinking.

Inside, I shuddered too, but not just for Rialta. Her eyes were opening—now she had a chance to have a life. I shuddered for all the people I've known who actually used their own version of Rialta's disastrous list, never feeling OK enough to try to succeed, and not seeing what they were doing until decades later. Some never see.

Self-esteem has become a politically unpopular term recently because it's been so misunderstood. Having good self-esteem does not mean thinking that you're *better or worth more* than everyone else. It does not mean thinking that you're entitled to use and abuse others. It doesn't mean having an inflated ego, and thinking you're so cool when you're not. And it's not about having external things that make you *look* OK, like clothes, cars, or "cuties." Healthy self-esteem is about having internal things that make you *feel* OK. Things like courage, compassion, and confidence.

Self-esteem may direct your life more powerfully than any other aspect of your identity, so pay attention to it.

Ignore ignorant people who say that worrying about self-esteem is silly nonsense. Self-esteem may direct your life more powerfully than any other aspect of your identity, so pay attention to it. If your self-esteem is feeling a little punkish these days, don't worry too much. That feeling could be called the adolescent flu, because it's so common to teens. And just as with the flu, given a little time and a little patience, you can heal yourself. Your brain will do the healing.

THE ANTIDOTE FOR POOR SELF-ESTEEM: Your Amazing Adolescent Brain

If she were my daughter, I would have wanted to give Rialta a hug—a hug she would have probably pushed angrily away—because no one, not even a loving parent, can fix that awful feeling inside of a teen who feels really badly about herself. Ironically, lots of parents and teens lose their connections when loving parents keep trying to hug away those bad feelings in their kids. When you were small, that trick actually worked, and made both you and your parents feel better. But now, being smothered by Mom can make you feel crazy and snap out on Mom, who can then feel sad and rejected. This is another one of those bad circles that good families get caught up in. If this is happening to you, try explaining to your folks what you are feeling, and that maybe they can best help by just sitting and listening, instead of treating you like a baby and telling you dumb things like "you'll get over it."

By the way, you *will* get over it. Most kids go through a time when their self-esteem feels shaky. And most pull out of it before it seriously affects their lives. But if you see poor self-esteem controlling all of your decisions, see a counselor yesterday. You want to take a look at this before you actually use a "never-take-a-risk" list like Rialta's. If you look at the adults around you, you'll see many who started avoiding positive risks in adolescence, and then grew to hate both life and themselves as adults. This is not good.

BUT POOR SELF-ESTEEM CAN RECOVER IN ADOLESCENCE, THANKS TO YOUR MIRACULOUS BRAIN. Remember Chapter 1, where we talked about your evolving gray matter, and how you can program your blossoming brain for the rest of your life? Self-esteem is a perfect (and critical) example. The key to building your self-esteem is to try to get yourself to take positive risks, to try good things that you might fail at, such as grades, community projects, sports, music, leadership, and so on. You must try doing this, even though one part of you is yelling "DON'T DO THAT—YOU'LL JUST SCREW UP!" If you can push yourself to try these things, you'll start to hear new voices that slowly change your view of yourself, such as, "Gee, I made the swim team and even won an event. Maybe I'm not a total loser like I thought." Or "Gee, I didn't make the swim team, but getting cut wasn't the end of the world—I'm glad I had the nerve to try. What's next on my list?"

If you can't get past your fear, try this. Ask yourself two questions: First, "What am I afraid of?" Isolate exactly what your fear is. Your answer might be, "I'm afraid that I won't make the team, and I'll be disappointed." Then ask a second question: "Would feeling disappointed be a horror, or a frustration?" Many times, we confuse horrors with frustrations, and then become paralyzed, unable to take any risks. Horrors are World Trade Center attacks, not swim-team cuts. When we answer those questions, it helps us see that it's only *a fear of a frustration* that keeps us from trying challenging things. Remember, exploring new things is your number-one tool for doing your number-one job: *developing your identity.*

FORMING YOUR IDENTITY: CONNECT THE DOTS, AND COLOR

Speaking of identity, you have now completed the outline of your own. Like a paint-by-numbers picture, those four identity journeys—intellectual, moral, social, and emotional—provide you with a psychological sketch that you can begin to fill in with colors. The sketch (the four parts of identity) is the same for all of us. But the color choices you can make (those things that define you) are infinite, and they ultimately come together to form the unique portrait of you. That's the magic of adolescence.

However, like magic, adolescence can be a little scary at times. All of that churning and changing can take us to places where we're not sure if what we're feeling is normal teenage craziness or perhaps a real illness that requires treatment. Mental illness happens to teenagers, too. It might sound silly to say that, but, far too often, adolescent mental disorders are overlooked, hidden beneath the chaos that sometimes clouds the teen years. Statistically, the fact is that either you or someone you know will have a true mental disorder in adolescence. You need to know what distinguishes serious adolescent mental disorders from the normal disorder of adolescence, so that you can be in a better position to help either yourself or a friend get the help needed to get things back on track.

This next chapter is designed to give you this knowledge. As you will see, almost all of these disorders can be very effectively treated to help get back what they can steal from teen lives.

But there are things that no mental illness can take from a person: Qualities like compassion, courage, and character are far too powerful for any mental illness to conquer. How do I know this to be true? A couple of heroes of mine taught me, two of the most courageous people I've ever known. They also happened to be mentally ill. And they were teenagers. Turn the page and say hello to Graham and Rachel.

YOUR CRAZINESS

What's Normal and What's Not

"I know I'm, like, a little crazy. Isn't everyone a little crazy?" —Frank, age 12

I haven't met many kids who never worried about having a mental disorder. At one time or another, teens often worry that they might be developing some sort of serious disturbance. Because adolescent years can be so difficult and adolescent brains can be so unpredictable (see Chapter 1), it's pretty common for kids to occasionally fall into behaviors that can set off alarm bells. In fact, as you will soon see, "normal" adolescent behavior can appear very much like "abnormal" behaviors that are considered to be mental illness. In this chapter, we're going to sort all of this out, to help you distinguish the "normal" craziness from the "abnormal" stuff.

But before we go on, we need to chat first about why your stomach (and mine) starts getting a little tight simply because we mentioned the words *mental illness*. The fact is that, when you're mentally ill, you're caught in a very strange irony. Most mental diseases can be cured or controlled, thanks to the wisdom of today's world. And yet most mental diseases are misunderstood and feared, thanks to the stupidity of today's world.

Remember when we talked about how our culture is dangerously biased against people who are sexually different? Well, we also have a strange tendency to ridicule, fear, and even hate people who are mentally different because they are ill—*mentally* ill, that is. You've probably seen this. If a kid is hospitalized for diabetes or asthma (so-called "physical" illnesses), that's OK because that's "just an illness," you know? But if a kid is treated for depression or anxiety ("mental" illnesses), well, that's different. God knows what he's capable of. He can't be trusted to do the right thing. Like Graham, he certainly can't be sane enough to hold a public office.

> "Why is it," Graham challenged, "that everyone who's close to me—my parents, my friends, even my brother—keeps telling me to lie about why I went to the hospital? In the hospital, you guys [counselors] busted on me every day for two weeks, saying that the 'disease' of depression is nothing to be ashamed of, and that I was right in telling people that I was feeling suicidal. And now that I'm headed back to school, I'm supposed to lie about where I was? Like I was bad, and went to jail or something? Well?" he demanded, "Which is it? Am I or am I not supposed to be ashamed of being in a mental hospital?"
>
> I could only shake my head before he continued, but now in a smaller voice. "My dad said that I'll lose my race for class treasurer if the true story gets out. When I said I didn't care, he looked more upset. I told him that I wasn't willing to lie, just to avoid hearing the jerks laugh at me. I told him that it was important for someone to stand up for this. I said that there are lots of other kids who are too scared to admit that they have a mental disorder, and that if I take a stand, maybe the others can come out, too. Then I asked him why he was so proud when I took stands on other issues, but not on this one. He didn't answer me. He didn't even look at me."
>
> Graham took a deep breath and exhaled slowly, as if he was thinking of quitting an important fight. "You know what the real question is, don't you? The real question is should my family and friends be ashamed because I was in a mental hospital? Isn't that what's going on here?"

Graham had just been whacked by a dirty little secret. If you're different in this culture—nonwhite, mentally ill, Muslim, gay, whatever—you'd better act a little ashamed, and keep a low profile. We don't handle "different" so well in our society. Graham's father is probably right. Running for an elected office with a mental disorder just isn't done—even if the disorder is fully controlled. If you're "normal," you can be a real jerk and parade around however you like. But if you're "different," you'd best hang out in the shadows, even if you're a wonderful person.

As with any prejudice, this foul thinking oozed out of the swamp of fear and ignorance.

How did this happen? As with any prejudice, this foul thinking oozed out of the swamp of fear and ignorance. Many people act as if mental illness is an infection of the soul, a virus that contaminates all that is human and good about a person. If she has depression, she can't be dependable. If he's compulsive, he can't be courageous. And if she has multiple personality disorder, she's worthless, right?

Rachel sat and stared at the floor with the saddest eyes I'd ever seen in a 14-year-old girl. She didn't know it, but I had been in touch with school and county social workers, who had told me off the record that her father was probably an abusive monster, a phrase they don't use lightly. They were almost certain that he had been neglecting and beating Rachel's three- and five-year-old brothers for years. Rachel had been denying this to investigators, presenting difficulties for legal intervention. They referred her to me for treatment of a possible dissociative identity disorder (also known as multiple personality disorder). Her psychiatrist felt she was in the early stage of this illness, hearing a voice and losing memory for some time periods in the day.

In earlier sessions, Rachel seemed to be constantly testing me on trust issues. Her school records suggested she was mentally gifted, perhaps extremely so, yet her grades were poor. Her poetry suggested that she saw the world through the eyes of a tormented, bitter war veteran, yet with stunning insight into the human character and condition.

This session, she leaned forward in her seat and decided to take a risk. "I'm not dumb, but I act that way to get left alone. I really do have a dissociating disorder. I know, since I looked it up before the school sent me to the doctor. I've got another Rachel inside of me." She paused. "Do you have any idea what it's like to wake up in the middle of your life, in the middle of your math class, in the middle of your conversation, in the middle of your sentence, in the middle of your word? When you can't remember what the first syllable of that word was?"

"I know you're not dumb, too," Rachel continued, "but I don't know if I can trust you." With a sad laugh, she sat back and added, "I haven't met many adults I can trust. Kids are more moral, you know. If they're gonna hurt you, they'll do it in your face, right away. Adults lie. All the time, and then they tell you why it was OK for them to lie.

"I need you to fix me fast. So I'll tell you what that book said you need to know. I was sexually molested from the time I can remember until I was 8 or 9, by my father's friend. My father didn't know. Then I was raped twice by another of my father's friends, when I was 12. That stopped when I put a knife to his throat. My dad never knew. Nobody touches me now. Even including my boyfriend. I told him I can't be sexual, or even hug him. I told him why. He understands." As I tried to clear my emotional head from this incredible picture she was painting, she knocked me over again.

"I'm officially telling you that my father never knew any of this. I want you to write that down on your paper there."

I wondered what she was really trying to tell me, so I asked what seemed to be the obvious question. "Rachel, why would you not tell someone this stuff was going on?"

She looked at me as if wondering what it must be like to have a life as protected as mine. "You really don't know, do you? It's because when you tell, they all just lie, and do nothing. When you tell, you just get hurt more, and watch your baby brothers get hurt more."

I said something that I hoped would keep her talking. "I can't believe that, Rachel. We have laws today that . . ."

It worked. She jumped up and yelled. "Your laws SUCK. Before we moved east last year, I told. I told for the babies. And the babies got beat! On account of my telling! He doesn't beat me now; he's scared of me, but. . . ." She froze. With an icy voice she said, "You tricked me."

I walked to my desk and handed her a picture of our newly adopted two-year-old daughter. "That's Sarah. She came from a hell-hole like the ones you've known. She was born addicted to cocaine, and she was almost starved to death when she was a year old. Rachel, I give you my word as Sarah's father that, if you tell, no one will beat the babies. I don't know where you came from, but you're in my ballpark now. This just ain't gonna happen here."

> Rachel had kept her silence for years to protect her brothers, for whom she was really a mother in every sense of the word. She was being held hostage by a "father" who threatened to harm the babies if Rachel ever left, told about the sexual or physical abuse, or even killed herself. Rachel's heart and will were so strong that her mind finally broke under the incredible load she was carrying. Her disease of dissociating was her last-resort survival attempt. Even now, at age 14 and mentally ill, her convictions held firm.

As I said, Rachel and Graham are heroes of mine. They are my living reminders of something that you must remember whenever you are confronted with mental illness, either with yourself or a friend. *Mental illness is one aspect of a person.* It is not the person. The most wonderful and unique parts about us as human beings (such as our values, hopes, loves, and dreams) have nothing to do with being mentally ill. A person with a mental disorder is just that: a person with a mental disorder. He might be a wonderful person or a terrible person, but the disorder is not what determines if he's nice or nasty. Unfortunately, movies like *Silence of the Lambs* and *Halloween* have pictured mental diseases in ways that happen about as often as alien abductions.

The fact is that almost all antisocial acts are committed by "normal" people. When I worked in a "lock-up" mental hospital, we used to joke about how safe we felt once we were inside the walls with the patients, because so many of us had been mugged outside the walls by the "sane" people. Similarly, I've worked with many "normal" kids whose total lack of compassion made me wish they had picked another shrink to see. I've also worked with many "abnormal" kids whose strengths of character left me in awe. So be sure to separate any disease (physical or mental) from the person who has it, whether that's you or a friend.

So be sure to separate any disease (physical or mental) from the person who has it, whether that's you or a friend.

You need to do this even if you don't have or see a mental disorder, since just being an adolescent sort of qualifies as one. Most kids feel nuts at times, and many worry that something is more seriously wrong than just the "teenage flu"(normal adolescence). These worries can do a lot more than be unpleasant. They can rip holes in your already-fragile self-esteem (see Chapter 3), which can lead to more "crazy" thoughts, which can lead to more "crazy" behaviors, which can lead to more "crazy" feelings, and so on. This chain can spiral down to a lonely place where it seems impossible even to reach out for help, let alone to get better.

We're not going to let you crash like that. We're going to keep you out of that spiral by making you an expert on the most common mental disorders that can occur in adolescence. This will help you sort out the "normal" craziness from the more unusual problems that sometimes happen, so you can better decide when it's time to get some help (or to get help for a friend), and from whom. Let's start with the "from whom" part.

SHRINKS: The Helper Folks

Shrinks: This is a term that used to refer only to psychiatrists (we'll define these in a minute), but is now used by kids as a label for any mental-health professional. There are many such people around you to provide help whenever you find the sense and courage to ask for it. And don't worry about your business becoming public information. Professional helpers are bound by rules called *confidentiality* that make them the best secret-keepers you'll ever meet. In general, short of anything that could harm someone, whatever you confide in a professional helper must remain a secret. This makes the helper's office a special place, where you can say whatever you want, and no one will ever hear about it. Without your permission, professional helpers can never repeat what you say. These secrecy rules can vary a bit by the type of helper and your location. So, before you confide anything to these professionals, ask them to tell you their exact rules of confidentiality.

There are so many different types of helpers that kids get confused about the differences, and then give up on the idea of seeing someone. So here's the crash course on the types of mental health professionals you'll find around you.

Counselors, Therapists, or Psychotherapists: These are labels that can describe many types of people who may or may not have any particular training or license. Some are very highly skilled and educated. Others might be people who just called themselves therapists. Be cautious here, because these types of helpers might not be regulated by the rules of confidentiality, and they might not have any specialized training or education.

All of the helpers listed from here on are people with lots of training, certifications, and licenses. They've had to spend years in school, pass examinations, and usually do internships and/or residencies, places where they are carefully supervised and taught before they're let loose on the public. These folks all have to abide by strict rules of confidentiality. Like anyone else, they can still be strange (my son says shrinks are definitely the weirdest people he knows), but their titles give you some assurance that they know what they're doing. And they can be very good at helping adolescents.

School Counselors: These counselors are different from the ones noted above. Your school counselor typically has a lot of training and must pass state examinations to become certified as a school counselor. These folks are great people to see first, because they're right there in school, and they deal with kids so much. If they can't help you themselves (or if you feel uncomfortable talking to someone you'd see everyday), they will get you to the right person who can help.

Licensed Clinical Social Workers: These are social workers who take specialized courses and training to provide mental-health services. They also must take state examinations and be supervised in training. They do not prescribe medications. They might hold a doctorate degree (Ph.D., Ed.D., Psy.D.) and therefore be called "Doctor," but it's a different sort of doctor than your family physician.

Psychiatrists: Medical doctors who take further training in mental health are called psychiatrists. They also must take state examinations and be supervised in training. These doctors can also prescribe medication when it's needed.

Psychiatric Nurses: In many states, nurses can obtain additional training, degrees, and supervision to become certified to provide mental-health services. In some states, they can prescribe medications, although usually in collaboration with a psychiatrist. They also might hold a doctorate degree (Ph.D., Ed.D., Psy.D.) and therefore be called "Doctor," but, again, it's a different sort of doctor than your family physician.

Psychologists: This is the title of someone who has completed a doctoral degree in psychology, and who then undergoes supervision and state examinations. Although these people are referred to as "Doctor," in most states they do not prescribe medications.

That pretty much sums up the list of helpers, with the exception of the most special helpers of all: the nonprofessional helpers. These are the front-line troops who are much more responsible for helping you than any of the pros, because they often are the ones who convince you to get help. People such as teachers and tutors, cops and coaches, firefighters and friends, all of those people who care about you, are lifelines who can keep you safe when you are caught in a bad adolescent storm.

I have met lots of kids who were amazed to find out how many adults around them really cared about their welfare, often adults they thought hated them, like a teacher or coach.

BUT YOU HAVE TO LET THEM KNOW WHEN YOU'RE WORRIED ABOUT SOMETHING. Aside from that TV guy who talks with dead people, I don't know any mind readers out there. I have met lots of kids who were amazed to find out how many adults around them really cared about their welfare, often adults they thought hated them, like a teacher or coach. You'll never find out who truly cares until you ask for help.

Let's see, did I leave any helpers off the list? Oh yeah, YOUR PARENTS! Another large bunch of amazed kids I've known are the ones who were stunned to see their parents love and stand by them when bad teen times hit. As with teachers and coaches, often you get locked into never-ending battles of power and control with your parents over stupid stuff like curfews and homework. You never get to see that these middle-aged morons who make your life so miserable actually love you to death and would take a bullet for you.

It's really quite sad. The depth and strength of the love of your parents usually ends up buried under the endless layers of quibbling garbage. Yet, under fire, when some teen tragedy hits, I see most families forget the dumb stuff and focus on what's really important: loving each other. That's when I see amazed teens seeing their amazing parents in a whole new light. It's such a shame that we can't tap that goodness more in good times.

I ask you to take a leap of faith and consider using that first line of help when you need help: Mom and/or Dad. They might be very

"I LOVE MY FATHER, BUT HE'S DIFFICULT TO TALK TO. BY THE WAY, ARE YOU GOING TO BILL ME FULL PRICE FOR THIS SESSION, DAD?"

different people than you think, if you give them a chance. If they have serious problems themselves (such as being active addicts or abusers) then, yes, bypass them, and get to the next sane adult helper on your list. But if you're just trapped in that typical "they're-dumber-than-paint" view of your folks, take a risk and a minute to talk to them. I know they seem crazy to you much of the time, but if you take a chance, they might actually be smarter than paint.

WHY YOU SHOULD GET HELP

First, allow me to save you a lot of repetitious reading over the next few pages that I'd otherwise have to bore you with, by saying the same thing about seven thousand times. The following sentence applies to every illness discussed in this chapter: IF YOU HAVE ANY DOUBTS ABOUT WHETHER OR NOT YOU NEED TO GET SOME HELP, THEN YOU DO (need to get some help). Just being upset and confused qualifies as a great reason to see someone. Shrinks specialize in helping people who are upset and confused, as well as in seeing people who have specific mental disorders. Plus, as you will see, almost every disorder is easier to treat the sooner it is treated. Delaying can mean adding months or years of needless pain.

Finally, as you will also see, we are very successful at treating these things. Even if the shrink says, "Go home; you're only as 'crazy' as everybody else," at least you'll have that peace of mind. But know that teenage mental illness is far too often overlooked because just being a teen can at times mimic some of these illnesses. So if you're going to err, err on the side of safety, and go see someone.

Which, of course, you won't do because you're just like adults—we all would rather get a root canal than see a shrink. What is this about? How did the shrinks' waiting rooms become scarier than the dentists'? Let's find out.

WHY YOU WON'T GET HELP

That first visit to the shrink is really difficult for a good many kids, for a few lousy reasons. First, there's that dumb stigma against mental illness and treatment that we just talked about. It's difficult to do something that is mocked so much. Second, adolescents are fanatics about doing things on their own. You're supposed to push adults away, and do everything solo. This is how you grow to become independent. Asking an adult for help can feel like a terrible defeat of your independence. Third, and perhaps most powerful, is the normal (and healthy) adolescent drive for privacy. For some teens, just thinking about pulling out their personal thoughts with a stranger can seem like pulling out their fingernails.

The monsters we create in our minds grow much larger when we won't confront them.

But most adolescents who muster the courage to walk into a shrink's office feel better walking out, even after one meeting. Not because shrinks are great, but because the simple act of overcoming our fear and talking to someone really helps a lot. That first session helps us to feel not so alone. And we feel a bit of strength in ourselves because we were able to take some steps to push back against whatever was hurting, shaming, and scaring us. The pain is still there, but it "shrinks" down a lot (pun intended).

Remember the relief you felt many years ago, after finally looking under your bed (with your Nerf bat in hand), for the unseen monster that was terrifying you? The relief you'll feel in facing your feelings is much the same. The monsters we create in our minds grow much larger when we won't confront them.

So if you're ready to go monster hunting, let's push on to look at the most common categories of teenage problems, and see how the "usual" issues look different from those that are actually illnesses requiring treatment. These categories include acting-out behaviors, moodiness, food problems, and anxiety. Got your Nerf bat ready?

ACTING-OUT BEHAVIORS

Acting out means all those things you do that get adult eyebrows and voices raised. That might include releasing a bunch of mice in assembly, or releasing a bunch of threats in anger. Most forms of acting out are usual for teenagers, such as harmless, irritating pranks. Some acting out is unusual, such as frightening fury. Knowing the difference between the two types, the usual and the unusual, will help you decide what to do, whether it's you or a friend acting out.

ACTING-OUT BEHAVIORS, USUAL TYPE

To some degree, acting out (being disruptive) is part of your normal teen experience. A few things happen to make this so. First, as your intellect grows, you become a lot less impressed with the intelligence of adults, and you're not as willing to do what they say without questioning it. It's not that adults get "dumber," it's just that you get smarter. So, by comparison, adults are not nearly so impressive to you.

Second, those drives for autonomy (being in charge of your self) grow very strong, and you don't want others to be in charge of you. That's a good thing, because now is the time when you need to start making more decisions for yourself.

And third, you can start to feel a bit aggressive as a result of your physical and hormonal growth. This, again, is a normal and healthy part of your development. Mix those "normal and healthy" feelings together with a brain that sometimes can't prevent runaway impulses (see Chapter 1), and you get acting-out behaviors of the normal variety. Which, as Jeremiah can attest, can be disastrously funny.

> Jeremiah was working very hard to act ashamed about what he had done. He knew it was very bad, yet, at the same time, it was

making him laugh as he told the story. "When Mr. Mott announced to the class that my brain was nothing but 'elephant crap,' I sort of snapped. He says that all the time to embarrass kids for doing bad at algebra. He makes the girls cry, and he doesn't care. He calls them 'feminist babies' and tells them they're wasting their fake tears on him."

Jeremiah paused to camouflage a laugh with a cough, as he pictured the next part of his story. "Well," he coughed again, "wouldn't you know, that day the circus had paraded elephants into town right past our school. So I said, 'You'd better be careful, Mr. Mott. There's a lot of student brains on the road out there. You never know what could happen.'" Jeremiah's grin disappeared. "I didn't mean to threaten him. That's not what was in my head. I was really trying to make up a joke as I talked, you know? But it didn't come out right. Mr. Mott went wild. He got right in my face, called me a punk, and dared me to do something. Then he called my parents and told them that I threatened him, and he sent me to the principal.

"That night, with my friends, an idea just came together. First, I added water to this big bucket of wet putty stuff that was in my garage. Then Jason turned it disgusting brown with dirt and grass, to make it look like elephant crap. My little sister Brittany added stuff from her chemistry set that made a horrible smell. Then we put it in a bag and labeled it 'CAUTION—MR. MOTT'S STUDENT BRAINS.'" His half-grin returned, along with his cough. "I took it to class just to show around, you know? But, as we were waiting for Mr. Mott, the smell got real bad, and I panicked. I climbed on top of his desk and hid the bag on top of the light. It was the only place I could think of where he might not look, and where it might not smell."

Jeremiah coughed a lot now. "Mr. Mott walks in and starts to drone on about quadratic equations, when I notice that the light is dripping brown, smelly stuff into his open briefcase. The bottom of the 'brains' bag was soaked and leaking. I guess I shoulda' used a plastic bag. Kids are all staring at the light above Mott's head, when he starts sniffing and saying, 'What *is* that stench?' He looks up just as the bag slithers off the light and explodes like a shit bomb, right in his briefcase. It was like Dumbo took a huge, flying dump on his desk. I mean SSSSPPPPLLAAAATTT!

"The fake crap flew everywhere. Kids were screaming and jumping out of their desks. Mr. Mott was covered by the stuff. He, like, couldn't move until Francine started puking. Then he starts screaming at her to stop puking, like that helps. Some other kids started gagging like they were gonna' puke, too. Mott was screaming so loud his words made no sense—'PHLLAAAGGA, SNARFLEXES GODAMMINUTIES—AAARRRRRGGGGHHHH,' words like that."

My belly laugh made Jeremiah pause, "See—you think it's funny, too. So why am I in such big trouble?"

As I wiped tears from my eyes at the hysterical picture he had painted, I shook my head. "Jeremiah, I'm afraid that in the game of adolescence, a lousy sense of judgment is rarely excused by a great sense of humor."

Is that ever true. In fact, humor can be a big contributor to adolescent acting out. Sometimes, an impulse can seem far too funny to resist (particularly in boring situations like algebra class), and the possible consequences of the action simply don't appear on your teenage radar screen. This type of occasional occurrence is called normal acting out. But when the occasional occurrence becomes a daily kamikaze run at the Mr. Motts of the world, it's time to consider the possibility of a more serious disorder than normal adolescence.

ACTING-OUT BEHAVIORS, UNUSUAL TYPE

When you turbocharge that typical teenage tendency to rebel and not do what you're supposed to do, you can get into three patterns of behavior that can put a major hurt on your life: Oppositional Defiant Disorder, Conduct Disorder, and Attention-Deficit/Hyperactivity Disorder.

Oppositional Defiant Disorder (ODD): Where Teen Rebellion Happens All the Time

This first one is probably the disorder most teens are falsely accused of having at some point in their adolescent careers. Real ODD is pretty much as it sounds: being in the faces of most authority figures most of the time. Teachers, coaches, cops, and, oh yes, especially parents, find that, no matter what they ask, the ODD kid says or does the opposite. If this is you, you might find yourself preprogrammed to hate and resist most anything that is asked of you. To qualify for this label, you have to be doing this for at least six months, doing it to more than one authority person, and doing it so much that your life is going down the tubes (school, sports, and so on). Usually, this stuff starts between ages 8 and 14, and the fights are verbal, not physical.

Teachers, coaches, cops, and, oh yes, especially parents, find that, no matter what they ask, the ODD kid says or does the opposite.

We don't know for sure what causes this disorder, but we do know that most ODD kids had tough times as infants. They were hard to comfort and often pushed away anyone who tried to pick them up to soothe them. They typically had a condition called colic, in which they cried almost nonstop for months without any apparent cause. One theory says that this situation might cause parents to start to shy away from their babies because they can't seem to help them. This, in turn, might make these babies even more upset and less able to be comforted. The theory holds that this vicious circle of mutual rejection causes a big gap to occur between the child and parents, a gap that only worsens over the years. And there is probably some genetic aspect to this, as well.

So do not take ODD behavior personally, whether it's yours or a friend's. ODD is a specific disorder with a specific cause that is treatable. It is not a character flaw or moral failing.

Kids suffering from ODD should get help yesterday. Left untreated, it can progress to the next and much more serious level of disruptive behavior: Conduct Disorder. You do not want to go there.

Conduct Disorder (CD): Anger Locked and Loaded

A few kids with ODD can graduate into a much more serious pattern of conflict called Conduct Disorder (CD). This is where the verbal assaults cross over into the physical. CD kids beat, bully, cheat, steal, rape, and do whatever they choose without giving a damn about anyone else. Because you're reading this book, this is not you. But if you know a kid who has Oppositional Defiant Disorder, do whatever you can to convince him to get some help now.

Conduct Disorder is very hard to treat, and kids who have it usually end up with criminal records.

Attention-Deficit/Hyperactivity Disorder (ADHD): It's Hard to Know Who Has It

If there is a maddening disorder in the teen world, this is it. Maddening because it's so hard to figure out what it is, what it isn't, when it could be, and why it's not. Confused? Welcome to the club. Let's look at what is known about ADHD.

The symptoms run like this: ADHD kids are inattentive (can't pay attention), disorganized, overactive, and impulsive. Some are mostly inattentive, others are mostly overactive, and many are only impulsive. Yet many can sit stone still and play a video game for hours and hours. They have to be this way for at least six months, and they have to be this way at school, home, or with friends (two out of three qualifies). There is no blood test or MRI that can diagnose ADHD (as of this writing), so the kids who are this way are labeled only by observing symptoms, symptoms that are amazingly similar to the symptoms of normal adolescence. That makes it pretty subjective. That makes it pretty scary.

The first scary fact is that, although 5 percent of American kids have ADHD, 20 percent are diagnosed with it. That means that 15 out of every 100 kids in the nation can get medications they don't need. Which brings us to the second scary fact. Most of the medications used to treat ADHD are quite powerful, and they can have substantial side effects. Some of these same drugs often are abused by illegal users, with disastrous results.

So what distinguishes ADHD from normal adolescence? In "normal adolescence," a kid can focus with a mental discipline, if she chooses to try. She simply finds the work boring, stupid, or whatever, and stops trying. The true ADHD kid finds it impossible to focus, even when he truly wants to, and tries very hard to.

If you have any doubts, go see the shrink. DO NOT, DO NOT, DO NOT simply take your friend's medication to see if it helps you. This could seriously hurt you, particularly if you're depressed or anxious, which, as you'll see, are other reasons kids sometimes can't concentrate. See the experts. They sat through years of boring school so they would be able to answer your questions.

MOOD DISORDERS

Acting-out disorders affect our behavior, but mood disorders are illnesses that affect how we feel, how we see life, and how others see us. That's what we call our *mood.* When you think of yourself or a friend as being "up" or "down," "hyper" or "laid-back," you're describing a mood. When you have a mood disorder, something takes control of your mood and forces it to be something it normally wouldn't, and makes you feel differently from the way you would normally feel. This could result from genetics, brain-chemical imbalances, physical diseases, drug use, or life events (like car crashes or divorces).

Throughout our lives, moods can change a lot and still be considered "normal."

Throughout our lives, moods can change a lot and still be considered "normal." That's because the events of our lives can shape how we feel. Yet, at one point in our lives, our moods can dance all over the place for no apparent reason, and it's still "normal." Would you like to guess when that might be?

ADOLESCENT MOODINESS, USUAL TYPE

If adolescence had a coat of arms, it would likely be a picture of moodiness, whatever that would look like. It might look like Arthur.

> "Sometimes, I can't put on the brakes in my brain. I swear, I'm fine one minute, and then my mother will say some little thing, and I go off. I mean really off. I'm, like, mad yelling, just because she joked about my hair or something. A minute later, I'm happy again." Arthur looked a little embarrassed at this next part. "Then, when my mother looks at me like I'm nuts, I act like nothing happened. I can do this so well that sometimes I get her thinking it never really happened, like she's the one whose nuts. Jake [his friend] says I'm a manic-depressive [has bipolar disorder]. He learned about it in his psych class. I guess that's pretty bad, huh?"

It might be pretty bad, but it's not manic-depressive (bipolar disorder), something we'll discuss shortly. Jake's experience is pretty normal for a teenager. That developing brain of yours can often have some flimsy emotional brakes (see Chapters One and Three) that can let your moods swing wildly at times, and go to some impressive extremes, making many kids (and more parents) wonder whether some not-normal thing is going on. The fact is that normal teen moodiness can seem very similar to many mood disorders (illnesses) that happen in adolescence.

For example, most teens report feeling depressed, thinking about death (but not about killing themselves), and having mood swings at stressful times during adolescence. That's normal. Not pleasant, but normal. When you're stressed, that's where your heads can go for short periods of time. But these second-string imitations have little else in common with the real disorders. The differences between the minor and major versions of mood problems have to do with how severe they are and how long they last.

ADOLESCENT MOODINESS, UNUSUAL TYPES

When your moods begin to have a bad effect on your life, you may have a mood disorder that needs treatment. If school, home, friends, or activities are suffering because of how you're feeling, the odds are that you're suffering, too. When moods become really severe and long lasting, when they start to become the rule and not the exception to your daily life, it's time to see a professional. Here's what the unusual mood problems of teens look like.

Depression: Where You Have to Rally to Feel Only Awful

Anna walked in like she was trying to keep from throwing up. Taking slow, deliberate steps, as if she had to think about every one, she stood frozen in the middle of my office, finding the task of picking out a seat overwhelming. When I made a dumb joke about my clients being frightened of my furniture, she frowned at first, and then smiled weakly when she realized that she was supposed to laugh in response. But that forced smile was the best she could do. As small a thing as that was, I could feel how hard she had worked just to smile. Her pain filled the room.

At first, she would offer only one-word answers, as if each was a tremendous effort for her. No, she wasn't sleeping well. Yes, her appetite had disappeared. No, she wasn't doing any of the sports she used to love. Then, speaking like a 60-year-old 17-year-old, she interrupted me, impatient with my multiple questions.

She spoke with a sigh. "Let me make this quicker for you. The world seems, like, all gray to me now. Nobody knows what I mean by that, but it's true. Nothing has any color, taste, excitement, whatever, and I can't even say why. My father keeps asking if I'm doing drugs." She laughed sadly. "I tell him I'd feel better if I were doing drugs. He keeps telling me to 'think' my way out of this, that I'm not trying hard enough, that I need more sleep and vitamins and stuff. My mother finally made him bring me here. But this is stupid and pointless. Nobody can understand what this is like. This 'gray' thing is just me, just the way I see the world."

With another sigh, Anna slowly honored my request to follow me into the hallway, where a bunch of teen artwork was hung on the walls. Her eyes grew wide as she stared in amazement at a painting done by a depressed teenager. It was a landscape painted entirely in gray.

Any adolescent worthy of the title of "teenager" gets depressed from time to time. In fact, everybody gets on the "down" escalator for a day or a week now and then. Life is like that. And these "downers" are probably not all that bad for us. They eventually help us truly appreciate the good things, times, and people we have in our lives.

But when that "down" escalator becomes a free-falling elevator that crashes into the basement of sadness and stays there, it's time to worry about the disorder of *clinical* (serious) *depression.*

Clinical depression is not just a sad feeling. It's a dangerous disorder that requires immediate treatment by professionals. The symptoms run like this: feelings of hopelessness and/or worthlessness; cutting off from friends, family, and activities; drops in grades; eating too much or too little; sleeping too much or too little; lots of physical aches and pains; thoughts of death and dying. A final symptom that I'd add to that list is drug use. Kids often use drugs, especially alcohol and marijuana, as a way of "treating" depression on their own (as we'll discuss later, that trick never works, and it frequently leads to full-blown, lifelong addictions).

At least four of those symptoms must be happening for at least two weeks to officially qualify as clinical depression, but the hard part is that depression can sneak so slowly into your brain that these symptoms don't get noticed for a long time. So try to check in on yourself once in a while, to nab this disorder quickly, before a depression takes over.

Many teens tell me that, in the beginning, becoming clinically depressed makes everything seem "gray," as if life loses its color and excitement. They don't feel like doing the things they used to love. Everything becomes an exhausting effort. Music, laughter, food fights, sleepovers all become stupid, as if a huge "whatever" attitude takes over your soul. So keep an eye out for this in yourself and your friends. Clinical depression is a very common problem with adolescents these days. If you (or a friend) should ever qualify for that title, there's some bad and some great news that you should know.

Adolescents feel emotions, good and bad, at least as powerfully as adults.

The bad news is that teenagers in particular often suffer silently and needlessly from depression, sometimes for years. Teen depression often doesn't get identified and treated because it's teen depression. Your age becomes a problem in three ways. First, adults can forget how powerfully adolescents feel things, and so not consider that you might be really, really hurting. Parents sometimes think that, because you're not a grown up, you can't suffer like a grown up. It's not that they don't care, they just kind of forget. It's like that "puppy-love" prejudice. Adolescents feel emotions, good and bad, at least as powerfully as adults. Many shrinks believe that you feel many things more intensely than adults.

Second, kids are amazingly good at hiding personal issues, even serious diseases like depression. And when you're clinically depressed, sometimes you're feeling so bad that you can't even see that you're feeling so bad. When you're in the middle of a depression, it's like not being able to see the forest for the trees. The depression distorts your view and makes you forget that you used to be happy, and that you deserve to be happy.

Third, depression in teens can look nothing like depression. Some kids get real nasty and angry as a way of trying to fight their pain. They push everybody away, so no one is left close enough to see the terrible sadness beneath the sarcasm.

The great news is that when we are smart enough to see it, we are very successful at treating depression. So if you have any doubts about possibly being depressed, PLEASE, PLEASE, PLEASE do not try to "tough it out." If I had a nickel for all the depressed kids who later told me how stupid they felt for initially trying to push through this disease on their own, I'd have a lot of nickels. If you're in doubt, get help NOW! If you're not careful, depression can take a lot from you. It can take your soul. And if you're not careful, depression can lead to this next disorder, which can take the rest of you.

Suicide: Do Fear the Reaper

One of the not-so-pleasant side effects of your expanding mental skills is the realization that death is a reality of life, and that can be overwhelming. As a little kid, your brain really couldn't grasp that concept very well, so you were able to mostly ignore it (unless you lost someone very close to you). But as your brain does that adolescent "question-everything-I-was-told-as-a-child" review, occasionally, you can get stuck in thinking and worrying a lot about death and dying issues. For example, many adolescents get upset about death because, as they think through religious questions, they might give up their belief in an afterlife, a comfort that helps many of us handle death fears.

This type of worrying is not unusual in adolescence, but it is a good reason to talk to someone. Most teens just bury these heavy thoughts and fears, and struggle on. But talking them out really does help.

Although occasional thoughts or worry about death is not a disorder, if the thinking moves from "I'm scared about dying" toward "I wish I were dead," it is time to get some help, NOW! The odds are that you really don't want to stop living, but that you really want to stop hurting from something. Those death thoughts are symptoms that life has become too painful. But instead of thinking about ending your life, shouldn't you think about ending your pain? Seems simple enough, until ending your life looks like the only way of ending your pain. That's when you are truly in trouble, particularly for someone dealing with this with an adolescent brain.

The fact is that there are always much better solutions to ending pain than ending life. But three downsides to having an evolving teenage brain (see Chapter One) can mean that you might not live to see those options. First, adolescents sometimes have trouble controlling impulses. Second, teens often feel things (like emotional pain) so intensely that they can't think their way out of a problem. Third, they sometimes can't fully understand the consequences of some of their most critical actions. This means that kids who suicide have no way of truly seeing the impact of a decision to kill themselves. Unless, of course, they believe in miracles. Halbert's beginning to.

"Did you ever see that Christmas movie [*It's a Wonderful Life*] about this guy who kills himself, and then this angel shows him how the world would be without him? That was me, sort of." At 16, Halbert looked like any other teenager you might meet. A little metal on his body, a few braces on his teeth, and a lot of shaggy hair covering scars on his head.

"I can't really say why I did it. I know I've been down for a long time, but there didn't seem to be any point in telling anybody. What could they do? I just pretty much hated my life, and I guess, myself. I wasn't trying to hurt anyone. I figured that they'd hardly miss me, since I act so nasty all the time.

"That night, I decided to drink my father's beer in the basement. He hides it there from my mother. After I had four or five cans, I remember my head getting really weird, like something was daring me to do it. So . . . I. . . ." Halbert's voice trailed off into nothing. Then, without any explanation, he fast-forwarded to weeks later.

"You know who really made me understand? My little [14-year-old] sister Mina, of all people." Halbert paused. "I guess I can't call her 'Moron Mina' anymore. Everybody else, my parents and uncle, and even a teacher who came to see me in the hospital, they were, like, super sweet and concerned. They all acted sorry for me, and kept asking how they could help, and all. That was nice, but none of it seemed real to me, you know? My parents looked whacked out, like smiling zombies, like they weren't real. I felt like nobody was being real.

"My little sister didn't visit me. My mother said it was because she was so busy with school, but I knew that something was up. When I finally went home, she wasn't there all day. When she finally came home, I went to her room and, like a jerk, I said, 'What's the matter, 'Moron'—aren't you glad to see me?'

She looked up at me, making this growling noise, like the Exorcist girl. Then she attacked me. She went nuts—punching, kicking, and screaming so loud that my parents came flying into the room. My head was still bandaged, and she didn't care. She screamed that she wished I was 'f'ng dead,' that I'm an 'F'ng A' hole.' She screamed this over and over, so much and so loud that she threw up. This is from a cheerleader girl who never said 'damn' in her life. "My parents thought she was having a breakdown or something. They kept telling me that she didn't mean what she was saying, but I knew she meant every word."

Before I almost made the same mistake as Halbert's parents, telling him she probably didn't mean that she wished him dead, Halbert showed me what was real.

"She's right. I was an 'F'ng A' hole.' And she should want me dead for what I did to her. When I saw how mad, scared, and hurt she was, I finally saw the truth about what I had tried to do. That was when I understood how messed up I was. I was so far gone that I couldn't see what was real, what I had done to people who love me, people I love. My sister was the only one who showed me straight up. I guess I owe her now."

Halbert had shot himself in the head. The surgeon said that Halbert's survival was a "one-in-a-million" occurrence. The bullet "miraculously" caused only minor damage.

Do you believe in fate, God, or angels? Halbert didn't use to. He says he's not so sure anymore. When I asked if I could use his story in this book, he said sure, that maybe his "miracle" had some purpose. He hoped his story might make some other kids pause and think before putting guns to their heads, as well as to the hearts of all those people who are left behind, like Halbert's "moron" sister.

You need to know the facts about suicide, so that you'll be in a better position to help yourself or a friend if this disorder strikes near you.

And in the hope of moving guns away from heads, we need to talk about the mythology of suicide. With this topic, bad information kills. It can make people respond in bad ways that can put kids at greater risk of dying. You need to know the facts about suicide, so that you'll be in a better position to help yourself or a friend if this disorder strikes near you. As you are about to see, the odds are that it will. You need to be prepared. So put away your books and take out a pencil. It's suicide quiz time.

Answer true or false:

1. Hardly anyone kills him- or herself.

Answer: FALSE. Last year, 2 of every 10 teens in this country either attempted suicide or were close to it. This means the odds are very high that, as I'm talking with you, suicidal thoughts are talking with someone you know. Keep an eye out. In addition to the symptoms of depression listed previously, watch out for friends who suddenly do things like use a lot of drugs (especially alcohol), give away their prized possessions, contact all of their past and present friends ("goodbye" meetings), and/or get heavy into death themes (in talking, writing, or music).

2. Only depressed kids kill themselves.

Answer: FALSE. Suiciders come from many different places. Some are angry kids, trying to "pay back" parents, teachers, or other kids they think are being unfair to them. Others are teenagers who suffered some loss that might seem small to onlookers, like the rejection by a boyfriend or girlfriend. Many are "copycat" suicides, where one kid's pointless death seems to inspire others in the community to be just as pointless.

3. Kids who are depressed attempt suicide only after long bouts of depression.

Answer: FALSE. Many kids suicide after only a week or two of sadness. Another down side to being an adolescent is that it's often very hard to believe that time heals all wounds (it does), and that you'll survive any tragedy if you just keep putting one foot in front of the other when things get tough (you will).

4. Once a kid takes antidepressant drugs, she's no longer a suicide risk.

Answer: FALSE. Often, the risk of suicide is greater just after someone starts a medication. The reason is that the drug can initially give depressed kids just enough motivation to carry through a suicide plan. I've seen this tragically happen where a kid's "friend" gave him some antidepressant pills that he stole from his home. Please don't ever medicate yourself or a friend. Handing out stolen pills is like doing open-heart surgery on your friends—unless you've been extensively trained, you stand a good chance of killing someone.

5. Kids who make weak attempts, or who "just" threaten suicide, never do.

Answer: FALSE, FALSER, AND FALSEST. "Weakly" attempting suicide or talking about it makes you much more at risk of actually dying. Amazingly, some people like to mock kids who talk about dying or have unsuccessfully suicided by saying, "He's just looking for attention." If I may use my daughter's favorite expression, "Well, hellllloooo!" Yes, this behavior is very much an attention-getting device, just like the screaming of people drowning in pools. If they don't get the attention (help) they need, they may die. Which brings us to the subject of what to do if (or when) suicide comes knocking on one of your friends' doors.

Suicide Prevention Hotline: (Write Your Phone Number Here)

Of all the stomach-turning sentences in the world, one of the worst comes from the friend of an adolescent suicider who says, "She used to say that suicide junk all the time—that's why I didn't tell anybody." These are words whispered by hollow-eyed kids who can't get pictures of their friends' coffins out of their heads. You do not want to be whispering those words. It seems that every year I get to meet at least one teenager who tried unsuccessfully to save a friend from suiciding by talking to him all night, instead of calling parents or police.

If your friend called you up and gasped that she was having a heart attack, would you guess at whether she might survive? Would you play doctor on the phone, or would you dial 911? Easy call, right? Then why do so many kids guess about their friends' suicidal intentions and try to do telephone, Internet, or in-person "therapy"? The ironic thing is that shrinks never "guess" when a kid calls up and says she's going to kill herself. We take their word for it and get them help

ASAP. And contrary to what you see in the movies, we don't fix suicide problems on the phone. We simply try to keep people safe until the rescuers (parents and/or police) can get there. The only phone work is to keep them from pulling a trigger until help arrives. The real treatment for suicidal thoughts is long, complex, and often risky. It is definitely not a game for amateurs, no matter how caring.

As soon as you hear that "S" word, get a message to your friend's parents or to the police.

Yet you will likely be the first person to be able to help a suicidal friend, because you will likely be the first person he will tell about his twisted thinking. Kids typically share their suicidal thoughts with other kids first (and, far too often, last). This means that you are the most important rescuer in the loop. *You must resist your natural, caring urge to try to help your friend by becoming his shrink.* You can be a wonderful resource to other teens who are having problems, except when the issue involves suicide. As soon as you hear that "S" word, get a message to your friend's parents or to the police. If you're on the phone as your friend is holding a gun, keep talking, but signal your own parents to secretly let them know what's happening, so they can make the calls while you keep your friend distracted (say you need to go to the bathroom).

Will your friend get mad at you for ratting her out? She might, but I guess you need to ask yourself what the nature of true friendship is all about. Many say it's about loving a friend enough to do what's best for her, even if you lose that friendship as a result. What's best for your friend is keeping her alive. I've yet to meet a kid who was sorry that his suicide had been prevented—*every single near-suicider I've ever known has sooner or later become happy that he survived.*

So love your suicidal friends. Love them enough to risk losing their friendship by giving them their life. To help you to do that, see the DOs and DON'Ts about suicide calls from friends on page 130.

Had enough talk of suicide? Me too. For a lifetime. Let's move on to look at another teen mood disorder that can seem so similar to normal adolescence that many of you get treated for a disease you don't have. Kids call it being manic-depressive. Shrinks call it bipolar disorder. Kevin's mom called it hell. The lines on her face told me she'd seen it.

CRITICAL DOs	CRITICAL DON'Ts
Take all threats seriously.	Guess about threats or blow them off.
Watch your friends.	Think this can't happen to you, your friends, or family.
Get adult help IMMEDIATELY!	Try to fix this yourself.
Love your friend enough not to care if he or she gets mad at you.	Love your friendship more than your friend.

Bipolar Disorder: The Real Deal

"Kevin had been depressed for some time. I don't know how long exactly, because he keeps to himself so much." This exhausted mother laughed a dark laugh here. "I should say he used to keep to himself. He was getting worse and worse, until he couldn't get out of bed to go to school anymore. My friend said to give him these antidepressant pills which she didn't need anymore for her own kid who had been depressed. She said they were like a 'gift from God' for her kid.

"At first, they seemed to be a miracle for Kevin too. The next day he was up at 5 A.M., all dressed and ready for school. It was amazing. He was just so up and positive, saying that he couldn't wait to get back to school, that he had all of these projects that he had thought up all night. The next few days were like more miracles. He seemed to have endless energy to do schoolwork, staying up working after I had gone to bed, and up in the mornings before I got up. I was thanking God for this miracle. But it wasn't God working with my son.

"Last night, he starts telling me that he has to transfer out of his school, that his teachers and classmates are all too stupid for him, that he has 'mental powers' they can't understand, and that they're jealous of. When I asked what he meant, he got his chemistry binder out that he had been working feverishly on for days. With a weird smile, he shows me the pages and says, 'Can't you understand it. Mom? It's a formula for making people invisible.' Then he laughed a weird laugh, and spoke some gibberish phrase. I looked at the binder pages, and I wanted to cry. Dr. Bradley, his writing was all gibberish too!"

Mom started to weep. "That's when I realized that he was sick. I stayed up all night with him to be sure he didn't hurt himself. HE STARTED SCREAMING AT ME TO GET AWAY FROM HIM, THAT I WAS WITH 'M FORCE,' ONE OF THE 'SECRET POLICE' TRYING TO STEAL HIS SECRETS. HE INSISTED ON TAKING MORE OF THOSE PILLS EVEN THOUGH I PLEADED WITH HIM NOT TO. HE STARTED PLUGGING ALL OF THE ELECTRICAL SOCKETS WITH FOIL SO THAT THE 'M FORCE' COULDN'T SPY ON HIM." Mom worked hard for a minute to collect herself. "Sometimes he'd stop and start to cry and beg 'Mom, please help me,' but then he'd run away and lock himself in a room.

"He's sleeping, finally, now. He took a bat to bed with him in case he gets attacked by the 'secret police.' I need to know what to do when he wakes up." Her fears and her tears broke through once again.

"WHAT IN GOD'S NAME IS GOING ON? IS HE CRAZY? IS HE POSSESSED?"

"Yes," I thought to myself. "He is probably possessed. By a demon known as bipolar disorder."

Not all that long ago, Kevin *would* have been suspected of being possessed by a devil. He's an example of what bipolar disorder can look like if it's not quickly treated. Although there are various forms of this illness that can be much less severe, they are usually marked by longer periods of depression (usually months), followed by shorter bursts of manic activity (for days or weeks), during which kids can do some strange things. Like speak too much and too fast, jump from one subject to another to another, as if they are on drugs, or think they have super powers. They might stop bathing, eating, or sleeping, or even hear and see things that aren't there. These scary symptoms all result from a brain chemistry that goes out of whack. Any one of us would act the same way if our brain chemistry was altered in the same way as occurs in bipolar disorder.

This used to be an adult illness that rarely hit a kid. But, recently, it's occurring in lots of children and teens, and we don't understand why. Explanations include things you can't control (like genetic changes), plus two factors that you can control: stress and drugs. A lot of shrinks are convinced that the never-before-seen stresses of your adolescent world trigger this disease earlier than they did in prior generations. Twenty percent to 40 percent of the adolescents who become severely depressed (and that's a lot of kids) see their disease evolve into bipolar disorder within five years.

Another group points to the never-before-seen levels of drug use, saying that putting powerful drugs (especially stimulants like speed, cocaine, and ecstasy) into a brain that's rewiring (see Chapter 1) may trigger serious mental diseases such as bipolar disorder. Makes you think, doesn't it?

Try to keep those dramatic pictures of Kevin in your head if you worry that you're manic-depressive (bipolar). The odds are that you are not. As I said earlier, when we talked about "normal" adolescent mood swings, being a teenager means that your moods will shift around a lot in the course of a day. It's part of the normal teen experience, and the mood swings will improve as your brain rewires through adolescence. These "normal" moods are short lasting (for hours or days) and usually have some explanation that makes sense, at least to you. The disorder moods last much longer, and the kids struggling with them usually say that they can't explain why they feel that way.

But if you have any doubts, get to the shrink fast, for three reasons. First, this is another disorder that can be treated very well. With medication and therapy, the symptoms of bipolar disorder can often be completely eliminated. Second, if you start treatment early, you can avoid those horrific scenes that terrified Kevin's family. If Kevin had gotten immediate help, he might not have fallen into the really bizarre behaviors. Third, get help quickly, because the longer you live with this disorder, the harder it can be to accept help. Some kids start to "enjoy" feeling manic, and they don't want to get better at the cost of losing the feeling of being superhuman. Because your teen years can be so tough at times,

With medication and therapy, the symptoms of bipolar disorder can often be completely eliminated.

becoming Superman or Superwoman can seem like a very attractive alternative to the feelings of vulnerability that are so painfully common for so many adolescents. But whatever you do, don't ever allow anyone to use anyone else's medications. Kevin's horrific episode of believing he was superhuman was actually triggered by taking those pills that Mom's "caring" friend offered. Sharing pills is not caring. It can be killing.

And while we're talking about teens trying to become superhuman to cope with stress, it's time to chat about another group of disorders that urges kids to become something that is not human. But whereas bipolar disorders come from a chemically unbalanced brain, this next cluster of disorders comes from a values-unbalanced world that tells you that you're not worth anything unless you almost look like you're dying. A world that, at the same time, addicts you to frighteningly fattening foods that load you with life-threatening pounds.

EATING DISORDERS

Being an adolescent is a tough enough time on its own. As you saw in Chapter 2, the physical changes kids go through can make you very self-conscious about your appearance. Then, as you saw in Chapter 3, your self-worth often crumbles when you crash into adolescence. And, as you saw in Chapter 1, your teen brain tends to feel things very strongly, often overreacting in ways that can be harmful.

On top of this mix, our world has added a culture that adores thinness yet promotes fatness. This has created a generation of adolescents struggling with food problems like no other before.

Normal Eating Struggles: CAN I MONSTRO-SIZE THAT FOR YOU?

Something weird has occurred over the past few decades. What used to be considered a normal body is now called fat. And what used to be considered a normal meal is now called skinny.

In Chapter 2, we discussed how our culture somehow changed the rules about how peoples' bodies are supposed to look. This has gotten so far out of hand that the Miss Americas of the past few decades (the "ultimate" of female beauty?) have all been malnourished according to medical standards. In other words, we have now defined beautiful women as females who are *slowly starving to death.*

What makes this particularly nuts is that our view of food has gone in the opposite direction. What used to be considered a normal meal is now looked at as starvation rations. In this country we eat too much, too often, and we eat too much fat. America is the butt (pun intended) of food jokes in other nations. Where most of the world's population is fighting starvation, many of us are quite literally stuffing ourselves to death. Overeating-related illnesses (such as diabetes, heart disease, and obesity) are off the charts. Yet we continue to promote all the wrong foods, even to small children, which shape their lifelong eating patterns in ways that may literally kill them.

Every day, you are hit with many powerful suggestions (slick ads) to eat junk that makes you fat. But starring in that Triple-Barfo-Burger ad is a pencil-thin girl being adored by 10 lean guys (just how many Triple-Barfos do you think they eat?). All of this craziness is not lost on teenagers. More than 80 percent of the girls in this nation report being upset with their weight. Serious eating disorders (which we'll discuss shortly) are epidemic among females. And record-high numbers of boys are now hurting themselves with too much or too little food.

There are some secrets that true friends don't keep when the lives of their friends are at stake.

When this constant battle between wanting to starve yourself and stuff yourself stays even, with neither side getting the upper hand, I'm afraid that's called normal. Unhappy, perhaps even miserable sometimes, but normal. That's the price we pay for living in this world that can't make up its mind about fat versus thin. As long as your weight stays within normal ranges (according to your physician, not your pop star), and you are not doing any of the scary things we'll discuss shortly (eating disorders), you're probably OK. But should any of the following behaviors look like you (or like a friend), get help quickly. The longer these diseases go untreated, the harder they are to fix. They're nasty, painful, and potentially fatal.

And if you see a friend keeping her eating disorder secret, please remember our chat about friendship and suicide. If she's doing something that can kill her, it's time to rat her out to her parents, a teacher, or a counselor. There are some secrets that true friends don't keep when the lives of their friends are at stake.

Abnormal Eating Struggles: Where The Food Craziness of Society Gets into Your Head

Marcy's hands and arms were hard to look at. The bones were precisely outlined in places where a 14-year-old's muscle and fat should have been. What flesh remained was bruised and battered by countless intravenous (medicine injection) sites and a blood-clotting problem, both results of Marcy's determination to "stop being fat."

"I'm out of the hospital for now," she said weakly, "as long as I eat enough to . . ." she paused here, "to gain a little weight," she said. "To stay alive," I thought. She struggled terribly with those last words, just as I knew she struggled terribly to swallow food. "You said that you wanted me to tell you the truth about how I feel. What I feel is that I'm fat. I know I'm sick and all from not eating, but I still look fat—to me. I know everyone else thinks I'm skinny, but they're wrong. They can't see what I see." Her voice became even weaker now, as if the life force within her was slowly draining. "I can't do what they [her parents] want, you know. Everyone keeps trying to scare me into eating by saying I'll die. But another thing they can't see is that I'd rather be dead than fat. The world hates fat people. What's weird is that I don't mind fat people. I see them just like people, like anybody else, you know? But the world . . ." she shook her head, "the world says if you're fat you're worthless, like you have no right to live."

After she sat awhile, Marcy laughed a very hollow laugh. "My father used to have a bumper sticker on his truck that had a picture of a crossed-out fat woman. It said 'NO FAT CHICKS IN BIKINIS.' He still had it on there the first time they took me to [the eating disorders hospital]. The social-worker lady pointed it out to him, and he ripped it off. He was embarrassed. He lied and said it was on there when he bought the truck, but I remember the day he put it on. He was laughing and showing our neighbor. I remember thinking, 'He's right. Fat chicks are disgusting. I'm disgusting.'" After a hollow sigh, Marcy offered a frightening mental picture of herself. "I guess I'm about to become the crossed-out girl on that bumper sticker." She suddenly raised her voice as if to cut me off from offering to help her. "There's no way out of this, you know."

Marcy was wrong. There are ways out of these eating disorders, but they are very hard work, for two reasons. First, because we don't fully understand what causes these disorders, we have a difficult time treating them. We suspect that there are a lot of causes, some genetic, some brain chemical, and some from life stresses that swirl together to make proper eating seem impossible.

Second, these illnesses are tough to treat because the world around these disorders is a disorder itself. Just as that bumper sticker proved, the way our culture views nonskinny people is absurd. It's a prejudice in every way, one as hateful and as dangerous as the ones about sexual differences and mental disorders. Add "fat" jokes to your list of ways to pointlessly hurt good people who happen to be different. As Marcy proves, that garbage can kill.

The serious versions of adolescent food struggles come in three versions that have a few deadly things in common. They mostly strike women, they can be fatal, and they come on so slowly that no one seems to notice that something is wrong until after a lot of damage is already done. And just as with suicide, it's usually a kid's friends who know long before adults that something is wrong. So, just as with suicide, you might well end up being a friend's lifesaver by letting adults know what's going on. Keep your eyes open. Here's what you might see.

Anorexia Nervosa (Marcy's Disease)

Kids with *anorexia* eat almost nothing because they're stuck looking into a trick mirror similar to those at amusement parks that make you look heavier than you are. If you and Marcy stood over a pond and looked at her reflection, you'd see a frighteningly thin girl who was starving herself to death, and who desperately needed to eat more. Marcy would look at that same reflection and see a frighteningly fat girl who was eating herself to death, and who desperately needed to eat less. Understand that, when a kid suffering from anorexia tells you that she's fat, she's telling you the truth—the truth for her, that is. So just telling her to eat more is like telling her to stand in front of a speeding truck. She truly believes the distorted picture that only she sees in her mirror.

Anorexia, which usually affects younger female adolescents, always becomes visible, because there is no way to conceal the weight loss for long. And before that, a bunch of other symptoms appear, like menstrual-cycle interruption, stomach and sleep problems, and complaints of always being cold. Many anorexic kids also get into prolonged, intense exercise jags.

Bulimia Nervosa

Bulimia is when kids eat large-to-huge amounts of food (binge eat), and then get rid of it by forced vomiting or taking overdoses of laxatives. The part of this disorder that kills is the puking and/or laxative-induced diarrhea. Those behaviors can do terrible damage to a body, damage that initially remains unseen because, amazingly, that overeating/vomiting cycle can maintain a normal-looking weight for a period of time. This makes the disorder very hard to spot at first. But eventually, bulimia causes nasty things to happen, like rotted teeth, perforated throats, and stopped hearts (not very attractive, don't you think?)

Like the anorexic kid's reflection, a teen with bulimia also suffers from a distortion that she can't escape. This one has to do with feeling that the food she ate is like a poison that she has to get out of her body. The feeling of a full stomach becomes agonizing. Although anorexia seems to get most of our attention, bulimia gets more of our young women, with estimates of this disorder running as high as 20 percent among college females. This means 2 of your 10 female friends might be struggling with this life-threatening illness right now.

Obesity

This disorder of overeating now qualifies as an epidemic seeping our nation with a deadly efficiency that would make the most devoted terrorist envious. America-haters can forget about launching anthrax or smallpox attacks. All they have to do is sit back and wait. Most of us are eating ourselves to death. Think I'm kidding?

As I write, the statistics show that more than half of America's children are overweight, which means that they are shortening their lives (and making themselves much less healthy) if they don't change their food habits. Estimates of obesity (being grossly overweight to an extent that threatens health) run from 15 percent to 30 percent of our kids. And that's a figure that's doubled in 20 years. Carrying around too much weight causes a bunch of nasty disorders that cause early death and make the living years much less worth living. That list includes diabetes (where kids need insulin shots every day) and high blood pressure, two diseases that cause early death and strokes. Sleep apnea (where kids can't breathe while they sleep) makes the obesity hit list, along with depression, poor self-esteem (see Chapter Three), and drug abuse.

The best help you have to offer is just being a friend, and that really helps a lot.

Obesity is a particularly vicious disease in that it runs in a circle that makes itself worse. Just as with other eating disorders, there are a few different causes for obesity, but one big one is that heavy people often overeat to find emotional comfort and to punish themselves. Why do these folks need comfort and self-punishment? Largely because of our insane need to criticize, ridicule, and even hate nonskinny people.

> "You know," this 15-year-old girl offered sadly, "being obese means everybody sees your disease. I know lots of teenagers who steal, do drugs, and even beat up on little kids. But they're thin, so nobody ever knows what they are when they walk through the mall. They can pass for nice kids if they want. Other kids like them more, the teachers like them more, and so do parents. When I think about this, I feel mad and hopeless about my weight. It makes me feel like eating way too much. Sometimes, even my own father says. . . ." Susan couldn't finish her sentence.

So if you want to help this society (or just your friend) lose some weight, first try losing your own bias against heavy people, and simply accept them for who they are, for their worth, not their weight. Try to leave the weight issue out of your relationship. "Curing" someone who is eating herself to death is a complex and difficult process best left to the professionals. The best help you have to offer is just being a friend, and that really helps a lot. The LAST thing you want to do is be critical and make someone feel even more self-conscious. Don't ever think that an overweight friend somehow doesn't worry about her weight. Today's adolescent world will allow her to think of very little else.

As I leave you with some DOs and DON'Ts about eating disorders, let me emphasize two points: The first is that the longer you struggle with these diseases, the longer it takes to get better. The second is that the younger you are when you get help, the greater the odds that you can fully recover. If you or a friend has one of these disorders, "waiting it out" is only making things much worse. GET EXPERT HELP NOW!

CRITICAL DOs	CRITICAL DON'Ts
Get help yesterday.	See whether it gets better on its own.
Get adults involved.	Gamble with these life-threatening disorders.
"Just" be a friend (that's a lot).	Try to "fix" a friend; never be judgmental.

Adolescents who worry too much about their weight brings us to the last group of disordered teenagers we need to discuss: Adolescents who just worry too much.

ANXIETY DISORDERS

I'd be hard pressed to name 10 teens I've known who were not anxious much of the time in adolescence. Teen years can be so rough at so many times for so many kids that worrying about stuff is just part of your daily routine. But there are normal and abnormal ways this worrying can happen.

Normal Adolescent Anxiety: "What? Me Worry?"

Simply stated, teenagers worry. About everything. There are so many stresses, conflicts, and challenges to today's teenage life that the trick is to learn to stop worrying once in a while and enjoy these years a bit. Normal levels of adolescent anxiety mean that you're pretty much able to do want you want, even though you worry about it. For example, if you were able to try out for the school show, even though you couldn't sleep the night before the auditions, I'm afraid that's normal. And if you got yourself to that party, even though you got belly butterflies about not being cool enough, well, that's normal too. As hard as these things are, they actually make you tougher, helping you to learn about yourself and gain confidence in your abilities to meet challenges. Like they say, what doesn't kill you makes you stronger. But if you see yourself worrying a lot more than your friends, check it out.

Abnormal Adolescent Anxiety: "What? Me Worry?"—All the Time

When worries start to take control of your life, preventing you from doing what you want to do, it's time to consider the possibility that the worrying might be excessive. The problem is that, because worrying is part and parcel of the teen experience, many kids don't realize when something unusual is going on with them, which puts them at great risk. For example, far too many kids get far too heavy into drugs (including alcohol, and especially marijuana) as a way of trying to live with feelings of anxiety by "medicating" themselves, which often leads to addiction. Many other kids experiment with the "wrong" drugs that can make anxiety disorders a whole lot worse, and put them into tailspins that land them in hospitals or worse places. So if you or a friend seem anxious, you have another good reason to stay sober. But that doesn't mean that you do nothing.

Far too many kids with anxiety illnesses struggle through life suffering terribly and needlessly, because anxiety disorders can be cured or controlled very well. So read on to see whether you find yourself or a friend among these anxiety disorders. You might save a life.

That's because these illnesses can make living so painful that dying can start to look good. Far too many adolescent suicide notes talk about being unable to live with overwhelming fears. This makes shrinks absolutely crazy, because anxiety is so easily treated. So don't make shrinks any crazier than they already are—get help for yourself or a friend if you have any doubts.

Generalized Anxiety Disorder

Anxiety becomes a disorder requiring treatment when it starts to stop you from living your life the way you want. When you find yourself avoiding things you love (like sports or parties) because they make you too anxious, you might have the illness of generalized anxiety disorder. In addition to avoiding activities, the symptoms can include extreme shyness and nervousness, sleep problems, excessive aches and pains (like stomach problems), risk-taking (as a way of covering up fear) and drug use (as a way of self-medicating the bad feelings away).

And, sometimes, anxiety can take a form so powerful that kids actually believe that they are dying. It's called a panic attack.

Panic Disorder

Think of the scariest moment of your life, perhaps during a terrible nightmare in which you knew that you were going to die some terrible death. Your heart pounded so hard that you thought it would explode. You panted so fast that you felt like you were suffocating. Sweat poured out of you as if you were in a sauna. You might have had agonizing chest pain, nausea, and numbness, just like with a heart attack. Now picture this happening to you out of the blue, with no apparent cause, perhaps while you're just relaxing and watching a funny movie. If nothing physical is wrong, you had a panic attack.

If nothing physical is wrong, you had a panic attack.

These episodes do a lot more than just give you some bad moments. They make life miserable and often impossible, because these attacks can occur anywhere, at any time, with no warning. Kids with panic disorders can become afraid to do anything, to go anywhere, or even to hang out with friends, because the thought of having a panic attack in public is unbearable. These kids may quit school, friends, sports—everything, and just hide out in their rooms, thinking that they're nuts and no one can help them. They "know" that nothing is wrong with them physically, but, just like being in that nightmare, they still "feel" like they're going to die. This seems so frightening and crazy to them that they sometimes never tell anyone what's going on—not even a best friend.

Obsessive-Compulsive Disorder (OCD)

This is another "Top 40" disease that many teens are sure they have simply because of the title, because adolescence is a time of obsessions, when things get into your head and seem to almost take over your brain. Like with sex, cars, sex, clothes, sex, love, and don't forget sex. That's mostly the fault of adults, who seem to have lost control of our world that now pounds you with these suggestions to act out with sex, drugs, and aggression. You can't look at a TV, a magazine, or even a newspaper without seeing these suggestions. They literally surround you. Usually, though, these normal obsessions come and go, and they don't really control what you do. Normal obsessions don't keep you from school, activities, or friends. But when thoughts in your head take over your life in a way that stops you from living as you want, you may have OCD.

There are two parts to this nasty disorder that usually hits males in their early- to mid-teens, and females later on. The first is a true OCD obsession, an overpowering, unwanted thought that you know is crazy but that you can't get out of your head until you perform some action. These thoughts might have to do with excessive cleanliness, safety, or fears of God punishing you if you don't repeat some prayer over and over. This is considered an anxiety disease, because if you resist the urge to do the action, you end up with terrible, paralyzing anxiety that can literally bring you to your knees with fear.

The compulsion part of OCD is the action that you must take to relieve the anxiety of the obsession. This might be something like praying when you don't want to, having to keep some clothes from getting "contaminated" by outside air, or doing what Michael was doing.

> Michael's 14-year-old eyes were pleading with me, even though his mouth stayed closed. In his eyes, I could see intense pain, shame, and humiliation, all imprisoned by fear. He desperately wanted me to find a way that he could tell me what he needed to say, without him having to say it. "I, like, can't tell you what I'm doing because, that's like a rule in my head, you know? If I tell anybody what I'm doing, it will get worse." He hurriedly added the next part, terrified that I would just

send him away. "I know that's crazy, that it makes no sense. But at the same time, I believe it, if that makes sense." After searching my eyes for understanding, he turned his eyes downward in defeat, certain that there was no way out of his prison of irrational fear.

Weeks later, I learned that Michael was wrestling with a life-consuming compulsion to place imaginary "cushions" on every sharp corner of every object in the world. If he failed to do so, his brain would obsess on the sharp corners, telling him that people would hit their heads on them and die. His brain also told him that if he shared that secret with anyone, he would no longer be able to cushion the corners and save lives anymore. He had agonized secretly with that horrible fear for two years. When I told his father about this, he seemed angry and frustrated. "Why doesn't he just stop thinking like that? Is he trying to get attention or something? Maybe I need to get in his face. He's got to stop this!"

Michael's dad reacted just as most of us would if we didn't understand what OCD is about. From the outside it seems obvious that, if Michael would try hard enough, he could stop. Because his dad loves him, it seemed the loving thing to do to scare him into stopping. Loving parents in particular can often look like abusive beasts when they are trying their hardest to help their kids. Strange, but true. But with OCD, taking the linebacker approach never works. The more stressed you make someone with OCD, the more OCDish you make someone.

As weird as it sounds to your parents, most kids hate having to take drugs, for reasons that tie right back into your development.

Keep Michael's fear-wracked brain in mind if you're worried that you have OCD. If you can live your life normally, then you probably are only as obsessive and compulsive as the next kid. But if you can't get control of these thoughts and actions, and your life is suffering, get some help NOW. The sooner you start treating OCD, the easier it is to treat.

Here are some DOs and DON'Ts to consider if you're considering the possibility that you or a friend might have an anxiety disorder.

CRITICAL DOs	CRITICAL DON'Ts
Get it checked out immediately.	Let the disorder grow by waiting.
Remember that anxiety can be a disease.	Assume that your pain is normal.
Avoid all drugs (including alcohol).	Medicate yourself or a friend.

That concludes our little tour of the common mental disorders of adolescence. If you remember one thing, please let it be that a mental disorder should be no more of a "label" than diabetes or asthma. These disorders are all just one aspect of people. Don't ever let them become the people themselves.

There is one final aspect to mental disorders that we need to discuss before we move on: medications. The fact is that most of the disorders we looked at are most effectively treated by a combination of talk therapy and medications, AKA drugs. Which brings us to that question I hear monthly from at least one kid: "OK, Doc, let me get this straight. You want me to use pills to stop using weed?"

MEDICATIONS

Having confronted the difficult task of seeing a shrink and facing some pretty tough issues, an adolescent who has a mental disorder often faces yet another hurdle in her journey to get well. She is told that drugs might help—the prescribed kind, that is. For most kids, that's a big problem.

As weird as it sounds to your parents, most kids hate having to take drugs, for reasons that tie right back into your development (see Chapter 3). The first is autonomy (being in charge of yourself). Part of your job as a teenager is to want to do everything on your own. This urge is normal and critical to help form your identity. So being told that you should take a drug to help you help yourself can sound like a terrible dependency on something artificial, outside of you. It sort of feels like a failure, like having to admit that there is something that you cannot do.

The second reason kids hate medicine is control. Again, your normal and healthy adolescent nature tells you to seize control of your life at every opportunity, and to resist things that try to control you. Prescribed drugs can sometimes sound like adult controls, personality-altering chemicals that might take charge over you in some way, by changing something about you that seems a bigger problem to your parents than to you. And, to you, it might feel like it's part of your personality that the adults want to "drug" away. Sometimes, that might be true. At least that's what Morissa thought. But truth is more often in the middle.

> Morissa was really angry that I asked if she was taking the medicine her psychiatrist prescribed. "No!" she snarled. "They're nuts if they think they can make me take that stuff. My parents and teachers just want me to stop getting in their faces. Well, too f'ng bad! If they don't want to deal with it, then tell THEM to take the f'ng drugs. If I don't like something, I say it. That's who I am. I'm no f'ng wuss like my brother. I'm not kissing their asses like he does. AND IF YOU DON'T LIKE IT, TOO F'NG BAD FOR YOU, TOO! THIS IS WHO I F'NG AM! I'VE ALWAYS BEEN LIKE THIS, AND I ALWAYS WILL. THIS IS MY PERSONALITY. SO YOU GOT ANY F'NG QUESTIONS?"
>
> I let this 13-year-old girl sit for a minute, while her angry words echoed in her head. They seemed to slowly quiet the fury in her eyes. I took a chance.
>
> "Morissa, I'm sorry. I didn't mean to say that there is something wrong with you—but what if there is?" The rage returned in her eyes. "Hear me out, please," I begged. "You can say things straight up, but can you hear things straight up? If you want me to talk with you like an adult, you need to let me know. Because that means holding onto your temper and dealing with stuff that's not so easy. You up to it?" Slowly and coldly, she nodded yes.
>
> "OK," I said, "Here it is. I think you're right. I think your parents don't want to deal with who you are. They do want you to be a clone

of your 'perfect' brother, and that's wrong. What's more, I think they have a problem with anger in general. They hate any kind of conflict, and maybe that's why they want you to take the pills, thinking it will make your anger go away, and then their lives can be perfect. I'll tell you what I told them: That's never going to happen. Your anger won't and shouldn't go away with some pill. I said that you should be angry, and that the family needed to deal with why." When a hint of a smile appeared on Morissa's face, I promptly squashed it.

"Now, here's your part. Yes, you have a right to be angry. No, you haven't the right to assault people with your anger like you do, 24/7, for all these years. Morissa, if I get in your face screaming 'f'ng' names, does it sound like I'm trying to tell you I'm angry, or just hurt you? And are you likely to listen to what I have to say, or just rage back, or run away?" Her drooping head told me she knew all of this, so I continued.

"I know you know this, and I think that you can't stop the rage even though you want to. I think you know that something goes wrong when you get mad, like a runaway train in your head. So here's your challenge questions: Do you just want to rage, or do you want others to listen to why you're angry? Is it your 'personality' to be someone who likes to hurt others, or someone who doesn't want to be hurt?"

When she just nodded again, I knew her answers. "Morissa, you're telling me that you can't be who you are, or who you want to be. That means it's time to take a look at taking the medication. Not to change who you truly are, but to allow you to become who you truly are. Get it?"

She just sat and looked so sad, I almost wished for the raging Morissa to return. "OK," I shrugged, "I'm shutting up. It's your turn to 'f'ng' talk." She laughed a small laugh, but it was the first laugh I'd ever heard from her. "Sometimes," she sighed, "being mad feels a lot safer than being hurt, you know? I guess I'm afraid if I take the medicine and stop being such a bitch, I'll get hurt more. Then I'll be weak. It just hurts really, really bad to hear my parents describe me as the family screw-up."

I shook my head. "Morissa, when you rage, you become weak, not strong. Everyone just dismisses you as some lunatic they don't have to listen to. If you really want to 'get' to your parents, all you have to do is calmly tell them how hurt you are. I guarantee they'll listen, and you might even see some tears in their eyes. Just now, when you told me how sad you feel, being seen as the family screw-up, you brought tears to mine."

Morissa's struggle against medications presents my best argument for taking them: If they allow you to become who you think you truly are, who you truly want to be, then they are not changing you—they're allowing you to become you.

Medications don't make any-body do any-thing. There is no pill that makes you do homework, stop raging, respect your parents, or quit doing drugs. The very best a pill can do is to allow you the choice of doing those things. Whether you do those things is up to you. For example, lots of kids with ADHD don't do their homework. So we give them medicine that helps them concentrate better, and you know what we find? Some still don't do their homework. Not because they can't anymore, but because they just don't want to.

As you saw in this chapter, many kids have disorders from brain-chemical changes that can make them do things they don't want to do. Like rage, feel anxious or depressed, or screw up in school. Taking a prescribed drug levels the playing field, so that a kid with a disorder can have the same choices as any other kid.

If you have asthma, would you refuse to take a pill that allows you to do what you want, and be who you want? Or would you argue that gasping for breath and being unable to run is part of your personality, and shouldn't be medicated away? Diseases like depression leave your spirit gasping for its emotional breath. Shouldn't they be medicated, as well?

Prescribed vs. Illegal Drugs: Who Says Paxil Is Better than Pot?

Good question. In answer, I'll spare you all of the legal, moral, and scientific reasons for now (although we'll get to those in following chapters), and instead leave you with that same argument for why you should consider medications if they're suggested: It's all about having choices. Street drugs are all about wimping out on life by making problems temporarily disappear, or by making life seem temporarily different. Pot can make you stop worrying that your life is going nowhere. But your nowhere life is waiting for you when you come down. Booze can give you the nerve to talk with girls. But your killer anxiety awaits you with your hangover. Ecstasy can make you feel loving and loved. But your agonizing loneliness crashes back in as you crash out.

Illegal drugs fix nothing. They're just short-term chemical lies to fool your brain into thinking that you're OK when you're not. Because they work so well in putting you into a temporary la-la land, they are also terribly addicting—not just "craving" addicting, as with crack, but "escape" addicting, as with weed. In Chapter 5, we'll talk about those drugs specifically and show you how addicting they are, especially the ones most kids never worry about (like alcohol and marijuana).

Street drugs are all about wimping out on life by making problems temporarily disappear, or by making life seem temporarily different.

The legal drugs we give to teenagers are not addicting, and they help you stand up to your problems in the real world—to engage them, challenge them, and fight with them toe-to-toe, so that you can have those choices of being who you truly are.

My final warning on using street drugs to try to medicate yourself is the same one we give to physicians: We all have the potential to become addicted. Humans shouldn't prescribe drugs for ourselves because we're too potentially nuts (yes, even, or especially, doctors) to be trusted with access to chemicals that can make our problems temporarily disappear. And if you doubt that, then tell me why alcohol, the one drug adults can "prescribe" for themselves, *produces at least 30 times the number of addicts than all of the other drugs combined.*

So if you or a friend is struggling with this issue about taking a prescribed medication, do a couple of things. First, ask a million questions of the doc who's telling you to take this. After all, it is your body. Second, get on the Net and research the medicine on serious, scientific Web sites. There's lots of good data out there that can help you understand more about a drug.

Finally, think about a trial run. The bottom line is that no one can make you take any drug you choose not to take, so it's up to you. Try the med for a while, and see whether or not it helps. After verbally wrestling with Jon on this suggestion for more than 6 months, that's what he finally decided to do.

Jon was one of the most stubborn kids I've ever known. Even though terribly depressed, he was never too down to argue about anything any adult ever advised. The problem was he was so good at it that he would always win his arguments, and lose his happiness. After telling me that I was the biggest pain-in-the-ass shrink he had met yet (a true compliment), Jon finally agreed to a trial use of an antidepressant. After three weeks on the drug, he walked in trying to hide a grin, a thing I had seen perhaps twice in six months. He was still stubborn, but now he was also funny.

"If you ask me how I am feeling on the med, I swear to God I'll stop taking it," he fake-threatened. Then he laughed: "I can't believe what a sore loser I am. OK, OK, it helps, all right? You win. You were right. Now rub it in. I know you're just dying to say 'I-told-you-so, nanya-nanya-nannnyyya.' Go ahead, take your shots."

"Jon," I laughed, "given the forced choice, I'd taunt Mike Tyson before you. But I'll make a deal: Tell me whatever you want, and I'll never ask again—at least in this session."

Jon turned serious, but his face looked so different: Serious no longer meant sad. "For the first couple of weeks on the medicine, I was sure that nothing was happening. Then, on Monday, something weird happened. In the hall at school I, like, found myself talking with some kids I hardly knew, and I wasn't scared. I've wanted to do that for years but never felt like I could. Maybe I don't have to be 'The Invisible Man' [his name for his depressed, shy self] at school anymore."

Jon paused, thought some more, and then decided to share his thought: "I hate to say this, because I'm so scared of jinxing myself, but I think that I feel, like . . . happy? Not "high" happy, just feeling OK. I'm not sure I ever felt OK before in my life. It feels really, really good. It feels like you said it might—that maybe I can start being who I want to be." Feeling better didn't mean he stopped feeling stubborn: "So, Doc," Jon smirked, "why didn't you tell me before that I needed a medication?"

Jon's parting shot proves to be a great way to end this section of this book and move on to the next. His fight against taking a medication (and admitting that he had a mental disorder) came from more than just being a teenager. It also came from the shame and guilt that our culture dumps on those of us with differences. Jon's fight to become himself speaks to the awesome power that others can have in shaping what we believe, how we act, and, in the end, even who we are.

You could call that "power of others" your *culture,* and, as you're about to see, it will try to fight you for the very control of your life, of your identity. You need to know this force well, to know when it starts to shape you into someone you might not be.

So, if you're up for the challenge, turn the page. It's time to look at your world. But be ready for some shocks.

YOUR WORLD

Putting the Pieces Together

"Parents point to their kids and ask, 'Why is it that teens do so much sex, drugs, and rock 'n roll (violence)?' I point to the world and ask, 'Why is it that teens do so little sex, drugs, and rock 'n roll?'"
—Dr. Michael J. Bradley, age 52

Part One of this book put you under a microscope, to look at many of the forces inside of you that shape who you are. But that's only half of the growing-up story. For, as I'm sure you've seen by now, much of who you are comes from forces *outside* of you, from ideas in the world around you.

All of us (not just adolescents) are so controlled by the world around us that people argue all the time about which forces are more powerful: those inside a person or those outside. Scientists call this the "Nature versus Nurture" debate. Most agree that both Nature *and* Nurture weave the cloth that makes us who we are as people—that inside *and* outside forces swirl together to shape our values and beliefs, strengths and weaknesses, and in the end, our successes and failings as human beings.

If that's true, it presents a very scary problem: how do we know if those outside forces shaping us are good or bad? We often can't judge whether they're right or wrong, because sometimes *we don't even see these outside forces.* That's because *we're so used to seeing them* that they

"NEVER MIND WHAT SUSIE'S MOTHER SAID. TWO-PARENT FAMILIES ARE *NOT* A CULT!"

blend into the background of everyday life. This is like that "can't see the forest for the trees" stuff. We just react to these things by acting a certain way, without realizing that we're doing it.

We see the incredible power of outside forces in something that we touched on earlier: female attractiveness. Do you think you could be "told" by outside influences what type of female body you would think is attractive? No? You might want to read this next part first, before you decide.

We see the incredible power of outside forces in something that we touched on earlier: female attractiveness.

Researchers recently did this incredible study of the population of a remote, isolated island (no TV), where, for many hundreds of years, heavy women were seen as much more attractive than thin women. Then, just a few years after these folks got satellite-beamed television, all the women were suddenly starving themselves to get thin. Centuries-old traditions proved no match for the TV "babes." The power of what these people saw on TV, for just a few years, wiped out their ancient beliefs about what makes women attractive. Think that was a fluke? Think again.

Nigerian women always did lousy in international beauty contests due to two factors. First, the African women cared so little about these silly events that they barely drew enough contestants. Second, as with many African cultures, heavy females were seen as more attractive, and so they were always picked to represent Nigeria (ever seen a chunky Miss World?). Then, in 2001, they wised up and intentionally picked a skinny woman to represent them at the Miss World competition, *even though the Nigerian judges did not find her physically attractive* (some dissenters called her "a white girl in black skin"). She became the first African winner in the 51-year history of that international competition, and she got lots of publicity back home.

At about the same time, the South African TV network (seen across Africa) chose a skinny winner in its "Face of Africa" beauty contest (that network also carries mostly American shows). *Within one year,* heavy African women were seen as unattractive (particularly by people under 40) in their own countries, and "skinny" became queen in a world that had prized heavier women since the dawn of history. A minor problem here, according to researchers, is that, by nature, African women tend to be heavier. But that's OK. They've begun starving and running themselves into shapes they were never intended to have, just like Western women do.

Still think people can't be easily influenced by their environment?

The rest of us are no different. Research has shown over and over that each of us will doubt *and often change* our own values if the world around us constantly tells us that what we think is wrong. Standing up to the opinions of others is something that can wear down the strongest and smartest of us. Even a kid like Ian.

At 17, Ian seemed to have it all. Very bright, straight As, lots of friends, successful parents, and three scholarship offers from three of the best universities. But he was miserable.

"Look, I know we've been over this a lot. And I know who I am now, and what I believe. But what I believe can't be right—IT JUST CAN'T. Everybody else I know, and I mean *everybody*, chases money—everyone except me. I'm sure I'm just naive or immature. Something must be wrong with me—I know it!"

Ian looked like he had lost his best friend. It turned out that he had. "Last night, Josh [his lifelong friend] told me that he was just bullshitting all those times when he said he'd join AmeriCorps [a volunteer service program] with me after high school. We always planned to take a year off before college to help poor people, and to grow up a little before going to college. He said that the real reason he was ducking college was that he felt he could never compete with kids like me, and never make the money he thinks I will make. He said that after graduation he's joining his father's remodeling business. He absolutely *hates* that work. He's only doing it for the *money*. All these years, I never knew Josh was only about *money*."

Ian shook his head sadly. "God, it was like talking to my father. My dad hates, *really* hates, being a lawyer. He hates it so much that he can't sleep, and he gets sick to his stomach all the time. All he talks about is retiring. Last week, I said, 'Dad, why do you do a job you hate? Why not be a high-school teacher, like you always wanted?' He said, 'This is the only way I can make the kind of money I make. This is what you do when you're a grown-up.'"

Ian squashed the stretch toy on my table, much as the world squashed his values. "Then my father offered me a new Mercedes if I take the Harvard scholarship." He held up the flattened toy, as if it were him. "Picture *me* driving a *brand-new Mercedes*. What a joke! I hate those cars. Nobody understands! I don't give a crap about 'THE MONEY.' Sure, I want to live decently, have a family, and all, but I don't care about Mercedes or mansions. I just want to do something with my life that makes a difference in the world, that makes it a better place because I was here. That's my idea of being rich: going to a job that you love going to, and not have it feel like *work*. That's why I broke my butt in school—to be able to do things that make me *happy*, not *rich*. To me, those are not the same thing. But that makes me messed up, at least according to everyone around me: my parents, my brother, my teachers, and now my best friend. It's really the whole world versus me. Can I really be right?"

After a moment, Ian smiled a sad smile. "So, Dr. B, can you turn me into a kid 'Who Wants to be a Millionaire'? Because I really don't."

Ian was in the middle of a fight for his very life. What was *inside* of him (his identity) was not acceptable to what was *outside* of him (his world). He had to choose one and disappoint the other, because there is no way to please everyone when it comes to making identity choices. The power of those outside influences was making Ian doubt himself. Just like those "heavy-is-beautiful" people, he was getting worn down about holding on to what he believed.

Ian's fight is your fight: discovering who you *are,* while very powerful forces in the world tell you who you *should* be. You need to know about these forces, so that you can best deal with them. These things are most powerful when you can't really see them or understand their influence over you.

The trick is to actively sort out the good from the bad, instead of just going along with the flow.

There's good and bad in each of these parts of your world. Some things these inside and outside influences suggest can save your life. Sometimes they suggest things that can end it. The trick is to actively sort out the good from the bad, instead of just going along with the flow.

Sorting all this out is what Part Two is about—looking at your world in five pieces: your *parents*, your *family*, your *peers*, your *school*, and last, but certainly not least, your *culture*. In fact, because so many folks say that your culture is the most powerful force in your life, maybe we should tackle that one first.

YOUR CULTURE

Separating Who You Are From What's Around You

I look at my parents and I see
people, sane and loving, but stupid and boring. I look at
my world and I see
people, crazy and selfish, but exciting and cool. I look at
my mirror and I see
me: sane and crazy, loving and selfish, stupid and exciting,
boring and cool.
In my mirror I don't see me. I only see
them.

—Unsigned poem

If whoever left that poem in my waiting room reads this book, please contact me. I love that piece. It describes so many things so very well that I had to share it here. To me, it is a snapshot of adolescent struggle for identity. It shows the wrenching crash that occurs inside of teenagers, as the old values and beliefs of their parents smash head on into the new values and beliefs of their adolescent world, of their teen culture.

Culture means the things that make a particular group of people who they are, and the things that make them different from other groups. These include beliefs, attitudes, behaviors, language, and customs. Body piercing, for example, is a custom mostly seen in today's youth culture, a fashion that makes that group different from other groups (such as parents who can't even look at a pierced tongue).

But be very careful here. Talking about people as having a certain culture can be dangerous, because some misinformed folks can assume that everyone in a certain culture is the same. That's *labeling*, which is another form of prejudice. Some of you do this to adults. You think that because someone is grown up, they think and act a certain way. Some adults (and parents) do this to you. They assume that they know who you are, based on the clothes you wear, the words you say, or the number of holes punched in your body. This is insulting, stupid, and sometimes even dangerous. Prejudice between parents and teens causes each to move further away from the other. Emotional gaps between people quickly fill with fear, anger, and bitterness, all things that kill love, which, in the end, is the thing that keeps us all safe.

Remember, *the fact that you live in a culture does not mean you* are *that culture*. As I said in the Introduction, just talking about a teen "culture" is misleading, in that inside that huge group called "adolescents" are many smaller groups that are very different from each other ("jocks," vs. "nerds," vs. "skaters," vs. "preppies," and so on). And within those smaller groups are also kids who are still very different from each other.

Finally, there are those kids who aren't in any group. These adolescents make up the largest group of all. They're just people—individual, unique teenagers trying to make up their own minds about what's right and wrong, without joining any particular group. These kids become rightfully angry whenever they read books (like this one) that generalize about teens.

The worst influences on today's teens are those created by the adult world.

So what's the point of talking about the teen "culture," if it doesn't represent who you are? The point is about *power* and *control*: seeing the *power* that the culture has to change you, and getting the *control* you need to resist unwanted ideas.

We are all changed by the forces in our world, some of which come from *outside* of our culture. The worst influences on today's teens *are those created by the adult world.* When we look at three life-threatening behaviors of adolescent culture—sex, drugs, and "rock 'n roll" (violence), it becomes clear that *adults* tell kids that these are cool, normal, and fun things to do.

You don't produce the music, movies, or ads that push these ideas. *That's on the grown-ups.* Adults sell products by using sex, drugs, and even violence to appeal to dark urges inside of people. They think it's all great fun, until you start to do exactly what you're shown in the music, movies, and ads that rain down on your heads. Then people start yelling that kids today are so bad. This is crazy.

The fact is that, as a group, the same adults who judge you for being into sex, drugs, or violence *would have done these same things* if they had been teenagers today, because of the tremendous influence of culture. Its power can be frightening. Study after study shows how it messes with heads, and, as you're about to see, it's been messing with yours.

I need to remind you about your head, and about those critical changes going on in your brain wiring (see Chapter 1). The bottom line is that our world has plunked you into a culture that forces you to deal with life-threatening issues like sex, drugs, and violence at the absolute worst time in your life. First, your brain is just now developing the parts you need to make good decisions, control impulses, and understand the consequences of actions. And second, as we speak, you are hard-wiring your brain with habits, beliefs, and values *that can stay with you forever.*

So, if you're ready, let's take a quick tour of your culture, to see how it's doing. The odds are that you're doing better than it is. We'll start with the bad news, so we can end with some good, because we're going to need it. Get ready for sex, drugs, and rock 'n roll (violence). Your culture is *like none before it.*

ADOLESCENT SEX: This is Sexy?

I was stunned when the speaker put the question to this group of one hundred 10th graders. During a high-school seminar on reducing pregnancy, he asked how many girls in the room were virgins. Before anyone could jump in to say that wasn't a great question to ask, one girl slowly raised her hand. Most of the kids started to giggle, and then a lot of the boys began laughing, taunting, and mocking her. It was just terrible. I wanted to do something, but the auditorium had collapsed into chaos, and no one voice could be heard.

As I helplessly watched this poor girl's face burn red with humiliation, a weird and wonderful thing happened. A chant started to grow from within the audience that slowly swelled louder and louder until it finally silenced the bewildered boys: The *girls* were all chanting "SHUT-UP! SHUT-UP! SHUT-UP!" with one voice. After the boys did shut up, the girls' chant quieted down until it was silent, and tension filled the room.

Finally, a very brave girl named Chandra stood up, turned to face the loudest boys, and said, "How dare you? HOW DARE YOU? All you creeps do is use us for sex and then throw us away like yesterday's dirt, and talk trash about how *easy* we were, and how cool you are to get us. You like trash talk? OK, here's some for you. I ain't no virgin, but I ain't laughing at her. You wanna' know why? 'Cause I wish I *WAS* her. I wish I was as smart as her to know that I *didn't* have to have sex with creeps like you, just because *you* say we're not cool if we don't do it."

There was dead silence in that room as she walked up to the biggest loudmouths and got right in their faces. "There," she said, "There it is. Now, you go ahead and laugh. I really want to hear you laugh now, funny boys. Laugh now, or sit down and shut up, 'cause you don't know what the hell you're talking about."

Those boys were twice Chandra's size, and half her character. Character beats size every time. Slowly, they sat down with the reddest cheeks of all. Standing her ground, she turned to the "virgin," nodded and said. "You go, girl. You go." That became the new chant as the girls all stood up and applauded. The boys just stared at the floor.

Something huge happened in that room today.

—From the personal journal of Dr. Michael Bradley

I tell that story every chance I get, because it shows where hope exists in the face of an out-of-control world that has rewritten the rules about sex. Our hope for sexual sanity lies with kids like Chandra *who think for themselves.*

If you look at our American culture, you'll see that it's obsessed with sex. It's everywhere. As if sex is not a powerful enough urge on its own, we seem to be a society of crazed sexual maniacs who can't resist putting sex into every possible aspect of our world. Chapter 1 gave you some of the numbers on this. All you have to do is watch TV for 10 minutes to see it. The problem is that it's there so much *you don't even notice it anymore*, much like background noise. But, like that jingle that gets stuck in your head because you've heard it a million times, these sexual messages can get stuck in your head and change who you are.

In the past decade, that sexual bombardment has exploded into your world. Rates of sexual activity among even young teens are way beyond anything seen in prior generations, with 38 percent of 9th graders being sexually active, and 24 percent of those having multiple sex partners (four or more within 12 months). While the numbers bump up or down a bit from year to year, kids are having sex, and lots of it. They're also having all the nasty little problems that tag along with being sexually active, things that they don't sing about in the music videos.

More than one-third of American girls now say it's OK for their boyfriend to slap them for insulting him in front of his friends.

Like pregnancy and sexual assault. And although teen pregnancy rates have recently dropped a little bit, *35 percent* of girls in America accidentally become pregnant *before they celebrate their 21st birthday*. Sexual and physical assault now hits 20 percent of teenaged girls. Last year, 10 percent of American high school girls were raped—*10 percent*. Some researchers say rape is skyrocketing because of "date rapes" (girls being raped by a boyfriend), but we're not really sure, because this is a crime that mostly goes unreported. When asked why they didn't press charges, most girls felt that they had "brought it on" themselves, or they were too ashamed to tell anyone.

Speaking of girls not valuing themselves, "relationship" violence has become so frequent that it seems almost normal to kids. *More than one-third* of American girls now say it's OK for their boyfriend to slap them for insulting him in front of his friends.

Finally (and maybe not coincidentally?) teen mental disorders like depression, anxiety, and suicide are also off the charts. These things

"I'M NOT SURE IF I'M GAY OR STRAIGHT. WHAT'S IT CALLED IF YOU ONLY SLEEP WITH TEDDY BEARS?"

have all occurred as kids began having sex so much. That doesn't mean that having sex caused these problems, but, at the same time, maybe there is a link. We really don't know for sure. Which brings us to the big question: *Is it OK to have sex as an adolescent?*

Answer: That's a call you have to make. The fact is that no one can stop you from being sexually active. Another fact is that, for many kids, it seems nearly impossible to *not* have sex, because of the pressures of your culture. My job is to lay out some facts and observations for you to mull over. You have to decide what's best for you. But be sure that it's *you* doing the deciding for you, and *not* your culture. You and your culture may not agree.

Your culture says that having casual sex is fun, risk-free, and doesn't hurt anybody. That also happens to be what most boys (and most men) say. That's not what most girls (or women) say. Sex is not the same thing to boys as it is to girls. Since the dawn of time, men and women have seen sex differently. What's news is that, recently, girls seem to be accepting the boys' view of sex, at least publicly. But privately, many girls are not so happy about it.

What Boys Say and What Girls Say: What Do You Say?

Whenever teens are asked about their sexual activity, two things keep jumping out of their answers. The first is that casual sex, once only common among boys, is quickly becoming common among girls. Forty percent of young women at college recently said that they had "hooked-up" (had sex with someone they didn't care about) at least one time. The second thing that keeps showing in the answers is that boys and girls are still very different in their views about having sex, casual or not. When asked how they felt about it, the boys thought it was all just great fun. The girls either had mixed feelings or regretted doing it. This differing view of sex is best seen in the following survey question: When asked to describe who they had sex with, the boys mostly said "with some girl I know." The girls said "with my boyfriend."

This all fits with what we know about what sex means for women, versus what it means for men. Most women see sex as a very special way of showing love for someone very special to them. In other words, females hold the *emotional* parts of sex as most special. This seems to be part of the female nature. Most males, in contrast, see sex more as an adventure, a way of having fun without getting caught up in feelings like love. They can value the *physical* parts of sex more than the emotional. "Best friends with benefits" (casual sex partners) is a phrase I've heard from lots of guys—and never once heard from a girl. To be sure, there are some exceptions to these trends, on both sides. Occasionally, I do meet boys who see sex as an act of love, versus those who act at love to get sex. But these guys seem to be increasingly rare.

However, most guys are not quite the pigs that some girls claim they are. They're just programmed by nature to be this way sexually. It's only as men age and mature a bit that they learn to control these "sex-with-anybody" impulses, and start to value the emotional parts of sex more (although, as you've seen, some adults never do).

I've also met some girls who claimed that casual sex is just fine and fun with them, as well. But as I got to know them, I didn't believe them. They always seem to be girls wrestling with some loss or pain that gets numbed through casual sex. The real crisis that worries experts is this recent change that is occurring, where girls are caving in to the male view of sex, rather than being true to their own nature, and to whom they truly are sexually. Attempting to be someone you are not can cause you a lot of pain. Karen found out how much.

Karen ran down the list of her drugs with me. This 17-year-old was in way over her head. The hair on my neck was starting to rise. The pattern looked almost suicidal, as if she might be hoping to die. She spoke calmly, with the thousand-yard stare of a combat soldier. "And I also do ecstasy a couple of times a month."

"Why ecstasy?" I asked.

She gave me that "he's-a-dinosaur" look. "For the sex, of course. I've got a sex problem. I, like, sometimes can't get it on with guys at parties."

Attempting to be someone you are not can cause you a lot of pain.

Once in a while, a client will say something that makes me pause, looking for some sensitive question, to figure out what the heck the person is saying. This was such a moment. "Karen, do you think you're supposed to . . . sorry, strike that question. How often do you have sex with guys at parties?"

She looked upset with the question. "Just like my friends, maybe a couple times a week. Some weeks, none. Why? You think I'm a whore, or something?"

"Do you want to be having sex like that?" I asked.

At least she had some life in her eyes now. She was mad. "What's wrong with that?" she snapped.

"Maybe nothing," I shrugged. "I just wanted to know how you felt about it."

Her anger slowly melted into tears. Then she cried and cried and cried. . . .

Karen had been seduced more by the culture than by the creeps. She was ignoring her own feelings that were telling her that having sex was bad for her. She thought that the world around her must be smarter than her own feelings. As she saw it, sex was everywhere around her, and it seemed to be normal and expected. Her friends, her music, her videos, even her own father were all into sex for sex's sake. But, as she found out, sexual values are very serious parts of your identity that must come from *within* you, and not from a culture that seems to have lost its own values and identity.

That culture lied to Karen in another way, as well. It told her that emotional conflict and guilt are always things to be put to sleep with chemicals. The truth is that *our conflicts are usually nature's way of trying to tell us that something is wrong in our lives that we need to fix.* It's kind of like a toothache. You can just numb the pain with drugs, and avoid dealing with an infection (that may kill you one day). Or you can see the pain as a signal that you need to find and fix that problem inside of you. That choice is also yours. You must make up your own mind, because your culture has made up its mind: It hates dentists. It loves painkillers.

ADOLESCENT DRUGS: A Crisis Inside a Crisis

Listen closely, because I have a terrible secret to share with you. What I am about to tell you is a huge lie in which most adults participate. I can almost guarantee that, if you confront them with the facts I'm about to give you, they'll probably deny them.

Your teen culture lives in the middle of a huge drug culture that is not even yours. This is a place where most people do one particular drug all the time, often daily. That drug is one of the deadliest and most addictive substances known to man. It's used so much and by so many that, when the federal government attempted to outlaw it, the drug users forced *The United States of America* to back down. Pushers who make and openly deal this drug make billions of dollars, and they have turned many of this nation's neighborhoods into deadly drug zones. The drug, of course, is *alcohol.* The culture, of course, is your parents'. The denial, of course, belongs to all of us.

Alcohol: It's Not "a" Drug—It's "the" Drug

Would you like to hear a very funny phrase? It's "drugs *and* alcohol." You see it everywhere. Shrinks who deal with substance abusers are called drug *and* alcohol counselors. In school you have drug *and* alcohol education programs. Your phone book has a listing for drug *and* alcohol rehab centers. Even self-help groups act like these things are different: *"Hi. Welcome to Alcoholics Anonymous. Cocaine addict? Oh, you're looking for Narcotics Anonymous—down the hall on the right, just past Gamblers Anonymous, but before you get to Overeaters Anonymous."*

Addictions do have some differences, but they mostly have a lot of similarities: They all serve to help us avoid our feelings. When you hear experts yelling at each other about whether a drug is *physically* addicting or *psychologically* addicting, you are hearing a silly argument, but one that users use to justify their use. A drug proven to be *physically* addicting is one that creates physical changes that cause a person to crave a certain chemical. Drugs claimed to be *psychologically* addicting are said to serve some other purpose in your life besides to stop cravings. It's like with cigarettes. The physical addiction is actually easy to beat. Every smoker I know has successfully "quit" a hundred times. After a few days, the brain cravings start to stop. But the *habit* of smoking (the psychological addiction) is a monster to beat. It's not the physical cravings that pull smokers back to their poison. It's the *psychological* cravings. Things like stress relief and comfort are what nicotine provides to help smokers feel better. That's what all illegal drugs are really about: escaping from how we feel.

When we avoid calling alcohol what it really is, a *drug*, we stop seeing that it serves the same purpose as any other illegal drug: *to escape our feelings*. But, in this culture, the drug of alcohol has been marketed by clever pushers into being seen as something else. And that deception is a killer that almost took out James. It feeds a monster called denial, a killer that can infect both teens and parents.

Even as he walked into my office, I had second thoughts about what I was about to do to James. I hated the thought of betraying anyone's secrets. When I first met him, at age 15, he was pretty much a full-blown weed addict, something that frightened his mother so much that she asked me to help him to stop. Although his father was always too busy to come in, eight months later, James was a "success" story—completely marijuana free. The only problem was that he was now a slave to booze.

When he slumped down in my couch, his face forced my hand: Lifeless eyes ringed by huge dark circles, contrasted by a pasty white complexion. This kid was dying. "James," I began. "I'm afraid I have to tell your parents about your drinking. That's a secret I can't keep any longer." I waited for his explosion and was puzzled to see none. Baffled, I went on, explaining away my guilt. "You've got to understand," I apologized. "I can't do anything while you drug [drink alcohol] as much as you do. The amount that you drink *could* kill you fast, and *will* kill you slow. You look *awful.*" I paused, and then added, "Do you feel as bad as you look?"

James sat and ignored my question, instead just staring at me through those sick, hollow eyes. "Go ahead," he finally sighed with a half-smirk, as if trying to muster enough energy to be sarcastic. "You go tell my old man [his father who drove him that night] that I'm a drunk. In fact, Doc, I'll go get him for you. He's sitting in his truck. You wait right here." His sad smile confused me.

After 10 minutes of overhearing murmuring, angry voices in the waiting room, my confusion disappeared as James returned with his father. The stench of too much beer rushed into the room in front of this man. Dad's face was beet red, his eyes were mirror glassy, and his words were drug slurred. "Wha's this crap about beer being a drug?" he demanded. "I haf' a few beers. You sayin' I'm druggie? This is bullshit. And so what if James has a few [beers]? He stopped doin' drugs [marijuana] when *I* started to let him drink at home. It wasn't this bullshit therapy stuff, like my wife thinks. It was my idea that got James better, not this bullshit." He turned to his son. "Les' go, James. We're getting the hell out of this bullshit place."

As he left, James turned with that same sad half-smile, and shrugged. Though his mouth spoke no words, his eyes seemed to say, "*Try to understand, this is my life. Not much anyone can do, you know? Peace, Doc.*" I never saw James again.

All of the whining you hear about "drug" (non-alcohol) use by teens becomes a joke in the face of facts that show the secret love affair adults have with booze. They simply flat-out refuse to admit that alcohol really is a drug, let alone an extremely dangerous one. Want some facts? Be sure now, because beer might look a little different to you after you read this.

Alcohol is a reality-altering, mood-altering, highly addictive poison. At very low levels of use, the bad effects are very small. But the bad side effects increase dramatically as you use more of the substance.

Booze alters reality by enabling people to change what's real in their life—for a little while, anyway. Given enough of the drug, they can temporarily believe things that are not real, and not believe things that are real. You can get drunk with someone you hate and think you love them—until you sober up. You can get drunk with someone you love and think you hate them—until you sober up. Alcohol makes scared people think they're brave, makes shy people think they're friendly, and makes messed-up behaviors you wouldn't do sober seem as if they're OK (like driving too fast or having sex). This is how it alters reality—until you sober up.

Given enough of the drug, they can temporarily believe things that are not real, and not believe things that are real.

It's also a mood-altering drug. For many, it brings on a "high," a kind of "everything-is-great" feeling. But lots of folks find that, instead, they become very depressed, surly, and nasty on this drug (one of the reasons so many suicides occur on booze). And after the "buzz" passes, everyone who uses this drug feels down. That's because, over time, alcohol acts as a chemical *depressant*, causing its serious users to become seriously depressed. This makes them want to drink more, creating a vicious circle that's caused by this next vicious fact.

Booze is also highly addictive. For adults, it produces more drug addicts than all the other drugs combined (although for teens, there's another number-one addiction I'll shock you with shortly). The more alcohol is used, the more it rewires the user's brain toward developing an addiction to alcohol. Like a great sales campaign, *it creates its own market in your brain* by actually changing your wiring around, so that you can start to crave the chemical of alcohol. And if addiction runs in your family, the odds are that your brain is already prewired to become addicted much faster than other kids. So if Mom, Dad, Grandmom, or Granddad has a problem with alcohol, you're taking a big risk every time you take a big taste.

Finally, alcohol is also a *poison*, with terrible side effects, both short- and long-term. I'll never forget an experiment I saw in school, in which they put a super microscope on some guy's liver as it tried to remove alcohol from his bloodstream. The alcohol molecules were literally blowing holes in his liver, like artillery shells exploding across a field. You could actually see how the liver was desperately trying to repair itself faster than the new "incoming" shells of alcohol, but it was losing the race. Many people eventually lose that race big time, dying from liver diseases that kill you in ways you don't want to know about.

Alcohol blows away other parts of your body as well, including your stomach and, especially, your evolving brain. A very frightening study just released proves that old scare line: *Alcohol affects adolescents very differently than it does adults.* The MRIs (brain pictures) of kids who abuse booze show that alcohol blows away the parts of your brain that handle memory and learning (called the *hippocampi*). The teen drinkers' hippocampi (that's the plural of hippocampus—your brain has two) were *10 percent* smaller than those brain areas of sober kids.

Do you know how, when you wake up after drinking too much you feel as if you were poisoned? Well, *you were*! And if you don't believe me, ask your gut after you've filled it with booze. Your stomach makes you puke as a last ditch survival effort, to get rid of what it knows is a life-threatening poison that can kill you quickly as well as slowly.

The short-term risks of booze can be just as deadly as the long-term ones. Every weekend, tens of thousands of kids drink until they pass out. Seems harmless enough, even to some parents. Some kids even like to brag about doing this, like they scored the winning basket in the playoffs. "Just let him sleep it off," everybody jokes. The punch line is that *thousands of those kids never wake up.*

When you watch a sleeping drunk, what you're looking at is a drug overdose, every bit as deadly as the fabled heroin overdose. Drunk, "sleeping" kids are not sleeping; they're in comas that can kill them in two ways. First, drink enough, and you'll drown the part of your brain that makes you breathe. That's not good when you're "asleep." Second, many kids vomit during these "sleeps," and then inhale, and choke to death on their puke. Also not good.

So, if a friend drinks until he passes out, don't roll him into a corner to sleep it off. Your friend has overdosed and needs medical attention. And if he's doing this regularly, the odds are he's an addict and needs help. Don't guess about this. Too many of us do, and as a result, we have body counts like the following:

- For every 1 American that dies from drugs, 15 are killed by alcohol.
- *Fifty percent* of this nation's homicides, suicides, and driving fatalities involve booze.
- *Twenty million to 24 million* Americans currently suffer from serious problems (health, family, work) related to drinking. And this stuff is *legal*?

This adult blindness to booze spills over into your own world like a poison. The teen numbers are even scarier. Read these facts slowly, to let them sink in:

- One in four American kids lives with alcoholism and alcohol abuse in his or her family.
- More than *50 percent* of 7th through 12th graders drink.
- *Twenty percent* of 7th through 12th graders drink weekly.
- Eight percent of these young people binge drink (five or more shots in a row) each month.
- Fifty percent of teen suicides involve alcohol use.
- *Forty-five thousand* teenagers were badly injured last year mixing boozing with driving.
- *One in three* teens rode with a drinking driver last year; 8,000 never rode again.

These numbers make the "drug" body count look small. Last year, we lost far more adolescents to alcohol than were stolen from us by heroin, cocaine, pills, and ecstasy, *combined*—so somebody, please explain to me how alcohol is not a dangerous drug!

We don't have a National Booze Czar, or a War on Wine. We actually sell, tax, and profit from this particular drug in ways that might draw the envious admiration of the worst opium lord in the world. Picture a foreign gangster desperately holed up in his hideout, with attacking drug-agent helicopters hovering overhead. He glances at his satellite TV and catches a famous American commercial. In disbelief, he watches soft, fuzzy, winter camera shots of Christmas-adorned sleighs. They're carrying loving, devoted, drug-bearing, red-blooded American families to warm gatherings to celebrate a joyous day, by using a dangerous, highly addictive, reality-altering chemical that is fully government approved. *"This holiday message brought to you by your local connection. We urge you to do your drug responsibly. Have a safe, wonderful day."*

American adult culture has fooled itself into believing that the most lethal drug we know of (alcohol) is a national pastime.

Is this a great country, or what? American adult culture has fooled itself into believing that the most lethal drug we know of (alcohol) is a national pastime. Not to be outdone, your teen culture has managed to fool itself into believing that the other most dangerous drug out there is really harmless.

I'll bet you your favorite CD that you can't guess what it is. I'll even give you a clue: Although booze *kills* more kids than all the others *combined*, this drug *hooks more teen addicts* than all the others *combined*. It's known as that "safe" drug, you know, the one you can't get addicted to because it's not really a drug. The one that won't make you wreck your car. Or so I've been told by all the weed addicts I've known who've wrecked their cars.

Marijuana: The "Booze Lie" of Your Culture

Adolescents have been watching adults closely. I'm so sure of this because of how neatly teens have adopted the very same denial techniques about marijuana that adults use about alcohol. It's almost funny, until you see the terrible toll that alcohol and marijuana denial takes on lives, adult and adolescent. Michael worries that his story might sound too familiar to you.

> Michael gazed through his haze at his friends, as their slurred voices faded into mush. That faint voice once again nagged at him from deep inside. *"What's wrong with this picture?"* it kept asking. The scene seemed harmless enough. Just the nightly gathering of "the gang": ex-military, now-college-student friends who gathered late each night to "have a few beers."
>
> It had all started innocently as an occasional meet. Then, a few Fridays gradually grew into every night. A few cans gradually grew into a couple of quarts. A few missed classes gradually grew into academic probations. Everything grew gradually except the denial. That grew fast.
>
> "Look at those draft-dodging, pinko-hippies," Jim snarled, as he did every night after his second quart of beer. "Smoking their goddamn dope, polluting their pinko-brains. What a bunch of druggie losers. I still think it's time we f'ng tuned them up." Michael looked closely at Jim. His eyes were glassy with cheap beer, his face was red with misplaced rage, and his words were suddenly hollow and stupid. Jim was reading Michael's thoughts, but he couldn't see the worst one.
>
> "What?" Jim demanded. "What the hell are you lookin' at? Every night lately you sit there and stare at me, like you think you're better than me. You think you're better than me? You think you're better than

us?" Right there, Michael's denial about booze shattered like an amusement-park mirror, revealing the ugly truth behind it.

Without a word, he slowly got up, poured out his beer on the ground, and walked away. Jim, the leader, screamed after him. "YOU WALK OUT, YOU DON'T EVER COME BACK. YOU HEAR ME? I'M TALKING TO YOU. YOU HEAR ME?" Michael heard. He knew that Jim was right. He was never going back. He never did.

—From the personal journal of Dr. Michael Bradley

That memory about the power of denial flashes through my head at least once a week. That's because at least once a week I listen to a kid like Kim, telling me how her use of weed is definitely *not* a problem.

"You know, I, like, don't *need* it. I could stop anytime I wanted, and I wouldn't, like, miss it. I just do it to be social, you know, only with my friends—well, mostly. And, besides, it's not like I do drugs. Weed is only like drinking, but without the hangovers. It's a lot safer. You can't get addicted."

"Kim," I asked, "Did you see today's paper? A U.S. government study found that, last year, more kids went into rehab for marijuana addiction than for all of the other drugs—*combined*." She didn't believe me. Then she didn't believe the article when I showed that to her. "Kim," I asked, "what proof *would* you accept?" When she sat staring blankly, I tried a different approach: "Back when I was in college, I used to hang out with some friends. . . ."

Of course, my story didn't make a dent in Kim's denial. She pointed out that, while I was drinking every night, she smoked only two or three nights, and, oh yeah, most mornings. And, occasionally, at lunch. This is what denial looks like. When you're in the grip of drugs like alcohol or marijuana, it's easy to see what you want to see, to keep using. But denial is particularly deadly with weed, because the side effects seem so slight and so harmless—or so it seems at first. The fact is that *marijuana is so dangerous because it's so "safe."*

When I did drug rehab work, I used to pray for clients who were alcohol, cocaine, or heroin dependent—anything but cannabis (weed, marijuana, dank, hashish). Kids hooked on alcohol, cocaine, or heroin were a lot easier to work with, because their drugs usually made them physically sick (we'll talk shortly about these other drugs and their effects). So it was a lot harder for them to deny that they had a problem with whatever.

But the "cannabis kids" . . . they were (and are) the worst. Their drug doesn't give you a terrible hangover, like booze does (at first); it can't kill you, like heroin can; and it won't keep you up for 48 hours, like cocaine will. By comparison, it looks "soft" and safe. Kids can (and many do) smoke several times a day and still go to school, talk nicely to their parents, and stay mellow. Really mellow. *So mellow that many lose their lives.* Not by dying, but by *existing without living.* This point is very important to understand, because although it applies mostly to marijuana, this same idea applies to the use of any illegal drug. Here's how it works.

In case you haven't noticed, life can be hard. Often, we get stressed, agitated, and upset by problems and challenges that confront us, particularly during adolescence. School, sports, relationships, bullying—these can be very painful at times. Painful enough that we all wish for some way to avoid the stress. The best stress reliever is to rise up and confront the challenge, because this is nature's way of making us stronger and tougher. Facing the problem gives us confidence that we can handle stress and gives us the courage to go after whatever goals we choose, no matter how difficult. So don't be too upset when things are hard for you. That's how we grow to be strong.

The best stress reliever is to rise up and confront the challenge, because this is nature's way of making us stronger and tougher.

Just as with physical strength, emotional strength grows from challenges, hard work, and self-discipline. These efforts will leave you with a few "scars," emotional prices you pay in tough fights where you don't back down. Like getting cut out from a cool crowd, for not drinking at their party. Or being mocked, for hanging out with the "loser" kid. But scars are not always bad. They hurt when you first get them. Then, later, they become powerful reminders that you're tougher than you think if you don't let fear of stress make your choices for you.

Which is an important thing to learn, something that the adult culture seems to have forgotten: *The point of life is not to live a spoiled, self-centered, stress-free existence.* Whatever you find to bring meaning to your life, I can guarantee it will *not* be to party 24/7. Most of us try that a bit, but many of us discover how stupid and senseless a life that is. It gets real old, real fast. Truly happy people are those who constantly find new challenges and ways of growing. They're never satisfied with just doting on themselves, erasing all stress or worries. They understand that some stress and worry is just part of the game of life, something that makes them tougher and wiser as they chase their goals. They know that the really wonderful things that life has to offer don't come cheap or easy. They come at the cost of challenging ourselves.

Go and tell that to a "cannabis kid." He'll laugh. But if he listens at all, he'll probably also want to get high to put your words out of his head; because marijuana, that "safe" drug, whispers softly into kids' ears, saying things like, *"Hey, feeling stressed out about your nowhere life? No sweat, man. Don't stay up all night worrying and thinking about changing. Don't try to push yourself to see if you can do something hard. Don't find the guts it takes to try something you're afraid you can't do. Just take a few hits. It'll all be cool."*

And sure enough, the warmth of the weed suddenly makes everything cool. As promised, your stress goes up in smoke—temporarily. Along with your motivation, your striving for excellence, and your courage to confront life-limiting fears and anxieties—and that can be forever. This is how marijuana helps you to exist without stress—*by helping you to exist without living.*

This kind of escaping turns out to be incredibly addicting, particularly for adolescents. Remember Chapter 1's chat about how you hard-wire your brain in adolescence? Escaping is a perfect example. The more you avoid stress, the more you need to avoid stress. The fewer times you face up to fear, the more afraid you become. That's how marijuana, that "nonaddicting, nondrug" has now smoked more kids into addiction-treatment hospitals than all of the other addicting drugs *combined.* It's not number one for nothing.

So the next time you hear someone say that weed is not a drug, and is not addicting, try making a bet: Ask them to name the drug that has more teen addicts than any other. And bet big, because you're going to win.

And while we're exploding the myths about marijuana, here's the last one you should kill before you buckle up: "*Weed won't impair my driving like booze. I drive a lot safer when I'm high.*" Oh, really? Research proves that pot slows reaction time, impairs judgment, and cuts back your peripheral vision. Marijuana makes people *feel* like they're driving better, much like acid (LSD) did with an old friend of mine who swore that he "saw" the answers for world peace whenever he tripped. Because he amazingly couldn't remember this war-ending formula when he came down, he decided to write while tripping. The only problem was that his "words" looked like they were written by a berserk bubble-jet printer. But, much like the weed addicts, he kept trying for years and years. He was so sure. It's called denial.

Other Drugs: Same Dope, Different Day

Illegal drugs all share a few effects in common: they all change you temporarily, they can all addict you quickly, and they can all kill you permanently. Because weed and booze mangle more teen lives than all the others combined, those are the drugs I wanted to talk about the most. But before we move on to the other "second string" drugs, there's one final fact you might mull over about all drugs: Virtually every adult addict in this country started to take drugs as a teenager. We know that the younger someone starts messing with drugs, the greater the odds of becoming addicted. Doesn't that make you wonder what that "harmless" drug experimentation might be doing to new adolescent brain wiring?

Virtually every adult addict in this country started to take drugs as a teenager.

These other drugs are used much less frequently, and by far fewer kids, although one is making a run at the titles held by alcohol and marijuana. Although you are unlikely to do these, you are likely to see other kids putting these drug guns to their brains. If so, just like with suicide, remember that key phrase as you consider what to do about a friend who's in over his head: *Love your friend more than your friendship*. Sometimes, that means ratting him out to save his life. Did I mention that life can be hard?

Amphetamines (speed): These drugs come in powders or pills that can be swallowed, snorted, or smoked. A popular favorite is Ritalin, stolen from some kid's little brother who has ADHD (attention deficit/hyperactivity disorder). Another is taking handfuls of over-the-counter cold medications that contain decongestants. Kids on speed will have bizarre energy bursts, talk nonstop, bounce all over the place, not sleep, and think they're super-cool when they look stupid. You might not want to tell them, though, because they can also be wildly sensitive, raging, and willing to fight over nothing.

Amphetamines work by stimulating your body, like a super-charger does with a car engine. The only problem is that super-chargers blow up engines that weren't designed for that stress. Speeding "blows up" kids physically in a bunch of ways, because, like those engines, your body wasn't designed for that stress either.

Cocaine: Kids snorting "coke" (it's usually a powder) will look much like kids on speed, with the added attraction of pupils dilated wide enough to drive an ambulance through. Which may be a good thing, because, contrary to the myth, coke *can* kill. Take enough, and you will go into a coma, along with getting heart and lung damage. One form to watch out for is the bargain-basement version called *crack*, which is smoked. It initially seems cheaper than "regular coke," but, over time, it's really much more expensive because it's wildly addicting and can ruin decades of your life in just a few days.

Ecstasy (E, MDMA): This is one of the newer crossover drugs (a mix of two or more other drug types) that deserves special mention here. "E" is usually a mix of a hallucinogen (see below) and an amphetamine that gives kids a "warm, loving" feeling that many people claim can't be addicting. After all, what can possibly be addicting about a warm, loving feeling?

> Tony looked like he was describing the face of God when he talked about what ecstasy did for him. "I can remember that first hit like yesterday. It was incredible! Amazing! Suddenly, all the anger I had for my father was gone! For the first time in my life, I was at a concert, and I *wasn't* looking for a fight! I felt like I loved everybody, and everybody loved me. And this wasn't a drug like heroin that you could get addicted to. And it made me this great person—until I crashed. Then I was a bigger bastard than ever. I hated that! So I did some more E, and some more E—it went like that for a while. I had to keep taking more to get the same high as the first time." Tony's face just glowed as he remembered that feeling. Then the glow disappeared.

"One day, at school, I, like, woke up. A cop was putting handcuffs on me, and I saw this huge bag of E on the table in front of me. I was, like, in this awake dream or something. Then I remembered how I think I had been giving handfuls of E to any kid in the hall that day, 'cause I loved them so much, you know, and I wanted them to feel good, like me. I swear, I wasn't dealing, I was actually giving the shit away." Tony paused and picked at his nails. His voice got very small. "You know, I stole from my grandfather to buy those pills. I think I told you, he's got cancer. . . ." Tony couldn't say the complete truth, that the man he stole from, his grandfather, was dying. He couldn't even look at me as he spoke. "That's messed up. That's really messed up. What's more messed up than that?"

I tried to answer him softly. "Tony, what's more messed up is that a 15-year-old boy has to take a pill to feel loved. Maybe that's the most messed-up thing of all."

Ecstasy is so new that we don't know very much about it. While the jury is still out on whether E is physically dangerous or not, every week a researcher pops up with some scary findings about what it might be doing to kids. But because there is no hard evidence yet that E can harm you physically, kids are taking this *lack* of information to assume that it's safe to use. Which is kind of like finding a strange fungus on the ground and thinking it's safe to eat because no one said it's bad for you.

Another reason to be careful about E is that it's often mixed with other drugs to cause other effects. And sometimes the users don't even know until the effect of the added drug kicks in. For example, a new version called "Sextasy" mixes Viagra (a sexual-potency drug) with E to produce things like four-hour erections. This has landed quite a few "studs" in hospitals with some unusual injuries.

The final point of debate on E is about whether it can be addicting or not. This is another question you need to decide on your own, now that you know what addiction really means. As you think, know that use of this "nonaddicting" drug shot up *71 percent* last year, with *12 percent* of your friends now using it. Want to guess what the next drug might be to challenge marijuana for the "most kids addicted" title?

Hallucinogens: These are a wide variety of chemicals that do a wide variety of things. These drugs are known by names like LSD (acid),

DMT, 'Shrooms (mushrooms), and Mesc (mescaline). They all can produce hallucinations (seeing things that aren't there) along with some side effects like anxiety, paranoia, sweating, pupil dilation, tremors, and rapid heartbeat. By the way, if you think these mushrooms are like the deadly ones you have to be sure you never eat, you are correct. Which raises an interesting question you might pose to a user friend: "Just how reliable and upstanding is your drug dealer?"

If you get enough, you go comatose and can die, particularly if you drink on top of the pills.

Opioids (heroin, codeine, oxys [Oxycontin], Percocet): These chemicals all make you sleepy and not care much about much, like a huge "Whatever." If you get enough, you go comatose and can die, particularly if you drink on top of the pills. Heroin is the biggie here, suddenly popular as the result of a killer lie put out by pushers that you can't get addicted to heroin if you only snort it (instead of injecting it). Oh, OK. Sure. Isn't it amazing how many people turn to pushers to get their information on drugs?

Phencyclidines (PCP, Hog, Tranq, Angel Dust): These are actually surgical anesthetics that can be eaten, smoked, or snorted. They act like hallucinogens, cutting you off from reality and making you think and act really weird, but with an aggressive edge at high doses. These are the kids you hear about who required three cops to subdue them because they were so nuts and so dangerously strong.

How Drugs Are Used

Two things make discussions about the risks of drug use difficult. First, when kids say that they're not doing drugs, they usually mean that they aren't doing *pills, heroin, or cocaine*. You have to ask separately whether they are doing booze, weed, or ecstasy, because so many kids don't think that those things are drugs. Hopefully, if that was your position before, you might think twice after reading what you've read. Whatever your opinion now, please remember that from here on out, whenever I say "drugs," I mean all of them.

Another frustrating (and dangerous) thing about drug discussions is trying to decide the point at which drug use becomes a problem. It's kind of like speed limits on roads. Many kids think doing the speed limit of 55 mph (using no drugs) is just fine. Others push the rules a little to do 60 mph (use once or twice). Still others think that 65 mph is safe (perhaps using once a month). Then there's the 75 mph group, who use once a week, but they're sure they're OK. Finally there's the 90+ mph crowd, who use more than once a week, but say that's fine, as well.

So where do you draw the line? Who's to say what speed is safe? Can't the 110-mph gang argue that going that fast is OK, since they haven't died yet?

Fighting about "safe" levels of drug use is just like that. It's very hard to say that this amount is safe and that amount is dangerous. In general, though, there are a few rules that can guide you through these issues. First, it's very clear that the faster someone drives, the greater the odds they'll get hurt. Likewise, it's very clear that the more drugs someone uses, the greater the odds they'll get hurt.

Second, it's very clear that driving faster allows the next level of speeding to occur. Hardly anyone drives 55 for years, and then, one day, suddenly does 110. Usually, you slowly move from 55, to 60, to 70, to 75, until, one day, you suddenly realize that you're doing 110. Likewise, it's very clear that using one level of drugs allows the next step of drugs to become more possible. Hardly anyone goes from zero drug use to shooting heroin in one day, or even in one year. Usually you move slowly from one level of use to the next.

In the world of drug treatment, we divide kids who do drugs into different levels of use. This is to help people sort out how fast they're "driving," what the risks are, and how serious their problems might be. The first level of use is called *experimentation*. This is almost always done with cannabis or alcohol, and almost always as a party (social) activity, with friends at sleepovers or hang-out times. Most kids call this partying, and they don't believe that this is doing drugs at all. This level of use is hard to see because, at first, not much changes in a kid's life.

Many of these experimenters move on to the next level, called *misuse*. Like stomping on the accelerator pedal in your car, everything starts to go faster here. Use of alcohol and cannabis moves from "just" occasional weekends with friends to include weekdays, and sometimes alone. Drug choices move from "just" booze and weed to possibly include pills and powders (opioids, amphetamines, and hallucinogens). At this point, life starts to come unglued for most kids. Grades drop, sports become too hard, and friends shift from "happy" kids to "druggie" kids, at least according to Kelly.

> Kelly's scared 16-year-old eyes flitted all around the room, as if she was waiting for the cops to kick in the door. "You promised this was confidential, right? You can't tell anybody what I just told you about the drugs I'm doing, right, since oxys and weed can't hurt me, right?"
>
> Hoping to duck that question for the moment, I had one for her. "Kelly, how can you sit there and tell me that drugs haven't hurt you? In six months of use, you've gone from first honors to Fs, from all-state lacrosse player to always-stoned spectator, and from 'happy-to-be-at-home' to 'I'd-rather-be-in-hell.' You see none of this?"
>
> Kelly's eyes stopped moving back and forth, but they were still scared. "I do see one thing," she admitted. "Every day now, I have to choose who I'm going to hang out with that night: My old "happy" friends who don't do drugs, or my new "druggie" friends who do. More and more, I pick "druggie." My happy friends make me feel weird now, like I don't belong anymore. I used to think that it was them who changed, but it's me. I don't feel as good as my "happy" friends anymore. But I know I'm still better than all of my "druggie" friends. I guess hanging out with losers helps you not feel so bad about being a loser."
>
> Kelly's honesty was too much for her to take. Her eyes widened and filled up as she stared at mine, like she had a million things that she needed to say. Instead, she looked at her watch and made her choice about who she was hanging with that night. "I forgot to tell you that I have to leave early tonight, OK? I'll call you to set up my next appointment."
>
> We both knew that she wasn't going to see her "happy" friends. We both knew that she was not coming back. Only she knew how much pain she was in. Only I knew where she was heading.

Kelly was headed for the next step into hell, called *drug abuse*. Here, drugs become the center of a kid's life, pretty much ending it. *Abuse* leads to things like truancy, fighting, stealing, even drug dealing to support drug use. This is where the risks of suicide and accidental death go off the charts. And it can still get worse. A whole lot worse.

Dependency is the last stop on the runaway train of drug use. The only purpose in a drug-dependent life is to stay high, 24/7. Death no longer seems so scary, so with these kids, anything goes: prostitution, violent crime, contaminated needles, risking AIDS, starving—whatever, just as long as they can get high. This is a short and miserable life.

If those four stages of drug use sound like a ladder down into hell, you have the idea. Most kids stay on the top rung of that ladder (experimentation) and have the good luck (and that's all it is) to be able to snicker at the antidrug ads that predict terrible times for kids who use drugs. But here's the billion-dollar question: *Who knows which of those snickering kids will slide down that ladder into hell?* Although no one can predict that, I can tell you that *the last one to know is the kid who slips.* It's called denial. My years of watching too many kids slide into hell has left me with two absolute truths that prove the power of denial:

The only purpose in a drug-dependent life is to stay high, 24/7.

Not one snickering experimenter ever intended to be a dying addict.

Every dying addict always intended to be a snickering experimenter.

So how do you guess whether or not you might be the kid who slips? Here are a few factors that increase the odds that "only" smoking marijuana or "only" drinking might lead to madness. First, if your family has a history of drug problems (alcohol included), the odds are much higher that you will, as well. Some part of drug addiction seems to be passed along genetically (although many addicts have no history of family drug problems).

Second, kids who feel crappy about themselves (see Chapter 3, on self-esteem) have much higher rates of addiction. Third, teenagers who have a hard time making and keeping friends also slide down that ladder faster. Finally, kids with parents who don't care, are over-controlling, or are too permissive often end up on a first-name basis with a pusher.

Use these factors *as precautions, not predictions.* Having many or even all of those problems in your life does *not* mean that you will become an addict. Many kids who come from bad places like those are actually safer from addiction because they've seen the ugly realities of drug use up front. Watching a drugged-out father slapping his kids while slurring his curses can be the best antidrug message you'll ever see, if you use that experience to be smarter, and not just crazier, than the old man.

If you have these factors in your life, they should be like flashing yellow traffic signals saying, "Slow down—Watch out—Be very careful." Once denial infects your soul, you can be broadsided by a truck of addiction that you never saw coming. No one ever sees that truck. *No one.*

In Part Three of this book, we'll talk about some specific strategies for dealing with drug issues in your life or in the life of a friend. Try to remember the things you learned here about drugs, for the odds are huge that you will be dealing with addiction in some way in your life.

And now, it's time to push on to the last piece of bad news about your culture. Having seen the source of the other two problems (sex and drugs), would you like to guess where this next problem originated? And while you're guessing, whose teen culture do you think was more violent: yours, or your parents'? Better not bet on that second question. You might be in for a shock.

ADOLESCENT ROCK 'N ROLL (Violence): It's Not What You Think

Everybody knows that teens are incredibly violent today. Every time you watch CNN, it seems there's a new story about some berserko teen killing somebody, right? And no matter what we do, we just can't seem to stop it. In our courts, we now prosecute teenaged children as adults, execute some, and give others (some as young as 11) life sentences, but kids keep killing. In our schools, we use metal detectors, armed guards with dogs, undercover cop-students, and even lockdown searches, but kids keep killing. Everybody agrees that kids are just a bunch of homicidal maniacs. That's what kids themselves say. No one knows how to solve this runaway epidemic of teen violence: cops, teachers, prosecutors, or parents. No one, that is, except the quiet, nerdy researchers who study youth violence, and who keep being ignored by the beautiful, bubbly, blonde TV news reporters who just gush over violent teen stories.

These research nerds have a suggestion to reduce the teen-violence epidemic: Just turn off the TV. *This works, because there is no teen-violence epidemic.* In fact, you guys are the *least* violent generation of adolescents we've ever known since we began to keep these records. Confused? Join the club. Teen experts don't understand why you guys are doing as great as you are, either, considering the violence-saturated world in which you are being raised. Still don't believe me? Let's look at the numbers.

The FBI research folks say that adolescent homicide is *half* what it was when your parents were teens. The Centers for Disease Control (CDC) found that school violence is down, anywhere from *25 percent to 40 percent,* over the past 10 years. Columbine-type shootings are like airplane crashes—horrors when they happen, *but they hardly ever happen.* And just as flying is much safer than driving, kids are much safer at school than they are in their own homes. Yet, when we ask, everybody (teens included) thinks that the teen world is a war zone. This is just one of those myths that takes on a life of its own, and "news" people are largely to blame. When a very few crazy nightmares like Columbine happened and got all kinds of publicity, everyone assumed that every school had its own suicide assault teams, poised to strike.

The FBI research folks say that adolescent homicide is half what it was when your parents were teens.

It's like those crazy rumors that go around school and are repeated so often that they seem like they *must* be true. *("PSST! Sarah's brother knows this guy who lives next door to the cousin of this janitor who was married to a nurse at the hospital. She told the janitor, who told the cousin, who told that guy, who told Sarah's brother, who told Sarah, that Mr. Backhair, the gym teacher, used to be a woman.")*

But the teen-violence myth becomes easier to believe when you look at the level of violence that our culture bombards you with. How does it do this? With music, media and movies—things all controlled by adults, incidentally, not teens. I won't repeat the TV-violence statistics you saw in Chapter 1, because all you need to do is watch TV for an hour. If you don't see gunfire within 37 seconds of watching, you're watching The Weather Channel. Your generation "plays" at violence, *but mostly as entertainment, not as a way of life.* Your parents' generation seems to truly love violence just for the sake of violence. . . .

What a dad said:

> "Are you saying that *I* created this violent culture? I hate this violence as much as anyone, and more than most. It makes me nuts. Just the other night, my 12-year-old son asked to walk to the mall, and I said no. He went crazy, demanding to know why I said no. I didn't know how to answer him. It's not what he thinks, that I don't trust him. It's really because I'm terrified of the world around him. I can hardly look at a newspaper anymore without reading about some kid getting attacked or abducted or molested. When I say that, he gets mad and yells that he can take care of himself. But how do you defend against a gangster with a gun? Every day, you read about some teen shooting. A kid carried a loaded gun to my son's *middle school,* for God's sake. So what do you think gets carried to malls? I feel like I'm punishing my son because the world is violent. And I'm not even sure that it *is* more violent than when I was a kid. I ran everywhere all alone when I was 12. I'd be gone for 6 or 8 hours, and nobody got upset. So why can't he? Am I being over-protective? And my poor daughter, I know I'm much more protective of her than I am even with my son. Is that fair, just because she's a girl? I don't know, it's all so confusing. One strange thing I do know is that all the teenagers I know seem so *non*-violent. Another thing I do know, that this confusion makes my kids hate me sometimes. How can I explain it so that they understand?"

Overall, your teen culture is incredibly *non*-violent toward others, which is truly an impressive tribute to your generation, given how the world has changed. For example, although most adolescents in America can now get a loaded gun within 12 hours, hardly any kids take advantage of that "opportunity."

However, while yours is the least homicidal generation, you still have more killers than any other. You guys kill *yourselves* at *four times* the rate of your parents' generation. In Chapter 4, we talked about suicide and some of its causes, but this violence-loving environment must share some of the blame. It's incredible that your generation has managed to shield others from the effects of this, while at the same time turning weapons so often upon yourselves.

And while we're talking about aspects of your culture that make it different from your parents', here are a few others. *Today's adolescents are more giving than any other generation.* Rates of volunteer activities have never been higher among your age group, which is another incredible accomplishment, given that you live in a very cynical, self-serving world. In record numbers, you do things like fix up run-down houses, work in soup kitchens, tutor disabled children, help out in senior citizen centers—this list of "giving" activities runs a thousand times longer than the list of teen problems. And the list of kids who have the courage to do these things runs a thousand times longer than the list of kids who mess up.

Another unique thing about your peers (and one of my personal favorite teen accomplishments) is the explosion of peer mediation programs, where kids help other kids peacefully resolve conflicts (could this be part of why there is so much less violence in schools?). As I read the newspaper, I often daydream about having the "unsolvable" world conflicts placed before a teen mediation panel. As naive as that sounds, understand that I've seen "war zone" schools be retaken by kids who simply stood up and said, "We've had enough!" and who worked at ending bullying and violence in their schools.

And I've seen a very violent youth prison cut assault rates by *90 percent* when the kids there took the same stands. In both the schools and the prison, these things could only happen with the heavy support of the adults who were in charge. But they also could only happen *because the kids believed that they could change things.* Once that belief took hold among those kids, violence didn't stand a chance. *Belief in the power of good turns out to be an incredible weapon against evil.* Don't ever be afraid to pick that one up. And keep it locked and loaded.

Belief in the power of good turns out to be an incredible weapon against evil.

So there you have it: a snapshot of the good and bad parts of your world. Before we conclude this tour, I need to point out the most important thing you should know about these dangerous parts of your culture: *They cannot overcome who you are, if you know who you are.* The stronger your sense of identity, the weaker the effects of your culture. Kids who fall hardest into the clutches of craziness are those who don't know much about themselves, such as who they are, or what they believe. Insanity floods into empty spaces inside of people.

So fill in your gaps—work to build your identity at every opportunity. Look, think, talk, question, write, and challenge. Which is interesting advice, considering that this next chapter looks at what can be the most powerful identity-controlling force in your cosmos. In fact, I think I see it peeking over your shoulder right now, trying to see what trash you're reading. *"Hi, Mom and Dad."*

YOUR PARENTS

Who Are They, and What Are They Trying to DO??

"Son, could you let me finish one sentence before you start to contradict me?" —Arnold, age 43

I have some good news and some bad news. The good news is that your parents will have more impact on shaping who you will become than any other influence in your life.

The bad news is that *your parents will have more impact on shaping who you become than any other influence in your life.*

For many kids, that news is OK, because their parents are OK. They have a set of values, they don't do crazy things, and they put their kids' needs first. They are "adults who are grown-ups," as kids describe them.

But for kids like Dylan, that news is not OK. His parents are adults, but not much else.

Dylan had an incredible mind for a 15-year-old. If he could ever beat his weed habit, he had a shot at doing anything he wanted, which for now was to be a video producer. In fact, he had an idea for a TV spot that I thought was so good that I suggested he submit it.

"I'm, like, sick to death of these public-service antidrug ads. You know, the ones that tell these loving, concerned parents about bugging your insane kid not to do drugs? My ad would be a little different.

"All the scenes would show just the bodies of people who are talking—no faces, but you can hear the voices. It opens with a principal and a cop sitting at a table with a kid, and the principal is on a phone with the kid's mother, and he's saying, 'Mrs. Jones, can you come down to school immediately? I'm afraid your son has a drug problem.' The screen cuts to Mom at home holding a cell phone, talking to the principal. As she stubs out a cigarette in an overflowing ashtray, she knocks over a beer bottle in a group of empties. With a slurred voice, she says, 'Dylan? Drugs? I can't believe that.'

"Then Mom calls Dad on his cell. His phone rings on his car seat next to a bag of pot. He picks the phone up, and you see a cloud of smoke as he exhales. With a weed-tight voice, he says, 'No way! Dylan? Drugs? That's nuts! I'll meet you there. I'm sure it's a mistake.'

"The final scene shows the first table, as everyone turns towards the door as it opens. The principal says, 'Mr. and Mrs. Jones, thanks so much for. . . .' He pauses, as the camera moves up to show the glassy eyes on both parents. 'Uh, Dylan,' the principal says, 'you can go now. I think I need to speak with your parents—alone.' The scene closes with a written message on the screen. It says, 'Want drug-free kids? YOU FIRST!'

Dylan's video was pretty much a scene from his own life.

Dylan would be upset to learn that his parents are the most powerful influence in his life. He made me think of my son's tee shirt. On the back, it reads "You can pick your friends, and you can pick your nose, but you can't pick your friend's nose." On the front, it reads "You can pick your nose, but you can't pick your parents." That front message is pretty scary when you look at all the research that shows that your parents have more impact on shaping your identity than any other part of your world. This means that blind luck selects this most powerful influence on your adolescent life.

The secret to handling this influence well is to see your parents' lives as menus of sorts, as collections of ideas about how you might want to live your own life. Some of their ideas will be excellent. Others may be terrible. But if you can see your parents more objectively as people, human beings with good and bad points, strengths and weaknesses, you'll do a much better job of sorting out what you want to copy, from what you want to cut.

Living your teen years without seeing your folks as human beings sets up an endless fight between those nonhuman creatures known as *parents* and *teens*. The odd thing is that, as different as those things are, they can also be almost the same.

Parents and Teens: The "Mirror Wars"

Parents are people. I know you know that—sort of. But one of the curious things about being someone's child is that you grow up seeing your folks not as *people*, but as *parents,* which are entirely different creatures, at least to kids.

Teenagers are people. I know your parents know that—sort of. But one of the curious things about being someone's parent is that you grow older seeing your kid not as a *person*, but as a *teenager,* which is an entirely different creature, at least to parents.

A person is a being with feelings, thoughts, good points, bad points, dreams, fears, hopes—you know, like a *person*. That is someone you usually respect, talk nicely to, listen to, and generally get along with. For the most part, a *person* seems rational and logical, and doesn't make you crazy when he or she says or does slightly annoying things. You forgive or overlook a lot with a *person*.

When we start labeling people, we stop seeing them as human beings.

I know this, because both the teens *and* parents I work with treat me like I'm a person. That's very nice. But too often, they don't see each other as people. That's very sad. That's what happens when people start to see each other only as *parents* or *teens,* and not as *people.* Those labels, as with all labels, can cause a lot of problems. When we start labeling people, we stop seeing them as human beings. That makes it much easier to hate, harass, and hurt them. It also makes it a lot easier to believe crazy things about them. Once you label someone, and do not see him as a person, arguing with him is like arguing with a mirror: *Your anger bounces right back at you.*

Labeling can even cause a kind of peculiar blindness, where you can see the world only from your side of things. It's called Me-opia.

Shared Blindness

Parents and teens both have a kind of blindness. Teens have always had a kind of blindness that their parents call being self-centered. It's seen in that unending battle over check-in times:

Parent: "I need you to call me to let me know that you're OK."

Teen: "If I know that I'm OK, why should I have to call you?"

In a teenager's head, that line makes perfect sense, because most of you think of issues only from your view of the world. That's normal for most kids. It's just a function of your brain (see Chapter 1) and development (see Chapter 3). It's very hard for you to see beyond your own world and consider things from the view of a parent. This blindness makes teen-parent relationships very hard.

Parents have always had a kind of blindness that their teenagers call being over-controlling. It's seen in that unending battle over check-in times:

Parent: "I need you to call me to let me know that you're OK."

Teen: "If I know that I'm OK, why should I have to call you?"

In a parent's head, that line makes zero sense, because most parents think of issues only from their view of the world. That's normal for most parents. It's just a function of their love and fear. It's very hard for parents to see beyond their own world and consider things from your view. This blindness makes teen-parent relationships very hard. And when we go blind in a relationship, we use labels to fill in all the parts of a person that we can no longer see.

Like when a person is labeled as a *parent* (by her teen), she can become nothing but a jury/judge/jailer, a controlling, insane monster who enjoys thinking of new, nasty ways to make life miserable for her teen. And a person labeled as a *teenager* (by his parent) can look like an arrogant attitude on legs—a terrorist who loves starting painful fights that hurt others, just to hurt others. These creatures labeled *parents* and *teens* aren't thought to have any soft feelings that get hurt, good intentions that get trashed, or deep sadness that never gets voiced. Only *people* have those things. This kind of thinking is what starts "mirror wars"—circles of hurt that never end.

Yet, when an adolescent or a parent says something that hurts a *person,* I see them stop and think about what it was like for that *person* to be hurt. Most will then apologize, and feel bad for hurting that *person*, and try to not do that in the future.

But when a teen *hurts a* parent, *or a* parent *hurts a* teen, *I see very few stop and think about what it was like for the other to be hurt. Most never apologize for hurting the other. They each tell me that apologizing is a dumb thing to do because the other is not really a person, and an apology would only be seen as a sign of weakness. They each tell me that the other doesn't actually get hurt, like a person.*

Well, they do. I know this, because, when we're alone, they show me. Parents and teens do get wounded by each other, and they both hurt from their pain. Both cry, thinking that they've lost each other forever. But you'd never guess it, seeing them together. Usually, everyone's so busy keeping their game faces on that they snicker at a suggestion from me about sharing their hurt feelings with each other. After all, *parents* and *teens* are not *people*, right?

One night, one parent and one teenager found out differently. But it didn't start out that way. It started out as it always had: like a mirror war.

> Joe the father squared off with Joe the son. In seeing them separately a few times, I had never realized how identical they were until I watched them go toe-to-toe that night. Alone with me, they were very different from each other. But together, they looked almost exactly alike, as if they were one person arguing in a mirror: Neither could see the person in the other. They could see only their own rage in the other.
>
> Dad took the first shots, after his 13-year-old son waved him on, as if to say, "Go ahead—take your best shot." Dad waved right back as he spoke. He looked like "nothin' but nasty," just as his son had described him.
>
> "This boy is disrespectful, foul-mouthed, and lazy. He hates us—no, no, he 'despises' us, as he loves to say. He has no shame, no regrets for treating us like dirt—he has no feelings at all. There's no heart in him. I'm sending him to live at a military school next month, and he couldn't care less about leaving us. You know what he said when I told him? He said, 'Fine. I'll f'ng leave tomorrow, 'cause I can't f'ng

be with you another day.' The father turned and blasted his son. "YOU DON'T GIVE A DAMN ABOUT ANYONE BUT YOU. YOU'RE THE MOST SELF-CENTERED, SPOILED BRAT I'VE EVER SEEN. I'M ASHAMED THAT YOU'RE MY CHILD. I DON'T WANT YOU AROUND MY FAMILY."

The father's "mirror" (his son) yelled right back. Just like dad, he was "nothin' but nasty" as well. "YOU WANTED ME GONE A YEAR AGO, THE FIRST TIME I EVER DARED TO TALK BACK TO YOU. I'LL TELL YOU THE EXACT DAY YOU DECIDED TO GET RID OF ME. TELL THE F'NG TRUTH! YOU'VE HATED ME EVER SINCE I DARED TO TELL YOU THAT I WASN'T GOING TO YOUR STUPID CHURCH ANYMORE. I EMBARRASSED YOU IN FRONT OF GRANDPOP. I SAW IT IN YOUR FACE. YOU CAN'T F'NG STAND IT WHEN ANYBODY DOES ANYTHING YOU DON'T LIKE. YOU'RE AN INSANE CONTROL FREAK, YOU KNOW THAT? I'LL BE SOOO HAPPY TO GET THE HELL OUT OF YOUR INSANE ASYLUM. AND I'M NEVER COMING BACK. NEVER!"

Both of their faces had the exact same look, as they both turned to me in the exact same manner, both holding up their hands as if to say about the other, "See, he's not a person. He has no feelings. No love, no remorse, no sadness, no fear. He's just an unfeeling bastard. It's hopeless."

I made them both even angrier by betraying their secrets, and exposing their hearts.

"You know what's really weird?" I asked. "What's really weird is that both of you are liars, and yet both of you think that you're so straight up." I turned to face the senior side of the mirror (dad). "Yesterday, you sat in that very spot and wept for, what, 10 minutes? You were nothing but pain, and hurt, and loss. You said your gut was tearing in half when you thought about sending your son away, because you love him so much, and you would miss him so terribly. And now you sit here and talk like that? You're a liar!" Before dad could react, I turned on his son, the junior side of the mirror, whose astonished chin was about to the floor.

"And you're a bigger liar," I continued. "Last week, you sat in that same spot as your father and cried more than him. You told me about how hurt and scared you felt about being sent away. You told me stories about how you used to be so close with your father, and how horrible it felt to be at war with him. You told me that when you had a bad fever in 6th grade, you woke up in the middle of the night to find your 'insane control freak' father laying on the floor next to you, staying awake all night to be sure you were OK, and . . ." Here, Dad cut me off. He was listening.

"I didn't know you knew I was there," he said with a husky voice. "Of course I knew," his son answered, "I know all of the stuff you've done for me . . ." His voice choked and then trailed off in confusion. A long silence set in that begged to be shattered.

"You guys are something, you know that?" I said. "You're great at the fighting, in-your-face, 'you-lookin'-at-me' stuff, but you're really, really bad at telling the truth. The truth for both of you is that your anger is nothing but a cover for your pain. Neither of you thinks that you're strong enough to tell the truth—to show the hurt under all that rage. Because, then, you'll have to admit that you love each other, and that's harder to do than hating each other. You want to be tough guys? Fine! Try being tough enough to take a risk. Try being strong enough to tell the truth—that you're each hurting each other because you love each other, and you miss each other. Tell me I'm wrong. I'm listening."

The mirror was quiet now. Each face was amazed to see tears in the other. Each face was silent, overcome by waves of hurt, loss, and love. Then, the mirror finally disappeared. The parent and the teen looked at each other, and each saw a person. For a moment, they connected.

CONNECTIONS: What It's All About

Ever wonder about what makes some families so happy and successful? The answer is *connections*. These are invisible lines of love that bind people together: husband to wife, and parent to child. When these connections are strong, they're like steel cables that keep people from drifting apart, even in bad times (like rough teen years). When these connections are weak, small problems become huge fights, causing people who truly love each other (like parents and teens) to drift farther and farther apart, to a point where they can't see the other as a *person* anymore. Finally, the distance grows so great that they can't send or receive love. That's when the connection finally snaps.

Does that sound silly to you? Well, think for a minute. Can't you remember feeling close with your parents at some time in your life, a time when it felt good and safe to be with them? It's not like you thought about "connections"; it's just that it felt natural and right. What you felt was exactly what a connection is.

Now do you feel distant and apart from your parents, like there's this wall between you? And even explaining a simple feeling to them seems like so much effort it's not worth it? Perhaps it's getting harder to see them as *people,* and not *parents*? If that's happening with you, the odds are that your parents are having these same symptoms, as well. You're both feeling the loss of *connection.* That turns out to be a contagious and costly disease, but one that can be cured, and even prevented.

To do that, I'd like to strengthen those ties between you and your folks. The way I suggest doing this is to sneak you into their world, to give you an inside look at what goes on in the life of a parent. You might find a lot of surprises. You might also find that your views of your parents might be very different by the end of this chapter. They might be, like, *people*?

Who Are These Guys (Parents)?

It's quite absurd when you think about it. If you're going to do it right, what job on this planet can possibly be more challenging, more personally demanding, more frustrating, and, at times, more scary, than being a parent? Each child is a completely different set of challenges, and each kid is constantly changing. There is so much to learn so quickly about so many things, it feels completely overwhelming.

But you get no training, no practice, no trial run to see if you're any good at this before you make a commitment. You have to just jump in and make it up as you go along. It's nuts!

I can so clearly remember the day my wife went into labor with our first child. She was fine, but *I* had a hard time breathing. It was wonderful and exciting and all, but I also had this sensation, like when you first get on some killer theme-park ride, and it's slowly climbing to that first awful drop. You think that maybe you made a terrible mistake, and you're sure you can't handle it, but it's too late to get off. So you just grab on and grit your teeth. Suddenly, I was being hurtled at light speed from a free, do-whatever-I-want lifestyle to . . . *what*?

I had no idea of *what*. Now how was I supposed to be, act, and talk? I'm not a parent, for God's sake, whatever that is—I'm *me*. You know, *me*: motorcycles, racquetball, sports cars, last-minute scuba trips to the islands, eating out whenever I feel like it, staying up all night if I feel like it, sleeping all day if I feel like it. Now, overnight, I'm supposed to become station wagons, car seats, and diaper bags (*diapers? Are you kidding me?*). And no sleep, no time, no money, no trips to the islands.

Panic started to settle in. I am not kidding when I said I had trouble breathing.

Then, my son was born. I held him in the first minute of his life. He opened his worried eyes and looked dead-on into mine, like he was searching them to see if I was up to the job of being his parent. He grabbed my thumb with his tiny hand, still searching my eyes with his. Finally, I told him that we were his family, that we loved him, and that everything was going to be all right. As silly as this sounds (talking to a newborn and all), I remember hoping that he would believe me, because *I* didn't believe me. I didn't know if everything would be all right. I was terrified. But my son sighed contentedly, closed his eyes, and went to sleep, as if he believed me. Whew! He bought it.

That was the first of a million and three scenes where I faked my way through some situation with my children, acting like I knew what I was doing, when I hadn't the foggiest idea, trying to make them feel secure and loved—and parented by someone who knew how to do this parent thing—all the while, feeling like I didn't.

Parents are not born, trained, or bred as parents. They're just regular people who kind of get drafted.

I share my story with you because your own parents have stories very similar to mine. Parents are not born, trained, or bred as parents. They're just regular people who kind of get drafted. You can read all the parenting books, and take all the parenting classes, but the fact remains that no one knows how to do this parenting thing until they've done it. There simply is no way to know what it's like until you've been there. Even then, you're constantly faced with new parenting problems you've never seen before, because your kids keep growing and changing, and each child is so different. It's a lot like being thrown into a deep lake to learn how to swim—over, and over, and over. You never "get it right," you just get it done—as best you can. You learn to deal with constant self-doubt, worry, and fear. You also learn the art of "faking it" very well, trying to give your children the confidence that you're in charge, and that you know what you're doing—even when you don't.

And you get to do all this while juggling all your other problems. Like tight money, tough marriages, and terrible jobs you can't afford to quit—because now you have kids. Somehow, you learn to cope with more than you ever thought possible.

Most of all, you learn to hide all of this worry from your kid. Like a good actor, you build this "parent" character that your children think is all you are. They have no idea that you used to be motorcycles, scuba diving, concerts, and clothes less than 10 years' old. To your kids, if you play the role well, you were *born* a parent: dull, predictable, lifeless, and corny. They think you *like* dumb cars, stupid clothes, and cheap vacations. They think you *enjoy* budgets, recycling, and harassing over homework. They think you get *excited* about two-for-one sales and back-to-school nights. Some parents can run this act for 10 or 12 years and do OK. Some even get a little smug, thinking, "Hey, this is no big deal. I can't believe those other parents can't control their kids. My 10-year-old is a perfect child because I'm such a good parent."

And then adolescence hits. BAM! It all comes apart. One day, your kid suddenly exposes all your weaknesses. She knows just how to push your buttons to turn good old calm, unshakable dad into a raving lunatic, stammering and staggering as he reels from insult after insult, trying to regain control. Your old parental smugness becomes a cruel joke, as you remember that you don't know what you're doing—and now as a parent of an adolescent, no less. That child who sweetly did everything you told him suddenly turns and snarls, "No! I'm not going, and you can't make me!" And you have no idea what to do.

Just then, do you know what feeling comes creeping back? ". . . it's like when you first get on some killer theme-park ride, and it's slowly climbing to that first awful drop. You think that maybe you made a terrible mistake, and you're sure you can't handle it, but it's too late to get off. . . ."

So what exactly are they trying to do? Your parents are trying to do a bunch of things that they know about. They have a list of things that they want to see happen in your life. We'll get to those in a minute. But they're also doing something else that greatly affects your relationship with them *that they don't even know is happening.* It's called grieving.

Ross's dad was very sad. "I know this sounds dumb, but I can't get what happened out of my head. My 12-year-old son and I are very close. I love him more than I can say, and I respect him as a person, for all the wonderful things he is, you know? I really, really like hanging out with him, just watching how he handles the world.

"Last night, I go to the basement to nicely remind him to get ready for bed, like I've done on most nights forever, and he suddenly turns and snarls at me, yelling, 'DONT SAY ANOTHER WORD, ALL RIGHT? JUST SHUT UP AND LEAVE, ALL RIGHT?'

"I know this stuff is normal for kids when they hit adolescence, and I know it's not how he really feels about me. And I know what he said is not such a big deal. But, at the same time, I don't know that, or at least it's hard for me to believe that. I felt very hurt. I felt like something great between us had died. I felt tears in my eyes, missing my sweet son who never snarled at me like that.

"The worst part is what I did with my pain. I turned it into anger. I wanted to slap my son around for daring to talk to me like that. I could feel a rage rising up inside of me, telling me to put my hands on this wonderful young man that I love so much, someone I've never even spanked.

"The ugly truth is very hard to say. I wanted to make him cry and be scared of me. It's like I needed to beat him down, to make him beg for my forgiveness. I started to think of ways to hurt him back, maybe with punishments, perhaps taking away something that he loves. At first, I fooled myself into thinking I would just be disciplining him for being disrespectful—you know, being a good parent and all. But the ugly truth is that I really wanted to hurt him back.

"I hate these feelings. I know better than most parents how stupid it is to hurt a kid for being hurtful. In my work, I tell other parents to not discipline their kids with anger. I preach fine words about 'teaching' kids to be better instead of 'hurting' them to be better, and there I was, fighting off an urge to demolish my own son.

"When I really get to the heart of this, I see that I'm grieving the loss of my son, of how he used to be. I miss my little boy so much that I get mad at this occasionally arrogant teen who took over his body. Yet, at the same time, I know that this is still my son, and that he needs me now, more than ever. I know this is not the time to pull away from him, because adolescence is such a hard time for kids.

This 'good parenting' stuff is so easy to say, and so hard to do. It makes you want to shake those parenting experts (like me?) who seem to talk down to parents who screw up (like me?).

—From the personal journal of Dr. Michael Bradley

Parental Grief: Did You Know You Died?

The first thing that your parents are trying to do is to grieve your death—that is, the death of the little child you used to be. But they usually don't even know this is happening.

Most parents fall totally in love with their children when they're small. Young kids are easy to parent. They do what they're told, they don't curse, they go to bed before 1 A.M., and, most importantly, they think their parents are great. Young children look up to Mom and Dad because parents can do so many things so much better. Like play baseball, solve math problems, or make bruised heads and hearts magically heal with a hug. While all this is nice for the kid, it's even nicer for the parents because they get all this admiration for doing things that are pretty simple. They can easily solve all the problems of their kid's world. That feels great to them and looks great to their kid.

To a teen, dad's throwing arm suddenly looks pee-wee league.

Then one terrible day, the parents' skills seem to crash. It's not that they've changed, but that their kid has grown into adolescence, a time when the parents' skills don't mean nearly as much. To a teen, dad's throwing arm suddenly looks pee-wee league. Mom's math magic can't cut Algebra II. And the painful emotional bruises of adolescent life can no longer be cured with that old hug. Overnight, the parents feel useless. They can't seem to solve any problems in their kid's world, and that feels awful to them. *But the kid hardly notices any difference. Suddenly, seeing her parents as sort-of-stupid just feels normal, as if it's always been that way.* But the fact is that parents see (and feel) a huge change. They fall from being number one to disappearing off their kid's list of admired people. That change causes sadness in your folks that is so strong we call it grief.

Other teen changes in you hurt your folks, as well. Have you noticed that you can be snappier at times, perhaps even vicious once in a while? Have you recently heard yourself saying things to your parents you wouldn't have dared to say when you were 10? Those changes (see Chapters 1, 2, and 3) are normal and are an important part of growing up. But they can hurt Mom and Dad a lot more than you think.

When kids say mean things to their parents, they are usually just reacting to some rule (like bedtime?) or punishment that they think is dumb or unfair. They're not trying to hurt their parents; they're just arguing back. But in arguing back, mean words that surprise the kids as well as shock the parents sometimes jump out of impulsive adolescent brains. When I ask kids if they meant those words, most tell me, "No, not really. I just get so mad at her dumb rules that I end up calling her a dumb bitch. She knows I don't really mean that." You think?

The parents think that the hurtful words were meant. They don't believe me when I tell them that their teen who says hurtful words tells me that she does respect her parents and feel close with them. They are further amazed when I show them the research that shows *most* teenagers respect and feel close with their parents, even though they sometimes say some lousy things to their folks.

How can this be, the parents ask? How can our teen seem so disrespectful, arrogant, and cold, and yet respect us? I answer, because you are taking his words too personally, and forgetting that kids often say things that they don't really mean. Plus, I add, you are grieving the old days when your kid used to tell you how great you were.

When a child becomes a teenager, the teenager stops doing some things that make a parent feel great, and starts doing some things that make a parent feel bad. She rebels and starts to disagree with her parent's opinions. Or he speaks his mind more, sometimes in ways that are not very polite. This is all part of growing up. But because the teen changes how he talks and acts doesn't mean that he changes his feelings for his parents.

Adolescents still see that a parent does respect-earning things, like work hard to provide money, take care of family members, and have a good set of values about things like drugs. What changes is that teens don't *tell* parents many good things anymore—but they sure tell the bad.

That's because your relationship with your parents can become more about control than caring. As you roll into adolescence, you push for more freedom and independence, as you should. But that can cause your relationship with Mom and Dad to become a contest of control. You and they can suddenly find yourselves on opposite sides of a contest about who's in charge of your life. Once that happens, your parents can literally feel as if the old "you" died, and that the new "you" hates them. That terrible parent pain is grief.

What Does Parent Grief Do?

A lot more than you think. Parents often take all that sadness and turn it into anger, without even thinking about it. Then they seem to turn cold toward you, treating you like some uncaring, irresponsible lunatic. Grieving parents can go in one of two ways. Some clamp down like crazy, making your life miserable, with punishments, policing, spying, and very few privileges. This, of course, only makes you angrier, which makes your parents angrier . . . it never ends.

About every young "freed" teen I've ever met was either depressed, or rageful, or in jail.

Other grieving parents can do the opposite, turning away from you, saying, "Whatever." They might quit parenting you, allowing you to do whatever you want, whenever you want, however you want. That might sound good at first, but it's not. Younger teenagers, in particular, are not ready to be cut loose yet. Like it or not, most still need parents to keep them from self-destructing. You

"FRIDAY NIGHT YOU STAYED OUT UNTIL 9:00, YESTERDAY YOU HAD COLA INSTEAD OF MILK AND THIS MORNING YOU FORGOT TO FLOSS. YOUR FATHER AND I ARE AFRAID YOU'RE GETTING TOO WILD."

may have seen this happen with a friend. Initially, the "freed" teen has a great time, but then things gradually come apart. About every young "freed" teen I've ever met was either depressed, or rageful, or in jail. Many die.

Finally, there's the group that represents most parents. They use both, the "controlling" and the "whatever" styles, bouncing back and forth, frantically trying to figure out which style works the best. One week, they're seeing how a no-curfew rule works (the "whatever" style). After you roll in at 4 A.M. a couple of times, they then try the take-aways (the "controlling" style). When the only thing left in your room that has not been taken away is the floor, the "no-curfew" rule starts to look good to them again.

A large part of this back-and-forth parent craziness has to do with their grief, with your folks missing the old "you," and trying desperately to get the old "you" back. But neither the "whatever" nor the "controlling" parenting style can get the old you back, because the old you doesn't exist anymore. This is a cold fact that your parents have to deal with if they are to make new connections with the new you. But doing this requires effort, by both them *and* you.

Don't let the grief of your parents over losing the "little kid you" cause you to lose your connections with them. Remember, in the family game, it's all about the *connections.*

So What Can I DO?

Dominick asked me that question. He thought my answer was pretty dumb. At first, anyway.

> Dominick sat and shook his head at me, slowly and sadly, as if he had heard the most lame idea of all time come out of my mouth. With a snicker, he asked, "Did you ever play football, Dr. Bradley? 'Cause if you did, you must have been lousy at it. In the middle of a football game, it's, like, not a good idea to give the opposing linebackers a hug and tell them what's *special* about them.
>
> "That's what you want me to do with my parents? Living with them is just that—a football game. It's all about who wins and who loses. I have to be tough with them, or they'll take over my whole life. I only get some freedom now because I go nuts on them sometimes. If I act all nice, they'll take advantage of me."
>
> I sat and wondered how to get around this 220-pound, 16-year-old football player. I decided I'd have to play his game. "Last week, Dom, you told me about that reverse [a trick football play] you ran that the other team was not expecting? It worked great, because it caught them off balance. It was not what they expected, and it was not what you had been doing up to then. You knew that if you kept doing what you'd been doing, the result would have been the same. So trying some really radical, bizarro move worked well, right?" He nodded.
>
> "Well, here you are again, in another hard game, this time with your parents. Up to now, you keep trying the same play with them, acting tough, and it gets you very little. So why not do some really radical, bizarro play, to catch your parents off balance? It might get you a lot further than doing what you've done. And, personally, I can think of nothing more radical or bizarro than the Dumpster [his nickname] giving his parents a hug and telling them something nice." Because he laughed, I pressed my luck. "Dom, what is special about your parents? There must be one good thing about one of them?"
>
> Dom looked liked he was giving the football away, something he never did. He answered with a sigh, rolling his eyes—but he

answered. "Well, my dad works like crazy in a job where they treat him really bad. I know he wants to quit, but he can't, 'cause he doesn't have a college degree, and they pay him a lot there. He does that for us, his family, you know? But I think it really kills him. The jerk boss gives him crap all the time for stuff he didn't do, and he has to stand there and get abused—and in front of the guys who work for him." Dom the Dumpster suddenly looked grown up. "That must really kill him, you know? How can he get up everyday at 5 A.M. and go into that place with that asshole boss? I couldn't do that. And he never complains to me or my little sisters. I only know 'cause I hear him talking to Mom late at night, when he thinks we're asleep." Now Dom looked a little ashamed. "One time, I think he was, you know, like, crying." He shook his head at himself. "Now that I think about it, I guess I've been like my father's asshole boss. I guess maybe I abuse him, too. And he takes it, mostly."

"That's it, Dominick," I said. "There's your reverse. When things are calm, sit down next to him, and tell him how much you appreciate what he does for his family. Tell him you're sorry for sometimes being another asshole in his life. *Hug the linebacker*. Maybe you guys can stop playing football and start being, like, a family?" Dom tried picturing that scene in his head. "I can't see me doing that," he said. "I just can't."

"That's the problem with reverses," I explained. "They're so different you can't picture them until you do them. *Just do it*, OK?"

The Dumpster laughed. "You shrinks get your ideas from sneaker commercials?"

"Nah," I retorted, "they stole that line from us . . . because it works."

Trick plays work so well because they upset everything and create new possibilities that people couldn't see before. Reaching out to your parents in the middle of a control contest, and telling them something that you love and admire about them, can create new possibilities. Like helping grieving parents see that they didn't lose their child after all. Like disarming parents' anger, and their need to control you so much. Like showing parents that you are more mature and thoughtful than they thought—so maybe they can trust you more?

It's all about those *connections.* When you stop fighting with parents and connect, you allow them to see the good parts of you, and you get to see good parts of them, as well. These good parts are never seen in fights. They only become visible when people stop yelling and try something else—like connecting.

"Healthy, Wealthy, and Wise": Your Parents' Wish List

So far, we've shown that parents are just *people* (with feelings), that they are learning this parent job as they go along, and that they feel sad that the old you "died" (that they lost their connections with you). Most of all, we've seen that when parents become scared or sad, they get mad—just like the rest of us. They cover their hurt with anger—just like the rest of us.

Parents are terrified of all the evils surrounding you in this nutso world.

On top of all those disabilities, let's add the list of things that your parents are trying to make happen in your life, because they love you. They want you to exit your adolescence healthy, wealthy, and wise. Sounds easy, doesn't it? That nice-sounding list turns out to be a real monster that eats connections for lunch.

Healthy: This category is about sex, drugs, and rock 'n roll (violence). Parents are terrified of all the evils surrounding you in this nutso world. Each day, their newspapers are stocked with stories of kids getting terribly hurt by sex, drugs, and rock 'n roll. The statistics are really scary. Much of what they worry about is keeping you alive. Their fear can make life miserable for everyone, as they fight to keep you away from the sex, drugs, and rock 'n roll.

Wealthy: This heading includes things like doing well in school, becoming self-reliant, and having a set of values to help you make good decisions. Most parents define wealth not just in dollars, but in happiness. The problem is that your definition of happy may differ greatly from theirs. For your parents, happiness includes all of those things they list under healthy and wealthy. They see your road to happiness as avoiding sex, drugs, and rock 'n roll, doing well in school, and so on.

You may see their road map for your happiness as one that ruins your fun. That's because the road to real happiness is often one that ruins fun—having fun and being happy are *not* the same things, although kids and parents often become confused about this.

You know all about fun. Sometimes, fun involves doing things that can hurt you. That kind of fun is *now, unthinking*, and *rebellious.* Happy is *long-term*, *thoughtful*, and *calm*. Fun is sneaking out of the house to hang with friends instead of doing boring, stupid homework. Happy is waking up the next day feeling good about having done the stupid, boring homework instead of sneaking out. Fun can be a drug to avoid feeling bad. Happy is the antidote to feeling bad.

Wise: This is a tough one to define. I think most parents define wise as meaning that you should turn out better than them—no kidding. Most parents (especially this one) have some regrets about their lives. Most can instantly tell you what they would have done differently if they could rewind the video of their life. If you ask, they'll tell you about mistakes they made, like going to school, not going to school; joining the military, not joining the military; making promises they should not have made, breaking promises they should have kept—a million and one things that all have one thing in common: They are all about a lack of wisdom. If you ask what that means, they'll tell you that they made these bad decisions for the wrong reasons. Like fear, or not believing in themselves, or taking the easy path. The greatest regrets you'll hear from adults are about abandoning their values, and giving up what they believe in. Many regrets have to do with people not knowing what they believe in, not knowing who they are. Now you know that another word for wisdom might be *identity*. As you saw in Chapter 3, identity is what you should be all about. But as you also saw in Chapter 3, your quest for identity can put you and your parents on opposite sides of that family fence.

So, although teens and parents all agree that *healthy*, *wealthy*, and *wise* sound like good goals, how parents get you to those things can start wars. Like I said, that list can eat your family connections for lunch.

How Do They Try to Do This?

Mostly, your parents try to get you healthy, wealthy, and wise just as their own parents did with them—with fear and anger. In the old days, fear and anger seemed to work great as a way of raising kids. I was a model child because I was terrified a lot. I didn't learn much about what was right or wrong. I just learned how to do what the scary adults told me to do. Adults like Sister Credenza.

Sister Credenza was a nun who taught my 8th-grade Catholic school class. Credenza's real name was Sister Cardoza, or Sister Carenna, or something like that. But she so closely resembled a large piece of dining-room furniture that she was always known as Sister Credenza to us 13-year-olds. But that resemblance was purely in appearance. In action, she was more like a battle tank.

One of her favorite methods of "teaching" right from wrong was to bounce bad boys' heads off of good slate chalkboards (the girls were subjected to less physical, though perhaps worse, "teaching" methods). When particularly peeved, she would grab an offender by one ear, run him up the aisle to the front of the room, and, with a pivot action that would impress an Olympic discus thrower, she'd whirl and bounce the sinner's noggin off the slate. Years later, I had an auditory flashback to these episodes while I was hitting golf balls. The noise was the same "thwok" as a good tee shot.

Dennis O'Leary was one of Credenza's favorite "thwokees." He was one tough Irish kid who seemed to have been prepared by Mother Nature for his encounters with Credenza. In 8th grade, his whole head looked a little too large for his body, with a huge, gnarly forehead that reminded me of one of those horned dinosaurs.

Toward the end of that year, O'Leary had taken a sort of suicidal turn in his Credenza confrontations, starting with smirking off her head "thwoks." Even while he was rebounding off of the slate, his grin was becoming obvious. This, of course, further infuriated Credenza, much like a heavyweight boxer losing his punch. With each of his successive trip to the slates, she seemed to add more and more force to the throws, while O'Leary added more and more grin to the rebounds. We all knew this was headed in a bad direction.

One rainy day in May, both O'Leary and Credenza seemed to sense that, with the season almost over (the school year), neither had established himself or herself as the clear winner in this game. O'Leary set the stage for the final showdown by drawing a picture of Sister Credenza (as a credenza with huge boobs and fangs) into his desktop—*in ink*. Ink was used on desks by Catholic school boys only

> for true suicide missions. Sure enough, Credenza saw the artwork, and the "Super Bowl" was on.
>
> Without breaking stride, she swooped down the aisle, grabbed *both* of O'Leary's huge ears, spun, reversed direction, and stormed toward the slates. Hitting speeds never before seen, she launched O'Leary at the blackboard from Adrienne Arinetti's desk, a good three feet away.
>
> The time to impact must have been about one-tenth of a second. Yet, I can recall that scene going into slow motion, like in a martial-arts movie. The most amazing thing of all was seeing a *grin* appearing on O'Leary's face as he hurtled toward his fate. What did he know?
>
> The answer arrived by sound. Instead of the usual "thwok," a "CRRRAACCKK" echoed around the room. A couple of kids screamed at the noise, covering their eyes to avoid seeing O'Leary's red-haired head shattered like an Easter egg. Instead, as the chalk dust settled, there stood a triumphant Irishman, wiping the blood of final victory from his forehead, gazing proudly at the hole his head, like some artillery shell, had punched through the slate. And he was *laughing.*

I was a "good" kid only because I did not share the kind of confidence in my forehead that O'Leary had in his. I was good to *avoid getting beaten*, not for the sake of being good. In fact, I knew very little about good and bad, despite years of "religious" education.

In those old days, a parent could keep a lot of the insanity away from kids by "policing" the world around them.

If you ask them, you'll find that your parents have their own "ridiculous-but-true" stories about being scared into being good. That's because, in the old days, you could more or less get away with frightening children into being safer. That's because the world around kids was a lot less dangerous. In those old days, a parent could keep a lot of the insanity away from kids by "policing" the world around them. Remember my mother tearing the underwear ads out of the Sears catalogue (see Chapter 3) to keep sex out of my life? My dad did his policing part, as well.

In 1968, my hoodlum friends and I were in my basement secretly listening to "The Devil's Music." Those were my father's words for the Doors (Jim Morrison) album that was around. He heard it playing, walked downstairs without a word, snatched the album off the turntable, smashed it against the wall, relit his cigar, and turned and walked upstairs—without a word. End of Devil's Music. There was no FM radio around, and no one had the bucks for another album. Back then, parents could smash, tear, and beat the evil away. At least to some extent. And all with no words.

Today, the insanity around kids is so complete, it pounds at them 24/7 and is available on demand. Smash a CD, and she'll copy it online in four seconds. Hide the underwear ads, and he'll hit the Web porn sites in three seconds. Smash a kid into a blackboard, and he'll call the cops in two. Or hit you back in one. Those old parenting methods are worse than useless in today's world. They keep kids from actually thinking about what's right or wrong, and instead make them think only of getting back at the parent. Yet those methods are what many parents have stuck with in their heads, because *watching one's owns parents is the only "parent training" people have for when they become parents themselves.*

Because the craziness is so much worse in your world, parents should *teach* kids instead of police them. The teaching method involves lots of words and thoughts. The goal must be to help teens to develop their own codes of right or wrong. This approach helps them to handle the ten thousand tough decisions they will face when their parents are not around. The deal is to help adolescents be safer by building identities, not jails. We call that respect-based parenting (versus fear-based parenting).

But this respect-based stuff is so easy to say, and so hard to do, mostly because your parents are stuck with their own parents' rules of how-to-raise-a-teen. These rules were written into our child brains as we watched our own parents be parents. And we tend to fall back on those outdated methods, particularly when we're stressed or tired. Even when we know better.

> "I had another one of my 'near episodes' the other night with my son. He's 13. In the past two months, he's suddenly jumping on every little thing I do wrong. If I mispronounce a word, or don't know the name of some current music or movie star, or even have my hair messed up, he loudly points it out, as if he can't believe how weird I

am. I know this is normal for 13, but it still hurts a little. After a day of taking shots like this, I was on my way to check the basement before going to bed. Ross was sprawled out in the family room, watching some show we both know I'd hate. He grunted an annoyed 'yes' answer when I asked if the basement had been picked up after he had been down there with some friends.

"I was really tired, and just wanted to crawl into bed (something else he now makes fun of), when I got to the basement landing and saw a huge mess. Junk was strewn everywhere, with popcorn bits and juice boxes left all around. I wanted to just explode. 'How dare he!' I thought. 'How dare he make fun of me, when he acts like a five-year-old doing a simple task. What's going to become of him? How is he going to manage his life if he can't manage one lousy chore?'

"As I started to clean things up, I felt angry blood rushing to my head. With each item I picked up, my rage increased. Soon, I was hurling toys into the closet. As the 'American Girl' doll crashed into the toy bin, I decided, 'Enough was enough, godammit! I'm getting his butt down here this instant!' I whirled and headed up the steps. In my head, an old scene flashed before my eyes: In my best intimidation stance, I was supposed to block his view of the TV, loudly and sarcastically 'thank' him for doing such a great job in the basement, and then wait until he dared to say something back. Then I would go nuts on him—in his face, screaming how sick I was of all this crap, his lack of responsibility, and so on. Maybe I'd shove him, just to make a point that he'd better damn well respect me! Then he'd learn how to be more responsible, and have a better life. So screaming at him would really be for his own good. Right. That crazy scene was a battle plan in my head. I was ready to go.

"Thank God for long basement stairs. As I climbed, a small voice inside of me started to ask where I'd played in that scene before. That's when it hit me: That was my own father's way of 'teaching.' And then I remembered how much I hated that, and how much it hurt, and how much it drove me away from him. I paused halfway up and sank down on a step, totally confused, but getting clearer. I started to remember who my son really was. Yes, an occasional slob, but also the most giving, courageous, and loyal 'slob' you'll ever meet. A young man with the heart of a lion, who at age 8 fought back his terror at seeing our family falling apart after taking in a difficult foster

> child. Even at that young age, and under that kind of fire, he insisted that we adopt that baby and make her part of our family. 'How dare I!' I thought. 'How dare I get so mad over something so stupid with someone so wonderful.'
>
> That old family rage drained out of me, like stale air from a punctured balloon. I felt more tired, but a lot wiser now. Yet one strange thing still bounced around in my head: 'American Girl' doll? Ross?' That's when it hit me. The mess was from Ross' five-year-old sister. I shuddered when I realized how close I had come to demolishing my wonderful son over something so stupid that was not even his.
>
> —Notes from the personal journal of Dr. Michael Bradley

If your parents ever act crazy like that one almost did, try to remember these things about them: They're people, they love you, and they're trapped between two worlds of how to raise kids. They're worried that, if they stop being tough with you, you'll end up dying from a heroin overdose. Their heads tell them that respectful parenting methods are better, but their guts tell them to go nutso, like their own parents would.

If you want the respect approach from them, you have to show your parents that it pays off. How do you do that? With connections (tired of that word yet?). When parents feel close to their kid, and feel like they have an idea of what goes on in their teen's world, they tend to stay a lot calmer and use the respect approach a lot more than the fear and control methods you hate.

You can make changes in yourself that can radically change how things go with your parents.

So a lot of what happens with your parents *is* in your hands. You can make changes in yourself that can radically change how things go with your parents. It's up to you whether or not you want to take a shot at making things different. What kind of changes? Funny you should ask.

How Can I Change Things?

By building those connections. You do that by talking, sharing, and hanging out—*with your parents.* If that sounds *totally* impossible, maybe it's time to get some outside help (see Chapter 4). Call a truce in the fighting, and say that you hate living like this, and that they probably hate living like this, so maybe it's time to sit down with a shrink to see if things can get better. I can just about guarantee that they'll go for it.

If that hanging-out idea only sounds *nearly* impossible, here's a trick to help you start to talk, and to learn about each other without getting into the curfew and homework fights. I know, I know—you get annoyed with books that have all those exercises and worksheets. I promised myself I would not do that to you in this book. But maybe we could make a teeny exception, because this trick works really well? It's called Larry King Live.

Larry King Live?

Interview each other. You go first. One session for Mom, and another for Dad. Put together a list of questions, and bring a tape recorder, so you can write it out later if you want (some kids use this as an extra-credit writing assignment for psychology, English, or even health class—the teachers love it). You might want to take them out to a coffee shop to do this (I don't know why, but people talk better there—perhaps it's the caffeine). Do this as if you've never met your parents, and you've been assigned to find out who they are—because, as you'll come to see, *you guys really don't know much about each other.*

Here are some interview questions you might try, but know that the best ones are those that you think of yourself.

Parent Interview Questions

- What were you like when you were 10 years old? 15? 20? 30?
- What's been your greatest joy in life?
- What's been your deepest sadness?
- What do you do when you're scared?
- What was the best sleeping dream you ever had?
- If you could change one thing in your life, what would it be?
- What did you love about your own father? And mother?
- What did you hate about your own mother? And father?
- When you were 15, who did you think you'd be today?
- Did life turn out like you thought it would?

- What do you truly believe about God and religion?
- What is left undone in your life that you want to do?
- What is it like being a parent?

After you've done their interviews, each of your parents should separately do yours. The rules are that 1) everyone gets to refuse any question he or she wants, 2) everyone agrees to tell the truth, and 3) everyone agrees to keep some answers secret if that's what the subject wants.

That's it. Seem silly? Try it and see. I'll bet you'll be amazed at how different the two of you will be when you stop being *parent* and *teen*, and start being, you know, like *people*. This kind of talking might even become habit forming, like that mocha latte at the coffee shop. There are worse habits you could pick up than hanging out with your folks at the coffee shop. So, if the interview goes well, consider making this a weekly show? You could call it *CONNECTIONS*. That show can change your whole world.

I'll bet you'll be amazed at how different the two of you will be when you stop being parent and teen, and start being, you know, like people.

And speaking of your world, it's time to move on to the next part that plays such a huge roll in shaping who you are, and what you might become. Unfortunately, there's more bad news here than good, because this particular aspect of your world has been under a vicious assault that has put it on its knees in our culture. It's on the ropes, barely hanging on to life, and tossed around like trash. It's become so endangered that, if we don't watch out, the only place you'll soon see it is in a museum. Yet study after study tells us over and over that this one thing is the key to keeping kids confident, caring, and connected. It's called *the family*.

YOUR FAMILY

They Make You Crazy, They Keep You Sane

"My family is like Leave It to Beaver *meets* The Osbournes. *One day we're great, the next we're nuts."—Jeff, age 18*

The group of eight teenagers settled into an uncomfortable silence. This was their third meeting, a project they had chosen as part of their 10th grade psychology class, to get an idea of what group counseling was about. Nothing much had been said up to now, just small talk, mostly. Lulls had happened before, but not quite like this.

This silence seemed to get louder the longer it lasted, like a radio turned up full blast when nothing is playing. A small cough echoed loudly off the classroom walls. The creaking of a chair attracted so many looks that its red-faced owner struggled to stifle the noise. A strange discomfort began to build, like a wave about to hit the group. There seemed to be an elephant in the room that everyone pretended wasn't there.

Something drew my attention to Lana. Judging by her face, she apparently had a bad cold—or maybe something else?

David finally shattered the stillness. With a forced laugh, he said, "This quiet reminds me of when my parents fight at home. Sometimes they won't talk for days. They can get really nasty."

David's easy manner told everyone he was just making that up to be nice, for some reason having to do with the "elephant" in the room.

Bridgette added her thought, which also seemed to be a lie meant to comfort. "My folks, they're really nuts. They, like, always say they're getting divorced, and they never do. They say they hate each other, but they always end up staying together. You can't believe what they say."

Each comment drove Lana's head lower. Finally, I had to ask about the elephant. "Guys," I said, "what's going on?"

Uneasy eyes all shot looks at Lana, whose own eyes were now filled with tears. "It's about me," she wept. "My parents had a fight, a *real punching* fight, in the parking lot, in front of the whole school, this morning. My father moved out of our house last week. He showed up today to try to make me go with him when my mom dropped me off for school. He's got a girlfriend that my mom found out about . . ."

Nobody moved a muscle, as Lana's shame shut off her voice. After a minute, she continued. "Davey and Bridgette, they're playin' [lying] to be nice. Their parents are still cool with each other. You can tell that, you know. You can look at kids and know if things are cool at home or not. I used to see it in other kids faces when their parents split. Then I'd be nice to them, like Davey and Brid are being with me. Now, I guess it's my turn to have that look, and have kids act nice to me."

Lana paused, sighed, and started picking off her nail polish. "You know what's weird is that I always used to tell my parents to get a divorce 'cause they fought so much, and I was so sick of hearing it, you know? And now that my father's gone . . . I'm scared. *Really scared.* I can't sleep at night because he's not there. I'm like this wimpy little girl who's afraid of the dark. I didn't think it would be like this, you know?" Lana's tears splashed over her broken nails as she tried hard to not cry. No one knew what to say.

I watched as these kids nervously glanced sideways at each other. They made me think of an army squad in combat, each wondering who was going to get picked off next, after half of them had already been hit. The fear in these kids was also of a death—the death of their families—from a deadly sniper called *divorce*. That's a shooter who hits more than he misses.

The terrible unfairness of this suddenly hit me. That with all the other worries they have, most kids today must also deal with seeing their parents split up. So who are they supposed to rely on? And

> where do we adults get the nerve to tell kids how to live their lives when we can't seem to manage our own? No wonder they think we're crazy.

Your family is another huge factor in your world that shapes your identity. It's another one of those things that is so close you can't truly see it. It just blends into the background of your life. But your family is a powerful force, giving you a million lessons about how to live family life that get wired into that developing brain of yours. These lessons will reach out through the decades and touch the family you will make one day.

If you have the incredible good luck of coming from a reasonably sane family, where people love each other, take care of each other, and stay together, you have wonderful things being written into your head. Like treasured old recordings, these will play back later for you when you have your own spouse and kids, helping you to do good family stuff without even realizing it. It will probably just come naturally to you.

These lucky "good family" people are the ones who look around and wonder why so many families are in such bad shape. They really don't understand how family members can be hurtful, cold, or uncaring toward each other. That seems so weird to them. It's not what they saw growing up, and not what got wired into their brains.

If you have the bad luck of coming from a family where things are nuts, those are the nasty recordings being burned into your brain that will play back later and can make you do nasty things with your own family—*unless you think about them now.* Thinking about the family craziness around you acts like an Internet filter for your brain, helping you to see the insanity for what it is, and not allowing it to become part of your hard-wiring—of your identity.

Boys who grow up in homes where women are abused often abuse their own wives *because it just seems natural.* Women who grow up in homes where women are abused often allow themselves to be abused by their husbands *because it just seems natural.* They don't really "see" the abuse for what it is. It's what they saw growing up, it's what got hard-wired into their brains, and it's what played back when they had families of their own. These are examples of how powerful your family can be in shaping who you might become.

But not all the boys from abusive homes abuse their wives. Many are kind and loving husbands who would rather die than ever abuse their wives. These are boys who saw, *really saw,* the abuse for the horror that it is, and vowed to never do that to anyone. They kept it from becoming part of their hard-wiring by *seeing* what was happening, *thinking* about what they were seeing, and *working* to become different from what they were seeing.

That's our goal for this chapter. To get you thinking about the things you may be seeing in your own family, to help you select the good stuff and filter out the bad. Even if you are one of the lucky few from good, intact families, read on anyway. You need to understand what this national family crisis is about, so that you can better help your friends who are dealing with these problems. And you also need to know how this mess is affecting your generation, because "family" is a powerful force shaping your values.

We're very bad at doing "family" in this culture. You could say that we suck at it.

Ultimate Parent Craziness: Blowing Up Families

Most of our marriages end up in divorce court. Many of the ones that don't are lousy marriages that limp along, often with ongoing problems of abuse, rage, drug use, and sexual cheating. Marriage counselors tell me that the most common marriage problems involve adults who expect to have a marriage and family *take care of their own needs*, rather than seeing a family as a place where you put your own needs aside to take care of others.

A child, not an adult, is a person whose needs should be met first in a family.

A child, *not an adult*, is a person whose needs should be met first in a family. But today, we have lots of "children" raising children, parents who decide that their own happiness comes first. These are the not-so-grown-up adults who trade mortgage money for motorcycles, homework-helping for happy hour, and worn-out spouses for shiny new ones.

The impact of this craziness on children has been monstrous, with pain and suffering that would make a terrorist drool: *Only 26 percent of this nation's children currently live with their biological mother and father.* That means three-quarters of our children have suffered through the death of their family.

But "death of their family" is not the wording most divorced parents use when they describe leaving their marriage. They mostly talk about how much better off the children are because Mom and Dad are so much happier apart. They usually say things like Susan's parents said to her. She knew it was garbage. She just didn't know that she knew.

Susan loved my stuffed Rocky and Bullwinkle characters. She was nuts about them. In fact, she couldn't put them down. In truth, this 14-year-old was desperately looking for anything to keep her from having to talk or think about her parents' upcoming divorce.

"These are great," she repeated for the third time. And then her face lit up with a big smile. "Last year, when we went to the state fair, my dad won me. . . ." She quit her story when she saw it ending with a warm memory of a family that was about to go up in flames. Her smile evaporated. "Anyway," she continued, "these are really cool."

I heard myself accidentally sigh before I spoke. I knew that what I had to ask would be painful. "Susan, can you finish that story about the fair?" At first, Susan acted as if she didn't hear me. Knowing that she did, I waited her out. Finally, she slowly shook her head no. "I'm not going there anymore, OK? That part of my life is over. It's dead. That's how I keep sane. I just refuse to think about it." She plunked poor Bullwinkle upside down on his head. "Time to move on, you know? There's no point in getting all upset. It doesn't do any good." Her voice sounded as flat as a computer voice. "Besides, my parents tell me that I'll be much happier [after the divorce], since *they'll* be much happier." She turned her face toward me, twisted into a half-grinning, half-crying look of pain: "Do you think that's true?" As I tried to think of what to say, she pushed harder: "Well, *do you*?"

This time, I sighed on purpose. I hate being asked that question. I always want to duck it, or lie. "No, I don't," I answered truthfully, as I watched her eyes fill up. "I think that's one of those things that we tell kids when we don't know what else to say. And I worry that it makes kids feel worse, because it doesn't fit with what most kids feel inside. Most kids just want the family to stay together, no matter what. Most kids want that a whole lot."

Susan's face was twisted again. One part of Susan liked that I told the truth. The other part hated that I told the truth. Tears ran down her cheeks as her voice cracked: "Why can't you just lie like them? Then maybe I could keep believing their bullshit and think that I will be happier. I hate getting upset like this. *I HATE IT! I HATE YOU! I HATE THEM! WHY DO YOU ALL JUST WANT ME TO FEEL BAD? WHY CAN'T YOU ALL JUST LEAVE ME THE HELL ALONE?"*

She cried hard for a long time. As she quieted, I sat and felt that horrible, helpless feeling of watching a car wreck that no one can stop. Susan seemed to read my mind. "The worst part of this is being helpless. There's nothing I can do. Nobody gives a crap what *I* want. It really, really sucks being a teenager in the middle of a divorce."

The Terrible, Secret Impact of Divorce on Adolescents

I'm sorry, I truly am. I've tried and tried to understand folks who say that teenagers whose parents split up don't get hurt very much. I've tried to believe that these kids can be made to feel as good, safe, and secure about their lives as children from families that stay together do. I've read books that say teens can have one of their parents only on every other weekend and Wednesday evenings, and do just fine. In fact, that's pretty much what I was taught in school.

I don't buy it anymore. I may be burning out, but I've looked too often into confused and frightened adolescent eyes that stare blankly back at me when I tried to sell them on this. Their eyes told me what my stomach knew: It's just a lot of crap that we adults use to justify our own failures to keep our promises to our kids.

Surprisingly, new research shows that even bad marriages maintain very powerful connections for children that help keep them safer. That's because as teens look out their bedroom window to see Dad packing up his car, they can feel the flesh-tearing pain of their family connections snapping, leaving them wounded in too many ways.

These wounds of divorce to a teenager are deep, ugly, and largely unseen, often boiling over years later, as acting-out behaviors like drug abuse and violence. Adolescents react differently from younger children to the death of their families. For example, many teens become darkly quiet. In keeping with their need to be cool (and not express emotion), they appear to shrug off the divorce, saying, "Whatever." If you've watched a friend go through this, you may have seen her distance herself from her family and friends, retreating into her room, or schoolwork, or sports, in what can look like a healthy reaction to the changes. But what you're seeing isn't healthy.

What you're seeing is pain. Teens may try to act like they don't care about divorce, but that's just a lie to cover pain. They may act tough and cool, but they're usually very soft inside. That distancing is a way of avoiding their feelings, and of ducking people they love, who they now fear might also desert them.

That marvelous expanding brain of yours allows you to be different from your parents, to learn from their mistakes, to become better than they are at some things.

Many kids feel embarrassed to be around their friends after their parents split. It can be too painful to keep telling the same ugly story, particularly knowing that it will be homeroom headline news on Monday: "*What*? His dad did *what*? Wait 'til the boys hear about this."

Worst of all, adolescents who watch their parents divorce can become cynical about *values*, which are so critical to your identity (see Chapter 3). In particular, the values that parents preached at you before they divorced become cruel jokes, stupid and painful lies. Values like "commitment," "responsibility," and "love" become only empty words, sounds without meaning. Worse, these words can become harmful debris, tricks used to get things before we tire of them and throw them away—things like spouses, children, and families.

So, if your family is exploding in a divorce, watch out for that falling debris. It's bad enough that you're losing your family. That hurts terribly. Yet, believe it or not, over time, that wound will begin to heal. But if you let the failure of your parents' marriage blow up your values, your *identity,* as well, that's a loss that can affect the rest of your life. Remember, *you are not your parents—you are you.* That marvelous expanding brain of yours allows you to be different from your parents, to learn from their mistakes, to become better than they are at some things. Things like math. Things like marriage.

Here are a few tips to help you do the very thing that, incidentally, your parents want from you more than anything else: *for you to become better than they are.*

WHAT CAN I DO?

Part Three of this book has a section on divorce that lists a few helpful tips kids have found that help them survive this terrible time. But for now, here are a few tricks to keep that craziness of adult divorce from hurting your adolescent identity.

First, if you've gone through this, and you're hurting, get some help (see Chapter 4). Divorce has somehow become so common that we forget how gut-wrenching it is for kids. Just because it happens a lot doesn't mean it's any less painful for any one teenager. The shrink can help you keep your parents' failure from becoming one you might repeat someday in your own marriage.

Second, whether you've been down that divorce road or not, take a look at your parents' marriage, to see what "marriage rules" might be getting hard-wired into your head. As with other influences on your life, thinking about whether those are the marriage values you want to have in your head is critical. Thinking about it acts as a filter, to be sure you take in only the good parts.

Do a marriage study of your parents' relationship. Watch them as they go through their days. Do they talk to each other? Do they listen to each other? Do they support each other? Do they handle conflicts well? Do they like each other? Are they friends? Do they admit when they're wrong? Do they apologize—*really apologize?*

Consider writing down what you see going on, both good and bad. Think about what things you'd like to see in your own marriage one day, and perhaps write those goals down, as well. Why? *If we don't think about our parents' marriage in this way, we stand a good chance of just repeating what they did, "for better or for worse."* If what they did wasn't so great, you must do some work to not repeat their mistakes. It may not be fair, but that's the way it is. Do this for yourself, so that you don't have to suffer the pain of a failed marriage. Even more, do it for the children you may have one day. As you likely know, kids become the innocent bystanders who get whacked in the crossfire when the adults can't solve their marriage problems.

So take a little time to spy on your parents' marriage a bit. If their marriage is great, that's your best bet to do as well as them. If their marriage sucks, that's your best bet to do better. Do this so that you never live this next nightmare of adult failures: parenting by yourself.

Single Parenting: Making A Crazy Parent Crazier

If you thought that parents didn't need any help being nuts, you were right. Yet, as if this parent job wasn't tough enough, our culture has found a way to put it right over the edge—with that post-divorce insanity called single parenting. If divorce ever visited that family on *The (Bill) Cosby Show*, I'll give you odds that Mrs. Huxtable would look like Peggy within a year.

Peggy rushed in and flopped down, as if she was tardy getting to the principal's office. She apologized for being late, saying that her boss was so mad that she had to once again leave work early for a kid crisis that he made her late, just out of spite. This single mother of three (4, 7, and 14 years old) looked 20 years older than her 36 years of life, with dark circles of exhaustion underneath her empty, frightened eyes. As she noticed (and then tried to cover) a tear in her stocking, she looked even more ashamed when she saw that the hem of her skirt was also torn and hanging down. As I talked, she kept trying to hide these things, hoping that I somehow wouldn't see them. The more she fidgeted, the less either of us could concentrate on the real issue: that her 14-year-old son had been suspended for fighting at school—for the third time in one quarter.

I was trying to think of some nice way to ease her embarrassment, when all hell broke out in my waiting room. Her 4- and 7-year-olds were punching and screaming at each other. Before we could react to that, her 14-year-old ran past the window, off into the night.

Peggy sat strangely, looking as if she was trying to make her body move, but found it wouldn't work. When I returned from the waiting room after stopping the fight, I found her just staring out the window, beyond tears. "I'm so sorry," she said. Her voice was so flat and gray that a listener might think she didn't mean it. But seeing her told me it was the best she could do. "I sometimes just can't move my legs at night when these things happen. I think it's because I don't sleep much. I have to get up at five to get things going, and I don't usually get to bed 'til midnight. My boss makes me work early now, since I can't stay late like he wants. I have to get my son to high school, my daughter to her school, and my baby to daycare in three different places, and. . . ." She stopped. "Sorry again," she said. "We're here for my son, not me. I'm just. . . ." Her voice trailed off.

I knew that, if she continued, she would tell me the same stories I've heard from a hundred single parents, about a thousand unsolvable problems that feel like ten-thousand-pound weights. Each time I hear these nightmares, I get a knot in my stomach. These are big problems, like no money, no time, no one to take over when you're puking from the flu, and no second car when the first breaks down. And smaller, spirit-killing problems, like broken screen doors that never get fixed, dripping faucets that never get repaired, and backed-up toilets that can't afford a plumber's bill. It all must feel so incredibly . . .

". . . hopeless," she continued. "I'm hopeless. I can't seem to get anything right." She held up her torn skirt hem as proof, and laughed a hollow laugh. "Everything in our lives is like this. Everything's broken or frayed or dented. I can't even cover it up anymore. I can't get my kids to the activities they want to join. Hector [her 14-year-old] just got thrown out of the school play because I can't take time off from work to help like the school requires. I've maxed out my credit cards, and we still can't get by on what I make. My ex, who's got a new family now, he sends money when he feels like it, but I can't afford a lawyer to make him pay what he should." Peggy started pulling at her torn hem. "We're broken emotionally, too. Big shock there, huh?

"The worst one is me. All I do is yell and scream at the kids. The only thing I can afford to give to my children is love, but now . . . I don't even do that. . . ." She moved suddenly into sobs. "It feels like I've got nothing left inside—NOTHING! I think they can feel that, and that's why they act the way they do."

When she quieted, she wiped her nose and shook her head sadly. "The last counselor we saw, he said I should ask Hector to help out, that I should explain to my son how hard things are. When I did, you know what Hector said? He said, 'That's not my problem. You and Dad should have thought about that before you had kids. You f'd it up, so you fix it.' Hector's right, you know. It's not the childrens' fault. It's mine."

That flat, gray look returned to Peggy's face. She was sad beyond tears again.

Single parenting is hell for parents. For most, it's a brutal, never-ending grind that slowly sucks the life out of once-nice people, making them scared, cold, and short-tempered. If things are cool between the split parents, *and* they help each other out, *and* they have the money to now run two homes instead of one, sometimes this can work OK. But, for most families, that's a Disney movie. Most alone parents end up like Peggy, slowly drowning in a cold sea of debt, doubt, and depression, and all the while thinking that the problem is that they're too stupid to do this right.

The real problem is that *this can't be done "right."* Single parents usually try to keep doing all the things they used to do for their kids because they feel guilty about the children getting hurt. So they try to squeeze 30 hours out of a 24-hour day, make 50 dollars go as far as 100 dollars, and give twice as much patience and tolerance as they have. If that sounds impossible, you have the idea. And then, when it doesn't work, they blame themselves for being weak.

Why tell you all of this? Two reasons. First, if you are being single-parented, try to look from your parent's side at things like that empty refrigerator. What you see is stupid macaroni and cheese again for dinner. That's an *annoying* feeling for a child. What your parent sees is yet another reminder that maybe she can't take good care of her children. That's a *horrifying* feeling for a parent. So, when she goes off on you for whining about the dumb dinner, cut her some slack. Understand that she's hurting—*really* hurting.

Being a teen means it's grow-up time in a single-parent home.

Second, understand that this *is* unfair to you. Being raised by one parent on one income was never your idea. There are so many things that you lose out on because your parents couldn't work it out. I don't have to give you the list—you're living it. As a child, it shouldn't be your problem. But as an *adolescent*, it is. Being a teen means it's grow-up time in a single-parent home.

I see many teens do just that—they grow up. Fair or not, they learn to gut out the missed dinners, missed practices, and missed allowances without complaining. They get part-time jobs, and then hand over the check to Mom without whimpering (maybe with a little whimpering). They take care of the younger siblings, allowing the parent to provide the illusion that everything's cool when it's not. They lie about how *they* made Mom make their "favorite" macaroni and cheese again, so that the little guys never know the scary truth that there's no option until payday. These teens are heroes in my book.

Is this stuff tough to do? Yes, it is. Is it a horror? No, it's not, according to most teens who grew up the night that Dad or Mom left. They say it sounds strange, but they feel kind of proud to make those sacrifices. They say they don't miss what they used to have as much as they thought they would. Many say they feel better about themselves: tougher, stronger, and more confident that they can handle challenges in the future.

It sounds crazy, but the pain of struggling in a single-parent home can be an unwanted gift to adolescents. Here, many learn a precious secret about life: *It's only through challenges that we see how tough we can be.* Becoming strong doesn't happen easily. You have to pay your dues. So, if the asteroid of divorce smashes into your world, remember that there can be an upside, as well: You might find that you're stronger than you think. You could even end up being a hero.

And if you're looking for other chances to be a hero after a divorce, just wait. Your opportunity may be just around the corner, disguised as this next weirdness our culture has created for families: merging two broken families into one new one.

Blended Families: Making the Impossible Harder?

I asked 14-year-old Randy what it was like going from the frying pan into the fire, surviving his parents split-up, only to find himself living with Dad's brand-new family six months later.

> This kid was the most arrogant, nicest teen I ever met. He had this strange manner where he was sarcastic and insulting all the time, yet

he never seemed vicious. I guess it was because he would tear himself down at the same time he'd tear you down. I guess it was also because somehow you knew he did this to keep his own pain away. My new haircut handed him an easy target.

"Your hair is really bad, you know? Do you go to some hair place where they experiment on you, or something? They should pay you to do that to you." His eyes showed no malice as he ran on. "You should go to my hair lady," he announced, sweeping off his hat and pointing to his own hair. "See this?" he asked, pointing to perhaps the worst set of cowlicks on the East Coast, "This is hair art, especially designed for skinny kids with no personality."

When I asked Randy how the blended family stuff was coming along, he tried some other joke about my clothes, but only got halfway through when he saw that I really wanted an answer. He really didn't want to answer. "The same, whatever, you know," he snapped in an annoyed voice. Then he rolled over, face down on the couch like he was signing off. "You're really annoying, even for a dweeb," he added.

After a few minutes, he sat up. "It's a freakin' zoo," he sighed in a defeated voice. "My stepmother's crazy. She doesn't want me hanging out with my old friends anymore. She wants me to get 'close' with her psychopathic twin daughters. They're nuts, and they hate me, which is OK, 'cause I hate them, too. We have these bizarre 'family' dinners every night, where my dad gets crazy and talks about this 'great, new family' we've got. I don't want a new family, and neither do the psycho sisters."

Randy flopped back down on the couch, staring at the ceiling. "The worst is my dad. He's got this crazed look in his eyes all the time, and he talks too loud and too fast." Randy's voice became very still: "I think it's because he knows he made this incredible mistake, busting up our family. I think he misses Mom."

A lot of divorced parents like Randy's father seem to catch a disease. You could call it The Brady Bunch virus. This bug makes parents think that it's possible to take a family, splinter it into two jagged pieces with a blunt axe called divorce, glue these two half-families to two other jagged half-families, and presto-chango, create two new, happy families. It's a kind of magical thinking, believing

"MY REPORT TOOK ME FIVE HOURS—ONE HOUR FOR RESEARCH AND TYPING AND FOUR HOURS TO GET MY SISTER OFF THE COMPUTER."

that sticking wounded kids into new instant families somehow makes everyone OK again. Jason knew that was crazy the first time he heard it. But instead of saying it, he acted it.

This 17-year-old boy was not at all what I expected. After meeting with his mom and stepdad for an hour, I began to worry that my coffee table might not survive an hour with Jason. Stepdad talked nonstop about Jason's rages at home, where he'd go nuts and punch holes in walls. When asked, Mom said nothing, and just stared out the window. When asked, Dad couldn't think of one good reason why Jason would act crazy. When asked, Jason offered 24 bad ones. And he offered them calmly and powerfully.

"Twenty-four hours a day, all I hear is what a "wimp" I am from Leon [his stepfather]. He and his son, my so-called stepbrother, love to hunt and fish and work on cars. I hate that stuff. You know what I like? I like reading, I like biking, and I like tennis. I'm sorry that those things are not manly enough for Leon. They make fun of me, asking me when I'm gonna' start knitting classes and stuff. It makes me crazy after a while, and, yes, Leon's right, I have freaked out and punched walls." He paused here, and searched me with his sad, scared eyes, wondering if he could risk telling me the next part. It made him feel ashamed. He stared at the floor.

"This last freak-out, I. . . ." Jason took a deep breath. ". . . I, like, started to cry." Jason paused here and looked up, as if waiting to see my disgust at his weakness. Seeing only concern, he relaxed a bit and continued. "Did Leon tell you that? Did he tell you what he and the boy said? They started mocking me, saying 'Ooooo, watch out. Mr. Tennis is real mad now. No telling what he might do. Ooooo, this is so scary.'"

The tears that Jason hated so much burned in his eyes once again. "The worst part of all this is my mom." Jason's voice began to choke here. His pain was heartbreaking. "Mom and I were alone together for 12 years before she met that jerk [Leon]. It was like me and her against the world, you know? My father just jetted out when I was four, and we had some days with little to eat. But we managed. We got through on our own. Now, I see how special that time was. We were really tight, like best friends." Jason had to stop speaking for a minute to collect himself. "Now, it feels like I've lost her. Whenever I complain to her, she keeps telling me about Leon's 'good points,' about what a good provider he is, and crap like that. I don't want his freakin' money. We were fine on our own. Why did she have to marry that creep?"

Jason sat for a moment and then spoke very softly: "I guess I feel like Leon took over my world, and took my mom away from me. I guess I feel like she picked him over me. I guess I feel like a loser wimp—just like Leon says. I even lost my mother."

Jason saw the difficulty in blending two families together from day one. Sometimes, it feels impossible to create close family bonds with the strangers who are forced on you as your new family members. Here's why.

The adolescent survivors of a family that is wrecked by divorce never go out and shop for a stepfamily—that's their parents' craziness. Mom and Dad are the ones who run around looking for a replacement husband or wife because they feel sad and lonely after a divorce. Finding a new spouse can feel like a miracle cure for their pain. If you doubt this, reread Peggy's single-parent story.

The teenaged children also feel sad and lonely after a divorce, but they know that starting up a new family is not the way to feel better about losing the old one. They know that the wounds of divorce are deep, and take a long time to heal, even a little bit. They know that they'll need lots of time to adjust to Mom and Dad not being together before they can even begin to consider the possibility of having to break in a new parent. Watching their parent finding a new spouse can feel like a terrible twist for their pain.

Teens say: "Man, I already have two parents telling me what to do. What do I need with a third? And are you kidding about me having three brand-new siblings? I'm supposed to be, like, family with these kids I've never met before? I don't think so."

Watching their parent finding a new spouse can feel like a terrible twist for their pain.

Teens think: "How can a parent who is supposed to love and take care of me do this to me? Doesn't he understand that I need to hold on to the broken pieces of *my* family? Can't he feel that I need his attention all to myself in the little time we have together?"

Teens feel: lost, lonely, sad, confused, hurt, abandoned, and scared.

Teens act: angry, mostly. And why not?

How would Jason's mother feel if, after the divorce, he went out, shopped around a bit, and then came home with an adult stranger and said, "Mother, I'd like you to meet Alphonse Catchafasoool. I know this may come as a shock to you, but he's going to be my new father and your new stephusband. He's very special to me, and he helps me feel good about myself. So I'm sure you won't mind becoming his wife. Oh, it'll take a little getting used to, I know. But after a while, you'll see what a wonderful man he is, and you'll come to love him as much as I do. And if not, well, too bad. I have a right to be happy, you know. I have to get on with my life. I can't just live my life for you, Mom—you won't be around forever, you know.

"And don't worry, you'll get used to Alphonse's odor. All chicken pluckers smell like that. After you've shared a room with him for a few months, you'll hardly notice it . . . Mom, what's wrong? Aren't you happy for me?"

That is pretty much what Jason felt his mother did to him when she found a new spouse and decided to create a new family. The new family can look like a dream to the parent, and a nightmare to the kid. I'm not sure who decided that you can easily turn strangers into siblings and parents, but I do know that they didn't come from a blended family. If they had, they'd know what a dumb thing that is to do.

Later on, in Part Three of this book, we'll talk about what you can do if this blended-family craziness falls on you. For now, understand that the blended-family craziness is running wild out there. So if you're stuck in a bedroom staring at a brand new "brother" who just moved in, and you're both feeling a little nauseous, blame The Brady Bunch bug.

What Jason's mom said:

> "What kind of a mother do you think I am? Do you think that I'd stick my son with some crazy stepfather just because I was lonely? Do you think my son's 17-year-old view is the correct one? There's a lot more to this than Jason says, or even knows.
>
> "Jason's biological father was the real creep. He was abusive to Jason. He left when Jason was four because I swore to him that the next time he beat Jason, I'd call the cops. I never told Jason that story because I never wanted him to feel like he was the reason his dad left. Leon loves Jason. He honestly does. They used to get along great until the day I announced that we were getting married. Jason probably hasn't told you about all the wonderful things Leon has tried to do for him, things that Jason just throws back in his face.
>
> "Leon is far from perfect. Don't you think I know that? He believes that teasing Jason is the right way to make a man out of him, to make him strong. I know that's wrong, and I tell him so when we're alone. But never in front of Jason. I don't want him seeing us argue. I don't want Jason to think that he can split us up if he acts crazy enough.
>
> "Because I don't fight with Leon in front of Jason, he thinks that I'm taking Leon's side over his. I'm not, but there's no way I can get Jason to see that without messing things up more. Jason and Leon each think that I favor the other. I'm stuck in the middle, trying to get these two insecure males to get along. You are right about one thing, though. I had no idea that mixing two families together could be so hard."

When you think of all that bad news about today's families, particularly if that bad news arrives at your door in a package marked "divorce," "single-parenting," or "blended family," think about what Jason's mom said. Remember that there are always two sides to every issue, and that you can't truly know your side until you've sat and listened to the other—*really listened.* When Leon, Jason, and his mom all sat down and started listening, instead of talking, things began to get better for all of them. Keep that trick in mind if you ever find yourself feeling like Jason. It's a lot cheaper than punching holes in walls. It works a lot better, too. And speaking of better things, would you believe that there is also lots of good news about today's families? Strange, but true.

The Good News

As bad as families can be, they've also never been better. Even though record numbers of families are in trouble, record numbers are also doing wonderfully well. In the "good old days" (before divorce became the norm), many more families stayed together. But good old days weren't nearly as good as we like to believe. Families staying together didn't mean that families were happy. The craziness that we see in families today is probably no more than what used to go on behind closed doors in the "good old days," and it probably is even less. What *has* changed is that there are fewer secrets than there used to be. And, in the long run, more open communication means happier families.

Kids who feel good about their families do much better in adolescence, and much better in life.

What has also changed is that more families do really well at the family game. Many adults have woken up to the fact that good families are the best bet for keeping adolescents happier and safer. Many parents today work very hard at keeping their families strong and loving, and the results are wonderful. Kids who feel good about their families do much better in adolescence, and much better in life.

If your family is not one of the happy ones, be sure to hang out with some that are. Study what goes on. Watch how those parents handle things. You will see that it is possible to set some limits on teens to keep them safe, and yet also give them some freedom to keep them independent. You will see that successful families can handle conflicts without screaming or threatening. You will see *respect* being shared between child and parent. See these things, and learn them, so that you may one day create your own family with this magic. If you have this respect in your family, you may not fully understand what magic it truly is.

If you don't have it, then you know.

Adolescents who don't find respect and love in their own families often find it by creating a second "family." Even teens from good families find great comfort and support in these second "families." But, just as with real families, these second families bring good *and* bad things to your world, and can very powerfully shape your lifelong identity. So, if you're ready, turn the page and take a look at your own second family: *your peers.*

YOUR PEERS

The Good, the Bad, and the In-Between

"When we started middle school, it was like everybody stopped smiling at each other. Friends were a lot of work. Now that we're in high school, it seems everybody has started to smile again. I like smiling better." —*Amy, age 17*

Katelyn sat stone still, with her wide, 15-year-old eyes staring through mine, as if I wasn't really there. This was normal for her. She was the only teen I ever knew who could outstare me. She seemed stunned by my question. I had asked if she ever thought of not hanging out with her three friends as much. "After all," I had pointed out, "this is the third or fourth week you've complained about how they're so into marijuana, and all they want to do now is smoke. Last week, you said you were furious that all they did was get wasted when there were 50 things that you wanted to do. You were concerned that they might pull you into doing weed. So maybe they're not good for you?" She stared so long that I wondered if she had heard the question. "Kate," I asked, "where are you?"

After another moment, she stirred from her thoughts. "You know," she answered, "I can't picture myself without my friends.

That's what I was trying to do just now. I was remembering how we've all been together since, like, 2nd grade. Whatever part of my life I remember, my friends are in it. They're kind of like family—no, they are family. They're family because, good or bad, they're still my friends. You don't throw family members away because they're bad or sick, right? You stick with them, even when you don't like them, or even when staying with them might hurt you, right?"

Kate repeated my question slowly, as if turning it over in her head. "Should I dump my friends because they're bad for me? That's like asking me to dump a part of me that I don't like. It feels like that's not even possible. You don't dump friends like you dump shoes, you know. Do you think that you can get new friends by, like, walking up to kids and saying [she used a Valley Girl voice here], 'HIIII! My name is KAAAATE. Will YEEWWW be MYYY friend?' It doesn't work like that. I think I should try to change my friends' minds about weed, or accept them as they are if I can't. The problem is that I can see myself starting to use weed, like them, after a while. But if I dumped them, well, I don't think I would be who I am anymore. I know this sounds weird, but it's like I'm not me without them."

After a pause, she added, "In the drug programs at school, they always warn about the peer pressure to do drugs. The peer pressure I feel isn't to do the drugs—the pressure I feel is to keep the friends. The drugs just happen to be mixed in there."

As Katelyn pointed out, your peers and the pressures they bring to you are not usually what you see on TV antidrug ads. They're much more complex than that. Just as you saw in Chapter 7 ("Your Family . . ."), peers, much like families, can bring good *and* bad things into your world.

The truth is that you and your parents are both right—and you're both wrong.

Peers include your close friends, kids you sometimes hang out with, and kids that you just know a little. This group is the next ingredient that you take from the world and mix into the recipe that shapes your identity. They are as important to helping you become you as any other part of your life, including your culture, your parents, and your family. For many kids, peers are the *most* powerful force in their lives, at least for a few years. They can control small things, like your clothes and speech. They can control big things, like your beliefs and values. So, when you remember how your evolving brain is hard-wiring itself for life (see Chapter 1), peers become another thing you need look closely at, to see what ideas they bring to your world.

But that's probably not how you see them, and it's likely not how your parents see them. You see them only as kids you know or hang out with, not as identity shapers. Your parents often see them only as bad influences who will make you do bad things. The truth is that you and your parents are both right—and you're both wrong.

Peers: The Good

Lizzie showed up in my office with two friends, without an appointment. Because she was only 14 years old, she had always been driven by her mom, until today. These kids had taken one-half day of bus rides to get to me. When I explained I couldn't see them for two hours, Lizzie jumped up to say that she'd try again some other time, but was cut off mid-sentence by her friends, who said very firmly, "We'll wait."

Two hours later, they marched into my office, the friends shepherding Lizzie, like sheriff's deputies. The oldest-looking girl of the group, Shana, had orange and green spiked hair, with three piercings that were visible on her lip, and probably many more in places I preferred not to think about. In that unusual body sat the closest thing Lizzie had to a mother. Shana started speaking as if she was 40. "Doctor, Lizzie has been bullshitting, uh, I'm sorry, I mean lying to you about everything. She does lots more drugs than she says, and she's having sex with about every creep in the park, and she ain't even using protection. This week, she stopped going to school, and her mother don't give a shi . . . uh, doesn't care. I'm, like, no angel, but I'm not gonna end up some loser, like my mom. Lizzie's, like, becoming a whore or something. She's gonna end up dead, and she don't care. She was going to school to be a hairdresser, but she's thrown out now 'cause she didn't show up."

Lizzie stared at the floor, red-faced as her peers, or her "pimp and pusher friends," as her mom had described them, delineated their concerns. I was fascinated to see Lizzie sit so still to hear all of this terrible information. The last time I had seen her with her mother, Lizzie went nuts when her mom noted only a small part of this dangerous behavior. That was a month ago, after which Mom no-showed for appointments and finally told me on the phone that she was "washing her hands" of Lizzie because she was so disrespectful. The answer to my next question explained this difference in Lizzie's reactions.

"Shana, why are you guys here?" Shana looked puzzled that I had to ask. "'Cause she's our friend, and we love her. We're not gonna just sit by and watch her get AIDS, or end up a drunk, like her mom. She's got to go back to school, or she ain't gonna have no life at all. You're a doctor, and a doctor's got to know the truth about a patient, to help, right?"

"That's right, Shana," I nodded, "And I'm going to need you all to help me help Lizzie, if that's OK with her." Lizzie very seriously nodded her assent. "You know what, guys?" I asked. "I think you've already helped her more than you can imagine. What do you think, Lizzie?" Lizzie began crying softly, as a child greatly relieved, and nodded again.

Parental News Flash: Peer Pressure Can Be . . . Good?

Lizzie's peers are not as unusual as your crazy parents might think. Kids *do* care about their friends' well-being. Sometimes they show it in bizarre ways, such as helping them do things that are bad for them (scoring drugs, for example); however, kids usually try to do what they think is good for their friends. You already knew that. But your parents aren't so sure. If you want your parents' view of peer pressure, give them this pop quiz:

According to research, what is the most common form of peer pressure in today's adolescent culture?

A. To do drugs.

B. To have sex.

C. To finish school.

When your folks pick A or B, you can make that annoying wrong-answer buzzer noise that your annoying history teacher makes when you get something wrong. The correct answer is C. The most common pressure kids put on each other is to *finish their education*, so that they can have a decent life. Peer influence is not the monster that many parents make it out to be. In fact, peers do a bunch of wonderful things besides help keep you in school. Without the things that peers bring, it's very hard for a confused teenager to grow into a happy adult. What sort of things? *People* things.

Peers As People Practice

Peers act as a kind of laboratory where you get to experiment with all sorts of relationship skills that are flat-out critical to helping you grow up. In hanging out with your peers, you learn about things like tolerance and prejudice, acceptance and rejection, loyalty and betrayal, caring and coldness, conflict and conciliation—and, of course, hate and love. Not a bad set of things to know about, don't you think?

Peers allow you to practice these people skills as a teenager, so that you'll be better at them as an adult. This way, you stand a chance of not screwing up your own marriage and family, as so many parents have done. In the game of relationships, the older you are, the higher the stakes. As a teen, you can mess up and hurt only yourself or a friend. As an adult, you can wipe out an entire family with one stupid move. Your teen peers allow you to learn these skills *before* you have two babies relying on your abilities to relate well to your spouse. They also act as a kind of "reality show," where you can learn a lot about life and yourself (your identity) without having to experience every "ride."

Peers As Identity Builders

Your peers can allow you to experiment with (and learn about) lots of things without having to do them all yourself. This approach comes in handy when you're talking about life-threatening activities. Watching peers struggling with drugs can make them seem a lot less attractive to you.

"Living through your friends" comes in handy in life-*building* activities, as well. Hearing peers talk about themselves and their life plans can open up new doors in your world, helping you to see wonderful things around you that you might have missed if your peers weren't around. Music, sports, books, careers, values . . . the list is as endless and varied as life itself. Think for a minute: Right now, inside of you, can't you see how parts of your friends have ended up in your own identity? And do you see how you've influenced them, as well? It's scary when you think of how we would turn out without having those "terrible" peer influences. And when truly bad influences do hurt your life, your peers can help out there, as well.

The unconditional love and support of a friend can be a light that guides you through some dark days.

Peers As Second Families

Your peers can be like another family to you, getting you through bad times that you can't or don't want to share with adults. The unconditional love and support of a friend can be a light that guides you through some dark days. We often forget how healing it can be to just talk a problem out with someone who cares. Someone who you can trust to hold and guard your deepest secrets. This might be the best peer influence of all. But there also can be a dark side to the tremendous power of peers.

Peers: The Bad

The first big downside to friends is what happens when you don't have any. Being a friendless teenager in adolescent America is one of the most painful things that can happen to you. Some say it's the *most* painful. A kid without friends becomes an outcast, suspiciously avoided, even by nice kids, who don't want to get too close for fear of catching that horribly contagious disease of being a "loser."

> Erica was horribly ashamed. That much I knew. She couldn't lift her 16-year-old head, wouldn't make eye contact, and acted like she shouldn't even take a tissue for her runny nose until I gave it to her. But ashamed of what, I wondered? What could a 16-year-old possibly do that could be that repulsive?
>
> "I have no friends," she finally mumbled after 10 silent minutes. Her voice had a terrible tone of defeat, as if she expected me to jump up in disgust and yell, "GET THE HELL OUT OF HERE, YOU LOSER. LEAVE—BEFORE ONE OF MY COOL TEEN CLIENTS SEES YOU HERE AND THINKS THAT I LIKE YOU."

The overwhelming shame in that simple statement, "I have no friends," stunned me. For a moment, I couldn't think of what to say or do. I thought about what a painful problem that was. I thought about how hard that was to change at 16. I thought about how life really sucks sometimes.

As if she read my mind, she opened up a bit. "I know I'm, like, a little weird. Other kids think I'm this joke. I guess I'm what you guys [adults] used to call a hippie. I like folk music, and I dress weird and stuff. My family moved twice in the past three years, once for my father's new job, and again when he lost that job, and we couldn't afford our new house. So it hasn't been easy to make friends, even if I could. I've always been bad at that."

Erica slowly, slowly lifted her eyes to meet mine, as if waiting for a rejecting look. Seeing only concern, she went on. "I see kids looking at me, sometimes. Nice kids, you know? Kids who probably I'd be OK with, if they'd give me a chance. And I think they're thinking about saying hi or something. But then the bitches always seem to show up, laughing, and saying this or that about my hair, or whatever." Now Erica's gaze held so firm that I hoped she would not see my worry that I wouldn't know what to say to her.

"It's really, really hard being alone, you know? It used to be OK, when I was smaller. My parents could, like, fill in for missing friends. But, now, it feels like they can't do that anymore. I think at 16 you have to have friends, or you just get cut out of living. That's how I feel—like I've been suspended from life—like I'm completely alone in the world. The longer this goes, the further away I drift from everyone. I think that keeps making me seem weirder to those kids who could be my friends."

Erica's words ring in my head whenever I get a phone call about a kid who has no friends. She exactly described that vicious circle that traps those poor kids who get labeled as "uncool" or "weird" by the "committee on cool" (we'll chat about that committee in a minute). The longer kids are isolated from peers, the more they are talked about, the weirder they seem to everyone, and the more they are isolated. It goes on forever.

Erica also exactly described the incredible power that peers can have in your life. Her pain marked the depth of the wound that results when peers are absent from a kid's life. But that same level of pain and damage can occur when peers are *present* in a kid's life. From what? From the *committees* and *soap operas* that they can bring into your world.

The Committees: Who Died and Made You Queen?

Ah, the committees! I hear from them at least once a week. You know, those kids who somehow ended up in charge of everything in your world? I'm not sure if they get elected, are appointed by the president, or just take over. They're unbelievably good at hiding their operations, so I've never been able to find out exactly how they come to be, but I do know they exist, and very powerfully. By carefully watching the teen culture, I've developed a few theories about how these committees function.

The committees must have secret monthly meetings in the middle of the night, at rotating locations, where they conduct their dark business. I know this because, over the years, not one of my teen clients has ever stumbled onto one committee meeting. There, the members hold secret votes on things like which music is cool this month and which is now stupid, what clothes are in this month and what is out, and whose party is worth dying to go to, and whose party you wouldn't be caught dead at.

The last vote of these midnight meetings is always the killer: *the kid coolness scoring*. The committee reviews secret files it has on all the kids in the world, and it decides who is cooler than whom. It's kind of like the pro sports all-star votes, but much more important. Although the scoring process is the most closely guarded secret of all, looking at kids who make the "ultra-cool" cut gives you some clues. It usually has to do with things like being athletic, good-looking (body and clothes), popular, and, sometimes, smart (smart can be a plus or a minus in different committees, as can being rich). Some committees seem to value other traits, like having a cool car, or being funny, or doing drugs. Strangely, many committees seem to like kids who are cruel, back-stabbing, and sarcastic (perhaps out of fear of being targeted themselves).

Although I joke about these "committees," kids ranking kids by their "cool" quotient is no joke at all. It can have a huge impact on your life, depending upon your ranking. Your score can also be

"OF COURSE I CAN ACCEPT YOU FOR WHO YOU ARE. YOU ARE SOMEONE I NEED TO CHANGE."

affected by a few boy/girl differences in the cool point systems. Males can get points for being tough, aggressive, and never showing any emotion except anger and sarcasm. Females get bonus points for the number of girls they can claim as their friends (even if they're not really friends). Males score higher for scoring (sexually). Females are put in a lose/lose scoring bind where having sex can cost points, and not having sex can cost points. Take a moment to guess at your own "cool" score. Think a bit about how it might be affecting how you value yourself—your self-esteem (see Chapter 3). Do well in this game of cool, and adolescence can be a magical time. Do poorly, and it can become a hell like Erica knew. But both winning and losing can have bad and good sides.

If you're a "winner," watch out—you could be heading for a fall. The good side of being rated cool is obvious, with all the preferential treatment you get. Like the commercial says, "It doesn't get any better than this." But that's only a temporary high-school illusion. The game changes radically when you graduate, and you may not make the next cut. Young adults define "cool" very differently than adolescents. This is where the downside happens.

When you're cool in school, your self-esteem can get falsely pumped up, to the point where you can start to think that you're cool for life. You can start to believe you really *are* worth more as a person than those "loser" kids. That's when you become what's technically known as a "jerk." Jerks don't fare well much beyond high school. A few manage to keep that game going for a year or two, but they look really silly past that. So, if you're a cool kid, understand that "cool" is a temporary illusion that will pass shortly. Work on your issues of character (see Chapter 3) if you want long-term "coolness."

Jerks don't fare well much beyond high school.

If your "cool" score puts you in the basement, I have good and bad news for you, as well. The bad news is that, if you're not careful, you can start to believe the crap that the cool kids may brainwash you with about yourself. You can start to tear yourself down because you don't look, talk, or act right. You've probably already learned how pointless it is to try to fake being someone you're not, so give that up if you haven't already. Spend your time finding out, and then being, who you are, not who others tell you to be (see Chapter 3). Like I said, the whole "cool" thing evaporates after high school, anyway. The only good things that kids take with them from adolescence are values, character, and identity, and these things have nothing to do with your "cool score" in school.

In Part Three, we'll talk more about the what-to-do-when questions about peers. For now, if you haven't made the cool kid list, don't despair. The older you get, the less kids care about this stupidity. After high school, this process goes in reverse. Things like caring, loyalty, and individuality (being different and unique) start to become valued. Things like aggression, sarcasm, or caring about being "cool" become stupid. This is one of the very few things that I can promise you. Time is on your side. Just outlast the jerks.

And, speaking of the jerks, watch out for them when it comes to another downside of peers: *the deadly gossip games.*

The Deadly Gossip Games: Where Soap Operas Can Kill

I've always been amazed at how popular soap operas are among some adolescents. Soaps are those syrupy, overacted, daytime TV dramas that show life as it really is. You know, like on *As The Stomach Turns,* where Doctor Charlotte, the ex-priest who had a sex-change operation before becoming a famous genetic scientist, lost her memory following a drunk-driving accident, where she killed Father Charles, the ex-famous, female genetic scientist who also had a sex-change operation before becoming a beloved priest. The episode ends with Doctor Charlotte having a flashback (while single-handedly fighting terrorists aboard a hijacked plane), in which she remembers that Father Charles was actually her clone, who married her stepdaughter, who had been abducted by aliens, who had sex change operations.... Well, you get the picture. TV soaps are like that. They show real life about as accurately as do the peer soap operas.

You can catch the peer soaps in the IMs (instant messages) on the Net and in the BRs (bathrooms) at your school. These are the syrupy, overacted dramas where some kids say and do lots of pointless things that seem designed just to bring attention to themselves. A lot of what happens seems like harmless, stupid stuff that only makes the "actor" look ridiculous. But one vicious part of the "soaps" *literally kills a lot of kids every year, and terribly wounds many others*: It's a bizarre hobby called the "Gossip Game."

The Gossip Game is a lethal pastime played by bored, small-minded kids who have no idea of the pain they inflict on other human beings. These teens might do less damage playing with loaded guns than playing with loaded words. They love to randomly fire off large-caliber words without giving a damn about who they might hit. They use killer words to spread gossip ("Did you hear what his mother did?"), tear somebody down ("Can you believe she wore *that*?"), and, my personal favorite, start fights ("Did you hear what he said about your girlfriend?"). The game might seem funny, until you see the body count this insanity can produce. My community has lost two adolescents in two years (one dead, one badly brain-damaged) to fights that began with rumors in chat rooms and ended with baseball bats on skulls. These mob actions were started by kids who love a game my grandmother used to call "let's you and him fight." Those kids are violence *carriers* (like disease carriers). They're never in fights themselves, but they're the first ones at ringside. In addition to the assaults that we know about, we also wonder how many suicides we don't know about that are triggered by this garbage. Did I mention that teen suicide is up *400 percent*?

The odds are that you'll never see this game result in a death. But the odds also are that you will see kids badly beaten up in the peer soaps—emotionally. And these emotional beatings can be much worse than the physical ones. You stand a good chance of being a target yourself. The non-lethal toll this takes on teenagers is hard to tally, but I see it weekly in my office. Kids are terribly wounded by the garbage that is dished out in these soap operas. The intensity can be incredible, and parents usually never know what goes on.

Kids are terribly wounded by the garbage that is dished out in these soap operas.

Zeke handed me a pile of e-mail copies. "Here," he shrugged, with red-faced embarrassment, "Here's how I ended up drinking that bottle of Nyquil last week. They read kinda' silly now, but they really got to me that night. I don't want to sit here while you read them. Is it OK if I wait outside until you're done?"

"Sure," I nodded, wondering what could be so bad in this ream of adolescent thoughts, all sent between 1 A.M. and 3 A.M. on a Friday night.

Reading the letters was like listening to an episode of the Osbournes—the curse words outnumbered the regular words so much that the messages were hard to understand. While I struggled through the piles of profanity looking for the story, in the corner of my eye, I caught Zeke watching me through the window. That must have been some night.

Finally, pieces of the tale began to emerge. Someone had started an e-mail rumor that Zeke's father was a convicted child molester. The author "considerately" copied Zeke. This mail had gone out to many kids, some of whom dismissed it as ridiculous. But it was too late. Like a vicious mudslide, this filth slowly gathered muck and debris until it took on an unstoppable life of it's own, bent on destroying whoever got caught in its path, innocent or not.

Kids started sending letters saying how they heard that was true, since they knew Zeke's father had been in prison. Other kids started producing names of little girls Zeke's father had "raped and molested." Still other kids claimed that Zeke's dad had approached them for sex. Then the real crazies jumped in, planning how and when they were going to beat up Zeke's father to ". . . teach that f'ng fag pervert to stay away from our sisters" and ". . . use my box cutter to fix that fag freak so that he can't [perform sexually]." One writer noted that she was telling her mom, who was head of the school PTA, and who would ". . . get the word out to all the parents."

Amidst this insanity were Zeke's increasingly upset responses. He slowly loses his cool, first denying, then pleading, then challenging, and finally threatening to kill some of the letter writers. Toward the end, he seems completely out of control, "screaming" his threats in ways that made no sense. The other kids began laughing and taunting him. It was almost too painful to read.

Zeke stood now in plain sight in my window, apparently feeling stupid for spying. After I waved him in, he sat down with a dejected sigh. "So," I tried to joke, "what's the embarrassing part?" He didn't laugh, and what he said made me swear to never joke like that again.

"It's bad enough that every kid I know in the world has copies of that," he said. "But the worst part has to do with my father." Zeke's voice dropped to a mumble. "He was in prison for a year before we moved here." Zeke spoke louder now. "But he's not a child molester—I swear to God! He used to drink a lot, and he got in a bunch of drunk-driving accidents. He was, I mean, he is an alcoholic. But he hasn't had a drink in three years, since prison. He's trying real hard now. And my family was trying to keep that all a secret, in the past, you know? We started over here, and nobody knows, especially my dad's boss. He'll get fired when this gets around." Zeke sat forward and hung his head down.

"I did this to my family. I told one person—my ex-girlfriend Karen. I think she's the girl who started the rumor. When she was my girlfriend, I thought I could trust her with my secrets. I thought we loved each other. When I broke up with her last week, she was really mad. She swore she'd get me back."

Zeke blew out a long breath. "And she did. She got my whole family." He stopped and shook his head. "Actually, I did. That's why I wanted to die that night."

Zeke didn't do this to his family. And neither did Karen, really. We did. In this culture we just love gossip, tearing people down, and fighting. We're junkies for bad news about other people. This is a dark side of all of us that keeps the teen and TV soaps in business. If they didn't have us as an audience, the TV soaps would disappear. If they didn't have us as an audience, the "Gossip Games" would disappear. If those kids trashing Zeke that night had minded their own business, Karen couldn't have hurt Zeke's family like that. It's the *audiences* that give these kinds of peer craziness their power. You can make it happen or you can stop it. You choose. But sometimes it's very hard to make courageous choices.

The bottom line of the dark side of peers (committees and soaps) is that they can seem so powerful at times that they can change you. Like a fascist government, they sometimes threaten you, to make you do and say what they want. They can make you feel that who you are is not good enough. They can distract you from your main teenage task of becoming who you are, of developing your identity.

Remember, being truly independent means being you—not who your parents are *and not who your peers are*. Independent means choosing your own values over those of others, *even if you pay a price*, such as being taunted or left out. That's easy to say, and hard to do late on a Friday night when a great Gossip Game called "Get Zeke" is playing on the Net. Writing in to say that this is cruel and stupid behavior might get you laughed at or shunned. Like they say, freedom ain't cheap. But standing up by writing in will do two things that can make the risks worthwhile. First, you'll let everyone know that you are a straight-up person. That, because you won't trash an easy target, you won't trash them, either. Kids worth caring about will see that as character. Kids who mock that shouldn't make your list.

But, second, and much more importantly, *you'll* know that you are a straight-up person. Taking tough stands like these helps us figure out who we are, what we believe in. You'll be amazed to see how seeing who you are brings you a great gift called self-acceptance, or being cool with yourself. And I can guarantee that you will find that being cool with yourself is a million times better than having jerk kids be cool with you.

So do a gut check. Listen to yourself as you hang out with peers. Think: Are you really being you, saying what you believe, or are you backing off your values and joining the crowd *because they are the crowd*? Are you willing to take a stand on what you see as right, or do you get intimidated by the "cool" people, like so many of us do?

Be honest, now, for the stakes of this game couldn't be higher: It's about *your identity*. If you feel you can be who you are with your peers, congratulations—for finding good friends *and* great identity. If you feel like you're two people, one you show to your peers and a second you keep hidden away, it might be time to stand up for something—like who you are. If not, you could end up apologizing to a shrink. You never want to do that.

If you feel like you're two people, one you show to your peers and a second you keep hidden away, it might be time to stand up for something—like who you are.

Daniel looked like a gangster with a bad diaper rash, waiting to get a tooth drilled. He squirmed, and fidgeted, and bounced all over the couch, very different from the laid-back, swaggering, 15-year-old thug who first visited me the week before. He opened the session with a two-hundred-word, never-ending, non-sentence: "I, uh, well, you know, I um, like, she's not, well, I didn't, well I did, I mean I did, but. . . ." After a big sigh, he finally completed a different sentence. "Damn, I feel like such a smacked ass." Then, whatever this was suddenly became my fault. "And you sat there and never said nothin'," he said accusingly. "You made me look like a jerk."

"OK, Daniel," I laughed, "I give up. You win. I'm guilty as charged. Is the accused allowed to know what crime he committed?"

Daniel looked appalled and puzzled, not sure whether or not I was being honest. "Are you playin' with me, or what? You really don't know?" he asked.

The truth was that I had a theory, but the issue was too explosive to raise with him this early in therapy. So I hung him out to dry. "Sorry, Dan," I said. "I'm really not sure. What are you talking about?"

Seeing Dan's eyes suddenly shoot to my daughter's picture on my desk confirmed my suspicion, but I kept silent. He needed to face up to this on his own. "On the way home last week, my mother told me about you, about how you adopted a black girl, and stuff." He paused again, likely praying that I'd make it easier for him. I didn't, because I couldn't, for his sake . . . I think.

"Don't you remember," he asked, "last week when I was talking about killin' all the Arabs and, and stuff . . . ?" His eyes pleaded with me, begging me to let him off his hook. Finally giving up, he finished his never-ending sentence by apologizing to my floor. "I'm, like, you know, sorry about what I said, you know, when I, like, called them sand-, you know, sand-niggers, and said they were animals, just like real niggers." Now, he looked up to see my face, but only for a second. He went back to his conversation with his sneaks. "I didn't know your daughter was black, so I didn't really mean that, you know? I don't think your daughter's an animal. I was just talkin', you understand? It's just talk. Everybody says that stuff."

A mix of anger, fear, and sadness swept over me as I tried to keep my feelings out of Dan's therapy. I thought of his divorced parents. I pictured his father, with his confederate battle flags on his Pennsylvania pickup truck, telling me how Dan's "bitch" mother deserted the family. I remembered his mother telling me about the years of beatings that finally forced her to run for her life from the marriage. As he sat and squirmed, my anger and fear cooled into the sadness—for Dan. I knew that his blind hatred was not his at all. It was just inherited from his father.

"Daniel," I asked as softly as I could, "Do you believe that 'sand-niggers' and 'real niggers' are animals that should be killed?" His eyes went wide at hearing his own words repeated, as if for the first time. He tried to hold to these insane "values" of his father, his uncle, and his peers—but were they his values, I wondered?

"Well, yeah," he answered with a voice too loud. "They should all be dead, if you really want to know. But your daughter's just a black girl. She's not what we call a nigger, OK?"

Trying unsuccessfully to avoid sarcasm, I said, "Well, thanks, I guess. But what about Sarah's (my daughter's) sister. Is she a nigger? And her birth mother, does she get in the club? How about her cousins? Do they deserve to be killed? Where do you draw your lines, Dan?"

I waited for him to get up and storm out of the office. Instead, he sat and looked like he was finally hearing something he very much needed to hear, and yet hated to hear. After silent minutes, he spoke again, but with a voice I didn't recognize. This one was quiet, subdued, and thoughtful. "I don't know," he sighed, "I don't know anymore. When my friends and I talk that 'kill all the niggers' talk. I always feel, like, a little sick. I thought it was because I'm a stupid wimp."

> "Dan," I said, "maybe your nausea is smart. Maybe that's your stomach's way of telling you that what you're hearing is a poison, at least for you. Maybe that hate stuff is not who you are?" He looked at me as if I had two heads. "Daniel," I said, "we need to chat a bit about a thing called identity. . . ."

So be sure to sort out the good from the bad when it comes to peer influence. The good can be wonderful, and the bad can be toxic. Both can influence your identity. See the attitudes and values of your peers as just another station on your radio of life, and you'll be OK. *You* pick from what you hear, to be sure it fits who you are. Don't let the "music" tell you who you are.

As far as peers go, you've now seen the good and the bad. What did we miss? Oh, yeah, the . . .

Peers: The In-Between

Here are a few other facts, neither good nor bad, about your friends that will help you understand what you may see going on around you. First, here are a few more boy/girl differences with peers. Girls tend to have larger groups of friends, and be more open, and share their feelings. Most girls are most happy to simply talk and share for hours. Boys tend to have fewer friends, and are *sloooowwww* to share their emotions. Males tend to do things together, like sports, music, or other activities, as their way of sharing and showing caring for each other (without actually *saying* that they care, God forbid!).

Second, peer influence gets smaller as you get taller. The older they get, kids are much less influenced by the attitudes and values of their peers. The high point for peer *pressure* is in middle school. However, your *closeness* with friends becomes much greater as you age through adolescence. By 11th or 12th grade, friends become more special, less numerous, and more tolerant of each other's differences. Jocks can hang out with smart kids, who can hang out with skaters,

By 11th or 12th grade, friends become more special, less numerous, and more tolerant of each other's differences.

who can hang out with musicians, and so on, without getting caught up in the "we're better than you" nonsense. This can be a great time to have a few really close friends.

Finally, in case you haven't noticed, kids change a lot through their teen years. Who you were at 11 will not be who you'll be at 18. Holding onto your friends can get tough, particularly because they're all changing, too. The odds of everyone changing in ways that will always keep them tight are pretty remote. Picture dropping 10 "bouncy balls" from a roof and expecting them to all stay together, and you get the idea. When circles of friends start to break up, it can be a sad time. It's hard to accept that things just aren't what they used to be between good friends, kids who thought they'd be buddies forever.

Mandy looked great. Her face was smiling and relaxed, wonderfully different from the struggling girl I'd last seen two years prior. Back home after her first year at college, she started to list all the reasons why she hadn't come to my office, before she got to why she had. "School is not the problem this time. I'm doing great. I just love it. And I'm not depressed at all anymore. Plus, I'm getting along great with my parents. So, compared to before, I'm, TAA-DAA, Supergirl." She laughed at hearing herself use her old fantasy nickname, but then her smile slowly disappeared.

"My problem is with the only thing I had going for me when I used to see you—my friends. Since I've been home, it's, like, really strange with us. I don't mean to sound like I'm so much better than they are, you know, because I know I'm not. It's just that we're so different now. We all seem to be moving in different directions, and seem to like different things.

"Susan's into politics, big time. That's great for her, but after three weeks of hanging out, I'm, like, sick of hearing about it. Franny still mostly parties. It's like she's stuck at 16, or something. That's gotten old for me. And I know I'm different, too. I'm all about becoming a doctor now. It's all I can think about. I probably bore them like they bore me.

"Now it feels so bad when we're together, like it's a funeral, or something. We don't laugh and get silly like we used to. It's like, what we had, died, but no one wants to admit it, and we keep hanging out. I can't wait until school starts in the fall to get back to my new life, and my new friends. But I feel like I'm walking out on my family. It feels very weird. And very sad."

Mandy was feeling more than sad. She was grieving that thing we lose as we grow, mature, and change: *We lose what used to be*, both in ourselves and in our peers. Some of us grow very close to friends as we struggle together through adolescence. It's kind of like soldiers who are in the army together. Those experiences make people very tight, as they survive bad times and enjoy great times together.

But, after that shared experience ends, kids move on to new things, with new people, who become new friends. Sometimes, the old friends just don't "click" anymore. Sometimes, you realize that, if you just met this old friend today, you'd probably not form a friendship because you're so different from each other now. Yet it seems so wrong to break away. Like Mandy said, it feels very sad.

If at all possible, try to keep those old buddies. Old friends are rare and wonderful, to be treasured and held onto through life. The good news is that, as an adult, most of your changes will be behind you, and lifelong friendships become easier to keep. The bad news is that you're changing so much through these adolescent years that most of your friendships won't survive.

Change is an unavoidable part of life. People who fight change end up being run over by it. So, as you grow, hold onto whoever you can, learn to let the others go, *but be sure you continue to grow*. Some kids hold on too long, and end up trying to keep 12th grade going on forever with partying, ducking college, and avoiding real jobs and real responsibility. These "endless summer" kids end up stuck for years, falling further and further behind in the game of life, until one day they wake up on their 30th birthday, still living in their parents' home.

Be sad and grieve the losses, but then get ready for the excitement of the new adventure that is before you.

You don't want to be blowing out 30 candles in your mommy's kitchen. Accept changes as they roll through your life. Be sad and grieve the losses, but then get ready for the excitement of the new adventure that is before you. As they say, when one door closes, another opens. But you have to be willing to close a door before you get to open a new one.

And speaking of closing doors, we're finished talking about your peers for now. In Part Three, we'll have some suggestions about how to handle specific situations involving friends. But now, it's time to move on to that final part of your world that shapes who you are, and who you will become. It's that building of burdens, that palace of pain, that address of agony, that monster of misery that causes my son to wake up every Monday morning screaming, "DAD—PLEASE, PLEASE, *PLEASE* TELL ME IT'S SUNDAY!!!"

YOUR SCHOOL

What It Was, Shouldn't Be, Isn't, and Is

"Parents forget what it's really like to go to middle school and high school. If they really remembered, they'd be a lot nicer when kids mess up."—Reynaldo, age 14

Paul was ranting about school, and about all the teachers who ". . . had it in for him." He was very ticked off. I mostly liked Paul a lot. He was very smart and very funny, constantly pointing out weird things about the world around him, like asking, "Why do they call it 'raw' sewage—do you know anybody who cooks it?" But he also made me nervous. At 15, he was big, loud, and angry at all adults. He'd study me with half-closed, almost sneering eyes whenever I spoke, as if waiting for me to make some mistake, to say one stupid thing, and he'd get up and walk out on me, muttering how worthless I was. I always felt that I was on thin ice with him, and that, sooner or later, he would figure out how worthless I was. It was just a matter of time.

When I realized that all of this was going through my head, I also realized that Paul reminded me of Martin Dienna, one of my high-school bullies. I was always terrified of Martin deciding that I was not cool on a particular day, an event that usually resulted in my head bouncing off a locker. Now here I was, 35 years later, afraid of Paul thinking that I was not cool. I had mixed those two guys up in my head. Feeling better that I had figured this out, I tuned back into Paul's rant.

". . . and then that bitch, Mrs. Monroe, she flunks me on the final. THAT BITCH FLUNKED ME! All for cheating on one lousy, stupid question. Kids cheat all the freakin' time! So I got in her face and told her that," Paul said proudly. Then he used a high-pitched, mocking voice (just like Martin used to): "'Noooo dice,' she says. 'The fact that others might cheat does not justify you cheating.'

"So I said, 'BUULLLSSHHHIITTTT' right in her face. I wasn't going to say that, but she deserved it. It's her fault for being such a bitch, you know?" Paul's voice dropped a bit. "That's how I ended up suspended. It's all her fault for flunking me, and then pissing me off. But it's worth it. I got her good."

Martin, I mean, Paul, paused here, expecting me to agree with him. His sneering face told me that's what I was supposed to do, or else. "Or else what?" I thought to myself. "I guess I better find out."

I held his gaze firmly. "Paul," I said quietly, "for weeks now, you've been telling me how this parent does that to you, and how that teacher does this to you, and how everything is everybody else's fault. Man, what's *your* fault?"

His eyes got narrower. "What's that supposed to mean?" he snarled.

I went for broke. "That 'bitch' didn't flunk you. You flunked you. She might be a bitch, but you made her 'bitch' job a lot easier by cheating, and then cursing at her just because you were mad that you got caught. That's on you, ace; don't hang that on her. You do this all the time, you know, talking about school like it's a Turkish prison or something. You don't get it. You don't see school for what it is. You've made it into some kind of grudge match, a blood game between you and those teachers. You think you 'got' her by cursing? All you 'got' is your third suspension and summer school. Do you really think that while you're there sweating away in July, that 'bitch' will even remember that you disrespected her? While she's sitting on some beach somewhere on vacation? Who got who here? You didn't get her. And she didn't get you. You—got—you. Get it?"

He didn't even blink an eye for 30 seconds. "Man," I thought as I waited for him to storm out, "he must be Martin's son or something." Finally, Paul's ice stare started to melt. "Ok," he said, "maybe I see what you're saying. Maybe I try to hurt all these people, and I only hurt me." He sat and thought for a minute. Then, in a challenging voice, he asked, "How come nobody ever said that to me before?"

I laughed. "People probably have, in softer ways that you didn't hear. It's scary to get in some folks' faces. For instance, when I was in school, there was this guy named Martin Dienna. . . ."

School is the last part of your world that has a huge role in shaping who you are becoming. It's another one of those "forest-for-the-trees" things that's so close to you it's hard to see the power it has in your life. You don't think about school as a "shaping influence" in your life. You just go there—seven hours a day, five days a week, nine months a year, for *thirteen years*. You do more school than any other part of your life, so you need to understand what it is and what it isn't, what's good about it and what's bad, and how it reaches into your head and messes with your identity.

Your School Is Only A Reflection of You

Paul couldn't understand what school was all about, and that was costing him, big time. What he didn't get, and what so many others don't get, is that school is like everything else in life—*it will become only what you make of it.* Get involved, and you can make it a much better place for yourself. Sit back and invest nothing, and that's exactly what you'll get in return.

The "love it" and "hate it" kids are easily identified by the time of day they get home.

In that way, school becomes as many things as there are kids who go there, because each person has his or her own view, level of involvement, and experience. For some, it's a wonderful, exciting, and challenging adventure, a place to build new skills, achieve thrilling successes, and build great friendships. For others, it's a jail—boring, insulting, and controlling—a place to learn nothing, to find only failure and isolation, until they finally escape. The "love it" and "hate it" kids are easily identified, by the time of day that they get home.

The "I like school" types (there are more of those than you might think) are all kids who get involved at school in some way beyond stumbling in at 8, and clocking out at 3. Bands, plays, student government, sports, community-service programs—these "silly" activities help make school a place where you feel like you belong, and where it seems the place belongs to you. A good antidote to hating school is joining activities.

But you should join for a bunch of other reasons, as well. You will find that these activities are at *least* as important in helping you figure out who you are as anything that goes on in a class. How?

In activities, you'll find yourself growing in ways that can't happen in a classroom. You'll be in new roles (like being a leader), trying out new ideas (like working together), and meeting new people. These "new" people may be the same folks you see from 8 to 3, but they're usually very different after 3 P.M. at school. Why?

Do you remember the first time you were in your elementary school at night? Can you recall how strange and exciting it was, how everything and everyone was so different from the daytime? The same thing happens in after-school activities. You'll see sides of kids and teachers that you never knew existed, and you'll learn things that you otherwise wouldn't know when everyone goes home at 3 P.M. Like the fact that Mr. Neveryells, the shy shop teacher, is an ex-marine. Or that Ms. Mumbles, the mealy mouthed math teacher, used to sing in Broadway shows. Or that Mr. Chesthair, the huge, intimidating gym teacher, is actually a nice, mild-mannered guy who loves stupid jokes and snuggling his four-year-old daughter.

Kids are also different after 3 P.M. at school. You might find out that Frank, the football phenom, loves tutoring little kids more than he loves to play football. Or that Connie, the class clown, becomes painfully shy and withdrawn when she's with only one other person.

As a boy, you might suddenly find that heavy-hipped Heather is the most beautiful girl you've ever known, once you get to really know her. As a girl, you could find that Nick the nerd is so thoughtful and caring that he suddenly doesn't look nerdy anymore—in fact, he looks kind of cute. Weird things happen after 3 P.M. at school.

The things you miss by catching the first bus home can teach you a lot about people, life, and your own possibilities. Hearing a teacher who was born in poverty talk about her struggle to go to college can make you think about trying that yourself, when you thought it was impossible. Hearing the big, tough coach talk about hating to fight can make you think that it's OK not to be a fighter. Hearing the senior talk about how she finally made it through chemistry can make you think that you can survive that class, as well.

Weird things happen after 3 P.M. at school. Kids and teachers put down the masks they wear during the day, and suddenly you can see the more complex parts of people, and you learn that they are usually not what you first thought. You hear about their triumphs and their failures, their shining moments and their regrets, what worked for them in life, and what didn't. So who cares about all that?

Your evolving teenage brain cares about all that (see Chapter 1). All that new wiring is begging you to learn all you can about all you can, to open yourself up, to see as much as possible, to help you learn who you are, who you are not, and what you might become in life. From your brain's point of view, your adolescent years are best spent hanging out with all kinds of people in all kinds of places in the world.

But you won't find these folks smoking in your basement. You have to take some risks, get outside, and try new things. So, if you haven't seen the inside of your school after 3 P.M., check it out—join something. You'll find that the serious learning is *not* all in the classroom, because school probably isn't what you think it is. In fact, adolescence may not be what you think it is, either. In fact, both teenagers *and* middle school/high school are fairly recent inventions. A quick history lesson will help you to get this, and then to understand what you see going on in your school.

WHAT SCHOOL WAS

Many of the school problems you deal with every day exist because of how the definition of middle school and high school changed over the past few decades. Up until 1940, what you call "graduating from high school" was about as common as getting a master's degree is today (doing six years of college). Most kids didn't do it. Very few families had the money to allow a 13-year-old child not to work, and to go to school instead. Public high schools were more like private academies for rich, smart kids who liked school and really wanted to be there. And teenagers, as we know them today, really didn't exist. After leaving elementary school, most kids simply went to terrible jobs, where they worked for 12 hours a day, six days a week. In the "good old days," there was no time for teens to be teens.

After World War II, life changed a lot. Money was easier to make, and more and more families could afford to allow their kids to go to school. Suddenly, everyone started thinking that *all* kids should go to high school, that this was a right of being an American child. Laws were passed that required it be offered to (not forced on) all kids. Now the kid that *didn't* go to school was looked at as being weird. It was expected that everyone would go to high school—that is, everyone who really wanted to. Gangsters who made trouble and kids who simply couldn't do the work were kicked out. This left classrooms still mostly filled with kids who really wanted to be there.

These school changes also created a brand new group of people called "teenagers," old children/young adults who now stayed in school until they were 18 years old. Adolescents started to develop their own culture, apart from the adults and the younger children, to include new clothes, music, speech, values, and so on. The adults started to think these teenagers were disrespectful and nuts. And the kids thought that the adults were controlling and crazy. Sound familiar? And remember, this was around *1950.*

Many kids in school in those days were not given the subjects that you're forced to take (math, science, and literature). It was decided that lots of kids were just not cut out to handle those kinds of subjects. They were picked for job training, instead. The boys could be plumbers, carpenters, electricians—whatever they chose. Girls pretty much had three options: typing, typing more, and typing faster. These kids were not expected to learn the other courses that were called the "academic" classes. And, again, kids who didn't want to be in school acted up and got thrown out. Bang-zoom. So school was still pretty much a place for kids who really wanted to be there.

In the 1960s and 1970s, another huge thing occurred that completely changed what middle school and high school were, and how they are today. It was decided that *all kids*—smart kids, limited kids, gangsters, job-trained kids, kids with learning problems—*all kids* should get the same education, in the same school, and usually in the same classroom, *whether or not they wanted to be there.* Laws were passed that made it nearly impossible to get even a violent kid removed from public school.

This change made teaching very different from what it used to be. Teachers were now confronted with trying to teach kids who *didn't* want to be in school (who had all kinds of problems that were never before seen in classrooms), while trying to keep the gangsters from hurting anyone. That was a tough trick. This was not the job teachers had become teachers to do. It might be an impossible job for anybody.

Predictably, things gradually fell apart in many schools. When they could, families fled to the suburbs, to recreate the old "private academy"-type public schools, which had fewer problems and more money. This left the folks with less money and more problems in the cities. Ignorant politicians love to say that troubled urban (city) schools fail because of lazy teachers and lazier kids. They love to point to successful, wealthy, suburban schools, saying, "If this school can succeed, then so can the city school." Of course, they never mention all of the terrible problems that only the urban schools must deal with, like poverty, disease, crime, and overwhelmed parents. Give me four aces every hand, and I can win at poker, too.

But those snooty politicians are getting their due. Some of the problems that used to be mostly confined to city schools are now showing up in some suburban schools; namely, sex, drugs, and poor test scores. The suburban schools are just now finding out what the city schools learned years ago: These problems are so difficult to solve that just being in a particular school can't do it.

Why the history lesson? The answer is because you are part of that history, and that history shapes part of who you are. Whether city or suburban, private or public, your school is dealing with difficult problems never before seen. Middle schools and high schools are not what they used to be, and neither are the kids who go there.

NO MORE PENCILS, NO MORE BOOKS, NO MORE TEACHERS . . . METAL DETECTORS?

In my day (and, likely, your parents' day), school was a safer, saner world in most ways. It used to be a more secure place, where kids could escape from the craziness of the culture. Those days are history. Adults did not have to deal with the out-of-control world (see Chapters 5, 7, and 8) that now reaches into your school life. For many kids, school can be a very tough place. In surveys of suburban and city students, most say that they could get a loaded handgun into school within hours. Most say that drugs are dealt in their building every day, almost openly. Most say that gay students are ridiculed and threatened, completely openly. Most say that minority students (be they African-American, white, Hispanic, Asian, Native American, Middle-Eastern, and so on) are frequently harassed and threatened by whatever majority happens to rule. School gangs, once seen only in old movies, are back with a vengeance in some areas.

School gangs, once seen only in old movies, are back with a vengeance in some areas.

In response, many schools are fighting back with metal detectors, drug-sniffing dogs, undercover narcotics agents, armed guards, and random searches. The situation has sometimes become bizarre. Last year, one South Dakota principal twice called surprise "lockdowns," where all of the students were forced to stand at their desks, while federal and local cops checked them out with drug-sniffing dogs. The police dogs made some of the students cry, which is understandable, because these kids were *four years old.* If that's not strange enough, the U. S. Supreme Court now allows schools to require drug testing for *all* kids in *all* after-school activities. In today's schools, before you can sing in a choir, you might have to pee in a cup.

Ironically, many American schools have become dangerous as the result of another killer found in the classroom that no metal detector can flag, one that nobody talks about, and one that hardly anyone believes is a bad thing. It's another deadly force called *academic competition.*

Naomi had the same "game" face I've seen on those Olympic swimmers on TV, just before the final races: exhausted, unsmiling, intense, and nervous. She even had that jaw-muscle-twitching thing.

"This is a complete waste of time," Naomi announced in a rapid-fire voice. "It's ridiculous and unfair that my parents are making me come here. I'd just refuse, except that my school also says I have to see you as a condition of my going back. All of this, just because I got a little emotional one day?" Naomi sat forward to take control. "Exactly how many times do I have to come here? Do you know how much time this takes up? Do you know how much [school]work I'm missing because of this nonsense? Everybody's yelling that I don't get enough sleep. Well, this waste is only going to make me have to stay up that much later. Do you think that putting this 'counseling' pressure on me is going to help me stay calm?"

Naomi's angry eyes slowly filled with tears, which only made her angrier. She tried whisking them away as fast as she could, hoping that I wouldn't see them, and that she wouldn't feel them. She could remove the tears. She couldn't remove the feelings. She lost control and began to say exactly all the things she didn't want to say—but so desperately needed to say.

"DO YOU KNOW WHAT IT TAKES TO BE NUMBER ONE [her academic rank] IN MY SCHOOL?" she yelled. "NOBODY KNOWS. DO YOU KNOW THAT KIDS DO THINGS TO TRY TO SCREW YOU, TO TAKE YOUR RANKING? TODAY, IN THE LIBRARY, I FOUND THAT ONE OF MY HONOR SOCIETY 'FRIENDS' RIPPED OUT THE PAGES I NEEDED IN A REFERENCE BOOK. WANT TO KNOW WHAT THE TEACHER SAID WHEN I TOLD HIM? HE SAID, 'TOO BAD. QUIT WHINING LIKE A BABY, AND SOLVE THE PROBLEM. IF YOU CAN'T TAKE THE HEAT, THEN MAYBE YOU SHOULDN'T PRETEND TO BE NUMBER ONE.'"

She was crying fully now. Her tears overwhelmed her need to hide them, and they dropped freely from behind her glasses. When she finally removed her glasses to wipe her eyes, I was struck with how she looked like a football player taking off his helmet after losing a big game: dejected, sad, exhausted. She spoke now very quietly, but with words that knotted my stomach: "The pressure is constant, and it's killing. I fall asleep thinking about school, and I wake up thinking about school. In the morning, my whole body aches, like I've been working all night in my sleep. My stomach hurts almost every day. I feel like I'm driving this car at 160 miles per hour, and if I don't slow down, I'll crash. But if I do slow down, I'll still crash. I feel like if I keep doing this, I'll die. And if I don't, I'll die." She looked up at me, no longer angry but pleading: "Please don't tell me that I have to stop. Can't you see that I can't stop? If I let up for one minute, my competitors will rip me to shreds. I'll never catch up. You're a doctor. You must know what I'm talking about. You had to have been ranked high when you where in school, right?" She looked to me for understanding. But she needed to understand something else.

"Naomi," I offered apologetically, "If I had to guess at my high-school ranking, it probably would have been 200 in a class of 1500. I got some honors, but I never really studied. In college, I ended up on academic probation after my first semester. My 'ranking' at that time was in the parking lot on my way home. Yes, I did eventually become a doctor, and yes, that was hard to do, and, yes, it did require years of intense study. But Naomi, please listen to this next part very closely. When I finally got serious about school, the only person I was competing against was me. The only person I was trying to impress was me. I didn't give a damn about my ranking against others. I only wanted to become a shrink. That's all I was in the game for. So what are you in your game for?"

Naomi sat and thought deeply. "I have no idea," she finally answered. "I guess this game [of being number one] became like an obsession. I guess I'm trying to impress everybody—my parents, my teachers, my friends—most of all, maybe the kids who are not my friends, the ones who hate me. I think it's something like that." She paused as her voice got tight, and her eyes filled again: "I just don't know if I can stop."

Naomi would have been much smarter (and happier) about school if she had learned what you're about to learn. Before you tackle serious school (middle/high school) you should know what school shouldn't be, what school isn't, and what school is. Then, maybe, you can make it what you want. Don't allow it to consume you like it did Naomi.

WHAT SCHOOL SHOULDN'T BE

Before we can talk about what school really is, we need to talk about how strange school can become for you if you're not careful. The strangest thing about these strange things is that they are as often caused by crazy parents as by crazy kids.

School Shouldn't Be the Super Bowl

But for too many kids like Naomi, it's a killer pressure cooker. These kids can be chewed to pieces trying to play this game [academic excellence] for all the wrong reasons and for all the wrong people. Have I mentioned how important identity is to feeling cool with yourself, that it's critical that you be who you are? The academic "Super Bowl" is a great example.

If you stay up studying until 1 A.M. every night because you truly love that stuff, if you thrive on that level of performing, if that's who you are (your identity), then that's great for you. You will love the game of school, and like who you are. You will compete with yourself, pushing yourself just to see what your limits are, just for *you*. That kind of pushing will only make you stronger and happier.

If, like Naomi, you're pushing yourself to impress the crowd, as a way of getting approval from others, that sucks for you. You will hate the game of school, and despise who you are. You will compete against others just to see who's "better," just to show *them*. That kind of pushing will only make you weaker and sadder.

The key is *balance*. For most kids, the ideal view is to always push yourself to always exceed your past performance, but never to the point where you become exhausted and crazy. You want to be "stretching and reaching" by working a little harder every semester as you progress through middle and high school, so that, by senior year, you're in shape to take on your next challenge (college, career, military, whatever). By the way, if you're slacking and thinking, "*Hey, I don't have to do well in school. I'm just going into the military or into a job, not to college,*" I have a flash for you. Unless Mickey Dees (McDonalds) is your life's ambition, you will need *exactly* those skills and disciplines of high school study to succeed, whether as an Army corporal or a union carpenter.

School Shouldn't Be Jail

". . . or prison," Monica nodded. "Ever since that stupid kid brought his father's gun into homeroom, school looks just like those prison movies. The first day we had the metal detectors going, it was weird. I got creeped watching everyone line up and empty their pockets, like we were going to jail, or something. Some of the boys were laughing and playin' around, you know, but they stopped smiling when the guards came. They had these big guards with clubs, walking around, pushing kids into line, and pulling out kids who weren't cooperating, and putting them in this, like, dog pen, or something. The boys stopped smiling then. They got that look, you know, like, scary? Like you see on prisoners' faces.

"When we got inside, it was real tense there, too. Everybody was angry and snappy, you know, feeling like we were all getting pushed around because of what one jerk did, bringing that gun to school. It felt like prejudice, you know? Like, just because we're teenagers, we must be dangerous, and can't be trusted.

"Since that first day, it's gotten weirder and weirder. Kids who never used to act bad have started acting all tough, and shoving other kids around. More kids seem to get in teachers' faces, you know, like they're the enemy now. We've had a lot more fights than ever before. I used to like school a lot, but now my stomach hurts every morning when I get near my school. It feels sad. And unfair! Why are we all getting punished? Don't they remember that it was us kids who turned in the jerk with the gun? If we didn't say anything, the teachers never would have known. Some kids say they're sorry they turned that kid in. Some say they wouldn't do it again. Some have started sneaking stuff in just 'cause it's a challenge, you know, like some crazy game. Before, if you brought in a knife, or whatever, it would be like, 'so what?' Now, it's like 'Wow, you're cool. You got that past the guards."

Monica sat for a minute, and then stole the thought right out of my head. "I think school is more dangerous since they started using metal detectors and stopped trusting us."

A lot of schools like Monica's are starting to look like jails. This is bad news, because nobody learns much in prison except how to become bad news. Once you start to treat people like dangerous animals, they start to feel and act like dangerous animals. Some parents argue that they have to turn schools into sort-of-prisons because kids are so much crazier than they used to be—*but are they*? In Chapter 5, we talked about how, in most ways, most kids are much *less* violent than before. Yet everyone (kids included) says that students are much *more* violent than before. So what created this myth?

Three things: First, the world around kids is much crazier than ever before (Chapters 5, 6, and 7). This helps the very few kids who do very crazy things to get a lot more dramatic (like with drugs and disrespect) than in the old days.

Second, we now force kids to stay in school who don't want to be there, who never used to be there, and who will do whatever they please while they're there. In many schools, there are "gangsters" who run wild, and there's little anyone can do about it. The law says that, short of their seriously assaulting someone, they have to be allowed to stay in school. If they want to be nasty, the teachers and other kids pretty much have to put up with it. In most states, it's nearly impossible to get a nasty kid expelled, and suspensions and detentions are jokes for hard-case kids. Sure, they eventually are moved to alternative schools, but in the months or years required to do that, these few thugs can change the climate of an entire school, making the sane 99.9 percent of the student body feel as if the whole school is out of control.

In most states, it's nearly impossible to get a nasty kid expelled, and suspensions and detentions are jokes for hard-case kids.

These first two changes bring new problems into our schools that used to stay out on the streets, and it keeps them locked in until 2 P.M.—drugs and disrespect. But drugs and disrespect are *not* dangerous weapons; they are dangerous *values.* Metal detectors can't fix dangerous values. In fact, they make them worse. They *increase* the values problem by making more kids want to do more dumb things, to rebel against unfair treatment (metal detectors, locker searches, drug testing, drug-sniffing dogs, and more) coming from that unfair myth about school violence.

And what's the third thing that keeps the school violence myth alive? Your TV set.

TV News Will Never Confuse You with the Facts

Television "news" is a powerful force in keeping the school violence myth alive. These days, whenever one kid (out of millions) does one crazy thing at one sane school, the TV talking heads go wild, making it sound like all kids are homicidal maniacs. This gets everyone believing that all kids are killers, and that we need these prison-type controls in all of our schools. What the talking heads don't tell you is that school shootings are like airplane crashes: They're horrors when they happen, *but they hardly ever happen.* Flying is *still* the safest way to travel, and kids are *still* safer in school than anywhere else (a statistical fact). Yet, the metal-detector rage marches on, even though it will never stop a suicide assault. The cops say that there is no way to defend a *police station* against a well-planned suicide attack, let alone a school.

This pointless prison approach is worse than pointless. As Monica said, it gets students feeling nasty and surly, which encourages many of them to act out by disrespecting teachers, other kids, and even themselves (by acting stupid or doing drugs). Some research says that these types of "safety measures" may *increase* violence, not reduce it.

This is what's called a *self-fulfilling prophecy*, meaning that we make happen what we *think* is going to happen, by believing rumors and myths. Have you heard of Columbine, that Colorado high school where two teenagers killed a bunch of people? Kids say that they hear Columbine mentioned a lot.

Have you heard of New Bedford, that Massachusetts school where kids planned to triple the Columbine body count? No? That's because a teenager stopped that massacre before it began, by ratting-out what the crazy kids were planning. But since that story was about a responsible kid doing the right thing, nobody remembers that one, or the thousands of similar stories about kids doing the right thing. Those stories are not interesting enough for the TV talking heads to spend time on. The talking heads get ratings only by yelling about how kids are so violent—even if it's not true.

Character Is the Best Violence Detector

Those folks in New Bedford were not saved by metal detectors or firepower. They were saved by "values power," by the morals of one kid who had the strength of character to stop the plot. My cop friends tell me that "values power" outguns firepower every time. They say that neighborhoods (or schools) where people care about each other are much safer than heavily armed communities where nobody gives a damn.

But giving a damn about others is not easy work. Having a school where the kids are respected for being responsible (instead of harassed for being hurtful) requires heavy dues. You have to pay for your freedom by getting involved, and putting yourself on the line. The quickest way to have cops and drug-sniffing dogs roaming your school is to sit back and let the crazies take over. *Allowing* drug dealers, gangsters, and vandals to do their business is the same as *approving* of them. If a community can't take care of itself, the cops are sent in to take over. Allowing craziness to go on in your school is inviting adults to take over your world and treat you like a prisoner.

I'm not suggesting that you openly confront drug dealers, bullies, or gangsters. I am suggesting that you do whatever you can to take a stand. That might be telling a dealer friend that it's time to retire. Or starting a student mediation program to stop bullying.

It might even be secretly turning a gangster in to the principal. Is that ratting-out a kid? Yep! Is that betraying a peer? Absolutely. That thought makes lots of kids pause, feeling weird about being disloyal and "narcing" on another kid. But being loyal to criminals is exactly how a neighborhood gets cops in its business. Being loyal to drug dealers in your school helps those "law and order" adults get what they want: to see you guard frisked, dog sniffed, and drug tested every morning at school.

Do nothing, and you become part of the insanity.

Deciding what to do about these things is a very tough call that you must make, whether you want to or not. Do nothing, and you become part of the insanity. Do something, and you take on the risk of being seen as uncool, or worse. The price of respect is high. It's called responsibility. If you don't want your school to be policed, then you must police your school. This is another one of those situations where growing up forces you to take a stand. That's just the way it is.

Now that you know what school shouldn't be, what do you suppose it isn't?

WHAT SCHOOL ISN'T

It's so much easier to talk about what school is *not* than what it *is*. That's because it is not what so many people think it is. The myths

"WHY IS IT IMPORTANT FOR TODAY'S KIDS TO LEARN ALGEBRA? BECAUSE I HAD TO LEARN THIS JUNK IN SCHOOL AND NOW IT'S YOUR TURN, THAT'S WHY!"

about school cause lots of problems for lots of kids, by giving them false expectations that soar hopefully in September, only to crash bitterly in June. When school turns out to not be what they expected, too many kids turn off their brains. And that's when too many parents turn into cops. So know, first, what school is not.

It's Not Relevant

School is definitely not relevant (useful), at least not in the way that parents seem to think it is. Most of the subjects you learn in high school you'll never use as a grown up. If you become a physician, you will need all of those science courses, but you'll never use European history. As a carpenter, you'll use geometry every day, but you won't see English Literature on the job site. As an adult, you might end up using some of your high-school courses, but, at best, most of what you learn is forgotten fast and forever after the final exam. If you don't believe me, go find your mom and ask, "Quick: What was the gross national product of Brazil when you were in school?" So when you whine that you'll never diagram a compound sentence in your adult life, you're probably correct.

But before you tear this page out, staple it to the school dropout form, and start running for your parents' signature, keep reading. The relevant fact is that the irrelevant facts you must learn in school do many critical things for you, even though you'll soon forget them. How could that be? It has to do with other things that school is not.

It's Not Easy

Or at least it shouldn't be. If school is easy, it's wasting your time. Like the saying says, the easy path is easy 'cause it's going nowhere. Doing something that is hard to do gives you a wonderful gift, even if you never do that thing again in your life. It gives you *discipline*: the quality that separates the winners and losers of the world.

Whether you're an athlete or an art teacher, discipline is the thing that makes you succeed. What is it? *Discipline is the ability to make yourself do hard, boring things that you hate.* Why would you want to do things that you hate? *Because doing anything you love requires doing some things that you hate.*

Most athletes hate lifting weights, running, and watching films of their mistakes over and over. They love playing their sport. But to play a sport, you must lift weights, run, and watch your mistakes over and over. It's a cost of that game that you have to pay to play. Most art teachers despise writing lesson plans, grading tests, and disciplining students. Yet teaching art requires you to do plans, tests, and discipline. It's a cost of that game that you have to pay to play.

The world is overflowing with incredibly talented people who never get to use their magic. Some are naturally gifted athletes who could play professionally, but who cut *themselves* from their teams by not forcing themselves do the boring work needed to get their talent to grow (like lifting weights and running). Others are naturally gifted teachers who could inspire students, but who also kill their own dreams by not doing the boring schoolwork needed to get a teaching degree.

Bosses (like pro coaches and school principals) know that most of what you learn in school will be useless in the job you want, but they still want good grades *even in stupid, irrelevant courses*. They know that doing boring work well is a test of mental toughness that shows you can handle the rough parts of a job. They know that the kid who blows off his "stupid" social-studies class in school is likely to blow off the boss's "stupid" requests, as well.

School should not be easy, just like boot camp should not be easy. Both places are designed to toughen you, to push you to accomplish things that you never thought you could. Both places should challenge you by making you hurt, sweat, complain, worry, want to quit, resist quitting, and then finally succeed. Growing strong happens only with hard work.

A "nice" boot camp instructor who lets soldiers slide through easily does them no favors. Those soldiers pay a terrible price when they are dropped onto a battlefield and learn that they don't have the skills to survive. Likewise, that "nice" teacher who passes kids for just showing up does them no favors, either. Those kids pay a terrible price in life when they learn that they don't have the skills to survive.

It sounds weird, but the sergeants and teachers who push you the most are usually the ones who care the most.

It sounds weird, but the sergeants and teachers who *push* you the most are usually the ones who *care* the most. Yet, those are the ones who are hated the most. Often in life, you'll find that your best "teachers" (be they instructors, coaches, or parents) are the ones who care enough to confront you and make you miserable at times by challenging you to be the best you can be. It's easy to be the smiling "whatever" teacher. It takes a lot to be the "tough" teacher who gets on your case, and demands that you do your best. *It takes caring enough to be willing to be hated.*

After spending 3 of her 14 years of life taking Spanish courses, Beth was furious when she got her first F on a report card for Spanish. Her problem was that she wasn't quite sure who to be furious with.

"At first, I, like, wanted to scream at my teacher for being a bitch. Mrs. Montoya is a hard teacher. She really expects you to study, and do your homework, and stuff. But then, I started thinking that that's her job, you know? She's supposed to get me to know Spanish. Then I got mad at my old Spanish teacher for not pushing me. I used to think he was so cool and all. He'd let me just do whatever, and give me a B. Now, I guess I'm mostly mad at me. Maybe it's time I, like, stopped yelling at everyone else when it's really up to me whether I learn stuff or not."

"Beth," I asked, "which person do you think cares more about you? Mrs. Montoya, or your old 'whatever' teacher?"

Beth sat and twirled her hair for a minute. She really didn't like her answer. "I guess I'd have to pick Mrs. Montoya, even though she really is mean to me. She takes a ton of crap from the kids in her class, whining and crying and arguing about how unfair she is. A couple kids' parents even went to the principal complaining about her. But she won't change. I guess her job would be a lot easier for her if she was like my old teacher. But then, I'd just waste one more year learning nothing, you know? But she really is a bitch to me."

I offered something that Beth had already thought of: "Beth, is Mrs. Montoya a 'bitch' to you, or to your poor study habits? Isn't there a difference?"

Beth just nodded glumly. She already knew that. Then she made me laugh with her next thought: "Three freakin' years of Spanish, and the only Spanish I know is, 'Yo, no comprendo.' That pretty much means 'I have no idea what you're saying.'"

Like Beth learned about Spanish, there's one final thing that school is not, something that too many kids don't understand until it's too late.

It's Not Personal—Unless You Start It

How many kids do you know who swear that teachers have it in for them, that they became teachers just to make kids' lives miserable? They tell story after story about how some teacher was mean to them for no reason, disrespecting them, and making them flunk. To hear them talk, the teacher walked in on day one, looked around the room, picked their unknown faces out of the crowd, and thought to herself, "Man, I really hate that kid in aisle three. I'm going to make his life a living hell."

The part that they usually leave out of these stories is all the garbage that they pulled *before* the teacher got an attitude—most of which *they don't even remember*.

"Wha, Wha?" Louis whined. "Wha'd I do?" He was responding to my laughter at his story about how his "nutso" teacher "wigged out" on him for putting his head down on his desk in class and sleeping

> while she was speaking. "Why'd she get so upset?" he had asked. "I wasn't bothering her. So I snored a little. She has it in for me." Louis was sure that all adults "had it in" for him, and, up until now, I couldn't seem to get him past that. It was time to get a little radical.
>
> "Louis," I said, "tell me your story again." As he spoke, I slowly lowered my head onto the couch pillow, closed my eyes, and pretended to snore. At first, Louis tried to finish his sentence, as if my sleeping was no big deal. When that didn't work, he got mad, and snarled that "this isn't the same thing."
>
> Finally, he had to smile when I opened one "sleepy" eye to stare at him. "Wha? Wha?" I slobbered, "Were you saying something?"
>
> "OK, OK" he laughed, "I give up. I guess that was pretty dumb, huh?" He thought for a minute, and then said something that wasn't dumb at all. "I don't really think of teachers as being people, you know? With feelings and all? I wasn't thinking that she would see my sleeping as disrespecting her. Maybe I do other things that get her mad that I don't. . . ." My "you got it!" nodding made Louis interrupt himself again: "You could let me finish one sentence, you know. Have a little respect."

I couldn't let him finish his sentence because I was so excited that Louis had "gotten it." He was finally seeing that, almost always, teachers are not looking for trouble, and, almost always, when trouble happens, it's from something that kids start by forgetting that teachers are people—"with feelings and all." They forget that, just like all of us, teachers' feelings can get hurt by acts of disrespect that are not intended as disrespect. Sleeping, talking, laughing, blowing off work, strolling in late—these actions that kids think shouldn't bother a teacher can hurt a lot. Score enough of these hidden disrespect points, and soon you have a teacher who is giving you those "I-really-hate-that-kid" looks. This is another way that school becomes what you make of it.

Are there bad, nasty teachers who start trouble first? Sure. But they're extremely rare. Teachers are like baseball umpires. They can make a bad call, but that doesn't mean they're doing it on purpose. They just make mistakes. If the player gets in the ump's face, screaming and yelling and disrespecting him, is that likely to encourage the ump to be nicer on the next pitch? If a student gets in the teacher's face, screaming and yelling and disrespecting her, is that likely to encourage the teacher to be nicer on the next test?

One of the unfortunate realities of life is that you will have to deal with imperfect umpires, teachers, bosses, sergeants, cops, and, oh yeah, parents. They will all make bad, unfair calls at times, and then you'll have to decide how you want to deal with it. You can't change the first call they make, but how you react to that *first* call can change the *second*. It's all up to you.

Now that you know what school was, shouldn't be, and isn't, it's finally time to look at what it is.

WHAT SCHOOL IS

When you really look closely at it, school is actually a lot of things that most of us would never guess. At least, not until we've been away from it long enough to be able to look back and see it for what it truly is. School truly is a tryout, it's freedom, and it's identity.

School Is a Tryout

One cynical-but-true view sees school as a game to get you into the next game. It's like moving up through the minor baseball leagues. You start off in A league, do well enough to go to the double-A league, work hard to go to triple-A ball, and one day have a shot at the major leagues. Similarly, you do well in school to get into a good college or job-training program, to one day get into a good job—the major leagues. Although school can certainly do that for you, it can, and should, be so much more.

School truly is a tryout, it's freedom, and it's identity.

School Is Freedom

Another view sees school as freedom. Don't laugh. Amazingly, it's true. This has to do with doors. One huge goal in the game of life is to keep your doors open as much as you can, which means to give yourself all the options to do whatever you want, whenever you want. That's called freedom. When you bag school, you close many doors on yourself—you eliminate all kinds of possibilities from your life. If, later in the game of life, you decide you want to do something, you might find that screwing up school will keep you locked out of something that you love. Doing well in school (by learning all that "irrelevant" stuff) can keep all your doors open, so that you have many more and better choices in your life.

School Is Identity

A final way (and the best way) to look at school has to do with your number-one goal in adolescence: figuring out who you are. In Chapter 3, we saw that, to do this identity thing well, you have to be exposed to as many ideas as possible, *even ones that you think are stupid.* To become who you are, you need to first know what all of the possibilities might be. Feeling confused and not knowing who you are as a teenager is OK—as long as you can admit that, and keep your mind open to all the things in the world. It's a bad idea to close yourself off to new ideas in adolescence by deciding that you know who you will be as an adult. Some kids make terrible commitments before they're ready. This can be a major mistake. For Matt, it was more of a "sergeant" mistake.

> Twenty-year-old Matthew looked great in his Army uniform. It seemed to fit him perfectly, as his words from three years prior promised it would. All Matt ever talked about when I knew him back then was joining the military. School was just a waste of his time, until he was old enough to become a soldier. He was positive the military would solve all of his problems. So much so that he used to get mad if I ever challenged him a bit by asking if he was sure he wanted to be a soldier all of his life. He didn't want to talk about it with me. He didn't want to talk about it with himself.
>
> From the neck down, it seemed that the old 17-year-old Matt had been right. He was trim, spotless, and wearing ribbons on his chest from his recent combat experiences. The picture from the neck up was very different. His face looked much older than 20, lined beyond his years. His eyes were strange to me. The old "in-your-face" fire was gone. Instead, these eyes stared back from deep circles, small and sad, even as he smiled weakly as we met at the store.
>
> Using his old greeting he joked, "Yo, Doc, whassup?" But this was not the same voice I remembered. This one sounded as hollow as his eyes looked.

One strange thing about being a psychologist is running into old clients on the street. You want to ask how they are, yet you don't want to make them feel uncomfortable by getting into subjects that are painful. Just asking how things are going can make ex-clients get into subjects they'd prefer to keep to themselves. As soon as I asked Matt how he was, I regretted asking the question. His smile ran away and his eyes flitted around him as if to see who might be listening to his answers, to see if he could tell the truth.

"I'm not good, Doc. All my life I was so sure that being a soldier was for me. I did great in training—boot camp, Airborne, Ranger school—I loved it, and they loved me. Couldn't get enough. Then, when I went into combat . . ., well, it wasn't the same. They keep warning you about that, but you don't really know until you've been there. The training, that was like a game, like when I played football. We'd yell about killing the opposition and all, but it was just a game. This, [being in combat] this was for real. You really end peoples' lives. My buddies [in combat] kept whooping, like we were winning some game. I just felt like we were murdering people. I know they wanted to murder us, too, but I can't make it right in my head, somehow. It didn't feel anything like honor, or courage, or all that stuff I used to talk about. It just felt wrong. . . ."

Matt paused and bit his lip, like he might cry if he didn't. ". . . [T]o me, anyway. I don't mean to knock my buddies. They truly believe in what they're doing, and it seems to be all right for them. I think I became a soldier for all the wrong reasons. That doesn't cut it when you end peoples' lives. You should know what you're about before you promise four years to your country. You should really know what you're about before you pull a trigger."

Some kids are sure that they'll hate science until they're forced to take a biology course.

Matt's first mistake was not in joining the military—it was keeping himself closed off from other ideas, thinking that, as a teenager, he knew enough about himself to make such a commitment. Had his mind been open, he might have discovered that he wanted to be a soldier for all the wrong reasons. He might have found a way to be who he truly was without first going through hell.

School can be a wonderful place to be exposed to a million different ideas about life that can help you learn more about yourself, if you can be open to the possibilities. Some kids are sure that they'll hate science until they're forced to take a biology course. Suddenly, they're amazed to find that they love it, and that they think maybe that's how they'll spend their lives. Others are sure that they'd love teaching, until they get to high school and see that they'd hate being in front of the class. Kids like Matt can get into discussions where they might find that there are ways to serve your country and find adventure other than joining the army (like joining the Peace Corps).

Being forced to take subjects you hate is just as important as taking the ones that you love. Finding out who you are *not* is just as important as finding out who you *are*. Both help you become much smarter about yourself and your choices, and help you not to screw up as much when it comes to making huge life promises like being a soldier, or being a parent.

Like that saying goes, you'll never know what you'll never know—if you never open your mind.

MORE SCHOOL SECRETS THEY NEVER TELL YOU

Many parents can get very weird about school. Some talk as if school is almost like a religion, as if it were something sacred, and that messing up in school is almost a sin. Others forget how hard school is for so many teens, and they get nuts if their kid doesn't get straight As. They act like you only have to show up to get great grades. But there is a secret reason for all this parent craziness.

For many parents, school was their only path out of poverty, their way to give themselves and you a decent life. They see your school as *your* ticket to a good job that will give you a decent life when you get older and when they are gone. For other mothers and fathers who are still struggling, school represents their child's only shot at getting out of a ghetto. So, when you mess up in school, understand that you are messing with your parents' deepest hopes, fears, and love for you. If you were them, you might get a little crazy, too. Unfortunately, too many parents don't explain the reasons for this craziness.

Many parents have forgotten other clues about school, as well, hints that can help you do much better at this game. Here are a few more secrets that my veteran teen advisors thought you should know about. Pass them on.

School Is Tennis

School is very much like tennis. Both school and tennis are not one skill; they are each many skills put together. To play tennis, you have to learn many different skills, and then practice each of them—a lot. Grips, backhand, forehand, volley, footwork, strategy, physical endurance. . . . Tennis is a lot more complicated than it looks.

School is a lot more complicated than it looks, too (and it's a lot harder than parents remember). Like tennis, school requires a lot more than one skill. It's a collection of many different skills that *do not come naturally* to many kids. School requires talents like organizing complex tasks, planning schedules, concentrating, studying, test taking, mental endurance, tolerating boredom, and so on. Each one of these is a separate skill that must be learned, and then practiced like crazy.

Not Everyone Is Good at Tennis

Or at school. Some kids have a terrible time trying to cope with middle school and high school, even though they try like crazy. Although parents are often quick to call kids lazy, some teens just don't have all the brain wiring in place yet to do well in school (see Chapter 1).

If you blow off schoolwork because you're bored, that is not a wiring problem; that's a discipline problem. But if you truly try as hard as you can and still don't do well, don't despair. As with so many other things, time is on your side. As your brain matures, the parts you need for the school skills will one day click into place. In the meantime, DON'T LET THE FRUSTRATION TAKE YOU OUT. Too many kids do too many drugs (particularly weed) as a way of easing the pain of messing up in school. The fact that you might painfully struggle to get Cs, while your friend happily cruises to get As, can become *your strength and her weakness*. Don't believe that? Read on.

You're Running a Marathon, Not a Sprint

School "sprinters" are those smart kids who just show up at school and do well. They never seem to open a book. The marathoners are those kids who go home every night and beat chemistry and composition into their brains, and sometimes still only get Bs. Want to guess who does better in college?

"As I started my freshman year, I was sure that I was going to do great in my first semester of college. I thought that the college should feel lucky to have me. After all, I was a scholarship student with honors from my high school, and I hardly ever cracked a book.

"In those first few weeks at college, I remember making fun of my roommate, Arnold. He was not the brightest bulb in the dormitory, and every day he'd rush off to the library to study, while the rest of us "geniuses" goofed around. We'd laugh and feel sorry for him. He wasn't smart like us.

"Three months later, my first-semester grades arrived early, with a note attached. It said that I needed to schedule an appointment with the Dean of Students to discuss my "future at this college." That note was stapled to a report card showing that Mr. Smart-Guy/Never-Studied/Honors-Student (me) was flunking out of school. I'll never forget standing there in my room, staring in stunned disbelief at my grades, with surprise tears dropping from my eyes. I picked up Arnold's report card, which he had left lying on the desk that we shared. He had made honors. I shivered, as a cold wave of reality washed over me like ice water. I had hit a wall. Being smart was no longer good enough. I had no idea how to do school.

"Arnold walked in, looked at me, and knew exactly what had happened. The "dim bulb" put his hand on my arm and quietly said, "Look, if you want, you can study with me at the library every day. I know a lot of tricks about learning stuff because things don't come easy to me. Maybe they'll help you, too." Then, without intending to be sarcastic, he added, "Even though you're really smart."

The lump in my throat kept me from saying anything. I do recall staring at Arnold, suddenly aware that being smart is like having a shiny, new guitar. It means nothing until you put it to use with your sweat, effort, and pain. Now the "smart" kid asked the "dumb" kid to

> share his wisdom. "Thanks," I finally choked out, "That would be great. I'm, uh, sorry . . . for acting like such a jerk."
>
> "Forget it," Arnold smiled. "I don't mind not being smart. That's the secret of my success. It makes me work hard."
>
> —From the personal journal of Dr. Michael Bradley

Arnold was like a marathon runner with schoolwork. He was not brilliantly fast, but he never quit running. The more schools I went to (bachelor's degree, master's degree, doctoral degree), the more I realized just how smart my "dumb" roommate was. On my first day at each school, I'd be amazed by how brilliant many of my new classmates were. On my last day at each school, I'd be amazed by how many of those brilliant students didn't make it to the finish line. I'd always be graduating with more kids like Arnold. They knew how to get past "The Wall."

Don't Fear "The Wall"

"The Wall" is that subject (often chemistry), year in school (often 7th grade), or type of school (often college), where you can no longer fake it and get through without really studying. Smart kids can pretty much show up at school for many years and get good grades. But, sooner or later, they all hit "The Wall," where they must actually start to study hard, or fail. Lots of smart kids pass without really trying for so long that they fall apart the first time they hit "The Wall." The earlier you reach this problem, the better. My roommate Arnold did great in college because he had hit his wall in high school. He arrived already knowing how to study well, something much more valuable than being smart. This was a tough lesson that Meghan learned, as well. But as Meghan's mom watched her daughter crash into "The Wall," I think it bruised Mom even more than it did Meghan.

> "My daughter Meghan is not a natural math student, and she has to work hard to do well. She was put into an honors math class because she did well on a state test, but she's definitely not your typical honors math student. She's extremely intimidated by the 'math brainiacs' who know the answers in class in a split second. When the teacher asks a question, and those hands go in the air immediately, her anxiety level goes through the roof, and she can't think. She slinks down when the

teacher asks a question, hoping she won't be noticed, because she's sure her answer will be wrong most of the time. Needless to say, math is her least-favorite class.

"We gave her the option (and very much encouraged her) to switch into the 'regular' math class, but she was too embarrassed to admit to her friends that she couldn't handle it (God forbid), so we decided to let her figure it out on her own. She works her tail off after school to stay on track, and she's unbelievably proud when she gets an answer right in class—unlike the other kids who take it for granted. I'm sure she's the hardest worker in the class, but most of the other kids are far superior in terms of their natural math ability. When the assessment test was given a few weeks ago to determine who out of the 35 kids in her class would remain in honors math, and who would be asked to go into the 'regular' class, Meg was very nervous, as you can imagine (way too much pressure for 12-year-old kids). Well, guess who got the second highest grade in the class? Yep, it was Meghan. And it was because of her hard work, not because it was easy for her. That was a huge life lesson for her—one I don't think she'll ever forget."

As long as you don't get too intense with the competition, as long as you are only competing with yourself, don't fear "The Wall."

This is why it's so important to keep yourself challenged in school with *some* courses that force you to study hard, make your head hurt, and keep you up worrying *some* nights. As long as you don't get too intense with the competition, as long as you are only competing with yourself, don't fear "The Wall." It will hurt a bit. *It will not kill you.* And remember where that easy path goes.

Grades Aren't Everything, *They're the Only Thing?*

It would be nice if grades and test scores weren't so important, but they are. School testing is a lot like the U.S. government: They're both very flawed systems, but no one's come up with anything better.

Ideally, grades should only be a tool for seeing what a student's strengths and weaknesses are, to help a teacher work with that kid. When you use grades as anything else, bad things happen. Recently, politicians have started to use grades and test scores as ways of deciding things, like which schools get closed, which teachers get bonuses, and which ones get fired. It's a simple and lousy way to make those types of decisions, one that is now used in most of the states in this nation. Using test scores alone does not take into account all of the many things that affect why some kids do well on some tests, and others do badly. But adults often like to pretend that things are simple when they're complicated—especially when they're very complicated. And trying to help kids learn is a very complicated business.

With that extreme focus on student scores, school has become a kind of sport where the goal is to beat out everyone else with your scores. Your state tries to beat other states, your district tries to beat other districts, your school tries to beat other schools, and you try to beat the kid sitting in front of you. Most schools even keep lists showing how you rank against your peers, as if kids are baseball teams. As a result, your grades and test scores have become the main focus of your school experience, and you pay a high price for that. How?

Most experts say that school should be a place where you learn about how to think well, and think about how to learn well. While doing that, schools should also teach you some information that will help you deal with the world. Most experts don't think that school should only be a place where you memorize a bunch of facts, many of which you don't understand, and most of which you couldn't care less about. Yet for kids (and schools) to do well on tests, teachers must spend their time *teaching students how to do well on tests*, instead of teaching how to do well in life.

Teachers used to tell a joke about having taught some incredibly important idea to a class, only to have a kid raise his hand and ask, "Is that going to be on the exam, or can we forget it?" Now, because of test-score pressures, that joke is no longer funny. Teachers are being forced to teach only things that will appear on some exam. Learning for its own sake has become a silly old idea. Today, it's all about winning test scores. That makes you the loser.

Forcing you to memorize the gross national product of Brazil helps you answer that one test question. Teaching you about how a gross national product affects people's lives helps you answer a thousand other questions about the world. And there are many other ways that you get hurt when your grades become like football scores to a Super Bowl team, or batting averages to a World Series contender.

Elizabeth sat still, but in constant motion. Without realizing it, she continuously wrung her hands, tapped her feet, and moved her chin. When I jokingly asked how many espressos she'd had that day, her blank look told me that this 13-year-old didn't have a clue that she was wired. "How long," I wondered, "has she been living like this?" Her anxiety made her answer my question before I asked it.

"I've had this sleep problem for about a year now. I need help because it's starting to affect my grades. I messed up a couple of tests this week because I was so tired from not sleeping. My family doctor says she won't give me sleeping pills unless I see you first. She doesn't understand."

"How badly did you do on those 'messed up' tests?" I asked.

She sat forward, as if we were finally getting to the important problem. She announced her messed up scores as if they were horrors: "A 98 and a 96!" she snapped. Now I was the one with the blank look. "You don't understand," she whined, "I always get hundreds and above, with the bonus points. I never do less than that. That's how you get into good schools and get good jobs. You're a doctor. You must have been number one in your school, right?"

When her question made me laugh, she broke down into tears before I could explain. "You don't understand. Nobody understands," she wept. "My family, my teachers, even my principal, they tell me every day how proud they are of me. I can't let them down. That's what keeps me awake all night. What would people say?"

After she quieted, I answered her question. "I don't know what they'd say, Elizabeth," I shrugged, "but I'd say that I was really proud of you." The blank look was back on her side of the table. "Proud of how incredibly hard you work at school," I explained, "proud of the community service you do, proud of how you help your overworked mom take care of your brothers. To me, that school ranking that you're killing yourself for seems a little silly next to all the truly wonderful things that you do."

When the blank look stayed in her court, I tried another approach. "On your intake sheet, it says you love the Phillies [her hometown baseball team]. What do you love about them?"

She spoke of how the Phillies always try, and always lose, but keep on trying just the same. She told of meeting some of the players, and how they do nice things for poor people in her town. "I'm proud of the Phillies," she said, "even though they never make it to . . ." she paused as a good thought crossed her face, "to . . . the World Series."

I acted shocked: "Elizabeth! How can you possibly love and be proud of people who are not number one?"

School grades should *not* be the World Series for teenagers. Yes, as I said earlier, you do want to learn the discipline of hard work, but it's important to keep a good balance and not get too caught up in the grades. You'll have lots of time for cutthroat competition when you get to the adult world. Besides making kids sick, fighting for grades as if it's the playoffs causes kids like Elizabeth to miss out on the really important parts of school that help you grow and find out who you are. *Remember, that search for identity is your number-one job right now.* By the way, knowing who you are will help you better handle that cutthroat competition when you're ready in a few years.

Besides making kids sick, fighting for grades as if it's the playoffs causes kids like Elizabeth to miss out on the really important parts of school that help you grow and find out who you are.

The ultimate joke about all of this testing pressure is that it not only doesn't help, *it makes things worse*! Research shows that most states using these kinds of tests have seen their kids' academic skills *decrease*, and have watched more of their kids drop out. Some schools have even been caught concealing their true dropout rates by falsely claiming that the dropout kids transferred to other schools. A school district near me is in the middle of an investigation because some teachers have been accused of changing their students' test scores to make their classes look better.

The decreases in skills are due to what we already discussed—when you teach for a test, you stop teaching important things. The dropout increase in these testing states came from struggling kids who were pushed into quitting because the schools didn't want these "loser" students dragging down their test scores. Research shows that these kids were pressured directly with words, or by being held back year after year from the grade level that takes that all-important test. This is academic success?

Seeing school only as a game for beating out other kids and getting high rankings has led to an epidemic increase in this next behavior, something done by some of the adults in some of the schools I just mentioned. Many people think it's a way to win when you're losing. It's actually a way to lose when you win. It's called cheating.

If You Cheat, You Lose More Than You Win

Cheating is at an all-time high among high-school and college students today, which is not much of a surprise to folks who work with teenagers. They understand that kids are no worse than before, but that the examples our adult world sets for them seem much worse (Chapter 5). Many kids say that the adult world tells them cheating is OK as long as you don't get caught. If you read a newspaper or watch TV, you begin to see their point.

Yet it was a kid who cheated big time who gave the best argument *against* cheating I've ever heard. And when he cheated, *he was following orders.*

> Dean stared at the brand-new league championship patch on his football jacket as if it didn't belong there. "I need to tell someone about this," he began. "This is really eating at me, but it's very hard to say. Please don't look at me while I'm talking, OK?" After I nodded, he leaned forward and held his face with his hands.
>
> "I made the winning score in our league championship game. It was a great game, with the lead going back and forth, like in a movie. I got sent in because the first- and second-string ends got hurt. I was playing good. There was only 30 seconds left, and we were on their eight-yard line, down four points. I ran a crossing pattern into the end zone, right into a pack of players. Our quarterback made a desperation throw that was too low. The safety [the opposing player] had me completely covered. We dove for the ball together, inside a mob of players. No one else saw the ball coming. He knocked it down on the ground, but I scooped it up. He and me were the only ones who knew for sure that I didn't catch that ball, that he had made the play." Dean began picking at the edges of his championship patch. It looked like he had been picking at it a lot.
>
> "I did like we're taught to do. I acted like I had made the catch. I jumped up screaming and showing the ball to the refs, and they

raised their hands [calling a touchdown]. They bought it. My cheating won us the championship.

"At first I felt great. I'm not even second string on the team, and here I am getting mobbed by all the good players, high-fiving me and all. It was weird—I started to believe my own lie, like I had made this great championship catch.

"After the game, we lined up to shake hands with the other team. All these guys from the other side were saying 'Great catch!' and congratulating me. That was making me feel a little bad. Then, I saw that safety in the line. When we got face to face, he stopped and just stared at me, you know? Didn't say a single word or nothing. He just stared in my eyes. Not a threat stare, more like he wanted to ask me something. He just stared for a minute, and then walked away, shaking his head. His coach, his team, even his family probably all thought that he cost them the championship, but I never heard him say one word about how I had cheated." Dean dropped his head, and then dropped his coat on the floor, like it was going into a trash can.

"I felt horrible. After we dressed, I went and told Coach what happened. He laughed, and said that acting was all part of the game. I asked him if acting was the same thing as cheating. He got mad, and said everyone cheats, and that it's only wrong if you get caught. He asked me if that safety would have told the referee the truth if he was in my place. I told Coach I wasn't sure what that kid would have done, that there was something in that kid's eyes, you know? Coach told me I was crazy, to just shut up and go celebrate. He yelled that I better not ruin the team's happiness by telling anybody what I told him. Then he wouldn't talk anymore about it." Dean kicked at his jacket on the floor. "I think he just didn't know what to say.

"I've had this dream a few times. It's like a slow-motion rerun of that play. I keep getting up and turning to the referee, and I can't decide if I should cheat or not. The dream always ends before I decide. It always ends with that safety just staring at me." Dean sighed heavily.

"I do know one thing. I know that if the ref made the right call, I'd be happier today, even if we lost that championship. That way, I'd feel like we played as hard as we could, and that we just lost to a better team. That would feel clean, you know? This win, this championship, doesn't feel clean. It doesn't feel like it belongs to me. That other kid, he should have this patch on his coat."

Dean lost a lot in the game that he won. But he found an important piece of himself in that end zone. "If I ever get another chance to cheat in life, I'm passing on it," Dean promised his coat. "Win or lose, from now on, I'm doing it on my own. I can't stand cheating. It tears me up."

Kids are right. At times, the adult world does seem to tell you that cheating is "all part of the game." Some, like Dean's coach, say it outright. Others preach that you shouldn't cheat, and then they do it. Still others say it's OK to cheat sometimes (like on a test at school), as long as you're not stealing or hurting anyone. Are there any adults who actually don't cheat?

At times, the adult world does seem to tell you that cheating is "all part of the game."

Manuel's father was too polite to speak too directly. He seemed very concerned that he not offend this American psychologist in any way. But his worry for his son forced him to speak of a subject that he found very difficult. His face showed the lines of a life of struggle, yet with the strength of quiet dignity and fierce determination. He had worked incredibly hard to fulfill his dream of moving his family from the desperate poverty of a poor South American village to this "land of opportunity—America." Yet, here he found a new kind of poverty that, for him, was even worse than the old.

"I mean no offense," he began in his heavy Spanish accent, "but I am most puzzled by many things that happen here [in America]. These things make me worry about Manuel, about how he is growing up. I fear that what he sees on TV and in the newspapers tells him that, in this country, all successful people cheat and steal, and that it's only wrong if they get caught." He stopped and seemed to search my face for any signs of insult before he continued. "I feel alone in this matter. I think I talk too much to Manuel about honesty, because he gets very angry at me now. I think he believes me to be old-fashioned, and not really American. I worry that he will follow the bad examples of the ball players, the politicians, and the businessmen that he looks up to." Dad's steely eyes misted over. "I don't think what I believe is important to Manuel anymore. I feel that I'm losing him to these bad men. How can I compete with them, with their cars, their houses, their money? How can Manuel attach importance to the words of his struggling immigrant father over those of these rich men?"

I wrote down this man's words because he so well summarized what so many other parents have said in many different ways, but all with that same pain. Parents do feel overwhelmed by the world that is presented to their children, a world that seems to say that cheating is fine as long as you don't get caught; that, as Dean's coach put it, ". . . it's all part of the game."

The fact is that cheating is *not* all part of the game. Every day, I am amazed by some selfless, caring, honorable act that someone around me does. Every day, I find inspiration in watching people (adults and kids) struggle through tough moral decisions, where cheating seems so easy, and yet they choose the harder moral path. But you have to go looking for these things. They're not nasty enough to warrant headlines. The media (TV and newspapers) love "successful people cheating" stories so much because *we* love those stories so much. We seem to find "goodness" boring. Tell the truth: If the TV news headline screamed, "MANUEL'S STRUGGLING FATHER TURNS IN $50 LEFT IN HIS CAB. FILM AT 11!!" would you tune in? The fact is that goodness makes lousy headlines, so we rarely hear about it. *But it is out there.* It lives in Manuel's dad.

Manuel told me about that $50, and said that his father "was a chump" for turning in the money. His father was devastated when he heard Manuel say that. Just as most other parents are when they feel overwhelmed by these stories raining down on your head that seem to say it's OK to cheat your way to success, to grab all you can and run. And just like Manuel's father, these parents can make you crazy by the constant morality lectures they rain down on your head. They make you crazy because they *are* crazy—crazy with worry, fear, and hopelessness about the world around you.

Lots of kids say it's hard *not* to cheat at school because everybody seems to do it. When asked, most kids say that cheating is OK, as long as you're not stealing (and many even say that stealing from strangers is OK). Dean (the football player) discovered that, at least for him, all of those excuses miss the point. He found out that *cheating is always stealing—it's always stealing from yourself.*

Whenever you cheat, you're really telling yourself that you're not good enough to win clean, that, on your own, you can never be as good as the competition. Do that often enough, and you'll start to etch that "loser" message into your developing brain. As with a cigarette habit, cheating can become a part of who you are, of your identity. Making a habit out of cheating prevents you from ever really winning in life, because every "win" becomes bogus, and every loss becomes even more painful. As with Dean, most people who've been through this usually say it feels better to have played your heart out honestly and lost clean. If that sounds like chump thinking to you, I understand. I would have thought that was dumb when I was a teenager. But it is the truth.

Please think about it. The stakes are high on this identity question. Dean thought about it and decided that he had to do something radical to live with himself.

> Two weeks later, Dean walked in with his football jacket folded up. His face looked tired, but somehow relieved. He unfolded his coat to show me the missing championship patch. "Is that in the trash?" I asked.
>
> "Nope," Dean smiled. "It's where it belongs. Today, I went and found that kid, the safety, at his school. I didn't think he'd recognize me, but he, like, froze when he saw me walking towards him. His friends were wondering what was up. I just handed him the patch without saying anything. I was afraid he'd throw it in my face or something, but he just smiled. 'Thanks,' was all he said. We shook hands, and then I left. It feels like I can sleep now, like a weight is off my neck. It feels like it's over.
>
> "It's weird," he said. "I always thought that 'doing the right thing' was what you did for other people. Now I know that you have to do that stuff for yourself."

Lots of kids cheat because they think they can't handle the challenge of honestly passing a test. They flunk themselves without even trying. That's *anticipating* failure. It's another one of those things where you make something happen by thinking that it will happen. Amazingly, this is the number-one reason that people fail: Not because they *can't* do something, but because they *believe* they can't do something.

Anticipation Is Where Games Are Decided

Yogi Berra, a famous baseball manager, once said, "Half of this game is 90 percent mental." Although his math was a little off, his message was right on. How you *think* about a task is just as important as your *ability* to do the task. If you don't believe that you can do something, you take yourself right out of the game. This is bad because, almost always, we think things will be so much harder than they truly are. We spend all of our time and energy *worrying* about doing something, instead of just *trying* to do the thing. We quit before we ever get in the batter's box.

If you asked me the secret of success in life, I'd answer that the first part is a kind of stupidity. Being "stupid" enough to think that you can do hard things *makes them possible*. The only people who get hits in baseball are those who have the "stupidity" to get into the batter's box. No one ever, ever succeeded by sitting on the bench and being "smart" enough to know that hitting a fastball is hard to do. "Stupid" people just get right at trying to hit the ball.

In school, this means doing things like forcing yourself to sit down and start that project you are so sure you can't do. And I mean *forcing* yourself. Many successful people sometimes yell and scream at themselves to get started on tough tasks, as if they were their own drill sergeants (I happen to be one of these). They do this to get themselves past the "I can't do this" fear. They find that, once they push themselves to take one step, their fear starts to evaporate, and the "impossible" task starts to get done.

It's that first step that is the hardest. Whenever you feel outmatched by a challenge, think *only* about getting that first step done. Focus only on each step at a time. If you look at all 20 steps of a tough task at once, it looks undoable. Doing one step at a time allows your brain to say, "Well, if we did that part, why *can't* we do the next?" That little thought is the secret to miraculous Super Bowl comebacks, and even more impressive failing-semester comebacks.

And while we're talking of miracles, here are a few tricks that kids have told me help a lot in the game of school.

SIX CHEAP AND EASY SCHOOL TRICKS

If you're struggling in school, trick number one is to get some expert help. Believe it or not, *your school wants you to succeed*. Even if they are the coldhearted jerks you think they are, your school staff needs you to pass, so they look better. Failing students make everybody look bad. So see your counselor, or principal, or whoever handles those things. They might have some ideas that can help a lot. Beyond that, here are some ideas that have worked very well for other kids when their grades started to slide.

1. Meet with your teachers.

Politically, doing this is a very smart move. Teachers never waste their time (or their charity) on kids who act like they don't care. Simply meeting with a teacher and asking for help makes the teacher want to see you pass. They'll only care if you do it first. Their help might be tutoring, allowing extra-credit projects, or even being generous with scoring on tests.

2. Use bribery (on you, not your teacher).

I have no idea where that ridiculous idea came from that you shouldn't be bribed to get good grades. Everyone is bribed to do well. Adults are paid for working. Even those "do-gooders" who help others for free are bribed: They get paid off in the "dollars" of good feelings that they get when they give. If your parents object to paying you for grades, read them the following paragraph.

It doesn't matter why or how you start to do well in school, it only matters that you do.

Parents who argue that kids shouldn't be paid for grades say that teens should learn for the "joy of learning," not for money. They say that something sacred like education shouldn't be muddied with bribes. These words are spoken by parents who've forgotten what it's like to be in school, forced to learn lots of boring, hard, irrelevant junk, very little of which you asked to learn. That "joy of learning" stuff applies more for middle-aged adults who go back to night school to take courses that interest them. *Even there, they get a bribe*: Learning about something that fascinates them. It doesn't matter why or how you start to do well in school, it only matters that you do.

Even if you start studying for money, over time, you'll begin to enjoy those feelings of being prepared, of learning new things, and of seeing pride in your parents' eyes. Those feelings become even more powerful bribes that replace the money bribes. That's how that "joy of education" feeling can actually begin to grow within you.

3. Don't do homework at home; do it in the library.

I've lost count of the number of kids who tell me how amazed they are at how fast and how well they work in the library, versus working at home. The secret is that, compared to your bedroom, your library is such a dull place. That's why schoolwork doesn't feel as boring there as it does at home, when it's competing for your attention against the TV, stereo, and instant messaging. Try the library for a week. You will be amazed at how much faster you get stuff done (and get guilt-free time for the TV, stereo, and instant messaging).

4. Get organized.

Are you sick of hearing that word yet? If not, then you're the one teen who isn't. Most kids who mess up in school are kids who can't seem to keep track of their homework, papers, and test dates if their lives depended on it. Their folders aren't nearly as neat as their rooms, and their rooms look like they qualify for disaster-relief funds.

If that describes you, please don't take this as a personal insult, for two reasons. First, as a neat freak who lives in a family with two slobs and two neat freaks, I've noticed that the slobs seem to be psychologically healthier people (and nicer, too). But they're really lousy at organizing things.

The second reason you should not feel insulted is that your abilities to organize and plan well come from brain parts that are not yet fully developed in adolescent brains (see Chapter 1). You might still be waiting for the "head hardware" you need to do school well on your own.

But this fact is *not* an excuse for not doing your work. Rather, you should view your "under-construction" brain much like that blind kid views his: Both brains are smart enough to do well in school. Both need special assistance with their challenges to get the work done, not dodged.

For the disorganized kid, that means seeing the counselor for help. It also means inviting adults into your life to help you manage it, something that probably sounds as inviting as dragging your fingernails across a chalkboard. I'm sorry to break this to you, but there is no other way until your brain finishes up its adolescent renovations. The terrifying teenage bottom line is that school is very hard to manage, even for kids who can organize well. If you're not one of those, view the help as a cast for a broken leg. Like the cast, the help is very annoying, but it will heal the problem, so you can soon run on your own. Getting help with organization can hard-wire those critical skills into that magically evolving brain of yours, *for life*.

5. Take 5-minute breaks every 30 minutes.

Meaning that you work for the 30 minutes, not the 5. When we study how you study, we find that after 20 or 30 minutes, your brain starts to stop. Pushing past a half-hour of hard studying can make it hard to maintain your focus. Often, that leads to finding yourself at the computer, halfway through Halflife at 1 A.M. (and your essay is still not done). Taking short breaks every so often is a great way to keep your focus sharp, stay on task, and do much better work, much more quickly. The breaks more than pay for the time lost, by helping you get the task done much faster.

6. Get sarcastic with yourself.

If you've pretty much quit on doing schoolwork, get in front of the mirror tonight, and sarcastically ask yourself, "Is 30 minutes of work *really* too much to ask?" Even if your assignments need more time than that, challenge yourself to do only 30 minutes. What *can't* you do for 30 minutes? That's nothing. Promise yourself that, even if you're not done, you can quit after the 30 minutes.

What's the point? If you're avoiding your homework completely, you're probably afraid of some feeling that you get when you try to face up to your responsibilities. Perhaps it's that lousy, jumpy stomach that people get when they start to deal with what they're ducking. Forcing yourself to do the 30 minutes will prove to you that that feeling is not a horror, and that you're tough enough to get through it, even if only for 30 minutes. Once you've challenged that feeling, you'll find it starts to shrink down, and you'll be able to work more and more. But you have to get in your own face for that first 30. Don't think about it—*just do it*.

There you go! Six cheap and easy tricks guaranteed to help you do better in school. If you see your counselor, she'll have at least another six tricks tailored to your particular challenges. These are not hard to do, yet they very often seem impossible to many kids. If you're one of them, ask yourself why. If your answer is that it somehow feels comfortable to screw up, and scary to try to do well, reread Chapter 3 and get some help. I promise you, life does not have to be that way. All it takes is for you to take a shot.

Your Parents' View: "And Now for Something Completely Different...."

When teenagers begin failing as students, their parents begin failing as parents. They usually start to do things that look ridiculous and maddening to their kids, and that generally make problems worse. For example, they'll yell, nag, threaten, punish, and endlessly repeat the same things that you already know are important about school. Things like how it helps you get a decent job, get into a decent college, and get a decent life. This is when you hear the phrase most hated by adolescents: "You're wasting your *potential*." These parent strategies, of course, just make you angrier, more rebellious, and much less inclined to do your work.

When teenagers begin failing as students, their parents begin failing as parents.

What's strange is that most parents know that these are dumb things to say and do, but they have to say and do them, anyway. That's because of a few things you should know about your parent's world.

First, your folks are used to having you do what they tell you to do. When you were smaller, they could scare you, or make you feel guilty enough to get you to do things like homework. So they try using these old methods that not only don't work now that you're older, they make you crazy. They haven't learned that they need to deal with the "teenage you" differently.

Second, when a kid starts to flunk, the parents also are told useless things that make *them* feel angry, rebellious, and less inclined to do their work. For example, your teachers tell your parents to "set limits," and "give consequences," as if they hadn't tried that already. The worst part is the embarrassing and infuriating looks they get from the teachers that seem to silently say, "I wonder what's wrong with these parents, that they could raise such a screw-up for a kid?"

Then there are the helpful parenting "experts," like your Uncle Louie. He loves to make your parents feel like wimps and failures by saying things like *"In my day, no kids flunked. No sirree! By gum, no parents would ever let us fail like you do with your kid. Why, my folks woulda' set me straight, yessir! My father was a real man. Why, I remember this one time I forgot to indent one paragraph, and my dad got his rifle out and shot me seven times, right through my head. Yessirree, bob, I never forgot to indent after that, no sir! Why, that kid of yours just needs a good beating!"*

The fact is that, when kids fail, they take beatings that don't leave bruises, *and so do their parents*. The kids *and their parents* are looked at and talked to as if they're lazy and stupid. The whole family starts to feel helpless and hopeless, and everyone gets snarly with each other. The unspoken truth is that everyone feels sad and scared. But, because we don't talk about those scary feelings, we just get snarly—which feels a lot easier and safer.

Mom described what she had done to get her 14-year-old daughter, Lindsay, to study. "We did groundings and punishments, like the school counselor told us to do. We took away her TV, stereo, phone, and computer. Her stepfather wants to take off the door to her bedroom so we can see if she's working, since she lies to us all the time about doing her work. I said no, and he washed his hands of her. We've taken away everything she loves, and she still won't try."

Lindsay just sat and stared furiously out the window. I guessed that she was waiting for me, her latest unwanted expert, to begin the "school is important" lecture. Instead, I just asked, "How's that stuff make you feel, Lindsay?" She went off like a volcano.

"IT DOESN'T MAKE ME FEEL LIKE WORKING!" she yelled, "IT MAKES ME FEEL LIKE SCREWING UP MY LIFE A LOT MORE THAN JUST FAILING SCHOOL!" After sighing loudly, she continued. "Look, I think I'm, like, a good kid. I don't do drugs or sex, like a bunch of other kids I could name who get great grades, and everyone thinks are wonderful. I don't hurt anybody, and I don't disrespect my teachers. But when my parents punish me like that, it only makes me feel like doing bad things, like hurting and disrespecting people. And hurting and disrespecting myself."

Lindsay turned to her mother, as if asking that she listen for a change. Mom looked away, but Lindsay spoke right at her. "Mom, I don't know why I don't do well in school. Honest-to-God, I wish I knew. Don't you think I hate failing all the time? Don't you think I'd like to get my work done? DON'T YOU THINK I LAY AWAKE AT NIGHT, CRYING, AND FEELING HORRIBLE ABOUT THIS? WELL? DON'T YOU?" she demanded, but her mother wouldn't answer. I could see Mom's eyes filling up as she looked away from Lindsay, trying to keep her pain to herself. She didn't understand that her pain might help her daughter where her anger could not.

"Ms. Taylor," I asked Lindsay's mom, "what are you feeling?" She flashed a furious look at me for my question, a motion that made the tears fall from her eyes, much to the astonishment of her daughter. "WHAT I'M FEELING IS NOT THE ISSUE. . . ." she began yelling, but then she let that tired dodge go. With a falling voice, she finally got straight with Lindsay, even though she still couldn't look at her. "Lindsay, I'm sorry. I'm . . . just sorry. I can't believe that, all this time, I wasn't thinking that this hurts you. It sounds stupid, but I guess I think that you do this on purpose to hurt us, and that you like not doing your work." As she got even more honest, Lindsay's mom finally turned to face her.

"The truth is that I'm scared and sad. I'm sad because you were always my perfect little girl. I guess I needed you to be perfect, to make me feel better, you know? I never felt good about myself, with my weight, and never finishing school, and all, but I could always show you off to everybody, to make me look good. So, when you started to fail, I got ashamed and sad—for me. I know that sounds awful, but that's the truth.

"But I'm also scared—scared for you. I know what life is like when you mess up school. It means taking crap from jerk bosses, never having enough money to pay the bills, and. . . ." She paused and looked at Lindsay, as if to see if she was old enough to hear the next part. Barely whispering now, she decided that her daughter was old enough: "And it means marrying someone just to get out of a bad place. I cry at night too, Lindsay. I cry, and I beg God to give you a better life than mine."

The anger seemed to have completely drained out of each of them. Lindsay suddenly looked and sounded very grown up. "Mom, I don't know why, and I'm not really sure about this yet, but I think that what you just said helps. I think now I can talk about my problem. Maybe it can change."

The cold, hard fact is that only *you* can make you study. Punishments might make some kids do better for a while, but that usually doesn't last very long. School can only be done well by kids who decide that doing well in school is *who they are*—that it's part of their identity. Sometimes, we figure this out by screwing up in school, and then feeling the pain of not succeeding—*of not being who we are.* That pain can give kids like Lindsay the courage they need to push themselves to do the work. If kids are punished into doing the work, they might not get to realize that *they themselves* want to do well in school. Doing well in school, just to avoid punishments, will not get it done in the long run. So, the next time you're waiting for your parents to kick in your door, loaded with threats and punishments for not doing your homework, do yourself a favor. Ambush them first, *before* the bad-news letter arrives from school. *You* sit *them* down and tell them what changes you think you need to make to do your schoolwork. *You* tell *them* that you're suggesting things, like no TV on weeknights, or reviewing your work status weekly with your teachers, until you're caught up. Move the talk away from ways to punish, and toward ways of fixing the problem. Remember, just saying "I'll do it" isn't good enough once you've screwed up. Now you need to put out hard and clear strategies that have a chance at really changing your study habits.

School can only be done well by kids who decide that doing well in school is who they are—that it's part of their identity.

The big secret is that your parents hate punishing you as much as you hate being punished. They get zero enjoyment out of grounding you and then having you stomp around the house banging things and muttering. They're looking for nicer ways out of the problem, just like you are, but they have to feel that things will get better. So do everyone a favor. Be the first one to take charge of your problem. Be straight up about screwing up, and offer real solutions. You might be amazed to see that their real interest is not in hurting you, but in helping you.

And speaking of being amazed, congratulations! You're mostly through this book. You've just finished your preparation for Part Three: the "what-to-do-when" section. Before we jump into those subjects, please know that, although everybody loves the advice parts of books like this, you've already read the most important parts. Parts One and Two help you to define who you are, which is the whole point to being a teenager. Knowing who you are helps you to solve your own problems, which is like writing your own advice book for yourself. And that will be the smartest book you'll ever read, guaranteed. No one—parents, shrinks, or friends—can know who you are better than you do.

So, if you're ready, turn the page, and let's get to the down and dirty of daily teen life. We'll run through the As to Zs of adolescence, starting with aggression, and talk about fun things like fighting and bullying. Which reminds me of my grandfather's ageless wisdom for dealing with bullies: *"Never forget this, boy: The bigger they are, the harder they . . .hit."*

YOUR DAY-TO-DAY LIFE

What-to-Do-When

"You know, when I think about it, for me, preschool was a lot more violent than middle school." —*Ross, age 13*

WARNING! STOP! GO BACK!
DO NOT PROCEED INTO PART THREE
UNLESS YOU HAVE COMPLETED READING PARTS
ONE AND TWO. FATAL COMPLICATIONS MAY
RESULT FROM READING PART THREE FIRST.

OK, OK, it can't kill you. But reading Part Three alone won't help you nearly as much. That's because the first two parts of this book are where you figure out your own "what-to-do-when" answers. If you've read those parts, you've seen that *your own answers* to your own questions are much more valuable than what anyone else can put together for you. Still, the answers you'll find here in Part Three will run a close second. Other kids found these ideas helpful when they stared down the same problems.

"KENNY HASN'T SPOKEN TO ME IN SIX MONTHS, HE WON'T RETURN MY CALLS AND HE GOES OUT WITH ALL MY FRIENDS. DO YOU THINK I SHOULD BREAK UP WITH HIM?"

The topics included here were picked by teenagers, friends you haven't met yet. They chose these as the situations and problems they thought might hit you most often. And again, the stories here are true, and the quotes are from real kids, although their names have been changed. The topics are arranged alphabetically, to make this a kind of encyclopedia in which you can easily flip to any topic you wish.

It's best to read all of Part Three once, even if every problem discussed isn't on your plate right now. As the smart karate masters like to say, *the best defense against danger is not being there when it happens.* Learning to avoid problems before they hit makes for a much happier life. Learning about these teen issues in advance of their happening can make for a much happier adolescence. And just thinking about these topics helps you to figure out more about who you are—your identity. Have I mentioned that building your identity is your number one job in adolescence?

Learning to avoid problems before they hit makes for a much happier life.

Aggression: How Come James Bond Never Looks Dumb When He Fights?

Grant seemed like a 14-year-old actor playing a role that was completely different from who he was as a person. His clothes, his muscle flexing, even his crooked, more-than-once-broken nose all yelled out "tough kid." Yet his soft words whispered "nice guy." Out loud, I wondered which was the real Grant.

"I'm both, I guess," he laughed, shooting me a look that said he thought I was smarter than I looked. "I fight if I have to, and I'm pretty good at it." He spoke without any swagger in his voice, as if he were talking about playing the guitar. "In the halls, there's always some thug trying to mess with you, and you have to stand up, or they'll mess with you all the time. I've fought a lot of kids bigger than me, and older, like seniors and juniors. I don't always win, but I never back down. I make them pay."

His business-like tone about fighting didn't quite fit him. "Grant," I asked, "how do you *feel* when you fight?"

Grant shot me my second "you're-pretty-smart-for-an-adult" look. But then he looked confused and sad. "It's weird," he said gently, as if being careful with his thoughts. "If I lose, I feel like an ass. If I win, I feel like . . . I don't know, like an ass, I guess. When other kids beat me, they mostly dance around yelling how they kicked my butt, and how bad they are, and stuff. So I feel bad, like a loser. When I win, I just feel embarrassed and stupid. It's not like on TV—real fights mostly look dumb. I want to run away. Usually, I feel *bad* for beating up a kid who was in my face a minute before. Can you believe that?" he asked, amazed at himself. "Once I tried shaking hands with a kid I whipped, you know, trying to make him feel better—like you see in old movies?" As I nodded "yes," Grant shook his head "no." "Man, was that ever dumb. He just started on me all over again."

"Grant," I said, "For all the fighting you do, you don't sound like much of a fighter, you know what I mean?"

He answered right away—he had been thinking about this: "I guess so," he agreed, "but what choice do I have? What would you do?"

Americans are world famous for being some of the most aggressive people around (see Chapter 5). We love anger and aggression.

Some adults like to put a nice face on this behavior and say that we're just "competitive," but the fact is that we love to dominate and intimidate others into doing what we want—or else!

The fallout of this rains down on your teen world. It shows in things like fighting, bullying, and sexual violence, problems that affect you much more than grown-ups. This is why they don't understand how tough your world can be at times. Most adults don't have to deal nose-to-nose with aggression like you do, particularly if you go to a rough school. Fistfights and physical intimidation hardly ever happen in adult settings. In addition, adults have many more options for handling aggression that don't hurt nearly as much as your lousy choices. For example, a grown man who walks away from a jerk challenging him to a fistfight is praised and admired by other adults for "taking the high road" and "being the better person." Very few people think badly of an adult who refuses to fight. Unfortunately, those rules don't apply to kids.

Grant had about as many choices as you when it comes to responding to aggression: *few and none* (also see "Bullying . . ."). Schools do what they can to help, but from a kid's point of view, there's just not a whole lot you can do *once aggression becomes accepted by the students as normal and OK* (again, see "Bullying . . ."). No matter how you respond, there's a downside—you just have to decide which downside costs you the least. Most kids just accept the occasional put-downs and try to avoid the thugs. And then they're the ones who look like wimps—no guts. Others let no insult pass, and rise up to fight, no matter what. They're the ones who look like hockey players—no teeth.

In deciding what to do, you need to find *your own* best answer. Some kids actually like to fight. Others get sick to their stomachs, win or lose. You must decide who you are on this issue. The wrong answer is the one that *somebody else gives you*. When Uncle Louie tells you to challenge the thugs to fistfights, he's telling you what he'd do (or, more likely, what he *wishes* he'd do). Getting into a fistfight because someone else told you to is always a bad idea. To help you decide your course, here are a few thoughts:

- **The older you get, the less this junk happens.** If you decide that you're not a fighter, that's fine. The odds are huge that you won't need to be a fighter as an adult (which is one of the many great things about being an adult). You just need to wait out this rough time.

- **Fistfights rarely go down like on TV, where the combatants shrug off vicious kicks and punches.** Strange, unpredictable things happen in fights. Three of the worst fight injuries I've heard about were in fights where no one landed a punch. In one, a kid swung on someone, missed, slipped on a wet gym floor, and suffered permanent and severe brain damage from hitting an open locker door on the way down. The second happened when a simple shoving match ended in lifetime paralysis after the "shovee" fell backwards down steps. In the third, a drunk kid fatally stabbed another for an insult that *was never said*. The whole event was a beer blur to the killer, *who had never been in a real fight before*. Think about the potential costs of playing Rambo *before* you lock and load.

Three of the worst fight injuries I've heard about were in fights where no one landed a punch.

- **Many kids make fights happen that don't have to.** Grant, for example, needed to learn when to go deaf. Simply pretending to not hear trash talk can keep far more suspensions (for fighting) off of your school record and far more teeth in your head. Many kids regret having tossed an insult at you the minute it leaves their lips. Losing your hearing allows those kids to quietly take back a challenge, without anyone losing any face (or any parts of their faces).
- **Booze often causes kids who are usually really calm to get really, really crazy.** When alcohol is involved, be extra careful about confrontations. Become even more hard of hearing when you smell beer breath.
- **Contrary to the TV myth, fighting tends to lead to more fighting.** Uncle Louie says that if you fight, kids leave you alone. The truth is that many kids fight to make what's called the "pecking order," an unwritten but well-known list of who's "tougher" than whom. Once on that list, you might hear your name called a lot by scary faces, as kids try to rearrange the standings. There will always be someone on that strange list who wants to get "ahead" of you, and that means that the fighting never ends.

Aggression also rears its ugly head in sex issues like date rape. Unwanted sex is *not* sex: It's violence. The problem is that, if you watch TV or listen to music, it can start to seem OK and somehow natural for males to demand sex, and to intimidate and even force women to give in. A lot of what you see on TV and in the movies, or hear in CDs or on the radio, says that women like being forced into having sex. It's crazy that I have to say what I'm about to say, but I've had too many conversations with too many boys who get confused by the perverted crap that they see and hear: *Women do not, repeat, do not find getting raped fun or sexy. They just feel horribly abused.*

Normal men *do not*, repeat, *do not* find raping someone fun or sexy. Any male who does might also enjoy torturing kittens. Forced sex is an act of cowardly aggression, nothing more.

Appearance: "YOU Are NOT Leaving THIS HOUSE Looking like THAT!" (teen yelling at his father, who is wearing black knee socks with plaid shorts)

When you think about it, it really is funny how much time and energy human beings put into fighting over how we look to each other. We have all these sayings, like "Don't judge a book by its cover," and "Clothes don't make the man/woman," and my favorite, "Small [clothing] labels can only be read by small-minded people." Yet fights about appearance still break out almost daily in many homes. *But those fights are not about appearance at all.*

Whenever people fight over stupid issues, the real fight is usually about something else, something not so stupid. When it comes to struggles over appearance (clothes, piercings, tattoos), those fights between parents and teens are really about things that are not silly at all, such as control, safety, independence, and respect.

From your point of view, you're fighting for independence and respect. After all, you're not far from draft age. Shouldn't you be able to wear what you like? And doesn't it feel insulting when people tell you that your clothes are not acceptable?

Your parents see the appearance issue as about control and safety. Control means how they're used to having you do what they tell you to do. That feels normal to them, because, after all, you are still their child. So, when they say "no" to a piercing, they are fully expecting that you'll say "OK," and walk away. When you start to argue and demand that you be allowed to do what you want, they feel like they're losing some control over you. Which happens to be true. That's the point of adolescence.

Your parents also worry about your safety. When it comes to piercings and tattoos, they worry that these might be hazardous to your health, which they can sometimes be. Ozzy Osbourne tells of how he almost lost an arm because of a tattoo infection (one-armed guitar players have very short careers).

Clothes can also be seen as dangerous by parents. When girls wear "daring" clothes, parents worry about what that "says" to boys, and what boys might then try to do to girls. Girls usually think their parents are sex maniacs or something for thinking that sexy clothes make boys think only about having sex. They say that they're not dressing to provoke boys sexually. The truth is that both girls and their parents are right.

When girls are asked who they are dressing for, it turns out that they dress more to impress other girls, and not so much for the boys. Girls get into fashion styles (be they grunge or sexy) as fashion statements, not as sexual statements. Most girls are not thinking that they are suggesting having sex by the way that they dress. But, as you saw in Chapter 3, girls and boys are very different sexually. Boys *do* get sexually aroused by sexy clothes on girls, and they do see dressing like that as an invitation of sorts. So both you and your parents are right when you argue your points about clothes.

So what's the answer to the appearance battles? Negotiation.

So what's the answer to the appearance battles? *Negotiation.* But make deals that relate to the real fights, not the silly ones. If the real fight is about control, show your folks that, if they give up some control over your appearance (like with a piercing), it will pay off for them. Like with you being more helpful with an added chore. Or by earning your piercing, with honors on your next report card. This is a "win-win" way of both sides getting more of what they want than if they go to war with each other.

If your parents refuse to negotiate at all, it might be time to ask them to sit down with you and a "helper" (such as a counselor or teacher). Sometimes, these "helpers" can help your parents understand that the teen years are much more peaceful when the family learns to negotiate well. I'll leave the subject of appearance issues with an interesting thought that Sean raised about tattoos.

> Sean had fought with his parents for months to get a tattoo. He finally earned their permission by getting straight As at school, something I'm sure they thought Sean couldn't do when they agreed to the deal. I was amazed to see two, then three, and then four weeks pass without Sean running off to Tiny's Tattoo Emporium for his five-color Grateful Dead Head. When I asked Sean about it, he smiled with some embarrassment. "Well," he explained, "I got to thinking. If I got a tattoo every time I wanted one, right now I'd be wearing Grateful Dead, *NSync, Power Rangers, and Barney [the dinosaur]. Once you have one, you have it forever. If you change, your tattoo won't. Kinda' makes you think, doesn't it?"

Try to keep those appearance issues in a good perspective. Don't tear your life apart over silly fads. When it comes to styles, look first at how much emotional energy you're putting into your appearance. If it's fun, then it's fine. If it's depressing, then it's dumb. If appearance issues are depressing you, it's time to remember what's important. It's time to remember your last birthday: Do you remember the gift, or the paper it came in (its appearance)? Don't get nuts over your own "wrapping paper" (appearance). It's only what's inside that counts. That's all that's ever remembered.

Blended Families: Does This Really Work Somewhere?

Sticking two half-families together as one makes a nice TV show, but a nasty real life for many teenagers. Chapter 7 talks a lot more about the problems of playing "The Brady Bunch," but here we'll talk about some tips to help get you (or your friend) through.

That emotional roller coaster you feel like you're on after becoming part of a blended family is not your imagination, and it does not mean that you're crazy. On the contrary, it's quite normal. It turns out that most blended families go through seven steps as they try to form one new family out of the pieces of two old ones.

The first step is called *fantasy*. That's where we think ahead about how great this new family will be. This, of course, happens *before* moving in together. The fantasy usually comes from whichever parent is getting married and trying to sell his kids on this idea of starting a new family. This fantasy thinking is usually as accurate as dreaming about how much fun Marine boot camp will be.

The next phase is where we move in together and start pretending we're The Brady Bunch—all lovey-family-dovey. The shrinks call this *fake assimilation,* meaning we act like there are no problems. That's easy to do when folks are visiting for a week. But when we realize that these folks are never leaving, we sink into the third phase, known as *awareness,* thinking, "Man, this is really hard. I hate having all these strange people around all the time."

All hell breaks loose in the next two steps, called *mobilization* and *action*, nice words that describe nasty battles over things like who gets the bathroom, who gets the remote, and whose parent gets to discipline. Assuming there are no fatalities, these families live on to see the final two steps, called *contact* and *resolution.* This is where the new family supposedly sits down and works out the tough problems they finally admit seeing.

Saying that blended families are made in seven steps is like saying that sausage is made in seven steps: These are neat ways to label some very messy scenes.

What do veteran kids (who've gone through this) suggest?

- **Lower your expectations.** Merging two families together is just hard to do, no matter what anybody says. Eventually, it will get better, and parts of it may even be fun. But don't get blown away with bitterness by believing that this new family will be all fun and games. You'll deal with it better if you have realistic expectations.
- **Raise your voice (in frequency, not volume).** Start talking. Let people know what and how you're feeling, from Day One. Don't hold anger or sadness inside, or it will swell and explode. If your new stepsister makes you crazy by getting hair on the toothpaste, *you have to speak up*. If you bring it up right away, you might be able to say, "I hate to whine, but could you do me a favor, and try to keep your

Don't hold anger or sadness inside, or it will swell and explode.

pink and purple hair trimmings out of the green toothpaste? I've got, like, a weak stomach, and all those colors are just too much for me in the morning." If you bury your complaints, you might suddenly hear yourself yelling not-nice names, and screaming, ". . . AND ANOTHER THING, KEEP YOUR STUPID HAIR OFF THE FRIGGIN' TOOTHPASTE . . .!" Which approach would make you want to help?

Speaking of listening, raise your voice in another way, as well. Ask your stepfamily what you are doing that is making them nuts. Remember that this is a tough time for them, as well, trying to put up with your little habits that make them nuts. Those silly family meetings that kids hate can help a blended family survive, by airing out problems before they become fist holes in the walls.

- **Keep your day job.** New musicians, athletes, and stepchildren should all follow that same advice, which means don't rely too heavily on your new "gig" (family). Take time to move slowly into the new family, by holding onto your old friends and activities. Some parents try to mash stepchildren together as if you should be instant best friends. Friendship takes a lot of time to grow, and it doesn't happen between two strangers just because they now share parents.
- **Give the rookies a break.** The odds are that both you and your new stepparent have never done this blended-family trick before. That means that you will both have to make it up as you go along, and you'll both screw up a lot in the beginning. That doesn't mean you'll fail in the end, provided you can talk things out. Try to set up weekly coffee dates, just for you and your stepparent, "minitruces" when the two of you can talk straight up about how you feel. The idea is not to argue about who's right or wrong, but to slowly learn about each other, so that you can slowly get better at getting along. It's not even important to come up with solutions at these meetings (although that's OK). It's more important to get to know each other, as you are in this new relationship. As you may know by now, that stepparent suddenly seems a lot different as your stepparent than as the person who dated your bio-parent.

Blending families is like blending paint. It takes a lot of trial and error to get it right. Take your time and keep your cool.

Bullying: Outlast the Bastards

He looked like the kid you'd pick to play a 13-year-old bullying victim in a movie—round face, round body, round glasses, and a silly first name that his mother wouldn't stop using, even though he had outgrown it: "*Paulie.*" As I spoke with him, I heard myself loudly calling him Paul, as if I was making some point. I guess I was trying to grow him up a bit, to make him less of a target (as if a better name would help).

"It was a great week," Paulie lied cheerfully. "Nobody gave me any trouble, although I did walk into a locker door. All your [antibullying] suggestions worked great. I really appreciate your help with that. Maybe now you could help me not walk into lockers. Heh-heh!"

His forced smile and weak laugh broke my heart. The school counselor had phoned to say that Paulie had been roughed up three more times that week, with one serious punch in the face. As always, he refused to say who had done these things to him.

I interrupted him so that he wouldn't have to keep lying. "Paul," I said quietly, "I know that your purple face did not come from a locker."

Paulie's eyes narrowed, and his smile evaporated. "Exactly what did they tell you?" he asked sharply, like a cop who was upset that secret information had leaked out. For years, Paulie had worked desperately to keep the bullying a secret. Like so many other victims of so many other crimes, he felt ashamed and guilty for being bullied. He had been pummeled so long that even he was buying the crap that bullies put out about their victims "deserving it."

When I told him what I knew, he looked hopeless, and then sad and mad. "CAN'T YOU ALL JUST LEAVE ME THE HELL ALONE?" he yelled. "It's my life and my problem, OK? You guys [adults] always make things worse by getting involved. Peer mediation [my suggestion from last week]! What a joke that is! I did peer mediation last year. Jeremy [his chief bully] talked real nice in there, and then shoved me down the steps when we left, saying I was 'dead meat' for ratting him out. He said that, before the mediation, he had decided to stop pounding me, but that now he would hunt me down the rest of my life.

"This week, I did go to the principal [my other "helpful" suggestion from last week]. He was a big help. He asked me a hundred times if maybe it was possible that I pushed Nolan first [another bully], making him hit me back. AND NOLAN'S A HUGE HOCKEY PLAYER. WHY WOULD I START WITH HIM?" Paulie cried bitter tears. "The principal kept asking me that same question, until I finally lied and told him what he wanted to hear, so that he wouldn't have to suspend Nolan, and make his father mad. Nolan's father is the hockey coach at school. So just leave it alone, OK? There's nothing anybody can do."

I felt exactly as worthless as Paulie looked. Fantasies of jacking his bullies up against a wall flashed through my head, just as they flashed through his mom's head every night. That Special Forces stuff would help us adults feel better, and make Paulie even more of a target. Even as I sat there, I could feel myself becoming the worst part of bullying for victims like Paulie: another adult who wants to pull away from him because he makes us feel so hopeless and helpless.

Bullying has become the latest-rage "X" sport in American schools (see "Aggression . . ."), with an all-time-high number of players. Although serious assaults in school have declined, surveys of kids show that bullying is off the charts, particularly for kids known or suspected to be gay.

Even when the actual bullying action isn't going on, the victim still lives his daily life just awaiting the next attack.

Bullying is different from assault in a couple of ways. First, the weapons of assault are usually fists, knives, or guns. The violence of bullying is less physical (slaps and shoves), mostly using words as weapons. Second, assault is usually a one-time event, whereas bullying usually happens over and over again. Even when the actual bullying action isn't going on, the victim still lives his daily life just awaiting the next attack. No joke—it can be the same kind of never-ending fear that wears down soldiers in combat. It can become part of your life. It can become part of your soul.

Assault is a 10-second tornado of violence, with bad physical wounds. But when you're assaulted, you usually get lots of sympathy and attention, and, usually, you heal up just fine. Everyone around you is outraged that someone would do such a thing to you, and the attacker is hated by everyone.

Bullying is an unending drizzle of mental violence, with worse emotional wounds. It can haunt you every single day, slowly wearing you down, until the words "worthless loser" are permanently burned into your identity, forever changing who you are and how you see yourself.

Adults who've never been assaulted or bullied are sure that being assaulted would be worse. Kids who've been bullied know that being bullied is worse. Assaulted kids end up in hospitals and crowded courtrooms. Their attackers end up arrested. Bullied kids end up in shrinks' offices and lonely bedrooms. Their attackers end up—*popular*. But not in all schools.

What's most interesting about bullying is seeing that *not all schools have bullies*. If you come from "Bully City High School," I know you find that hard to believe, but it's true. And how that happens shows us a lot about bullying. It's all about the *bystanders* and the *size of the audience* (or school).

Bystanders are the people who watch while some other poor kid is pushed around. When a kid is harassed in those larger "bully" schools, the bystanders tend to laugh outside, but feel bad inside. They might hate what they see, but they don't speak up when they're part of a huge crowd.

In smaller, "nonbully" settings, the bystander kids have bigger mouths and bigger hearts. These bystander kids more often get on a bully's case, saying things like "Knock it off. That's not funny." *Those six little words coming from most of the kids in a crowd can change a bully's ways faster than a S.W.A.T. team.* The magic fact is that, when a majority of students stand together and say it's time for that crap to end, *that crap ends*. The tragic fact is that, until those kids take control, there is very little adults can do to stop a bully. What happens is really up to you.

So, what can you do? That depends on your role in the bullying game. If you are a target, those same suggestions that didn't work for Paulie might not work for you, either, but you have to give them a try—sometimes they do work. Do these in the order they're listed here. The idea is to try the easiest, lowest-risk moves first.

Strategies for Bully Targets

1. Ignore the first few shots. Mr. High-on-life, the school counselor, is correct when he tells you that bullies are looking for a reaction from you. That's so hard to believe when you're in the middle of a taunting, but it's true. If you can, try just blowing off whatever is said, or keep walking when you get shoved. That's much easier said than done, but it's still your best first step in a bad scene: Try to show no reaction.

2. Tell the jerk to knock it off! If you've tried showing no reaction for a while, with no success, it's time for Step Two: Show a reaction. Tell him to stop. It sounds stupid, but some bullies don't think that what they're doing is bullying. These kids are amazed to find out that you really don't like the games they play (like smacking you and then yelling really loud, "QUIT HITTING ME!"). Some bullies are only amateurs—they just play at it a little. Firmly telling these kids that you hate what they're doing (without threatening them) occasionally ends the problem ("I REALLY, REALLY hate that. Will you PLEASE knock it off?"). Even if your bully is a pro, saying that won't make things much worse.

3. Don't be there. The best comeback to an insult is to not be around when it's thrown. Consider changing your routes to avoid running into No-neck Magursky (the universal bully) as much as possible. Yes, that's the "coward's" way out, but if that feels better to you than the other options, then maybe that's the way for you. Many kids (particularly boys) get confused about that "C" word (coward). Running from a fight does *not* make you a coward. It simply shows that, for you, the issue is not worth the risk of pain and injury. If you think you're a coward, picture No-neck attacking your mother or little sister. Do you picture yourself running away or taking No-neck on? Speaking of cowards, I personally walked four miles a day to avoid having to ride on the "bus from hell" with my own No-neck Magursky. It felt bad, but not nearly as bad as having No-neck's face in mine. We must all make our own choices.

The best comeback to an insult is to not be around when it's thrown.

4. Ask "What's up with that?" but ask in the right place. One right place is called *mediation*. It's far from perfect, but it's the next best step to deal with No-neck. Mediation is where you meet No-neck in a room with only you, him, and a *mediator*, who might be a teacher or another student (called a *peer mediator*). There, you can safely ask No-neck, "What's up with the bullying?" The trick is that, when No-neck tries to explain, he'll sound stupid *even to himself*, because bullying makes no sense. Without the laughter of his toadies or the fear of a crowd, No-neck's reasons for being a jerk will embarrass even him. Peer mediators and teachers will not be impressed if he says that you deserve it because you are a "loser." More importantly, there's a chance that No-neck will not be impressed with himself, either. That's where change becomes possible in people. If mediation had been around in my day, my legs might have been a lot less sore (from those four-mile walks).

A second right place might be alone with that bully. If your tormentor seems to love playing to the crowd (almost all do), he's less likely to pummel you in private. IF YOU THINK THAT YOUR BULLY IS NOT TRULY A VIOLENT WHACKO, but only loves the crowd attention, then confronting him alone might work. *If you have any doubts, then do not try this.* First, talk with a counselor to see if she thinks that idea would work with a particular kid. If he's truly violent, she will likely know that and suggest some other way.

5. Rat him out—particularly if you are getting physically pounded. If all other options fail, you may have to go to the principal, or even to the police (with your parents). This is the high-risk, last-resort option because it can label you as a rat, or wimp, or whatever. But if you've tried everything else, it's time to get tough, in return. Many bullies will get scared off when the heat becomes involved. Usually, No-neck torments other kids besides you, so he may have a record of doing this stuff, one that makes getting turned in a big problem for him. He even may be on probation for other things he's done. People like principals, cops, and judges really don't like bullying, and they're not shy about letting the No-necks of the world know.

6. Outlast the bastards. If you can, hunker down, and wait out the storm. The truly wonderful news is that this insanity will end if you can just plod through. As kids get older, bullying looks dumber and dumber to them. The whole bullying thing turns around. What impresses the heck out of 8th graders looks like sheer stupidity to 12th graders. "Revenge of the Nerds" is a fact of life. Older kids and adults are not impressed by who you can beat up. They are impressed by things like your friendliness, compassion, and honesty. Don't let the jerks pound these treasures out of you. I promise you that those qualities are what make you "cool" as you get older.

7. Beyond all else, limit the damage. The physical bruises of bullying are gone in a week. The mental scars can last forever, *if you allow them to.* If you let a bully start to change how you see yourself, you can become another bully inside your own head, one much more dangerous than No-neck. That bully inside can start to repeat No-neck's insults, telling you that you are a "loser" in every way. That bully inside can tear at your already-shaky adolescent self-esteem (see Chapter 3), but you can stand up to him by yelling at yourself!

If you find that you are adopting that "loser" label for yourself, and retreating from good grades or activities you love or want to try because you think you're not good enough, get in the mirror, and get mad! Yell at yourself, and say that the fact that No-neck can beat you up only means that *No-neck can beat you up—nothing more.* Admit that, and then let it go. Then ask yourself who you most admire in the world, who you want to be like. No-neck is probably not on that list, so stop making him your competition. Instead, look at what you find good about other people, and then start becoming like them. The odds are huge that the people you most admire are not bullies, and that the qualities you admire in them have nothing to do with fist fighting. Get really clear about what a real "loser" is (No-neck), and about who you intend to be as an adult. No bully can punch your identity away unless you allow it, and, in fact, do it to yourself.

Once he gets the idea that torturing people is not considered very cool by most of the kids in his audience, he'll start to back off.

Strategies for Bystanders of Bullies

Question: Who's the most powerful person in a bullying event—the bully, the victim, or the bystander?

Answer: *The bystander.* The bully and his victim are kind of trapped. The bully can change, but won't, because he gets some weird payoff for tormenting someone. The victim wants to change, but can't, because, well, he's the victim. But the bystander is the person with all the true power. The bystander can change things by speaking up.

The key to changing the bully's actions is his audience, meaning the bystanders. Once he gets the idea that torturing people is not considered very cool by most of the kids in his audience, he'll start to back off. Some schools have stopped bullying almost entirely by saying nothing to the bullies, and nothing to the targets. These schools have focused only on the bystanders, trying to get them to stand up and say what they think. That's clearly where the real power is. In light of that, here are a few tips on what you can do the next time you get a ringside seat at No-neck's show:

- **Distract No-neck by inventing an excuse.** As Paulie is cornered, act like you were sent to get him. Walk in on the bullying, as if you didn't know what was going down, and yell, "Paulie! There you are! Mr. Redneck is looking for you, and he seems mad about something. He said to get your face in his place, now!" Bullies get put off when they lose control of a situation. So acting like a teacher is around can end Paulie's torture session—for today, anyway.
- **Speak up, if you have the power.** Some very lucky kids are considered "cool," even by bullies. They usually don't get messed with. If that describes you, you might have enough power to call No-neck off without getting your own nose reshaped. If you're willing, go soft with the words. Try something like, "Yo, No-neck, enough, man. Let's go watch Mr. Redneck try to start up his classic Mustang." If you're feeling really brave, and want to tell the bully to back off permanently, try that only when you're alone with him. Appeal to his vanity. Let him know that he doesn't look cool picking on another kid. Try saying something like "What's up with that grade school stuff—you know, the bullying? Nobody does that anymore, you know."
- **Start the discussion.** The best solution is the one that takes the most time to help, but it can change things forever in your school. Start a conversation with other bystanders, perhaps in one of your classes. Get kids thinking about this whole idea of bullying, helping them to see that it will go on only if they allow it.

If you're a victim, remember that the most important goal in surviving bullying is to limit the bruises to your body. You may not be able to control what a bully does to your arm, but what happens to your heart (your identity) is up to you. A great First Lady (Eleanor

Roosevelt) once said that no one can make you feel inferior without your consent. Smart lady, don't you think?

Career Choices: "How Do I Pick a Forever Career if I Can't Pick Tomorrow's Breakfast?"

You could win the lottery before you could predict what your adult job will be. The odds are about as high. Adults who tell you to make career choices as a teenager are crazy. That is actually a very bad idea, for a bunch of reasons.

First, you're changing faster than the latest sneaker style. You have no idea who you will be at the end of this adolescent trip you're on, so how can you decide what kind of work you want to do in the future?

Second, the purpose of these teen years is to explore as much as you can, to learn as much as you can. Kids who decide at age 12 that they want to be a pilot can close themselves off from other ideas that may be much better for them. Remember, you have no idea what you have no idea about. Putting blinders on about other possibilities you haven't yet seen might keep you from a great job. Forget about the job you think you'd like, and start looking at all the things in the world you never thought about. Doing that will lead you to work you will love. If that journey brings you back to being a pilot, then you'll be all the more sure.

The best predictors of your success in a job are your interests, not your abilities.

Third, the experts tell me that the job you'll probably have as an adult *hasn't been invented yet.* The world changes so fast that the jobs needed to run it have to be created all the time. So it's pointless to pick a career now that may no longer exist when you're ready to do it. So put your time into learning about who you are, because your identity is your key to job success, as this fourth reason makes clear.

The best predictors of your success in a job *are your interests,* not your abilities. People who do the best in jobs are the ones who are similar to other people who are successful in that job. Being like cops and being unlike doctors means that you'd be a better cop than a doctor, *even if you have the skills to be a doctor.* People who hate what they do usually do lousy at it, even if they can do the job. And, as a bonus, they're miserable, as well.

Adults seem to be awful at picking two things: spouses and jobs. Usually, they screw up both choices for the same reason—*they never got to know themselves well enough to know what a good choice would be for them.* I don't have to tell you about the bad marriage choices (see Chapter 7). You've seen the mess those poor choices have created for your own parents, or for those of a friend. The mess that adults rarely talk about is how poorly they picked their job. They usually drift into whatever job pops up in front of them, grow to hate what they do, and think only of the day when they can retire. This means that they live, hating their lives, for eight hours a day, five days a week for 45 years, all because they didn't take the time to know themselves first?! That's nuts.

So what are the tricks for good career choices?

- **TAKE YOUR TIME.** Pick a career as carefully as you would pick a spouse. "Wasting" some time after school by exploring yourself and the world will be the smartest time you ever wasted.
- **Keep all of your options open (Chapter 9), by doing well in school.** It's possible that you might need chemistry one day. It's probable that you will need good grades every day.
- **Observe as many jobs as you can, by working or volunteering some time at various and different places (hospitals, building sites, law firms).** Watch what they do, ask a million questions, and drink coffee with those people. See if you seem to be like them.
- **Take all those dumb tests your counselor has that tell you about your interests.** As silly as they seem, they are actually telling you something more important about you than your abilities. They're showing you parts of your identity.
- **Ask yourself what you love, *what you would do for free.*** Then try to figure out how to get paid for doing that. Some kids love listening to and helping others. They often become shrinks. Others lose track of time building forts and tree houses. That's where carpenters are born. Still others love arguing over anything and everything, which is mostly what lawyers are paid to do. Harry Chapin, the late, great folk singer, once stopped singing right in the middle of a song, and, with a huge

smile on his face, said, "I have to tell you all that I still can't believe I get paid for doing THIS!"

- **If you're college bound, forget that junk about declaring a major right away.** Most college kids change their majors at least once. Approach your first year or two at college as a time to find out more about who you are. You can always take the courses you need later, once you discover what you love.

All those tricks lead you back to the same place: *you*. They're all about you finding out who you are. Once again, developing your identity becomes your best bet for a happy life. So, for now, focus on you. The rest of that career stuff will fall into place, as long as you keep your eyes open and your brain thinking.

Chores: "This Looks like a Job for Captain Eventually."

You'd think someone was being stabbed. Or at least getting their fingers broken. The screaming that goes on about teenagers' chores is pretty amazing.

The basic issue is that kids don't *feel* like doing them. Adolescents agree that they should have chores, and most agree that the chores they have are fair. The problem is that chores are so incredibly boring that teens always have better things to do at chore time. Which always happens to be the exact same moment when parents go completely berserk at the sight of uncollected trash. It's a cosmic thing.

Chores are another example of where you can get into serious fights over silly issues, because the real fight is about other things that are not silly at all (see "Communication . . ."). When you and your parents look at an overflowing trash can (your undone chore), you each see very different things. You see uncollected trash—no big deal. Your parents see defiance, immaturity, and a lack of love—a very big deal. Did I mention that your parents are crazy? Linda was sure that her mother was.

"I WANT THOSE DAMN CHORES DONE ON TIME, AS WE, THAT'S *WE*, AGREED! AND IF YOU CAN'T LIFT ONE FREAK-

ING 'PRINCESS' FINGER TO HELP OUT, THEN MAYBE YOU CAN'T LIVE IN MY HOUSE, THAT'S *MY* HOUSE, ANYMORE!" Loren jabbed her finger in Linda's face each time she yelled "WE," "YOU," and "MY." Mom's eyes told me that she was instantly sorry she had made that threat to her 14-year-old daughter, but now it was done.

As I waited for Linda to explode in return, I got another of my endless adolescent surprises. Cool as a cucumber, Linda studied her mother's red-with-rage face for a moment, and then slowly and very sarcastically asked, "Let me get this straight. You're putting me on the street because I didn't do the trash last night, right? Is that it? I just want to get the story accurate for the cops when they ask me why I'm sleeping in the park."

Mom looked like she was going to bust a gut. Linda's mocking answer had Loren gasping for breath, as if she was trying to take in too much air to fuel her next screamer. I decided to short-circuit the coming explosion. If I didn't, it seemed too possible that Linda might be sleeping in the park tonight. "Loren," I interrupted. "LOREN," I repeated loudly, to pry her attention away from her daughter, "Listen to me. What feelings are behind that anger you show when you see Linda's chores not done?"

This exhausted single mom looked completely turned around. She was so confused that now she could only speak quietly—and from her heart. "I get scared—and hurt, too, I guess. Scared because I have nightmares about dying and leaving Linda alone, unable to cope with the world. How will she ever take care of herself if she can't even do simple chores like laundry or cleaning? How can she run her life if she can't keep her room organized? How can she take care of her sister if she can't take care of herself?"

I couldn't let Mom off the hook without her saying the only thing that might make Linda consider doing her chores. "And the hurt part?" I asked.

"Hurt because, well . . ." Loren looked sideways at her daughter. ". . . well, hurt because when I see the chores not done, it feels like Linda saying that she doesn't give a damn about me or the baby. I guess then I feel even more alone. Alone and hurt for me, and alone and scared for her. I guess that's why I explode."

Linda stared at her mother in disbelief. "Why didn't you tell me any of that before?" she asked.

"Because," Mom said softly, "it's hard for me to say that to someone I think really doesn't care. Would it be hard for you?"

Linda's chores had little to do with chores. They had everything to do with her *relationship* with her family, although the chore part itself is important in a couple of ways. First, with most kids' parents working these days, there's never enough time to get it all done. Kids have to help out. Second, it is vital for teens to know how to cook, clean, and do laundry—especially if they're male teens (because it's expected of the females). Unless you plan to live at home forever, guys, these are survival skills. (By the way, gentlemen, I once had a female client who was a "cover girl" model tell me that her definition of a truly sexy man was a nice guy who knew how to sort laundry and change diapers.)

When parents come home and find housework done by their teen, you'd think they just got a birthday present.

But it's the relationship part of chores that is the most important piece. When parents come home and find housework done by their teen, you'd think they just got a birthday present. And if that work was not on the chore list, well, that's a New Year's Eve party for your folks. Those done chores are statements to parents that you do give a damn, and that you see how much work it takes to run a house. Besides that, those completed chores become report cards, telling parents that their kid is growing up and deserves adult kinds of respect. If you don't buy that, try doing extra chores for a month without being asked. I'll bet you dollars to doughnuts that new freedoms will rain down upon your head from your amazed and delighted parents.

A final tip: Most kids say that it's not the chores that make them crazy, it's their parents' *constant reminders* to do the chores that makes them want to scream (and not do the chore). Try setting up a system to remind yourself to get the job done. Some kids put up schedules on their walls. Others set alarms on wristwatches. All say that when they remind themselves, chores are no big deal. More than a few admit that it feels good to help out with the work at home. Kind of a growing-up thing.

Communication/Problem Solving: "If Yah' Keep Flappin' Yoh' Jaw, Son, How Yah' Evah Gonna Hear Mah Point of View?" (Foghorn Leghorn to the little chicken hawk who couldn't get a word in edgewise)

Foghorn's complaint is so funny because it's so true—*about us.* We humans are the about the worst communicators on the planet. Slugs communicate better than we do. That's because we see "talking" as just another weapon to pound somebody into doing what we want. "Listening" has become defined as that time where you plan your next verbal attack, while you ignore what the other person is saying. Nowhere is this more true than in a family in which a young child becomes a teenager.

Communicating well with people is a kind of a cure-all vitamin—it solves hundreds of problems all at once, because it gets to the *feelings behind the fights.* As you've noticed by now, most of the fights you have with people are not about the *things* you fight over, but the *feelings* behind the things. Drivers will have fistfights over parking spaces. Those fights are not over pavement, but over *feelings* attached to that pavement (like feeling bullied if the space is lost). Kids will fight over not being invited to a party. Those fights are not over parties, but over *feelings* attached to parties (like feeling worthless if you're not invited). This means that your fights with your crazy parents about chores or curfews are really about the *feelings* attached to chores and curfews (see "Chores . . ." and "Curfews . . ."). When you deal with the feelings, you automatically solve the 10 silly fights you have because of those feelings.

So the trick is to get to the feelings behind the fights, which turns out to be a tough trick. The main thing that stops us is that we believe that telling our feelings somehow makes us weak or vulnerable. Then, we fear, people will take advantage of us. Yet, as you'll see in a minute, the opposite is true. People are *less* able to take advantage of us when we simply say what we feel. And that also turns out to be a way of more often getting more of what you want.

However, we do easily share one feeling: rage. In fact, we're great at showing rage, but that doesn't really count as a feeling. Rage is only our cover for scary, hidden feelings like fear or hurt that we rarely (or never?) share. But shared rage is never stronger than shared fear or hurt—it's only louder.

Don't believe that? Well, which of the following would have more of a chance of changing you?

Option 1: Your crazed parent screaming, "I'M GODDAMN SICK OF YOU STUPIDLY FORGETTING YOUR FREAKIN' HOMEWORK!!"

Option 2: Your crazed parent confiding, "I'm terrified that you'll mess up school, and have a lousy life. I don't know how to help you, and that makes me sad. I get so scared that I can't sleep some nights. That's why I lose it and yell at you. I'm sorry."

If you picked Option 2, you have lots of company. It turns out that parents who scream at kids have kids who do less homework. And parents who quietly share their fears with kids have kids who do more homework.

Tantrumming, yelling, or threatening takes you further away from the things you want.

The same rule applies to your behavior with your parents. Tantrumming, yelling, or threatening takes you further away from the things you want. Speaking quietly from your heart is a much more powerful tool. Check out this example for yourself. If you were this parent, which approach makes you more inclined to compromise with your kid?

Option 1: Kid screaming, *"I'M SICK OF YOUR INSANE CONTROLLING CRAP, AND I'M NOT TAKING IT ANYMORE! I'M STAYING OUT UNTIL MIDNIGHT, AND THERE'S NOT A FREAKIN' THING YOU CAN DO ABOUT IT!"*

Option 2: Kid confiding, *"Dad, I get embarrassed when my friends have to drive me home at 10 because of my curfew. It makes me feel sad and hurt, like I'm being punished when I haven't done anything wrong. It feels like you can't trust me."*

Option 2 gets it done most of the time. Option 1 gets it done none of the time. Sharing feelings is a much more powerful way to talk. Isn't it strange that we seem so convinced that yelling and screaming is a better way to do family business?

Now that you know that the real goal in communicating is to share feelings, here are a few tips to help you through. And although we're using parent conflicts as examples, remember that these tricks work just as well with friends and enemies.

View communication as two very different steps: *Sharing* and *problem solving*. Sharing is when *feelings* are discussed. Problem solving is when *solutions* are discussed. DON"T MIX THESE TWO TOGETHER, OR NEITHER WILL WORK. You might even call a break in the talk before moving from sharing into problem solving.

Step 1: Sharing. Sharing is a truce time when people can feel safe enough to expose their hidden feelings. SHARING IS NOT A FOOTBALL GAME. The goal is to learn about each other, not to beat each other.

- **Say *feelings,* not *thoughts* or *demands.*** *Feelings* are short, simple, and powerful words like *scared, sad,* or *alone* ("Dad, I'm scared."). *Thoughts* are long explanations ("Father, I believe that the reason we don't get along is your lack of understanding of. . . ."). *Demands* are telling others what they must do ("You better get the hell out of my life!"). Thoughts and demands can be places to hide our feelings, and ways to play communication-ending games. Thoughts will be argued forever, and demands will be defied longer. Feelings can't be argued or defied. If you truly feel some way, no one else can tell you that you don't. Feelings are the ultimate in word power.
- ***Say* your feelings, don't *become* them.** Saying that you feel angry is fine. It helps parents to become supportive. Screaming that you're pissed off is not fine. It helps parents to become deaf. Once people start to yell, no good will happen, and a lot of bad can happen. If tempers get hot, call a timeout until you or your parents can calm down. Never hesitate to suggest letting a talk go until tomorrow. Very few decisions have to be made immediately. Very many decisions get screwed up because we think that they have to be made today.
- **Allow each side to speak without being interrupted.** When one is talking, the other should be listening—not to hear *if* what they say makes sense, but to understand *how* it makes sense—to *them.* You might think it's nuts for your crazy mother to get scared when you don't do homework, but if she does, *she does.* That's what she's stuck with, whether or not it makes sense to you. Is it fair to ask her to respect your feelings if you don't respect hers?
- **Stay on your side of the fence.** Don't judge another person's feelings. Telling someone that she "shouldn't feel that way" doesn't get rid of the problem, and, in fact, it creates another problem. She will still "feel that

way," and she now feels worse because she was told that she's stupid to feel as she does.

- **Let Dear Abby give the advice.** Don't play that adult game of telling people what they should do. We usually know what we *should* do—*doing* what we should do is the hard part. Telling Dad that he shouldn't scream at you doesn't help him much. He probably already knows that. Telling him that you feel sad and scared when he yells will help him understand why it's so bad. Understanding how we affect the people we love helps us find the strength to make hard changes.
- **Don't try to fix things—yet.** Be sure both sides have shared all of their feelings before moving on to Step 2.

Step 2: Problem Solving. Here's where the two sides offer suggestions about how to solve a problem, like curfew or chores disputes. The weird thing is that this step is actually the less important part of communicating well, but most of us skip over the sharing part every time. Often, just sharing feelings magically solves problems. But, if needed, here are a few tips on solving problems after sharing.

- **Negotiate, don't demand.** Negotiation is a great life skill to learn. The goal is to get both sides to win a little *and* lose a little. *In that way, everyone wins more than if one side bullies the other into an unfair deal.* That happens to be a scientific fact. Unfair deals never work over time, and they end up costing the "winner" a lot more than he or she would have gained by negotiating. For example, if you tantrum your father into taking on your chores, he'll be miserable, up your rear end, and not likely to give you rides when you ask. Those costs will outweigh what you gained by demanding. If you negotiated (and got less than you wanted), you'd actually gain more from your better relationship with Dad.
- **Make lots of options.** Ask both sides to think of a bunch of possible solutions before deciding on one answer. Possible solutions always help people think of other (often better) possible solutions. They kind of build upon each other ("Well, what if we took your idea about the weekend curfew and used it every other week?").
- **Take breaks.** If you find that you're going in circles, don't quit because you think it's a failure. Call a recess, knowing that it's just part of the process. It's amazing how those impossible Tuesday-night problems become so solvable on Wednesday morning.

- **Talk like Honest Sam, the used-car man.** Keep working calmly until you make your deal. Honest Sam never hears the word "no" as meaning that he's lost a sale. He never gets discouraged or takes it personally. He knows that "no" only means there's more negotiating to be done. Both you and your parents have something, and you both want something. Find that middle ground, where both sides win a little and lose a little. Better grades might earn you that trip where you miss some school. Wheel and deal with your parents, just like Honest Sam: *"Tell ya what I'm gonna' do, folks—just because you have such honest faces, and with today being my hamster's birthday. . . ."*

Many very smart people say that almost all of our conflicts, both in our families and in our world, result from bad communication. If they are right, that means that learning to communicate well (*listening, in particular)* might be the path to peace in our lives and in our world. In 50 years of searching, I'm starting to believe that. How about you?

Curfews: The Invisible Ones Work Best

At only 13 years of age, Cindy had mastered the swagger of a TV trial lawyer. Every time her parents suggested a curfew option, she would sigh, roll her eyes, and shake her head disgustedly. Slowly exaggerating her words for effect, she said, "YOU—ARE—NOT—LISS-ENNING. I told you, MIDNIGHT, not NINE!" Each time Cindy's eyes rolled, so did her possible curfew—backwards. You could feel the anger and resentment building in Mom and Dad with each shot she took at them. You could see her sarcasm convincing her parents that she was not responsible enough to be allowed out later. This was not going well.

"Cindy," I interrupted, "can I ask your parents a few things?"

"Sure," she snorted, "I told you they're stupid."

"Dad," I asked her father, "What are you feeling?" He looked like he was holding back an extreme urge to wring a 13-year-old neck.

"I'm feeling like now there's no way she's going out at night AT ALL. Listen to her! SHE'S CRAZY! She can't be trusted to . . ."

I cut Dad off: "Those are your thoughts—what are your feelings? Look inside a moment for some one-word answers."

Dad's eyes searched mine as he searched himself. "Sad, I guess," he finally said quietly. "And scared. Very scared."

When Mom nodded in agreement, I asked her to explain those feelings. "Sad because we used to be so close with Cindy," she said, as tears began to shine in her eyes. "We used to snuggle her to sleep every night. We've lost that. That 15 minutes every night was the best part of our lives—talking about our day, dreaming about our next vacation—things like that.

"And scared? Scared because . . . we don't know her anymore. She seems so angry all the time now, we really don't know if she's capable of staying safe. Maybe something is wrong with her mentally. How can we let her out late if she's not safe? What if something happened to her? What kind of parents would we be if we just let her do whatever?"

I turned back to Cindy. "You're up," I said. But that was before I saw that her eyes were shining now, just like Mom's.

"THIS IS NOT WHAT I WANT TO TALK ABOUT," she hissed with gritted teeth. "WE'RE ONLY SUPPOSED TO TALK ABOUT. . . ." Cindy's soft, bitter crying ended her sentence.

After a minute, I asked, "Is that hurt in your eyes?"

Cindy could only nod yes. "And loss," she added. "I feel so . . . lost. Like they don't know me anymore. Like I lost my family."

"Guys," I sighed, "Do you think we've got other things to talk about before we get to curfew?"

If you want a snapshot of how a parent-teen relationship is doing, ask about curfew. Some families stare back at you blankly, saying "Gee, we never actually set a curfew. She just seems to come in at appropriate times, or she calls to let us know if she's going to be a little late. It's never been a problem. We've never really discussed it." Others roll their eyes and pull out a 10-page document, signed and notarized, listing hundreds of curfew rules and regulations that have never worked, and probably never will.

The no-curfew families are usually much happier and quieter than the 10-pagers. That's because they've built a trust and respect for each other that *automatically* solves all those nasty little problems like curfew times (see "Communication . . ."). The 10-page folks have it backwards. They try to make trust and respect rise out of rules and regulations. That's like trying to grow gold out of garbage. If you're stuck in never-ending battles over curfews, understand that your real fight is about trust and respect. If you don't build trust and respect with each other, you'll never end the curfew wars.

Those magical qualities don't happen easily or accidentally, any more than a stone house builds itself. That one stone house is made of thousands of separate acts of sweat, effort, and love. Trust and respect are similar qualities, made of thousands of small, difficult acts of truth-telling, caring, and compromising—by both parents *and* their teens.

Trust and respect are similar qualities, made of thousands of small, difficult acts of truth-telling, caring, and compromising—by both parents and their teens.

If you're caught up in curfew wars, trust and respect are probably not overflowing in your house. If that's so, then you and your parents have also lost the closeness that you probably once had. Closeness is the first step to building trust and respect. If that's gone, get it back—now. Stop cursing about the curfews and start listening for the love—yours *and* your parents. Yes, it's still there, somewhere, buried beneath all the muck that covers it up when good people who love each other fall into bad ways of talking at each other.

If your parents didn't love you, there would be no curfew fights. If they didn't care, there would be no curfew to fight over. They wouldn't care when you got in or what you had been doing. So, first, get it into your head that your parents fight with you, and make your life miserable, *because they love you*. They might be really lousy at showing it, but they do love you. And you know that's true because you know kids whose parents don't care enough to fight with their children. If you can see your parents' meddling in your life as a sign of their love, you're halfway home to ending the curfew fight (along with a hundred others). Once you have that thought in your head, you might be able to calm down enough to take the next step in solving the problem: *communicating*.

Get everyone's *feelings* (not thoughts) about curfew out on the table. Yours will likely be about things like independence, respect, and trust. If you have curfew-free friends who laugh at you heading home at 9 P.M., mention humiliation as well. Put everything out CALMLY, so that your parents can get an idea of what it feels like on your side of the curfew clock. Ask them to listen to you—*really listen to you.* But don't tell them what's wrong with them. Just say what feels wrong to you.

Then, ask your parents to do the same. They'll likely speak of fear, control needs, and safety. Listen to them—*really listen to them.* Not to argue, but to understand. Try to feel what they feel. That sharing of feelings is where your curfew answers will be found.

When Cindy and her parents finally reconnected, they saw that her anger was all about her hurt and loss, not insanity. They realized that she was not crazy, or at risk. They saw that letting her out a little later helped her feel more trust and respect from them. Cindy, in turn, was able to see that her folks still did love her, and wanted to be closer to her. That helped her cut back her midnight demand to something her parents could live with. In other words, when that family fixed their feelings problem, they fixed their curfew problem. To help you fix your own, here are a few other points about your crazy parents to keep in mind as you negotiate your curfew:

- **Many parents cannot sleep until their kids are home.** As silly as that sounds, it happens to be true. The ones who tell you that are not lying. And most won't even tell you, because it's sort of embarrassing. It's a crazy parent thing, not being able to sleep until you know that your kid is safe. You might also have a lot of sleepless nights when you have kids. Before you start yelling, "But I am safe when I'm out late," check out this next tip.
- **The fact that you know you're alive does not mean that your parents know you're alive.** Teens get nuts with the "check-in" rules, where insane parents demand periodic phone calls to know that you're OK. It may feel like they're spying, but the truth is that parents worry about the unsafe nighttime world adults have left to you (see Chapter 5), and they frequently have nightmares about their kid's demise. Try to be understanding of these bizarre parent needs. They're crazy, you know.
- **Parent nightmares become realities (to them) when curfew hour passes without a call from you.** Their crazy fear that you're dead in a gutter somewhere becomes a certainty to them at precisely 15 minutes past your "due in" time. That's why, when you roll in 30 minutes late, they act like you shot Santa Claus, or something. What you're hearing in their yelling is not about 30 minutes. It's about fear. And love.

Remember the most important fact about curfews, and you'll have far fewer curfew conflicts: *Most curfew fights are not about curfews. They're about power, control, and respect.* Get to the real issues, and the curfew problem will solve itself.

Death: Sometimes, Fewer Words Mean More

I was shocked when so many kids suggested this topic for the book—shocked at the number of teens who had lost someone very close to them, or who knew a close friend who had. At 14, Holly had some words you might want to hear, whether it's you or a friend who takes that gut punch.

Holly caught me off guard. She had agreed to see me because she had become depressed in the eight months following her father's sudden death, but it sounded like she did not want to deal with her loss. Her mother told me that Holly never grieved, never even cried after her dad died of a heart attack one night. Mom told me that her daughter even insisted on going to school the morning after her father died, even though she and her dad were incredibly close. After hearing all this, I was expecting to chit-chat for weeks or months with Holly before she'd open up about her dad, if ever. In the first minute of that first session, she reminded me about the dangers of assuming anything about adolescents.

Holly politely ignored my stupid, opening chit-chat question about our home team being in the football playoffs. After staring at her hands for a moment, she began speaking in a soft, clear voice, with quiet words that froze me where I sat, riveted by the terrible picture she painted of that awful night. "When I sleep, no one can wake me up. I'm, like, in a coma. But that night, I woke up. It was 3 A.M. I saw red and blue lights flashing against my wall, coming through the window. I figured it was for our crazy neighbor, drunk again, or whatever. It was so quiet I could hear the clicking of those lights. I never realized that they make a clicking sound. The next thing I remember was hearing my mother crying weird, like, trying to muffle herself. I got up and went into the hall, and there was this big cop there, and he wouldn't let me out of my room. My sister started screaming and crying because they made her go back into her room, too. The cop shoved me back, and held my door shut. I heard the stretcher going down the stairs, past my door, and someone on a radio talking real low. I ran to my window and saw the stretcher sliding into the ambulance. My dad's face was staring out the window. It was blue. He was dead."

Holly suddenly looked up at me with her steely eyes to see my reaction. I had no idea what to do, so I did nothing. She studied my face a minute, and then decided to continue. "I'm sure my mom has told you that I went to school that morning. The reason I went is that I can't let this change anything. I have to keep my life going, or I'll go crazy." Then she answered my silent question about what she had been looking for in my face. Luckily, she hadn't found it. "The worst thing is pity. That's why I wouldn't go back to see those other doctors I saw before you. They acted all sorry and stuff. One of them cried. That made me hate them. Being pitied makes you different from everyone else. It makes you less than them. That morning, when I got to class, everybody just stared at me. Because my Mom called the school after I left, they knew what had happened, and they all looked sorry for me. Then the teacher and principal tried to hug me, but I ran out. They don't understand. Nobody understands. I don't want hugs and pity." Holly gritted her teeth. "I—just—want—my—life—back—the—way—it—was. When kids feel sorry for me, it just reminds me that I'm different from them now, and that I'll always be different."

After a minute of silence, I asked her as flatly as I could how she was different now. She answered immediately: "They all have their fathers. Some complain about their parents being divorced and all, but they still have their dads. They can go see them, touch them, and . . . well," she paused here, "smell them. I know that sounds weird, but I miss my dad's smell. You don't know that people have this nice smell until they're gone. He smelled like warm sweaters, and leaves, and stuff."

As Holly sat and remembered, those steely eyes very slowly rimmed with pain. "All I want is five minutes with my dad. To touch him, to say goodbye, to say I love him, and . . ." she laughed a soft, crying laugh, ". . . and to sniff him, one last time."

If you've lost someone close . . .

. . . there are no words that can take away your pain. Time is the only healer, if you can find the strength to just put one foot in front of the other for a while. You don't want to hear that when you're hurting like you're hurting, but kids tell me that time does ease the pain.

So does crying, screaming, laughing, raging—whatever you feel, as long as you can let it out. It's kind of like throwing up poison. It won't kill you if you can vomit it out. That's what grieving is all about. The only mistake you can make is holding it all in. But that's exactly what many teenagers (like Holly) like to do with feelings, particularly if they hate being different. If that's the case with you, see the shrink ASAP. You need to get that poison out of you, and the shrink's office is a private place to do just that, where nobody who counts sees or hears you (see Chapter 4). You don't have to worry about what the shrink thinks, and she probably will not be at your junior prom. So you can say and be whatever you feel with her.

Here are a few tips from other teens who have been there, to help you get through:

- **Let your friends know what you need.** People get very weird and clumsy around the subject of death. We don't know what to say, yet we always feel like we're supposed to say something. That's when we say the dumbest things, which is part of why your friends might make you so mad for a while, and why you might not want to be around them. Give them a clue as what works best *for you.* We all grieve in our own way. There is no one "right" way to get through this. If you hate sympathy, and don't want any of that "Oh, that's awful" talk, tell your buddies you want to be treated just like before. If you need a shoulder to cry on, tell them that, as well. It's too much to expect them to guess what you want.
- **Push back . . .** against the pain, however you can. Kids say that all kinds of strange things help a bit. Some make up scrapbooks about the lost one's life, a way of yelling to the world that perhaps death can end this person's life, *but it can never erase it.* Others plant trees, or volunteer time for some cause that their loved one loved. These memorials help remind us that winning in life is not in *how much* time we get, but in *how* we spend the time that we get.
- **If it's your friend who has lost someone . . .** reread the previous paragraphs, and let your friend tell or show you what he needs from you.

There is no one "right" way to be with a grieving friend. It all depends on your friend, and how he needs to grieve. As you hang out with him, you'll figure it out. Start off by being neutral, letting him know that you care, but avoid that "pity" trap. Use whatever ways you used before to show that you care. That might be saying it straight up, or it might be making fun of his hair. Use whatever worked before. Tell him that you're there, and that he needs to let you know what he needs. Then, let it go. Most folks need time away from the pain, and to see that some things in their world haven't been lost (like your friendship). That's how friends help friends heal from horrific hurts. They don't want you to be smart, they just need you to be there.

There is no one "right" way to be with a grieving friend. It all depends on your friend, and how he needs to grieve.

Two books on this subject that you might want to check out are *Straight Talk about Death and Dying,* by Robert Digiulio and Rachel Kranz, and *How It Feels When a Parent Dies,* by Jill Krementz. They're listed in the "To Find Out More" section at the end of this book.

Divorce: Stay Out of the Line of Fire

Chapter 7 ("Your Family") is required reading before you read this section. That chapter will give you what you'll need to make this section worth your while. Here, you'll find some divorce survival tips that teenage divorce survivors have asked me to pass along to you.

- **Be neutral, like Switzerland.** If there's a war between your parents, stay out of it. Maybe you do know who did what to whom, but maybe you don't. Perhaps the biggest thing I've learned in 30 years of hearing war stories is that there are *always* two sides to every fight, often only one of which gets published as the "truth." I stopped taking sides a long time ago. Mark reminded me why.

  Mark spent a full five minutes screaming at his mother for leaving his father. "AND YOU'RE NOTHING BUT A F'NG BITCH! WHY? WHY ARE YOU LEAVING HIM?" Mark demanded. "AND

DON'T GIVE ME THAT 'WE'RE UNHAPPY TOGETHER' BULLSHIT. HE'S DESTROYED NOW. HE CAN'T EVEN GET OUT OF BED SOME DAYS. YOU F'NG KILLED HIM. ARE YOU GETTING WITH SOMEBODY ELSE? MAYBE SOME SWEET YOUNG THING?" he taunted. "TRY TELLING THE TRUTH FOR A CHANGE! TRY NOT BEING THE BITCH YOU ARE!" Mark's heavy breathing slowly faded, as his mother fought back her tears.

Finally, she took a breath and started to say something, only to cut herself off. "I'm sorry, Mark. I've said all I can say. You're right to be mad. We've . . . I've let you down. I understand why you hate me. I'd hate me too."

Mark was back on her in a flash. "THEN UNDERSTAND THIS, GENIUS. UNDERSTAND THAT YOU'RE DEAD TO ME. I'M NOT YOUR SON. YOU'RE NOT MY MOTHER. A MOTHER WOULDN'T DO WHAT YOU'RE DOING. A MOTHER COULD NEVER BE LIKE YOU!"

Mom looked at me, confused for a moment. But then she answered her own unspoken question. She would say nothing more, and have her son hate her. She would do this to protect him from knowing that his father was involved with another woman. She would let Mark hate her as the "bitch," rather than destroy his love for his father by telling the truth. She loved her son that much.

Silently, I wondered if Mark would ever know how much. I wondered if I could love my own child that much.

- **Refuse the hate raps.** If your parents start acting like children, with each telling you how horrible the other is, cut them off. Mark's mother knew the first job of divorcing parents who truly love their kids: *to maintain the relationship between each parent and each child.* It's the *parents* who are divorcing, not the kids. Short of dangerous behavior on the part of a parent (abuse or addiction), the kids should never be asked to take sides. If you're getting hate rap from your folks, quietly remind them that you didn't ask for the divorce, that you love each of them, and that, if they love you, they'll leave you out of the war.
- **Leave rescuing to firefighters and shrinks.** Too many teens collapse while trying to carry their parents along after a crushing divorce. It's natural and nice of you to want to help out your folks after they've beat

each others' brains out in a divorce. You probably see one parent as more of a victim than the other, and you might have this urge to pitch in to help that parent feel better. That's fine if you take on a chore, and not fine if you take on a parent's emotional needs. You'll know this is happening if you find *your* gut in knots over *their* pain. Don't forget, *they're* the adults. Even after a terrible divorce, it's *their* job to take care of *you*, particularly since you got blown up, too. If you're feeling like a landfill for a parent's emotional dumping, call a timeout. Let that parent know that you can just about take care of yourself, let alone anyone else. Suggest that your hurting parent might want to chat with a shrink. Say that shrinks do cost more, but they hardly ever roll their eyes.

- **Get your own "ear."** As Chapter 7 makes painfully clear, divorce is a painfully unclear situation. You probably have about a million different feelings that you need to talk out, right at the time that your parents may not be available to you, either because they are just hanging on themselves, or because the feelings you have might be hard for them to hear. DON'T JUST SIT ON THOSE FEELINGS. That trick never works. All of that pain and confusion can haunt you for years. See a "helper" (counselor, psychologist), *now*. Find someone who is not caught up in the divorce who can listen to all of your thoughts and feelings. I promise you that you will be surprised how talking stuff out can make a lousy situation a little less lousy. If you don't believe that, then just go one time. The worst that will happen is that you'll waste an hour. If you don't, the worst that can happen is that you'll waste years.

If divorce has visited your family, whatever you do, *don't do it alone*. Caving in on yourself only makes things worse in the long run. Get those thoughts and feelings out. The bad news is that more than half of the marriages in this nation don't survive. The "good" news is that you have lots of company, lots of sympathetic survivors around you who have walked that trail you're walking. Remember, your parents' divorce is *not* your shame. It's only their failure.

Driving: Get the Pets and Children Off the Streets

Ahhh. Driving. That heaven of teens, that hell of parents. That glorious freedom of going wherever you want, playing whatever music you want, as loud as you like. Windows down and sunroof open, even though it's sleeting. Who cares? You're finally mobile. On your own. Asserting that wonderful rite of passage of asserting your right of way.

If there is one single thing proving that you're closing in on the end of adolescence, it's that driver's license. But, alas, all that magic can crash in the flash of a taillight, or in the screech of a tire, or in an instant of an impulse. Or, as with Michael, with all three.

Michael looked like he was chewing himself up from the inside out. The circles under his eyes spoke to his nights without sleep. Happier faces could be found on death row. He'd have to borrow the energy needed to die. Life was unbearably miserable as he awaited the dreaded phone call from the airport.

Yet life had been unbearably wonderful just a week before. School was closed for the holidays, the smug but beautiful Francesca Swartzlander had agreed (though reluctantly) to go out to dinner with him, and he had saved enough money to take her to a ritzy restaurant. Best of all, he got his, "TAA-DAA," driver's license. Life was good.

That good life went ecstatic when Michael's older brother Pete left his beloved, drop-dead-gorgeous, black Jaguar (with red-leather seats) while he flew away on a trip. Purely as a shot in the dark, Michael asked Pete if he could use the Jag to take Francesca out to the ritzy dinner. Pete would have to be nuts to go for that. Pete turned out to be nuts.

"Only, ONLY for the dinner, OK?" Pete insanely offered. "Otherwise, the Jag stays in the driveway. Deal?" Michael could not believe his luck. Escaping from a family that had no money, and hand-me-down clothes, Pete always felt bad for the brothers he left at home when he moved out and started his life. He saw this as a nice way of giving a poor kid a break. What a dope. "Deal," Michael pledged.

For the first two days, Michael actually managed to keep his word. For hours, he would sit dreamily in the Jaguar, smelling the leather, playing the stereo, and practicing his James Bond (007) lines for Francesca. Over and over, he imagined her smug but beautiful face struck speechless, only able to point, as the skinny, loser kid rumbles

> up in a killer black Jag. "Oh, this little thing?" he'd chuckle. "My brother and I sort of share this. It's kind of a secret. We, you know, don't like to show off. It's not right to make less fortunate kids feel bad." It was a great fantasy. This would be the best night of his life.
>
> "Hey," he suddenly realized, "I should be starting the Jag up every day to keep the battery charged. It's the least I can do for Pete." Sure—for Pete. It started innocently enough, starting up that beautiful beast, revving the engine a tad. Then putting it in gear—just to get the feel, you know. Hey, maybe let her idle up and down the driveway. That's legal—Pete said to keep her in the driveway. No problem.
>
> Problem. Michael's younger brother started to beg to be driven to the store with a friend. Michael felt his resolve melting in the warmth of that heavenly leather smell. What could go wrong? he thought. Besides, Jags need to be run to keep them in good shape (sure). "OK, twerps," he snickered. "Just to the store and back. And keep your pukey feet off my red leather."
>
> Thirty minutes later, Michael's eyes rained hard tears on red leather as he stared out the windshield at a once-gorgeous hood, now as twisted and crumpled as his shattered promise to his brother. He got to spend the rest of his vacation staring at a wrecked Jaguar, awaiting Pete's dreaded call to be picked up at the airport. It was a kind of walking death, only much worse. When that call finally came, Pete said just one, very quiet word—perhaps marking the holiday, or perhaps praying for the strength to not end the life of his younger brother. "Christ," was all he ever said.
>
> —From the personal journal of
> Dr. Michael Bradley, Christmas, 1967

I promised myself back then to tell that painfully true story to as many 15-year-old kids as would listen, hoping to save them from the agony of bending a car within the next year. The fact is that, at 16, too many of us are very lousy drivers. Some kids are excellent drivers. I often find myself amazed at how much better some very young drivers are than I am. So, if you are one of those great drivers, please do not be offended. However, the statistics are very clear: Sixteen-year-olds bend cars a lot.

I know you usually hear these warnings along with scary stories of gruesome injuries and death. Although those are certainly important,

I want to offer a less-dramatic reason why you should drive ultra (boring) safe: *Bending a car is a terrible experience, even when nobody gets hurt.* The embarrassing truth is that my 16-year-old friends and I began to slow down only after we had cried ourselves to sleep many nights after smashing up a beautiful car.

The hassle involved in even a minor accident is just incredible. There are debts, deductibles, paperwork, police, lawyers, lectures, and huge insurance increases that often end glorious driving careers before 17th birthdays. The worst part is the "what-ifs" that visit you all night: What if I hadn't passed, hadn't lit that cigarette, hadn't changed that radio station—the endless "what-ifs" can make you nuts.

An accident is a dark cloud that settles over your life for a while.

An accident is a dark cloud that settles over your life for a while. It's hard to understand how much this hurts, until you've rained hard tears on red leather yourself. I'm hoping to help you avoid that understanding with these few tips, sent to you by your peer drivers:

- **Drivers' ed works.** Besides getting you a healthy insurance discount, that course clearly makes you a much better driver. If Dad or Uncle Louie wants to teach you, remember that they're amateurs. They might teach you some very bad things that they don't even know they do ("Hey, Uncle Louie! What's the yellow light mean?" "*Floor the gas pedal.*"). Besides, many kids end up walking great distances home after having Dad's driving lesson blow up into a 60-mph screaming session on the freeway. There are two things that your crazy parents should never do: coach you in sports, and teach you to drive. Take the course.
- **Be sure you're ready.** I'm sorry if you're one of those great teen drivers, but some of the kids helping with this book said that they know they're not ready to drive (but they do anyway). They say that they get too mad when they're cut off, are distracted too easily, take risks they shouldn't, and have a hard time walking away when someone wants to race. This becomes confusing, because most 16-year-olds can handle the *skill* parts of driving. It's those *emotional* parts that bend teen fenders more often. For sure, there are many adults who can't handle the emotional demands of motoring, as well. But, at 16, it's harder. Think for a long time about whether you're ready before you start hammering your folks for the keys.

- **Don't drug and drive.** Few kids think that drinking and driving is a good idea, but many think that other drugs don't affect your NASCAR abilities. In fact, a myth has grown among teens that says weed actually makes you a *better* driver. This nonsense may have started with a study done in Europe that showed less aggressive driving behaviors among stoned drivers. Although that may be true, it's also true that marijuana messes with your judgment and reaction time. So if you're high and mellow, you're less able to avoid someone who's sober and raging. Driving at 16 is a big enough risk on it's own. Don't alter your odds by altering your reality.
- **Know that drugging and driving will produce insanity—*in your parents.*** And with good reason. You know all of those lectures that parents of teens get about letting kids make mistakes and having more freedom? All of those nice thoughts go up in nasty smoke when they smell the weed smoke in your car, or find the beer can in the trunk. Their "insanity" in grabbing your keys is not about drugs, and it's not about being control freaks. It's about *body bags and dead children.* Think for a minute: If you found that your own child was drugging and driving, would you, *could you* "be cool with that"? Even if it's "just" marijuana, or "just" a beer, these are things that greatly raise the odds that a hot car will become a cold coffin. Ask Freddie.

He walked in looking really rattled, a new thing for "Mr. Mellow." At 16, Freddie was passionate about two things: smoking dope and driving his new car. His first passion (weed) he had been doing for two years. He was a "weed warrior," a teen who was trying to get laws passed to legalize marijuana use. He ranted and raved about the "benefits" of weed use, and about the "stupid, oppressive" drug laws in America. He accused me of being weak-minded and of being taken in by the "establishment lies" whenever I raised any questions about his drug of choice. In fact, he would pointedly correct me anytime I called pot a drug. "It's not a drug!" he'd yell. "It's a natural herb. God put it on this planet for us to use, to stop all of our wars, to become mellow and wise."

His second passion was his beloved Toyota, a car he scrimped and saved to buy. He polished it endlessly and lovingly, as protective of his wheels as parents are of their babies. But tonight, he looked like he'd lost something precious to him. Like a baby, or a belief—or both?

> "I can't believe it," he said in a shaken voice. "I can't freakin' believe it. This just can't have happened. I must be tripping, or something. It couldn't have been the weed—could it?" His voice trailed off as he looked at me, remembering our many debates about marijuana being "harmless." But it was too late. Now he had to tell the story. "I was at a stop sign. I looked both ways before pulling out. On my right, I saw this old lady driving real slow, like, a mile away. I figured it would take her five minutes to get to me. I had lots of time. I glanced left, and then pulled out. And I smashed right into the old lady." Freddie looked like he was going to throw up. "It was real bad. She was all cut up, and bleeding, and crying, and stuff. I was thinking that she must have sped up, to, like, 130-miles-per-hour, to get in my way like that, because I knew she was way down the road when I saw her." Freddie paused, shrugged, and continued. "Then, this guy who was behind me stopped, who said he saw the whole thing. He said that the old lady was going real slow when I looked at her, but that she was only 20 feet away when I looked at her, not a mile, like I thought. That's when it hit me: If she was a mile away, how did I see that she was an old lady?"

If you drug and drive, remember that your parents will react as if you're playing with a live hand grenade. They shouldn't be "cool with that." If you drug and drive, remember that you *are* playing with a hand grenade. Should *you* be "cool with that"?

Drugs: Yes, Alcohol IS a Drug

If you haven't done so yet, read the Chapter 5 section on drugs (including alcohol) now. There, you'll find the "which" (chemicals are used), the "why" (kids use), and the "when" (it becomes a serious problem). In this section, we'll chat about the "how" part, as in how to look at yourself in a world that loves its drugs. These are the ideas that other kids (who live in the same drug-infested world) thought might be useful for you to think about.

- **It's your decision to make.** No one can make you use drugs, and no one can stop you from using drugs. Friends might furnish drugs, and parents might punish for drugs, but, in the end, whatever happens is totally on you. The problem is that, up until very recently, you didn't have to make any big decisions. When you were a child, all of that was done for you. Children just follow what they're told to do, or follow impulses to do the opposite, but they can't sit down and weigh out a lot of complex ideas (see Chapter 1). As an adolescent, you can, *and you must,* when the issue is drugs. What you do here can change the rest of your life. Don't do what most kids who use drugs do. Don't say "Whatever," and then let the world decide for you. Call a timeout, and think this one through carefully. Get all the accurate information you can about what drugs (and alcohol) are about, and decide for yourself. This is serious game time.

No one can make you use drugs, and no one can stop you from using drugs.

- **Listen carefully about drugs from both sides of the debate.** There's enough "drug information" garbage out there to fertilize the farm belt. On the one hand, there are folks who claim that smoking a joint will make you inject heroin (it won't), and that drinking a beer will make you an alcoholic (it can't). On the other side of the debate are those who say that weed (marijuana) can't be addicting (it can), and that alcohol is not a dangerous drug (it is). Anyone who sells simple answers to these questions is not selling the truth. The fact is that the facts about drugs are complex, and you need to weigh out what you are being told. When you see that someone is biased one way or another, be careful about relying on his or her information. But also remember that, because one side of a debate is wrong, the other is not automatically right. THINK THIS ONE OUT.
- **Not everyone uses drugs** . . . although it can seem like that. In fact, 30 percent to 40 percent of teenagers do no drugs at all. And a big chunk of the others do very little, often just once or twice. It can *seem* like everyone does drugs for three reasons. First, drugs are much more available (and often cheaper) than ever before. Second, if you hang out in a drug-using crowd, it will seem as if the "world" uses because *your* world is using. But that doesn't mean your corner of the world is the same as all the other corners. Third, some kids tend to exaggerate drug-use stories. Just like ex-soldiers, teenagers can get carried away with "war" (drug) stories to impress other people. Believe half of what you see, and none of what you hear.

- **Addicted? Compared to whom?** Because addiction happens in a bunch of ways, *any* drug can be addicting to *any* person. It's also true that most people who try drugs do not become addicts. Those are the scientific facts. The million-dollar question is how do you decide when drug use is only "fun" and when it's a problem? One way is to ask yourself what prices you pay to use drugs, like spending lots of money on smoke, or spending lots of time in court, or screwing up in school, or screwing up your connections (with your family, not your supplier). If you say that the "fun" of drugs is worth these kinds of costs, then it's a good bet you have a problem—because by the time you figure this out, it's usually too late. The drug already has its claws in your soul.

  The brutal reality is that finding out if you are a potential addict is exactly like playing Russian roulette: You'll know you're an addict when the round goes off (when you're addicted). And then it's too late. Addiction is a real horror show.

  If your crowd uses drugs, you're already in trouble. You won't see as clearly that you're getting in too deep. There are always kids around who use so many drugs that, by comparison, you look like the Pope. When you're knee-deep in drugs, a worse-off addict is a great friend to have—*he can make your life-ending addiction look normal.*
- **Addiction is an unwanted gift from a relative, which you can't give back.** If your old man, or his brother, or your granny overuses drugs or booze, you'd better think twice about using. Addiction can be handed down genetically, just like asthma can. The chance of your getting hooked goes way, way up if one of your relatives goes way, way down (on drugs). Remember that every addict started out using drugs "just for fun." In many kids, the monster of addiction is awakened by using drugs only "just for fun." If you inherited addict genes, using drugs causes those inherited addict parts of your brain to come alive. Once awakened, addiction is a monster you can never get back in its cage. Addiction is forever. Even when they stop using, addicts fight addiction *every day for the rest of their lives.* Is that risk worth a little "fun"? If you answer yes, are you sure that your little "fun" is truly just a little "fun"?

Addiction can be handed down genetically, just like asthma can.

- **Check it out.**

Cheri looked really embarrassed, and even more ashamed. This 17-year-old couldn't look at me, even after months of talking about some very embarrassing issues in her life. She had been able to tell me about all kinds of difficult things, like smoking marijuana, cheating in school, stealing from a neighbor, and having way too much sex. She always said that her pot smoking was from feeling bad about those other issues, and she said that she was rarely smoking over these past several months.

She raised her eyes just enough to glimpse the big baggie of oxys (a powerful, addicting painkiller) in my hand, which her mother had found in a hollowed-out book. Then, immediately, she hung her head back down again. "I feel really bad," she mumbled. "I know you trusted me when I told you I wasn't doing drugs." She raised her eyes to see mine. "But I was sort of telling you the truth, because I did stop here and there, for a day or two—well, maybe for a day," she corrected. Dropping her eyes back to the floor, she went on to miss the whole point of what was happening. "I guess you won't want to see me anymore, since you think I'm, like, this liar, and all. I really wasn't lying to disrespect you, you know. It's just that you wouldn't understand about the oxys—they're not the big deal that everyone thinks they are. So it's OK if you don't want to work with me now."

I let her hear her words a bit. Then, with a soft voice saying some hard words, I slammed Cheri—the addict Cheri. "Look. Maybe it's you who doesn't want to see me anymore. In fact, I'm afraid that you won't ever come back here. So now I'm going to say more than a shrink is supposed to say. Ready?" Her eyes got big. The addict Cheri knew what was coming.

"You know what's weird? What's weird is that you could tell me about cheating, stealing, and sleeping around, and that you couldn't tell me about taking pills every day for the past year. What's weirder is that you're still lying. Only now, you're lying to me and to you about not having a problem. Cheri, that lying is what makes it a problem. If it wasn't a problem, why lie? At first, you thought those other things you were doing were OK, too. You decided to stop them after talking them over. So, why not talk about the pill use? Answer: Because you know that the smart Cheri would want to stop. And the addict Cheri has no intentions of ever stopping. She won't let you stop lying.

"Cheri, the weirdest thing of all is that you feel ashamed for lying, when you should be puzzled about your lying. The only problem you see is that you think I'm disappointed in you. Cheri, listen hard: I'm not disappointed. I'm scared. You have a problem, girl. A big one. And you don't even see it."

One of the biggest symptoms of a drug problem in adults is *denial.* That's when you hide, lie about, or justify your drug use—to *yourself* as well as to others. Denial becomes even more powerful among teens, because it makes even more sense as a way of avoiding punishments or legal problems. Adults can be addicts completely legally (with alcohol), and they deny their addiction. Kids can't be legal addicts because their use of *any* drug (including alcohol) is *never* legal. So denial seems even more natural to a teen. That's how it becomes even more deadly.

So check it out. If you're using drugs, or drinking a lot, talk to a shrink about it. Get an objective opinion. If it's not a problem, you'll only waste an hour. If it is a problem, you might save your life. If you're unwilling to even consider doing that, you better get in your mirror and ask yourself what you're afraid of. You might be afraid of the truth, like Cheri. She never did come back. When it comes to drugs, the time to start being really scared is when your mirror becomes too scary for you.

For a good book on this subject, check out *Uppers, Downers, All-Arounders,* by Darryl Inaba. It's listed in the "To Find Out More" section at the end of the book.

Fighting (See "Aggression . . .")

Friends: You Can't Live with 'em, and You Can't Deport 'em

You have to read Chapter 8 ("Your Peers") first for this section to be of any help to you. That's where we lay out the reasons that friends can be such a powerful force in your life, for good and bad. Here, you'll find some specific ideas about friend problems that teenagers told me were important.

- **If you don't seem to have any friends, don't panic.** It's surprising how many kids report having few or even no friends. Many teens know other kids, but they seem to have trouble moving to the next step of hanging out with them. This happens for many reasons, such as starting a new school, being shy, or just being one of those kids who ends up as a loner. The good news is that the older you get, the easier it becomes to connect socially. Younger kids sometimes like to make a game out of excluding others from their friends circle. But that game gets old as teens get older.

  While you're waiting for that exclusion game to end, try slowly building some connections with kids you don't know well. Join activities where you're more likely to meet kids who are more like you (like clubs or community service groups).
- **Don't try to rush friendships.** Kids hate to be pressured, and they will back away. Instead, let friendships grow slowly. Look for chances to hang out with the group a bit, like going for pizza after a meeting. If you just put yourself into places like that, kids will eventually start to chat and include you in whatever next thing they're doing. Try to keep an eye out for other kids who are also not connected, and who would welcome having a friend in you. Sometimes, we're so busy being envious of the "popular" kids that we don't see other more approachable kids (who often turn out to be nicer, according to my sources).

  Try to keep an eye out for other kids who are also not connected, and who would welcome having a friend in you.

  Most of all, try to fight the thought that something's wrong with you, and that you'll be alone forever. The social game definitely gets easier the older you are.
- **Most kids end up doing what their friends do.** Chapter 8 talks about how peers can influence you. Keep that in mind as you watch your friends going through changes, good and bad. Be it bungee jumping or beer guzzling, the odds are that you will do much of what your crowd does. You don't *have* to share a bad habit to keep your friends, but it

usually ends up that way. As Chapter 8 explains, peer pressure pushes on everyone, adults and adolescents, for good and for bad. Once your identity is formed, you'll be steered less by your crowd, and more by your character. Until then, be careful. Think for yourself.

- **Whom do you trust?** Trust is one of those things we never appreciate until we get kicked in the teeth. That's usually when we look back and say, "I can't believe I trusted him." Trust is only as reliable as the person you give it to, which makes it tough for teens. Adolescents change all the time. So the person you hand a precious secret to may not be that same person in a month or two. You know this to be true if you've fallen madly in love with someone you can't stand two weeks later.

  Deciding who is truly trustworthy is a difficult art, even for old and wise adults who've been down the betrayal path a lot. The best way to guess what a friend will do in the future is to see what she's done in the past. If your new friend never seems to find a bad word to say about anyone, that's a trust plus. If you've been laughing with your new friend over some nasty secret she betrayed about her old friend, stop laughing—you might be next on the gossip gallows.

- **Speaking of gossip, don't.** Don't gossip, that is. Does everybody do it? Maybe. Does everybody enjoy this? Seems that way. Does that make it right? What do you think? You need to decide quickly, because gossip has become an epidemic problem among your generation. Not because you've gone nasty, but because you've gone Net. Electronic mail has raised gossip to a dark art practiced by instant-message thugs who can instantly kill a kid's reputation with a keyboard (see Chapter 8). It's kind of like a gladiator sport, where some poor kid gets tossed in the ring, and everyone takes a shot at him. It will stop only when enough kids say "STOP!" So if you see one of these assaults on your screen, think about signing off with a protest. Once the audience leaves, the show stops. It's all about getting attention.

  If you become a target of one of these "get her" sessions, also sign off. As hard as that might be, it's best to not play that game on the screen. Things only get worse the more you react. Yes, you will be the object of some snickers at school tomorrow, but, by the next day, the bottom feeders will have moved on to another target who's more fun. If you keep fighting back, the sharks stay around much longer. Your best defense is to just live your life, and ignore the insanity as best you can. Easy to say, hard to do. But important to do.

The biggest problem with friends comes from our fear of change. We humans love to pretend that everything stays the same, but that's a fairy tale we tell ourselves to try and not get scared so much. The only real cosmic constant is change. That means that you and your friends will change, too, if you are real with yourself. And that means that most of your friendships may not last. That's a sad fact, but an important one to admit. Important because if you keep yourself trapped in friendships or romances that have gotten old, you can shut down your search for yourself—for your identity.

In the name of loyalty and security, some kids hang onto people that they need to let go, so that they can move on to new things. You'll have plenty of time for "permanent" relationships as an adult. Adolescence is a time to stay as open as you can to new people, new ideas, and new growth. The best way to have "permanent" relationships as an adult is to define your identity as an adolescent. The price you pay to learn who you are is to go through lots of changes. One of those changes will be losing some friends. Don't let it make you crazy. It's just part of the plan.

Grades (See Chapter 9, "Your School," and Part Three, "School")

Homewrok ... Homwork ... Homework: It's Learning about Frustration ...

... and discipline. Your teachers will never admit to that. Sure, they're partially right when they say that homework is to help you learn the material that they give you in class. And they're also right when they say that the more you practice something, the better you'll get at it. But the real point of pointless homework is to learn to do boring, frustrating tasks that somebody else tells you to do *just because* (see Chapter 9, "Your School"). It's to help you build the strength to force yourself off of the computer, and away from the video game, and into math, history, or Spanish. That ability to stop yourself from doing what you feel like doing, and instead do some boring, annoying task happens to be one of the great differences between being a child and an adult. Adults can (supposedly) push themselves to do things that have no payoff for a very long time, like doing many years of school, or saving 25 dollars a week for 50 years (put that into your calculator, add interest, and be amazed at the total). Children do what pleases them at that moment.

Homework is like adult boot camp for kids who think they're ready to be grown-ups. Like boot camp, it should be frustrating, exhausting, and even make you want to cry at times. It's supposed to get you to wrestle with yourself, forcing you to get tough with that part of you who's a child and who wants to run and play, promising to do the homework "later." It should help you grow, and see that you are tougher than you think. In other words, just like school, it's *supposed* to be hard. If it's easy, it isn't making you any stronger.

That ability to stop yourself from doing what you feel like doing, and instead do some boring, annoying task happens to be one of the great differences between being a child and an adult.

Chapter 9 lists a few tips to help you with schoolwork (see "Six Cheap and Easy School Tricks"). Here are a few more to help you make it through homework boot camp:

- **Make wall charts.** Stop laughing—these things really work. Put a list that reminds you what's due when, and which test is on what day, up on a wall that you pass a million times a day. Many teen brains don't have the hardware in place yet to keep track of a bunch of assignments that they hate (see Chapter 1). The chart works like the nagging of your father, except without his annoying voice. Which is another reason why the list works so well. Dads magically cut back their nagging when they see that chart go up.
- **Use that 30-minute rule here, as well.** Chapter 9 talks about how your brain probably runs out of gas after 30 schoolwork minutes. Get that kitchen timer, and set it to 30 minutes. When it dings, don't work anymore. Reset it for 5 minutes. Get up, stretch, and punch the punching bag. When it dings, don't play anymore. Reset it for another 30 minutes, and sit back down with your books. You will be amazed at how that impossible problem you were stuck on suddenly looks doable. This works just like restarting your bogged-down computer.

- **Kill the stereo (and the TV, and the computer, and the satellite navigation unit, and the . . .)** I know, I know. You just can't do your homework without seven other noises competing for your attention, right? When you turn everything off, it's too quiet to work, right? I know all about that. I can't study unless I have a huge bag of tortilla chips at my side. And you know what? We're both nuts. People have studied how we study, and they've found that all those noises (to include my crunching of chips) only screw up our concentration and make homework harder and longer. Think about that. Doesn't it make sense? When it comes to getting your brain's attention, can David Copperfield compete with Dave Matthews? Can English Lit beat electronic mail? I don't think so.

  Try switching all the electrical devices off. If you absolutely have to, leave a radio on a classical music station, at very low volume. "BOOORRRIINNG" you say? Exactly. Like a cigarette junkie rummaging through ashtrays, your brain will desperately seek out something to do. It might even consider math.
- **Find strength in numbers.** Kids tell me that homework groups help a lot, particularly when you're reviewing for a test. Yes, there's the temptation to fool around with these friends instead; but, oddly enough, most of these groups help kids get a lot more done than if they worked alone.
- **"Dj'eat?" "Nah, dj'you?"** Your cortex (brain) is a Corvette, or perhaps a Porsche (maybe that purple one with the saddle interior? Yessss!!!). All three are magnificent "machines." Beautifully built. Fantastically fast. Those magical cars won't move an inch without fuel. Neither will your magical brain. Your brain simply won't work unless you feed it. You can't study on an empty stomach. And, like those dream cars, your brain runs only on premium fuel, not on soda and chips. That means foods like cheese, veggies, meat, and fruit—you know, real food (it's still sold at a couple of stores). Fries, barfo-burgers, and milkshakes will seize up your brain engine faster than you can say, "Double-size that." So do like the athletes do. Eat the right foods before you get into your game—of schoolwork.

There you go. These are some weapons to try in your homework wars. Kids tell me that these tricks are easy, and that they really work *when you find the "uumph" to use them.* If you can't seem to find the energy to try any of these suggestions, something else is going on, and it's time to talk with the shrink. Start with your school counselor, and see if together, you can sort it out. Don't just quit on homework. This is another one of those "serious game times" that can shape the rest of your life.

Homosexuality (See "Sexual Differences . . .")

Internet Insanity: Virtual Cigarettes?

Like medicine used properly, the Internet is a life-expanding miracle. Like medicine used badly, the Internet can become a life-ruining addiction. It all depends on whether *you* control *it,* or *it* controls *you.* If you're in charge, the Internet can be nothing but helpful. But the odds are that you or someone you know has become a slave to a screen. The hard question is, *how do you know when you're on line too much?*

Like medicine used badly, the Internet can become a life-ruining addiction.

The answer is to look at the price you pay to play (on the Net). If you're up too late, screwing up school, and dropping out of real-life activities, all because of having to be online, *that's a problem.* If you scream in pain because your parents pull the plug, *that's a problem.* If you find that you're on the Net three hours after you promised to get off, for the third time in three days, *that's a problem.* Richard had a problem.

> Last week, I thought Richard couldn't look much worse. Boy, was I wrong. He looked more 60 than 16, with scary dark circles under his lifeless eyes that told me to tell him that he needed to see his physician—a week ago. "God," he croaked, "do I feel horrible." Heading off my weekly question, he continued. "The most sleep I get is maybe 3 or 4 hours a night. Once . . ., no, twice, I was up all night, I think. I really don't know. I can't remember what day is what. I'm not sure I know my name. I, like, zonk out in school, and don't even know I'm asleep until some pissed-off teacher is shaking me awake."
>
> He took a few minutes trying to get his breath, holding his chest, and panting quietly. "And this is the latest problem. Sometimes I feel like I can't catch my breath, you know? Like I've been running, or

something. But I am definitely not doing much running. Mom tried doing what we agreed to last week, making me get off line at 10 P.M. I screamed and yelled and threatened her until she backed off." He shook his head at that picture of himself. "I guess that was pretty lame, huh? It was really just an act. I'd never hurt anybody. She went for my bluff." Richard took a very deep breath, and held it, trying to get his breathing under control, and then continued: "But I wish she didn't. I think I need someone to hide the phone line. That's the only way I'll stop [using the Internet]. I really can't stop on my own. But I go nuts if someone tries to make me stop."

I wondered what bluffing he would do when he got home and found that his mom had the house phone lines disconnected. She told me that she "would live without a phone rather than watch her son die in front of a 16-inch substitute for the real world." She said that she was at the end of her rope. So was Richard.

For some kids, a computer can do the same things as a connection (drug supplier): Both can whisk you away to a wonderful fantasy world, where stress and struggle magically evaporate. Like drugs, the Net can become a way to become someone you're not, to pretend that you're not pretending your problems away. But the more we run away from stress, *the more we run away from stress.* Soon, we can end up living in that fantasy world 24/7. As with Richard, we can bail out of the real world almost entirely.

If you or someone you know is taking the first steps down that path, here are a few tips that other kids say can help.

- **Keep a log.** Note how much time you're online each week (your computer can do this for you). Keep a running record, so that at a glance you can see if you're putting in too much time, or if weekly you put in more time on the Net. *Don't do this in your head.* We humans can't really trust our heads to be straight up when we're tracking a bad habit. Write it down.
- **Get that kitchen timer out again.** As with homework, plan out *in advance* how much Net time is OK, and then set the timer. No more of that "about an hour" stuff. "About an hour" becomes at least three hours very easily. When the timer gets to zero, you get off—immediately.
- **If you keep blowing past the timer "ding"** . . ., it's time to head to that

mirror and ask yourself what's up. Whenever we stop keeping promises with ourselves, it's time to start a conversation with ourselves. If you keep missing the ball, it's the batter and not your bat that has the problem. And if you're afraid to be this straight up with yourself, that's the sure sign you need to chat with the shrink. If someone doesn't get you back in charge of you, things will only get worse.

- **Involve your crazy parents.** Enlist their help before they rip the phone line out of the wall. If you tell them that you think you have a problem with Net use, *you'll calm them down*. If you *think* that it's a problem, I guarantee they *know* it's been a problem. If you go to them first, they'll be amazed and reassured by how grown up you are to admit it. Now you can work together with them on solutions that work better for all of you (like *calm* reminders, or rewards for limiting your use). This brings peace in the land. If you do nothing, they'll likely boil over one day and go King Kong on you, doing drastic things that are probably not necessary (like shutting off the phone lines). This brings war in the land.
- **Get that computer out of your room.** Now that you've picked this book back up after hurling it against the wall, please hear me out. One of the best diet techniques is to not have Twinkies in the house. Even the strongest willed among us do a lot better when our bad habit is not sitting in our room, softly calling to us. Out of sight *is* out of mind when it comes to chips and chat rooms. If privacy is a concern, I can about promise that your parents will be so overjoyed that you're moving the computer to the dining room that they'll swear to stay out when you're getting your mail. As with so many other things in life, the Internet becomes good or bad, depending upon how we choose to use it. In the end, it's just a question of balance. Don't tip over.

As with so many other things in life, the Internet becomes good or bad, depending upon how we choose to use it.

Love: How Can Something That Feels So Good Hurt So Bad?

"You can't understand," moaned Jerry. "No one can—not my parents, not my friends. They all just say, 'Jerry—you're only 14. You couldn't have been in real love. It was only puppy love. So Meg dumped you. So get over it!'" Jerry's eyes were wide with amazement and panic at how awful he hurt inside. He just could not believe it. He jumped up off the couch, turned around, and sat back down, as if he was trying to find some position that might make it hurt less. There was none. He shifted around nonstop, like he had splinters stuck all over him. Suddenly the name "Laura" began to echo in my memory. I started to feel a little uncomfortable myself.

"I can't eat, I can't sleep—school has gone all to hell, and this is finals week! I cry over Meg all night, every night—EVERY FREAKIN' NIGHT! I never cried in my life since I was, like, four, or something. And I don't even care, you know?" He paused, and got still for a moment. "Do you know?" he asked as he looked into my eyes. Before I could say the word "Laura," he decided on his own, and resumed his fidgeting.

"Nah. You can't possibly know what this feels like. Nobody can feel this horrible. Oh, man! Oh, man!" Jerry jumped back up, with nowhere to go. "Why'd she dump me? Why? We were in love for three months. THREE MONTHS! It was perfect. We planned to get married after college, and everything. Then, last week, she cuts me off—just like that. Tells me I'm a control freak. This makes no sense. This was not supposed to happen . . ." Jerry was about to add, "you know?" but he was sure that nobody knew.

I knew. Because I still remember Laura—from 1969. Jerry's parents used to know. They just forgot their lost teen loves. They forgot that lost teenage love hurts at least as much as lost adult love. Many say it hurts more.

Get ready to throw this book again: Your "perfect" relationship is not going to work out.

That cold, brutal, book-throwing fact comes from research that shows that, no matter how incredibly much you love each other, *your time together will end.* And so will other deep, completely committed relationships you will have, each of which will feel "forever" to you at one point, "never" to you at another, and terribly, terribly painful in between. And you know what? That's exactly how it's supposed to happen. With each painful, failed relationship you survive, you'll be a little smarter for the next one.

After loyally loving and then horribly hating Rex (who worships weapons and attack dogs), you'll likely shy away from the next boy who glues pictures of his pit bulls over pictures of his mom. After absolutely adoring and then desperately despising Ashley (who'd rather look at herself than at anything else in this world), you'll start to avoid girls who have more mirrors than thoughts. In other words, when it comes to love, we learn really well by getting our feelings beaten up really badly. Not every time, but as with Jerry's Meg and my Laura, some of our best lessons are learned in our worst days.

It's probably pointless, but I want to pass along some teen tips to minimize your painful romances with the raging Rexs and absorbed Ashleys of the world. These tips might be pointless because love is like a tidal wave when it hits. Few of us are able to stop and think as we're being swept away. Still, some of these might help if you use them before you go goofy. Good luck! You're gonna' need it!

- **Enjoy adolescent relationships, knowing that each will end.** If you can do this, you'll become much less likely to get your guts ripped out. Realize from date one that you will *not* be spending the rest of your life with any person you'll be dating as a teenager. This might help you to calm down and take things slowly and easily—which is better than constantly giving away your heart and soul, and then having these mashed person parts sent back to you in a box stamped "return to sender—postage due." Incidentally, kids tell me that these low-risk dates are also the most fun. There's much less jealousy, insecurity, and intensity, all of which are a lot of work, and not any fun at all.
- **Be friends first.** The best adult relationships are between lovers who are friends first. These are folks who are more interested in their partners being happy than they are in "owning" them. So the best way to practice for a lifelong relationship is to practice friendship. When you're friends first, you really get to know someone. That helps you be much wiser when deciding if you want to get serious. When you date first, you rarely get to know the real person behind the makeup and the cologne for quite some time, often not until after you're hopelessly in love with someone *who really doesn't exist.* That's because dating is an unreal sort of sport in which

If you let your pain out, it will begin to shrink, tiny bit by tiny bit.

people act in unreal ways just to make a good impression, not just to be themselves.

- **After disregarding this excellent advice . . .** and getting your insides ripped out by your latest mister or miz perfect, don't just shut down. No joke, the pain of a broken teen love can be horrible. It can do serious damage to you if you don't let it out somehow. Talk, cry, yell, scream, hit punching bags, whatever; but don't just sit and hurt. If you let your pain out, it will begin to shrink, tiny bit by tiny bit. Time and talk are the only pills for this ill. If your crazy parents blow you off, saying it's only puppy love, show them this book section, and then ask them to remember, really remember their own teen loves. I'll bet they get a funny look on their faces, and then become a lot more understanding. You might ask your dad if he was ever dumped by a girl named Laura.

Peer Pressure (See Chapter 8, "Your Friends," and Part Three, "Friends . . .")

Pregnancy: It Doesn't Get Much Tougher Than This

It was purely an accident of the alphabet that pregnancy followed love as topics here. Yet maybe this is exactly the place to talk about teen pregnancy, because about one of every five girls can expect to become unexpectedly (and unhappily) pregnant before she's married. Love usually has a lot to do with that statistic, and with many other bad numbers that follow. That same love that makes girls pregnant can get them into worse trouble unless they stop and think, very clearly, right when thinking clearly seems impossible. If you or someone you know becomes pregnant, you need to read this carefully. In this first section, we're going to pretend that you are female, and the one who becomes pregnant. However, boys and friends also need to read this, so that they can be helpful to the pregnant girl.

To the Girl: What NOT to Do

It's a lot easier to talk about what you should *not* do than what you *should* do. Please note that I'm giving you only some statistical facts about your options in pregnancy. This book cannot talk about the religious or moral issues involved in pregnancy options (such as abortion). Those are things to be discussed with your parents and religious advisors. Use the information here as a basic guide, over which you place your religious and moral beliefs.

- **Don't rush into a decision.** You need to sit and think—a lot. You need to sit and talk—more. The problem is that you probably just want the nightmare to be over, so you may rush into a bad choice, be it abortion, adoption, marriage, or single motherhood. Any of those options might be the best thing for someone else, but the worst thing for you. You have to choose for you. A few days probably won't make much difference, except to help you be smarter. Take the time. I know it hurts, and it's scary. *But you cannot rush this decision.*
- **Don't let your friends decide for you.** Your friends all know what they *think* they *might* do in your place. That's what they are telling you when they give you advice: *What might be best for them.* THEY DON'T KNOW WHAT IS BEST FOR YOU. As loyal and caring as your friends are, this is not the time to act on adolescent advice. Sorry, but that's just the way it is. You need to get older people involved, as hard as that might be. Use your friends as places to talk out your emotions, not to get expert advice.
- **Don't decide alone.** Get good adults involved. Yes, you *should* tell your parents, unless there is a real risk of someone hurting you. The vast majority of parents amaze their pregnant teen daughters with how much they truly love their kids—even in the face of this shock. When the chips are down, crazy parents usually put aside all of the craziness and focus on helping their daughter as best as they can through a very tough time.

  Also, get an expert involved, like a counselor, or doctor, or perhaps a relative who you know stays calm under fire and doesn't tell people what to do. The expert's job is to help *you* decide what *you* should do. You and your parents might not be able to think clearly for a bit, and having an "uninvolved" person involved in these discussions can help a lot.
- **Don't forget the adoption option.** Research shows that lots of teens get caught in a terrible place between not wanting an abortion, yet not wanting to raise a child. For many, adoption can be a great answer to that dilemma. In this nation, we have thousands of loving couples who are des-

perately seeking to adopt a baby. If you feel like there's no way out of this mess for you, consider the adoption option. It might be your "win-win."

- **Don't depend on the teen father, *no matter what he says.*** Sorry, boys. It's brutal-fact time again. Girls, here are four facts you need to know if you're thinking of relying on an adolescent boy to solve your problem.
- **Teen marriages and teen parenting don't work**. Eighty percent of teen marriages disintegrate within two years, throwing girls and babies into the streets or back into parents' homes. Most teen mothers never complete high school, and then they struggle to reach even poverty levels of living, earning half of the money in their lifetimes than what older mothers earn. This is no life for you or a baby.
- **Only one in five teenage fathers contributes money toward their baby**. And that one guy disappears within a year. Don't rely on the macho, meaningless words of teenage fathers. They have no idea what they're talking about when they promise to support their baby. These "fathers" are not adults, and they can't fulfill those promises. You'll end up on your own.
- **Half of the teenage fathers who move in with Mom and baby never make it to high-school graduation themselves**. So, even if the father sticks it out (and almost none do), he's headed for the same poverty train that awaits single teen moms and their babies.
- **In the past 10 years, we've thrown *64 percent* more children into foster homes.** This is a human tragedy. As an ex-foster father, I note this not to knock foster parents (the good ones are the Green Berets of the parenting world, doing work that became far too tough for me), but I've looked helplessly into the terrified faces of screaming babies who didn't know where they were and what happened to their mom. You don't want this for any child, especially yours. But that's exactly where your child could be headed if you try to play family with a boy who is pretending to be a man.

To the Boy: What TO Do

Be a man, but in ways that help. Be a man by staying by this girl, and supporting her in whatever decision she makes. Keep your arms open and your mouth shut. Like it or not, this affects her a lot more than it does you. This decision has to be mostly about her, not you.

Be a man by not lying by making promises you can never keep. If you're going macho, yelling about how you're going to raise your child, and all that, reread the facts above about where you're headed. Then, think about the nightmare you'll be pushing this girl and her baby into. You need to grow up a lot right now, enough to admit that you're not grown up enough to be a father or husband. It might kill you to say that to a girl (or crazy parents) who might be begging you to act like a hero and pretend that you're ready to be a husband and father. But, in your heart, you know that playing the hero would just be your foolish pride talking, not your head. If you truly want to be macho, be macho enough to tell the hard truth. Be tough enough to keep this girl and her child from living a terrible life that your pride could create by your playing at being a father. This is as serious as game time can get.

To Both of You: Slow Down

Yes, teen pregnancy is a car wreck. It's a terrible time that will leave scars, no matter what decisions you make. There is no perfect answer, so stop looking for that. The goal is to make the *least-bad* decision you can.

Yet, as scary as this is, lots and lots of people go through it and survive OK. In fact, most come out smarter and stronger *if, and only if,* they take their time, and think things through carefully, before they make their decisions.

Get all the expert help you can. Take your time.

Two good books on the subject you might want to check out are *Surviving Teen Pregnancy,* by Shirley Arthur, and *Teenage Fathers,* by Karen Gravelle and Leslie Peterson. Both books are listed in the "To Find Out More" section at the end of this book.

Problem Solving (See "Communication ...")

Racism: Some Bad Music Never Dies

Here's another topic that, as a teen in 1969, I never imagined having to write about in the twenty-first century. Back in the 1960s, many of us teenagers were sure that America was finally on its way to changing things for its minorities. But, just like that old rock 'n roll, racism refuses to die. Some say it's more popular today than ever, just quieter. But, sometimes, it's not quiet enough.

Lester had no intention of talking to anyone, let alone me. A middle-aged, white male did not seem to be the person to confide in, particularly after what had just gone down at school. At 17, Lester had the body of a hard man, and the face of a soft child. Today, that face showed more hurt than hate, more anguish than anger. Yet, it was his anger that forced him into my office to get a letter saying that he was ". . . not a threat to the safety or well-being of the school community."

He would only stare out the window as I asked him questions about how he ended up in the fight that day. Running out of time, I cut to the chase. "Look, Lester, I can see that you're furious about being sent here. I don't blame you. I'd be mad, too. But you can't go around punching out people who make you mad, you know?"

As his face slowly turned to meet mine, I watched him slowly change, from a pouting black boy, to an angry African-American man. His eyes locked on mine. "Anyone ever call you nigger?" he asked flatly. "And not just anyone," he continued, "but someone strange to you, someone you never saw before, someone who's got no business with you. Anyone like that ever call you nigger?" He paused, and then added, "Anyone like that ever call your mother a whore-nigger?"

His gaze was so intense that it almost made me look away. "Nope," I answered. But I heard a flip tone in my own voice. What was that about? Was I mad at his question? I shook off my thoughts of me, and pressed on with him. "Look, even as horrible as that must be, Lester, you can't react with fists. In the end, you'll lose that game."

I'm not sure if Lester ever blinked as he searched my eyes. Finally, he shook his head, and resumed staring out my window. "Man, you have no idea," he sighed. "No idea."

A few days later, my unflappable wife, Cindy, told a story. Her face was red with rage, her voice low with disgust. She had been walking out of a store with our three-year-old, mixed-race, adopted daughter, Sarah. As she passed a group of men, one began "whispering" intentionally loud enough for mother and daughter to hear. Referring to Sarah he said, "Well, well. Lookey here. There goes another one of those 'milk-duds' (a bi-racial slur)."

Cindy has never backed away from a fight in her life. She's a woman who stood night watch over houses in which minorities were being threatened. But, that day, for the first time in her white life, she felt the cut of personal racial hatred. And, for the first time in her life, she walked away from a fight, terrified of what racial hatred might do to a tiny three-year-old girl. She was still scared as she told the story.

My 50-year-old brain instantly went wild, with the rage of an adolescent. Suddenly, I had crazy thoughts of driving to that store, and shoving those punks up against the wall, begging them to swing on me. In two seconds, 10 "Rambo" scenes rushed through my head, of me terrifying them in return, making them cry and plead for forgiveness. A firestorm of fury had raced through me, turning all of my pretty antiviolence beliefs into meaningless ash. All it took was one racial slur—and I wasn't even there to hear it.

That's when Lester's face suddenly appeared in my mind's eye. I heard his voice: "Man, you have no idea . . . No idea."

Lester was right. If you're not a minority in this nation, you really have no idea what's going on. We like to pretend that we have no race issues anymore, but that's just a political sound bite. Efforts to fix some of the racial injustice of America are now being shut down as unneeded, because we "don't have racial discrimination anymore." You think?

If this trend continues, racial issues may become as explosive again as they were in the '60s, when racial strife almost destroyed America. We're already seeing racial gangs on the upswing in many areas, but this time with many more color choices than we had in the '60s. Black, white, brown, red, yellow—we have any color of hate you love. And of all the hatreds of the world, the rage of color ranks right up there with the worst. If we in America don't wise up, and remember our lessons from our racial past, we're doomed to relive them. And they weren't much fun the first time around.

So what can you do to keep the peace? Here are a few ideas from your peers:

- **Silence is deadly—you gotta' stand up.** The next time you hear a (chink/fag/jew/gook/nigger/polack/sandnigger/spic/wop—who'd I forget?) joke, remember—*there it is, right there in front of you.* That huge, unstoppable, overwhelming, senseless, war-starting monster called racial hatred. That thing that sounds so large, and distant, and unchangeable just popped up in front of you, *disguised as a joke.* Just a little thing? Perhaps, but still a thing that, in the end, connects with killing for hate. Whatever you do, you *will* make a difference, for better or for worse. You can laugh, and add a brick of hatred to that wall that separates people, or you can knock a brick out by saying, "Man, that's not funny." Is it only one brick out of a huge wall of hatred? Yes. Is it worth the embarrassment of taking a stand? That's your call. That's a call every one of us needs to make.

- **Just because you haven't seen it, doesn't mean it's not there.** If racial issues are cool at your school, that's wonderful. But don't get lulled into thinking that's the way things are for everyone. Racial bigotry can be real slick and subtle. For a while, much of it had gone underground because it was no longer so cool to be seen as a wild racist. But a lot of this hate is now oozing back out from underneath the rocks, where it was hiding. If you haven't seen it yet, you will shortly.
- **If you get slurred, ask yourself: "Who do I want to change?"** Beating up a bigot to end bigotry is like pouring gas on a fire to put it out. Oh, you're right when you say that the jerk might not start with *you* again. But he'll just go after a smaller, weaker version of you—this time, with hate furiously fueled by the beating you just gave him. In other words, the only thing you'll change are the odds of your little sister getting hurt. Don't waste your time trying to change ignorant people. Put your time in with the power people—*the bystanders.* If they see insults and fists flying back and forth, the bystanders only see a fight. If you can keep your cool, and let the jerk keep his teeth, the bystanders will see bigotry for what it is: ignorant, ugly, and dangerous. Not just for the victim, but for the *bystanders,* as well. It's the *bystanders* you want to change, not the jerk. When the *crowd* decides that bigotry is stupid, *only then* will it begin to end.

When the crowd decides that bigotry is stupid, only then will it begin to end.

Dr. Martin Luther King, Jr. showed us just how powerful a thing it is to respond to hate with calm and control. Many Americans forget how terrifyingly close we came to a racial civil war in the 1960s, and how he may have saved us from a bloodbath. So, take a page from Dr. King's book when you get slurred, and try saying something like "Man,

I don't hear anyone talking like that to you. What's up with you?" Then, walk away. He'll continue puking up hate at you, but that's good. That's *exactly* what you want the bystanders to see and hear as you walk. That's how you change things.

That might be the hardest walk you ever walk. But it might be the most important walk you ever walk.

Check out this book for an eye-opening tour of America's teen minorities: *Speaking Out: Teenagers Talk on Race, Sex, and Identity,* by Susan Kukin. It's listed in the "To Find Out More" section at the end of this book.

Rape (See "Sexual Abuse ...")

Religion: Where Struggles with Parents Get Personal

Belief in God is another issue that often becomes a battleground where teens differ from their parents (see Chapters 3 and 6), but this fight can have a vicious twist. Disagreeing with your folks' choice of diet is a lot easier than disagreeing with their choice of deity (God). Although they'll pout over food choices that could hurt your body, they'll panic over God choices that could doom your soul.

Before you brush off your crazy parents' fears, think for a minute: What if your situations were reversed? What if *you* truly, truly believed that *their* "bad" choices could cause them to spend eternity in hell? Would you just say "Whatever," or would you pull out all the stops to try to save their souls?

Think hard about that before you get into the next round of sparring about going to church, synagogue, temple, or mosque. Your parents might be crazy and controlling in other silly ways, but, in the religion fight, they might truly believe they must save you from an infinity of despair. They also might see your rejection of their faith as you disrespecting thousands of years of family history and traditions, things that saved some entire nations and peoples from extinction. Religion is an incredibly sensitive subject. We're not talking nose rings and curfews here. Now is when you must learn the art of *respectfully* disagreeing with someone.

This means you have to adjust your style of fighting with your folks. Remember that your parents' religious values may be the most sacred parts of their lives. Mocking those values because you disagree with them can wound your parents very deeply, far more than you might be able to imagine. Tread very, very lightly. Talk about how you see that those values are so special to them, and that you think that's wonderful for them. But explain that, at least for now, you don't hold their faith in your heart, although you wish you did. Raise the possibility that one day you might embrace their views, while you're telling them that you are not there right now.

Also, be open to their thoughts, and be open with yours, in return. Be open to the crazy possibility that their crazy views *might be right for you, after all.* Perhaps not now, but how do you know what you will think 10 years from now? Many young adults take on the religions of their parents after viciously rejecting them as teens.

The keywords here are *respect* and *love*. Love can survive religious differences. It may not survive religious disrespect. Religious disrespect can lead to war—in the world and in the family.

Rules: It's the How, Not the What

Rules can be comfortable guidelines, or barb-wire fences, depending more upon *how* they were made than *what* they are. When rules are made by one side and rammed down the other side's throat, they hardly ever work (see "Communication . . ." and "Curfew . . ."). The key is to have a system whereby you and your parents work together to set up rules you can both live with. Having a good system, where you work together, will actually cut the number of rules you will need down to a very few. In other words, a good system of making rules pretty much eliminates the need for them. But, before you start to wheel and deal on rules, it's a good idea to know what a good-rules system should be about.

It should be about control, but not in the way that many kids and their crazy parents think. It should not be a battle of kid *versus* parents, to see who's in control, but a project in which kid *and* parents work together, to slowly shift the control from the parents to the kid. In this game, parents should always be trying to give up the control, and adolescents should always be trying to prove that they're sane enough to take on the control.

It should not be a battle of kid versus parents, to see who's in control, but a project in which kid and parents work together, to slowly shift the control from the parents to the kid.

That means the parents' job is to be constantly willing to take risks to see their kid make good decisions, on her own. That means the kid's job is to be constantly willing to take actions to prove that she's grown responsible enough to take on control of her life. For parents, this risk might look like loosening up curfew, or allowing their kid to drive on a long trip. For kids, this growth might look like opting in at home when chores appear, or opting out at a party when kegs appear. When parents and kids work together like this, the results are amazingly good. When they don't, the results are amazingly bad.

The idea is not to be perfect, but to keep trying, and sticking to that plan of parent risk and kid growth. For example, if a kid rolls in with beer on her breath and keys in her hand, perhaps the car gets retired for a while, until she has proven that she's more responsible—not as a punishment, but just as a way of providing growth time, until she's shown she might be ready to make better decisions. Parents must always be willing to risk, and kids must always be willing to grow, even when this is scary for both of them. It takes guts for Dad to ever hand over the car keys after a drinking and driving incident. It takes guts for daughter to walk out of the next party "just because" underage drinking is happening.

I wish there were an easier way, but there's not. Peacefully shifting control from parents to adolescents takes courage and hard work on everyone's part. The only other option is war, a game that everybody loses.

Neil sat and stared at my clock, unwilling to answer any question I put to him. "So, why are you here?" I asked.

He loved giving me this answer: "For 50 f'ng bucks," he sneered, almost spitting the F sounds at me. "My parents are paying me to come here one time." Then he shook his head and snickered his disgust for them.

"So, why the hatred?" I asked. "Having met your mom, I know she's been up your rear-end all your life, but is that a reason to curse at her and threaten her all the time? She says you're smarter, bigger, and tougher than she is. So what's the point of terrifying her? Is this your way to get things changed?"

If looks could kill, I was a dead man. "That's right," he sneered again, "That's exactly right, Sherlock. That's exactly how I'll get everything I want." In fact, he was right. He had bullied his parents into buying him a car. He got up and put on his coat. "And what are you gonna' do about it?" he challenged.

"Not a thing," I answered, as he stormed out. "But thanks for coming in."

Neil never let me tell him that his parents were planning to take his car, and have him placed in a group home, if he refused to continue in counseling, as he just did. This was going to be a horror for them. It was going to be even worse for Neil. Neither side would win this war. Nobody wins a war. Some just lose more than others. In this war, Neil and his parents lost each other when Neil was removed from his home and placed in the custody of the state.

Don't take Neil's road. Use those paths of communication and compromise. I promise you, those trails will take you to much better places.

Running Away: A Smart Safety Valve, or a Lousy Life Choice?

Running away can be OK if it's done right. Or it can be the end of your life if it's not.

Most kids run away, in some way or another, at some point or another, in their careers as adolescents. In the vast majority of cases, they are gone for an hour or two, after storming out of the house after a fight, or so they think. The fact is that most of these "storm outs" occur in the *middle* of a fight, which is how this kind of running away can be OK. Leaving might be the thing that keeps the fight from getting any worse. That first type of running away is like a safety-release valve for anger. Let's call that a "type 1 run."

Type 1 runs are OK, as long as you eventually finish the discussion that blew up into an argument. If you can, before a "type 1 run," let your parents know that you will be back in a while, but that if you stay, no good will come of it. Help them see your jetting out, not as disrespect, but more as a way of avoiding further hurt for the family.

The next group of runaways, the "type 2 runners," are kids who are so upset that they stay out of the house for a night or two, usually at a friend's house. If you find yourself that mad, staying out a couple of nights in a safe house might also be a good way to take a break from the fighting, and sit and sort things out. But this must be done properly, as well, or it can make things worse.

First, explain to your friend's parents what happened in your home, and ask if it's OK for you to stay for the night. Being the parents of a teenager themselves, they'll understand. Next, call home to let your parents know where you are, and that you're safe. Put your friend's parents on the phone, to help calm your parents down. Calling your folks is a great way to avoid flashing red lights and handcuffs. Besides, your parents may also welcome an overnight break from the conflict, as long as they know that you're in a safe place. Again, tell your folks that this is just a temporary time, to let things cool down before you return home, and that you'll talk with them when you get back.

If things are truly so bad at your house that you can no longer live there, "run away" to some helper (cop or counselor), and tell the story.

The "type 3 runners" are the scary ones. These kids have no intention of ever going home. These are kids who hit the highway in search of freedom, love, and adventure. What they find is fear, loneliness, and abuse. Most of these runaways end up prostituting, drugging, and dying. This is not a way to go.

If things are truly so bad at your house that you can no longer live there, "run away" to some helper (cop or counselor), and tell the story. There are lots of people out there waiting to help you if you give them a chance. But they won't knock on your door. You have to go to them.

So if it's truly impossible to live at home anymore, if you're being abused, or if you're abusing others, it might be time to talk about living somewhere else, perhaps with a relative, or even in a group home. Sometimes, your seeking help will help the family understand that it's time to get the expert helpers (shrinks) involved, even if they refused before. Although this kind of "running away" may not sound as cool as hitting the highway, listen to the type 3 runners who survive and come home: They'll tell you that there is nothing cool on those dark and dangerous roads. There is a lot of pain.

"Sandi had been talking to this guy on the Net for a while. He said that he could get us jobs as models in New York City, and that we should stop taking all that crap from our parents. We had sent him pictures of ourselves, and he said he had lots of jobs for girls with our, you know, looks." As she said "looks," Shelby paused, and put her hand to her 14-year-old face, running her fingers over a fresh, gnarled scar on her soft cheek, a purple reminder of an untreated razor slash. "He promised us all kinds of money, and a place to live when we got there. So we split.

"The bus trip to New York was awful, but we were really excited, you know? Sandi and I were singing songs and playin' all the way there. It felt so . . . so free, like. We weren't scared or anything like that. If this guy turned out to be a creep, we'd just ditch him, you know?" As her fingers measured the length of her scar for the millionth time, she paused again. Her eyes darted around the room, as if she was afraid that somebody bad might be listening. When she seemed satisfied that no monsters were near, she started to weep.

"Nobody believes this next part," she cried. "He was a creep. He was . . ." her voice dropped low, ". . . a crazy pimp. He took us, like, prisoners, right there, at the bus place. He showed us a gun, and said he'd kill us if we screamed or made trouble. There were four of them, and they were huge. We were, like, frozen. We just did what he said. That's how we ended up, you know, doing what we did [prostituting]. My father, he can't understand that we didn't want to, and he keeps asking why we didn't just run."

Shelby's crying grew into sobs. "Please don't ask me about those two weeks, OK? I can't tell anyone about that. It's so hard to explain to people." She looked up at me. "Have you ever been really scared in

> your life, I mean, like, really, really thinking that you would die?" When I nodded yes, she calmed a bit. "Then, maybe you know. When you think you'll die, you do things that you thought you'd never do. And you become, like, a prisoner, or something, where you get too scared to try and get away. It's weird." She took a breath, and shook her head. "I guess I don't understand, either. It gets different sitting here, where it's all safe. It's hard to describe what you felt [her terror] when you're not locked in a room waiting to get . . . you know, raped."

If running away seems like the thing to do, take three thoughts with you as you go. First, know that when they pass the front door, most teen runaways *feel* like they want to run forever, but those feelings start to cool even as they get to the street. Almost *all* teen runaways head back home after a short time, because their feelings cool down after a short time. Second, know that most type 3 runners I've ever met (the kids who try to live on their own) have been badly hurt. Living on the street can mangle you in ways you can never imagine. And third, *every single type 3 runner* I've ever met regretted her decision.

Remember how to count. Resist that type 3 urge. Go with types 1 and 2.

School Attendance: The More You Miss, the More You'll Miss

If you or a friend run into this problem of ducking school, here are a few points to think about. Think fast, though, because truancy is like cancer: The longer it goes untreated, the more of your life it can take.

- **You have to go to school.** Chapter 9 explains why, but most kids know why school is important. It's just getting your rear end there that gets tough sometimes. Many states do allow kids to drop out at 16, but everyone knows that's a dead-end street for an adolescent.
- **The more you miss, *the more you'll miss.*** Truancy gets tougher to treat the longer it goes on. With each day that you cut, the harder it becomes to go back. This can quickly turn into a for-real mental disorder that may become impossible for you to beat on your own.

- **Friends can help.** If you're afraid to go back, level with your friends that this is not laziness on your part—*it's fear*. Let them know that you need help. Having them show up in the mornings to drag you out the door might get it done. If it's your friend who's ducking school, don't wait to hear from him—tell him you'll be there in the morning to pick him up, with a warm McMuffin in hand.
- **Helpers can help.** The experts (see Chapter 4) can get you past this. Sometimes a medication can make a huge difference in that gut fear you might be feeling.
- **Take small steps.** Try going back slowly, as in just in the door to the counselor's office the first day, maybe one hour of class on the second, perhaps a half day on the third, and so on. Believe it or not, the school staff will be very understanding of this request because lots and lots of kids have this problem. In fact, they'll be happy to cooperate, to help you get past this fear.
- **Rewards often work, punishments rarely work.** Once a school-skip problem hits hard, parents have already seen that punishing doesn't help. However, offering a reward to a kid who confronts her fear of school can help. Ask your folks if there is some reward they can offer. They're likely as scared about all this as you are, and willing to try anything. Don't threaten them ("*If you don't give me this, I won't go.*"). Rather, tell them straight up what that fear of school is like for you. Make it clear that this is not blackmail, but just a gimmick to help you stand up to your fear.

Beyond all else, don't start to think that stopping school is who you really are, part of your identity. View that urge to quit school as a virus, not a virtue. And know that it's a virus that can pretty much end your life if you don't get immediate treatment for it.

NOTE: Before you read the sections on "Sexual Abuse . . .," "Sexual Activity . . .," and "Sexual Differences . . .," it's *very* important that you reread Chapters 2, 3, and 5. There, you'll find lots of important information about sex. Much of that comes under headings like self-esteem, development, and aggression. You need to have this background information before you can make good decisions about sex. You might also take a look at the "Love" section here in Part Three. Go ahead. I'll wait.

Now that you've reread all of that stuff, here are some thoughts sent to you by other kids who have sat in your seat, and who have faced what you're facing on these topics. Again, remember that although these thoughts are addressed to the person who's dealing with the issue, you need to know this information, whether that person is you or a friend.

Sexual Abuse: Where Victims Feel Guilty

The case stories that I share with you in this book are kept in files arranged by subject. My file marked "Sexual Abuse Stories" is the thickest one of all. And it gets thicker and scarier every year. Although most sexual-abuse victims are girls, boys also get abused. In a sense, the boys may have an even worse time, because sexual abuse of boys is so rarely reported. We're just beginning to learn about the extent of sexual abuse of boys, which may be a lot higher than anyone thought. For now, though, girls win first place in the victim contest.

Last year, *10 percent* of the high school girls in this nation were raped—*10 percent.* Some researchers say that *30 percent* of America's women have experienced sexual abuse (forced, unwanted sexual contact)—*30 percent.* This is *not* a small problem. Here are some very important facts and tips to keep in mind:

- **Rape usually isn't what you think.** Most people picture rape as involving a masked stranger carrying a gun, kidnapping some random victim off the street. Denise said she would have preferred that.

After suffering for six months with daily blackouts (seizures) that her physicians couldn't explain, Denise spent another six months suffering through frustrating counseling that seemed pointless. This 23-year-old had been referred by her last neurologist, who told me, "Off the record, I'd bet she was abused as a child. I saw this once before. But don't quote me on that."

Her seizures were getting worse, the more we talked. She must have quit therapy 10 times, only to angrily return after her physicians told her there were no other options. Then, one night, after being hospitalized for what seemed the hundredth time, she came in and sat down, looking worse than ever. "I have something to tell you," she finally whispered. "I've known it for a while now, but I couldn't tell you. I couldn't tell anyone. I forgot it myself until a few weeks ago. I was hoping I could get better without having to tell this. Now I know I can't.

"My uncle . . ." She stopped, and started again. "When I was 13. . . ." She stopped again. Then she looked up, furious at me. "You know what I'm going to say, don't you? So don't just sit there and make me say it." She began crying, and yelled, "You don't care how hard this is for me."

I wanted to let her stop crying, but I couldn't let her quit now. "Denise, I don't know how hard this is. I wish I did. I only know that you must say whatever this thing is. It's no good if I guess, you know?"

She nodded bravely, and then finally let it out, along with her sobs. "My uncle . . . he did something . . . he . . . he raped me. He started . . . he started by saying he had to . . . to fix my hair, you know? He began grabbing at me. I was pushing him away at first, but then he pinned me against the couch. I think he was drunk, but he was big and strong." She paused again, to fight off her fear of telling. I could see her wrestling with herself, just as she had wrestled with her crazy uncle. She spoke through her sobs.

"Here's the worst part. My mother was just next door. His own sister was next door, and he's doing this to his sister's daughter? I kept thinking a million things, like 'this is not happening,' like 'he's just playin,' like 'will Mom blame me if she sees us?' and 'Dad will kill him if he finds out—my family will break up.' All those thoughts kinda' swirled around and around in my head, and then . . . it was over. My uncle, he says. . . ." she had to pause again, as her sobs got louder. ". . . HE SAYS 'THIS IS YOUR FAULT, YOU KNOW, AND YOU'D BETTER NOT TELL ANYBODY, 'CAUSE I'LL TELL THEM IT WAS YOUR IDEA, AND THEY'LL ALL KNOW YOU'RE A WHORE.'"

Ten years of locked-away pain poured out of her eyes. When she quieted, she seemed completely exhausted. In a flat voice, she finally said, "You know, that wasn't the worst part. The worst part is what he took from me. Not my virginity—my trust. The worst part is that he wasn't supposed to hurt me. He's family. Family's supposed to take care of family. I could never trust anyone after that—not boys, not friends, not even my parents, who I loved so much, and then shut out. It was like everyone might be crazy, so you can't be close to anyone."

She laughed a sad, bitter laugh. "Today, I read about that girl who got raped in the park by that rapist. At first, I was thinking 'how awful.' And then I remembered—I had been raped. And I thought, 'I wish I had been raped by a stranger, instead of my uncle. I think that would have been better.'" At last, Denise was able to look up at me. As she did, she shivered at these brutal, horrible thoughts that she had finally been able to face.

I hoped that that night was the beginning of the end of her rape.

- **Sexual abusers are usually people the victims know (like relatives or neighbors).** Those are people you are supposed to be able to trust. As Denise pointed out, when a relative abuses you, the sick sex part of it is a horror. But the shattered trust makes it worse. The shattered trust is why so many victims never tell, thinking that no one will believe them, or that they'll be blamed for "making" the attacker do what he did.
- **If you've been abused, tell someone, NOW.** I know it seems impossible. Just do it. This insanity goes on so much, I can about guarantee that any helper you tell (parent, counselor, doctor, cop) *will know without you even saying it that you did not want this to happen, and that you did not make this happen.* Most abusers threaten their victims into not telling. That abuse continues to abuse you every day that you keep it a secret, even if it ended years ago. Repeat this over and over until you tell someone what happened to you: THIS WAS NOT MY CRIME! THIS SHOULD NOT BE MY SHAME!
- **The worst wounds of abuse don't show.**

I thought Ali had told me the worst of it the week before. How she had been raped last year by a boy she hung out with in the park. She thought of him as her boyfriend. He didn't think of her at all. But the worst for Ali happened after that rape. "Last week, I only told you the first part," she said. "When I was crying last week, I wasn't crying for that first thing [her rape]. I was crying for what I've got to tell you now."

Ali seemed to shrink in size as she hunched down in the couch, like she was trying to become as small as possible. In a low voice, she told the worst for her. "I'm real ashamed to tell you this, and I don't know why, but I hung out again with him [the rapist], after he did that to me. I think I was afraid that he'd tell the other boys what he did, and they'd think they could do that to me—I don't know. Or maybe I wanted to make him a real boyfriend to make it [the rape] OK, or something. I just don't know." Here, Ali started to tremble terribly, as if ice water had been dumped on her.

In a voice that shook so much that it was hard to hear, she pushed on. "So he tried to get me again once, but I pushed him off. There were other kids around that time, so he stopped. Then, another time, he took me to a house where there was supposed to be a party. No one was there. Then he started again, just like the first time. I was crying, and I kept asking him to stop, and let me go home, but he wouldn't."

Ali's tears told me that now she was looking at her nightmare in her mind. She started to yell and sob at the same time. "THAT'S HOW I KNOW I'M BAD, THAT I'M A WHORE. I LET HIM," she cried. "I JUST WANTED IT TO BE OVER, SO I COULD JUST GO HOME. I FIGURED IT DIDN'T MATTER, 'CAUSE I WAS ALREADY DIRTY. I LET HIM—SO IT'S MY FAULT, UNDERSTAND? THE FIRST TIME, IT WAS RAPE, 'CAUSE HE BEAT ME UP. BUT AFTER THAT, I JUST LET HIM. THE SECOND TIME, IT WASN'T RAPE. IT WAS ME BEING A SLUT!"

When she quieted a bit, I asked her the questions she should have been asked a long time ago. "Ali, did you ever want to have sex with him?" With her eyes closed, she shook her head no. "Did you ask him to stop?" She nodded yes. "Did he force himself on you?" Again, she nodded yes, but she couldn't look at me. "Ali," I demanded softly, "Look at me." You could see the incredible effort it took for her to face the disapproval that she feared she'd find in my face. "Rape is unwanted, forced intercourse. You were raped, both times." She looked down again. "Please, Ali, this is real important for you to hear: Getting raped the first time hurt you terribly in many ways. Maybe the worst way was thinking that you were 'already dirty.' Thinking like that allows jerks like him to hurt you more. That trip never ends."

She sat for a minute, thinking, but saying nothing. Then, she shrugged and said, "It seems like there are lots of jerks in the world, you know?"

"Yes," I said, "especially if you happen to be female."

Once you make it clear that you don't want to have sex, that should be the end of the story. If someone keeps at it, he's crossed a huge boundary line from expressing love and longing into showing control and contempt. And if that sex goes on without your consent—if, like Ali, you just "let it happen," so you can escape, *you've been raped.*

And, like Ali, it's terribly important that you understand this. So that, unlike Ali, you don't start to call yourself names like slut and whore. Remember, in Chapter 3, we talked about the power of how you value yourself (your self-esteem)? Remember we saw how thinking of yourself in a certain way can make you act that way? For kids who are abused (girls *and* boys), the fallout from that unwanted sex is a perfect example.

Abused kids often give in to more abuse because they don't feel worth fighting for.

Abused kids tend to feel worthless. They tend to hang with people who treat them as if they're worthless. Abused kids often give in to more abuse because they don't feel worth fighting for. This is a never-ending, downward spiral. If you're there, STOP NOW, AND SEE A HELPER. Those bad feelings you feel are *not* about who you are or what you are worth. They are only about *what happened to you*—not because you *are* bad, but because you *were* unlucky—in the wrong place at the wrong time. You were run over by a truck called evil. You just happened to be in the way.

Sexual Activity: Do the Birds and the Bees Go through This?

Chapter 5 lays out the first set of things you need to think about before you think about having sex. You must read that chapter before this second list will make any sense. These are all thoughts sent to you by other teenagers who have faced these same tough decisions.

- **Don't get tangled in the "lines."** When boys want sex, they'll sometimes try to guilt, shame, or threaten girls into it. Here are some time-tested "counter" lines that girls recommend:

LINE	COUNTER
"If you loved me, you'd have sex with me."	"If you loved me, you'd respect my feelings."
"If you loved me, you'd have sex with me."	"Because I love you, I wouldn't make you do something you felt was wrong for you."
"Everybody does it."	"Go date everybody. I'm me."
"If you don't, I'll just get it somewhere else."	"Thanks for the disease warning. I'll get what I want somewhere else, too."

- **If you're going to have sex, do it knowing that your relationship *will* end (see "Love . . .").** This might be book-throwing time again, but facts are facts. The odds are about 10,000 to 1 that your present sex partner will *not* be your life partner, no matter how wonderful things might seem now. So, if you think that you're going to share your life with your present squeeze, the chances are that you're wrong. Sorry if I'm raining on your parade. I could never believe that, either. But it turned out to be oh-so-true. For me, and for everyone I knew.
- **As with drugs, everybody *doesn't* do it.** In fact, fewer kids are having sex these days. Not a lot fewer, but still, it's a trend. More kids are finding out that they don't need the intensity of a sexual relationship while they're dealing with so many other issues of adolescence. Radical thought, huh?
- **Drugs + Sex = *"Oh, No!"*** Most "disaster" sex (involving pregnancy, rape, and disease) happens in the warm glow of beer, ecstasy, and weed, which sobers up to the harsh lights of pregnancy tests, arrests, and infections. If your sex happens only when you're high, *think about it.* Not only do you risk disasters, you may be using chemicals to drug out your values.
- **If you don't want trouble, stay out of the jungle.** I couldn't stand hearing this story. Like a horror movie that was too scary, I wanted to

fast forward to the end. But Barbara had to tell every detail because she was so amazed. I wasn't so amazed, because this 13-year-old had already told me that this happened at a co-ed sleepover that no parents knew about. I wasn't amazed—I was scared.

". . . so after I pushed this kid off me again, Denise takes me in the other room and says that his mother just died a few days ago, and that he told her he's been in love with me forever, and that he just wants to hold me, since he's hurting so bad for his mother. I hardly knew him, but I felt real sorry for him. I, well, also had some beer. . . ." She left that thought where it was. "So he says he just wants to be held, and I say OK. He says he wants to sleep in the closet with me—no sex, or nothing, just to be held, like his mom used to do." Barb's eyes looked astounded at what she was about to say.

"So I go into this big closet with him. At first, he just holds me, but then he tries stuff. I keep saying no, but he won't stop. He starts telling me to shut up, and saying that I knew what would happen when I agreed to go into the closet with him. Finally, I screamed, and Denise opens the door and pulls him off me. She's, like, screaming at him, like, too much. He just laughs, and walks away. Denise told me that she made up the part about his mother dying. She just wanted us to be together because she thought we'd be a good couple. She's pretty stupid, huh?" Barbara asked.

I couldn't resist. "And you weren't?"

If you don't want to get hurt, stay out of harm's way. Empty houses, unsupervised sleepovers, drugs and kissing, older guys, late nights in the woods—these are all places where bad stuff goes down. If you go to those places, you're telling people like Barbara's creep to take a shot.

Sexual Differences: Any "Illness" Is in Your World, Not in You

It's disclaimer time. The leading medical/psychological/psychiatric groups in this nation say that sexual differences are just other forms of sexual expression. They are not seen as sick or weird by the folks who have studied them (see Chapter 2). Your own religious or moral views might strongly disagree with that, but that's what science has to say. If your views are different, please just accept this section for what it is, and place your own values over this information. The science offered here is not intended to replace your own religious views on sexual differences.

If you are not sexually different, the odds are that one of your friends is.

If you are not sexually different, the odds are that one of your friends is (see Chapter 2). So you need to read this section to be a better buddy to your sexually different peers. Those folks need good friends who have the courage it takes to stand with them against the gutless people who hate them.

Here are some helpful tips to keep in mind:

- **If you think you're different sexually, see a helper (parent, counselor, doctor).** You might be different, but you might not. Chapter 2 talks about how your sexual identity doesn't really get clear for a while. Don't "try it out" (have sex) to see. Having any sort of sex may only confuse you more. Get an expert helper involved, to sort through all of these issues. DON'T JUST GO UNDERGROUND. In spite of what the jerks say, sexual differences are *not* crimes, sicknesses, or moral failings. These are just differences.
- **Being sexually different has nothing to do with being a molester.** I shouldn't even have to say that, but my teen advisors say I must. For example, *a gay man has the same (or maybe even less) potential to molest children as does a straight man.* Molesting kids *is* a sickness (and a crime), whether the molester is heterosexual (straight) or homosexual (gay). Straight *and* gay men can be molesters, but the vast majority of both groups are not. Having sex with children is a repulsive thought to both straight *and* gay men. It is sexy to neither one.
- **Beware of the predators, straight or not.** Young teen girls are often sexually "hunted" by young men (18, 21, and older). These creeps play on naive girls who think they look "cool" running with older guys. Creeps can be sexually different, as well. So, if you're being pressured by one of those individuals (straight or gay), RUN to a helper.

If you're faced with any of these sexual issues, get all the information you can before you do anything else. This is serious game time.

For more information on this subject, check out these books: *On Being Gay: Thoughts on Family, Faith, and Love,* by Brian McNaught, and *Two Teenagers in Twenty: Writing by Gay and Lesbian Youth,* by Ann Heron. They're listed in the "To Find Out More" section at the end of this book.

Siblings: The Best Worst Friends You'll Ever Have

Whenever I do seminars for parents of teenagers, I'm always asked, "How do I keep my 12-year-old and my 14-year-old from fighting with each other?" I always answer, "By spacing their ages apart by at least four years." After everyone laughs, the parent always says, "Seriously, how do you stop the fights?" I always answer, "Seriously, by spacing their ages apart by at least four years." The laughter stops, because that is pretty much the best answer to stop the fighting.

Siblings who are close in age tend to fight more due to many reasons related to their close ages: jealousy, competition, friends . . . you name it. There seem to be a million reasons. And boredom. Many teens report that they pick sibling fights just to break up a boring day. The fact is that much of this is unavoidable, a fact that makes parents very sad, and fighting sibs very puzzled.

The kids don't usually see the fighting as that big a deal (depending upon who won the last round). To the kids, it's just business as usual. But they usually are surprised to see how upset the bickering gets their parents. This is another one of those "crazy" parent things. Almost all parents love their kids a lot, and seeing two people you love "hate" each other can make you crazy. It can make you wade into the middle of sibling fights and try to stop them, by asking dumb questions like who did what to whom. That trick usually starts more fights than it stops. Once a parent appears to be taking sides in a sib fight, she has just provided the ammunition for the next 10 fights. So, smart parents try to stay out of sib fights, to avoid taking sides. Of course, that then leads to "crazy" teens screaming that their parents don't care about them. Not a lot of great options here, but there are a couple that are better than nothing.

The first option is to talk with your warring sib. But talk in a new way, in a new place, perhaps with a moderator/helper (see

"Communication . . ."). It's really weird what hidden truths you can uncover when you just talk, straight up.

At 14, Vanessa had the "tough chick" act down very well. She was playing that role perfectly as her "perfect" 16-year-old sister, Emilia, attacked her with the list of "nasty" things Vanessa does that cause the two of them to fight. Sensing that Vanessa was winning the argument by laughing at her, Emilia went for her best shot. It was some shot.

". . . AND, WORST OF ALL," Emilia was yelling, "IS THE NASTY, PRINCESS, LITTLE-GIRL WAY YOU TALK TO MOM, KNOWING HOW SICK SHE IS. [Their mom had terrible problems from diabetes.] HOW DARE YOU TALK TO HER LIKE THAT WHEN SHE'S SO SICK?!" Emilia's best shot worked.

Vanessa suddenly jumped up, with raging eyes. "HOW DARE I? HOW DARE I? OH NO, EMELIA, IT'S HOW DARE YOU?! IT'S HOW DARE YOU TALK TO ME LIKE THAT, WHEN YOU'RE NEVER HOME WHEN MOM'S SICK. 'MISS PERFECT?' RIGHT . . . EXCEPT YOU'RE NEVER AROUND TO HELP. YOUR PERFECT SOCIAL LIFE, YOUR PERFECT BOYFRIEND, AND YOUR PERFECT SCHOOL ALL KEEP YOU AWAY, ALL THE TIME. AND ISN'T THAT ALL FRICKIN' CONVENIENT? WHO IS IT THAT EMPTIES MOM'S BEDPANS, MAKES ALL OF HER MEALS, AND HOLDS HER HAND WHEN SHE'S HURTING? THAT'S ME—MISS IMPERFECT. AM I A BITCH SOMETIMES? YES! SOMETIMES I GET SCARED, AND TIRED, AND DISGUSTED. AND ARE YOU EVER AROUND WHEN I'M CRASHING? NO! YOU'RE OUT RUNNING IN YOUR PERFECT WORLD WHILE I . . ." Vanessa paused here and exhaled loudly, suddenly looking very tired and soft, ". . . while I've got no sister to help me, to talk to, to, you know, be there."

Emilia just stared at the floor. Her best shot had bounced back and hit her right between her eyes.

So try the talking game, to see if it turns up some hidden cause of the feuding. If boredom is your reason to fight, ask your parents if they might pay you guys not to fight. No joke; if you get some daily reward for not fighting, it sometimes helps you break the *habit* of sibling fighting. Like a bad habit, fighting can seem to be the "normal" way of living with your sib. Rewards can help you guys look for other, less destructive, and less dangerous, activities to break the boredom. You know, like building thermal-nuclear bombs.

The ultimate irony here is that, in this game of life, your siblings will probably become the best friends you'll ever have. And they'll also have been the worst.

Sleep: You're Probably Too Tired to Read This

If I had to pick one factor in your world that affects you more than any other, it would be your sleep, as in your *lack* of it. If I could pick one magical power to fix teen problems like anger and anxiety, drugs and depression, failure and fatigue, that one power would be to get you to sleep 10 hours a night.

Of course, that means you'd be snoring in bed by 8 P.M. if your alarm goes off at 6 A.M. "No way," you laugh? Well, I agree that 8 P.M. is not likely to happen. But, before you laugh too much, check out these facts about sleep. They might keep you awake tonight.

- **Your brain requires 10 hours of sleep to work right.** Research proves that's how much your adolescent "sleep fuel tank" requires. When you get less, you start to pay a price with those problems I listed above. And the more sleep you miss, the harder those problems hit.
- **Your brain revs up in the late evening.** Which is why you start to party hearty at about 9 P.M., an hour after you should be in bed. Your brain has a thing called a "sleep clock" that tells you when to sleep and when to wake up. Left alone, your sleep clock might say "night-night" at 2 A.M., and "rise and shine" at 12 noon (which is about what teens do on weekends when they're left alone).
- **Your world demands that you be social in the late evening.** That makes it that much harder to get to sleep when the 'phoners keep phoning, and the messengers keep messaging.
- **Your school demands that you be smart at 7:30 A.M.** Which is exactly when your brain is shut down, as if you're in the middle of your sleep. Yet, you're supposed to be in the middle of geometry. Researchers have

found that up to *half* the kids sitting in those early-morning killer classes are actually much like narcoleptics, folks with a sleep disorder where they just zonk out. That's because you're trying to run your brain on 4 to 6 hours of sleep, when you need 10. Your car won't run without fuel. How is your brain supposed to?

- **No, you can't make it up on weekends.** Sleeping all weekend just screws up your sleep clock even more. It's about impossible to get up at 6 A.M. on Monday, when you got up at 3 P.M. on Saturday and Sunday.

So what can you do, besides enroll in night school?

- **Shoot for eight and one-half hours of sleep (maybe just eight?).** Although that's still not great, it'll get most kids by. I know that probably means a terrible shot to your electronic social life, but being asleep by 10 P.M. the night before might make you that much more attractive at 8 A.M. the morning after (and your brain will actually work, too). And you can do a *little* "catch-up" sleep on weekends without messing up your sleep clock.
- **Use tricks to move your sleep clock up toward that 10 P.M. slot, such as these:**

  Dim the lights at night. The darker you make your room, the more sleep chemicals you make in your brain. Cut back on the room lights around 8 or 9 P.M. By the way, your brain shuts off all those sleep chemicals when it gets light in your room. So switch *all* the lights on at 6 A.M.

  Hide the clock. Nothing keeps you awake more than watching your clock and worrying that you're not asleep by 12 midnight, 1 A.M., 1:30 A.M. . . . "*AAARRRRGGGHHHH!!!*"

  Eat to sleep. Avoid sugars and caffeine (soda, tea, coffee). Snack on things like crackers or pretzels. Turkey works great, too.

  Read to sleep. Boring books (this one, perhaps?) make heavy eyelids.

  Try one of those silly "white noise" machines that play continuous sounds of wind in trees, or ocean waves. Kids tell me that they work great.

  Don't force sleep. If you're tossing and turning, get out of bed, keep the lights low, and read some more (no TV/stereo/computer). When the lids start to droop, fall back in bed.

If all else fails, see your doc. After she recovers from meeting a teenager who *wants* to sleep at night, she'll chat with you about some short-term-use medicines that can help you move that sleep clock around, so that your own brain will eventually start to make your bed look really inviting at 10 P.M.

All this is not easy to do. It takes time and patience to retrain your brain to zonk out at 10 p.m. But it can be done. Adolescents who live in places like military schools find that it's no sweat resetting that sleep clock when you're forced to. And it's incredibly well worth doing. I've seen eight simple hours of sleep turn scores of heavily medicated, heavily troubled adolescents into happier, medicine-free teenagers. So, before you start taking antidepressant and antidistraction drugs, try a little anti-exhaustion sleep. You might be amazed at the results.

I've seen eight simple hours of sleep turn scores of heavily medicated, heavily troubled adolescents into happier, medicine-free teenagers.

Smoking Cigarettes: Who Gets the Porsche—You, or Your Pusher?

You've heard all the horror stories, and you know all the health risks that prove why you shouldn't smoke. Yet, for many of you, the scare tactics don't work. It's not that you want to die, it's more that you figure you'll quit in the future, sometime, you know, like *before* you get lung cancer. In other words, you admit that smoking will kill you, but, for some reason, you still feel a strong need to smoke now—*even before you're addicted and get those horrible urges to smoke.*

Those first few weeks of smoking cigarettes are when they taste *horrible* to a new smoker. They provide absolutely no pleasure at all. Many kids puke a lot, until they get the hang of working their addiction. They act like they like it, but any of us who've been there know that, for those first few weeks, cigarettes make your nachos taste nasty, your mouth feel musty, and your breath smell beastly. What are those first few weeks of smoking all about?

Posing. The need to look cool, or tough, or whatever. The need to act older than you are, streetwise, and all that. It's about image building. In the end, you begin smoking yourself to death because you don't feel good about your life. When you think about it, that's pretty sad. By the time smokers realize that they only look (and taste) stupid, it's too late. Those nice cigarette makers (you know, the guys with the great ads?) have you leashed on a dog chain called nicotine. And when they yank it, you jump, forking over *your* hard-earned cash to pay for *their* Porsches, by destroying *your* body. Now there's a great business.

The biggest joke of all is that these terrorists start poisoning you in your teen years, the time when you fight being controlled by adults. Yet, with the cigarette people, *you* pay *them* for the privilege of handing *them* a piece of *your* soul?! You have to admit it, those guys are geniuses.

If you haven't started to smoke, but are close, go to the convenience store—not to buy cigarettes, but to watch the young kids who do. Look closely at them as they light up. Do they look cool and tough? Or do they look like little kids trying to look like they're cool and tough? How do you want to look?

If you're already hooked and tired of paying for your pushers' Porsches, here are a couple of quitting tips from other teen addicts who've quit.

- **See your doctor.** He has a bunch of tricks that can help you get free, if you really want to get free.
- **See your parents.** They'll be so happy that you're taking back control of your body, you can probably talk them into some kind of reward to help you not quit quitting.
- **See what this is costing you.** Cigarettes cost a fortune these days. Total up your addiction-free savings over a lifetime. Then ask yourself, "Who do I want to buy that Porsche for: me or my nice pusher?"

Finally, if all of this talk about quitting your smoking makes you want to light up, know this: *More teens have quit smoking than ever before, and fewer teens are becoming smokers than ever before.* If they can do it, so can you.

Talking: How the Difficult Becomes Impossible

Back when you were a year old, your expanding baby brain needed to communicate with people so much that it drove you to learn how to talk. Learning to make sounds that make sense was an incredibly tough challenge for you. It involved a lot of frustration, failure, and even fear—fear of people not ever understanding you. Some toddlers get so afraid that they shut up and stop trying. That dooms them to years of painful struggle because there really is no other option: You *have to* learn how to communicate, whether with sounds or signs.

Guess what? It's rerun time, meaning that your expanding adolescent brain again needs to communicate with people, but this time on a *much higher level* than before. Your head is suddenly swamped with thousands of new, complex thoughts and questions that require a whole new level of language skills to communicate. But, much like that toddler, your brain might be racing way ahead of your mouth's skill levels. And, just like that toddler, it can get really frustrating for a while.

For a 12-year-old, Rob's writings were amazing, full of people thinking deep, complex thoughts. He loved to write—horror, comedy, whatever. He wrote so much that his parents were worried that he might be getting depressed, avoiding friends, family, and fun, often preferring to just sit and type.

He clearly was uncomfortable answering my questions. When I asked him what he enjoyed about writing, he sighed and looked at the clock, rolling his eyes when he saw that only 10 minutes had passed. "Sorry," I said, "I can see that coming here was not your idea."

Surprised by my words, and now blushing because he thought my feelings were hurt, Rob sat up and shook his head no. "No, no," he said, "it's not like that at all. I, um, well . . . I . . . did want to come, kinda'. But I . . . didn't want to, sorta, because . . . well, it's like this. . . . Sometimes I. . . ." Here Rob sighed loudly again, and sat back in the couch, silent and defeated.

Not wanting to mess up his thoughts, I sat quietly, but that just made Rob more uncomfortable. He kept adjusting his sneaker laces, glancing up occasionally at me, and then getting more agitated when he saw me looking at him. "Do you have to stare at me?" he snapped. Before I could respond, he took back those words he never meant. "Sorry," he mumbled. "Sorry for seeming like a jerk. I just . . . I'm so. . . ." He sat back again. "This is pointless," he finally added. "Not you . . . me. I can't say what I think. I never could. Just when I think I can say a thing, I lose it." Worried that I'd think he was stupid, Rob quickly added, "But I'm smarter than I sound." Then his face brightened a bit: "I could write this scene out great."

Many kids find themselves trapped in their own heads, with all kinds of ideas that seem impossible to say to someone else.

Rob had it better than many adolescents—at least he could write his thoughts. Many kids find themselves trapped in their own heads, with all kinds of ideas that seem impossible to say to someone else. Some teens talk nonstop about dumb stuff, never getting to their deeper ideas and feelings. Others just shut up entirely. If you find yourself knowing what Rob was going through, here are a few tips:

- **Don't shut up.** Like learning to "speak" with music, speaking your thoughts takes practice. Practice means that you're going to flub a lot until you get it down. Don't quit. The more you try, the better you get.
- **Don't worry about making sense.** If you stay with it, you'll eventually get out what you want, the way that you want. Let your words flow, like the first draft of a poem. You can edit later, if you want.
- **Ask your crazy parents not to interrupt.** And, especially, *not to finish your sentences for you* (doesn't that make you nuts?). Show them this book section. Ask them to remember their own teen talk problems. Explain that you'd like to have the time it takes to finish a thought, even if it doesn't make sense to them, or even to you, at first.
- **When pressed, write.** If you're under the gun to get ideas across to someone, and your mouth still isn't motoring as you'd like, write. As silly as it sounds, writing a letter to someone might help you get your points across better, and with much less chance of blowing things up with a bomb made of badly spoken words. Writing can come in very handy in the face of a four-week grounding. It also helps your brain train your mouth to say things the way you want.

In any event, don't mourn if your mouth seems full of mush these days. It's only a temporary condition. One day soon, you'll suddenly realize that your thoughts are zapping out of your head with laser-like precision.

Working: Keep Your Day Job

Jobs for teens are great. You'll learn as much important stuff in a lousy job as you will in a good school. Like discipline and hard work. Like how to handle people. Like why you should stay in that good school, and why you should get even better grades. School and grades can suddenly become relevant when you start your eighth straight hour of chopping onions at your local fast-food restaurant. But if you decide to work during the school year, keep these points in mind.

12 hours is okay; 20 is not. For most kids, working up to 12 hours a week during the school year works, but pushing beyond that gets tricky. Sleep (see "Sleep . . ."), grades, and moods start to suffer for the sake of a minimum wage. Unless your family needs your money for food, that's a bad trade-off. Working too much at a lousy job now can keep you in that lousy job forever, by causing you to screw up school. Over a lifetime, those school hours will pay off *thousands* of times better than minimum wage. Don't be a chump—play the game smart. Play to win the game of life, not just the first inning.

Don't run away to your job. When some kids are having trouble with grades, they can hide out in their jobs, taking on more hours as a way of avoiding doing frustrating school work. Feeling good about working hard at a job is great, as long as it doesn't replace feeling good about working hard at school. Remember that Job Number One *must* be school. Teen work is fine as long as it remains Job Number Two. If it becomes Job Number One, you may find that, as an adult, you'll need a Job Number Three just to make enough money to feed a family of four.

Well, there you are! Part Three is now yours to keep. Every answer to every problem of every adolescent's life in one book section—*I wish!* If only life were like that, wouldn't it be great? Have a hassle, look up the answer, and "*TAAA-DAAA,*" instant success. Then you wouldn't have any problems, or struggles, or sleepless nights, or nervous stomachs, or . . . or *joy.* That's right, no joy. Not the "yippee" joy of being given a car, but that deep-down joy that comes from working hard, saving, and then buying *your own car*. Real joy you get only after fighting for something, through problems, struggles, and sleepless nights. Real joy you get to feel only after you do something that's hard to do, something you are a little afraid of, something that you worry you might fail at. I've always been amazed at how much more teenage joy there seems to be in a "worked-for" 10-year-old Toyota than in a "given" brand-new BMW. In the end, for all of us, teens and adults alike, real joy is about *doing it on your own.*

The day that life becomes struggle-free is the day that life becomes no fun at all.

If someone ever writes a book that could solve all of your struggles, *don't read it*. The day that life becomes struggle-free is the day that life becomes no fun at all. The fun is in the *adventure*, in the *risk* of not being sure whether or not you can win. Think about this for a minute. Do you like to play easy games that are rigged to let you win, or do you find yourself pulled to those maddening games in which you lose a lot, but you keep going back, to see if you can finally win? And isn't that final win worth all of the struggle and frustration?

The "game" of adolescence is exactly like that. Lots of struggle and frustration, but also lots of final wins, if, and only if, you keep yourself in the right game, which is not the easy one. Avoid copping out to play the easy game, where you avoid all stress and always take the easy path. Stay in the harder game, the one where you push yourself, think for yourself, get straight up with yourself. That's the one where you learn about yourself, and you learn about life. That's the one that *builds your identity.* Books like this are here only to ease the way a bit, not to remove the struggle.

So use these tips the right way—to help you play that *harder* game *better*. Don't fear the struggles and the losses. They make your final win all the more joyful. Remember, *winning is most sweet to those who have tasted defeat.*

Speaking of accomplishments, CONGRATULATIONS! You just finished this book . . . almost. There's only the "Epilogue" to go.

And, speaking of winning and losing, aren't you curious to see what became of some of the kids you've met in these pages? Would you like to bet on where Gerald ended up (the boy in the "Introduction," who you last saw headed off to jail)? I'll bet you'd lose your bet.

Epilogue

We began this book by saying that there were three goals it should help you with: understanding your parents, understanding yourself, and getting some tips on how to handle common teen problems. I hope we've made a start in that direction. A start is the best we can hope for, because that's about the best any book can do for anyone. Books don't change people. Only life does that.

You've lived long enough to know that you get smarter at life only by living, by dealing day-to-day with your world, and by thinking. Always thinking. About who you are, what you're doing, and who you'd like to become. If you're honest with yourself and with others, and if you watch out for how crazy we can all get sometimes, you're headed for a happy ending. I know that's true because, believe it or not, *most kids turn out just fine—even in this crazy world that you live in.*

I, for one, don't really know how you manage to do that. I do know that I love the work I do because I also love underdogs and upsets in sports. To me, today's teens are underdogs, facing fierce odds against winning in this game of growing up. And yet they almost always seem to pull it off. Even those kids who seem so far gone, so horribly down that path of craziness, *even those kids* almost always get it together, in the end. I find that quite amazing. And inspiring. Like I said, teenagers are my heroes.

Speaking of heroes who beat the odds, I wanted to give you a "Whatever Happened To . . ." tour of where some of those teens you met in this book ended up. For example, do you remember Stan the Skinhead in Chapter 3? He was the kid you last saw looking over his shoulder for his skin "brothers," who weren't feeling very brotherly after he ratted out their leader. Care to guess where Stan the Skinhead parks his car now?

". . . in the faculty parking lot. Can you believe it? I've got MY VERY OWN RESERVED PARKING SPACE, in the faculty parking lot. I know you're green with envy reading this. Try not to get too down just because the craziest client you ever had has something his old shrink doesn't have: MY VERY OWN, RESERVED, PARKING SPACE. Well, OK, it's just at a community college, but I know that one day I'll have a job teaching at some Ivy League university. And that job will include MY VERY OWN RESERVED PARKING SPACE."

Stan's e-mail made me laugh out loud. More from happiness than from humor, but it felt wonderful, just the same. His note went on to explain how he finished college on a military college program, got discharged, got his master's degree, and landed his present teaching job. "And just to tempt fate, I also do some speaking at high schools about the dangers of hate groups. I should know, right?"

Stan then answered the question I posed to him at the beginning of our conversation: "What message would I give to teenagers reading your book? I'd say that Dr. Bradley is not a complete twerp; he's about 60 percent twerp, which isn't bad for an adult. But, since you'll never print that (shows what you know, Stan), maybe print this for your readers: 'Check out everything, but don't jump into anything while you're still a teen. Don't make big moves until you're older. You've got lots of time, if you'll only resist that urge to try and grow up too fast by starting a new life with a new family, whether that new "family" is friends, a gang, or a cult.

"Read my story, and think. When we're teens, we're all just too nuts to make huge commitments, like the bizarre one I did, just because I was looking for a replacement family. Personally, I think that's why many teens get into serious trouble: They're looking for replacement families while they still need their first one. Work on fixing the real family you've already got. Almost always, there's love there that lasts, even if it's hard to find sometimes. Replacement families are like those silly spare tires you get in new cars: They work OK for a little while, but, when the driving gets hard, they just blow apart and leave you stranded.'

"How's that? By the way, Doc, did I mention to you that I've got MY VERY OWN RESERVED PARKING SPOT . . .?"

Stan may have gotten his own parking space, but Lizzie did even better, considering where she ended up first. Lizzie was that girl in Chapter 8 who was into a bunch of self-destructive behaviors, the girl whose friends brought her in. After you last saw her, she was removed from her mother's house and placed into a bad foster home.

> "I ran away a lot," she wrote. "Those people were really mean. They used to hit the kids when we didn't do chores and stuff. We told on them, but no one believed us. No one believes teens, you know. I'm 22 now, and I still think that's true.
>
> "Anyway, the running away landed me in prison [juvenile detention]. I know that sounds bad, but I ended up in [a very good treatment center], where I kind of blossomed. The people there were great, both the staff and most of the kids. We got real close. That seemed to fix something inside of me. Thinking back, I now know I was looking for good people to be with, to learn from. All that crazy stuff I did was not me. I was just kind of screaming out for help, you know? Help, and love. Those things made a huge difference for me. I just finished my student teaching, and I'm interviewing for teaching jobs right now—teaching middle and high school, of all things.
>
> "And, to answer your question about what I'd say to adolescents? I'd have to say 'nothing.' Kids don't listen to that 'words of wisdom' stuff, do they? I don't think they can if they're hurting, and, if they're not hurting, then they don't need the words. They should listen, but they don't. That's because parents don't listen to them. It's just the way it is. . . ."

Sorry, Lizzie, but I disagree. I think most teenagers *and* parents do listen. And when you've been working with kids awhile, I'll bet you'll think that, too. But, for now, your non-answer to my question is just the kind of thing that perhaps kids should hear. Your directness will do you very well as a teacher of teenagers. In fact, your "non-answer" might have sounded so truthful that even a girl like Rachel might have trusted you enough to tell her own truth before it became her nightmare.

Remember Rachel (Chapter 4)? I think I get more questions about where she ended up than any other kid I've ever described. Rachel was that girl coming from about the worst place you could imagine, a place so horrible that she had to create another person inside of herself, just to stay alive. Some call that "crazy." I call it survival.

Rachel survived and even found happiness, after she finally told the truth about what her father had been doing all those years. She got a two-year associate's degree in child care, to help her find temporary work in day care, while she pursued her dream of becoming a lawyer to help abused kids. I lost touch with her some time back, but her last letter made my eyes fill up—in a good way. It seems that her identity was still unfolding, even after the brutal battering it took as a teen.

> "Dear Doctor Bradley,
>
> "It's me again, Rachel. Just sending you my new address, like you asked. Sorry I took so long to write. I've been working in this day care center for the past year while I finish my pre-law degree, and guess what? I love it! The day care, not the law. I'm at it all the time and love every minute. The little guys are so honest, so loving—I come alive doing this job. I've decided that the best work I can do is helping little kids and their parents to be OK, before any abuse starts, you know? As a lawyer, I'd be kind of getting these guys too late, after the damage is done. So I'm switching my major from pre-law to child development. At least that's the plan for now.
>
> "I've learned that you have to stay open to changing as you grow up, or you can end up losing yourself. Having already lost myself once [to her mental illness], I have no intention of ever going there again. I've met this great guy and. . . ."

If I could guess at what Rachel would have wanted to say to you, it would probably be two things. First, to "*. . . stay open to changing as you grow up, or you can end up losing yourself.*" She'd probably want you to keep your options open as you grow, so that you, too, end up finding what you love. Second, she'd want you to reread her story, to know that perhaps the strangest thing about life might be how the sun *always* comes up, even after the most horrific night. That, in life, what doesn't kill you does make you stronger—if you can find the raw courage to push through those dark nights.

Rachel would probably say, "Hey, if I made it through, so can you." In fact, I suspect that's what all of the kids you met in this book would say. Even Gerald.

Gerald was that first teenager you met, back in the "Introduction." He was the drug-involved kid who was arrested at that party. His parents were the ones who were using drugs themselves, lied about it, and then blasted Gerald for using drugs. He could be the poster boy for the title of this book, *Yes, Your Parents Are Crazy!* If you recall, Gerald's life was about as messed up as a teen's life can be, with a comatose girlfriend, courtroom hearings, and crazy parents. If he can survive (sort of), so will you.

I say that Gerald only "sort of" survived because of one down side to his story. In every other way, he turned out great. He stopped drugs, started studying, and went on to college, and even to graduate school. His real name appears in the acknowledgments to this book.

So why do I rate his survival as "sort of"? Because of his unfortunate choice of careers. Gerald became a . . . a . . . *psychologist.* I guess nobody's perfect.

Be well. Be happy. Good luck.

To Find Out More...

. . . consider reading any of these books. They will give you much more information on a particular subject you might want to learn more about. You can find these books at your library and at on-line booksellers. You might also check with your school counselor. It's a good bet that she might have these on her shelf.

Chapter 1: Your Brain

Strauch, Barbara. *The Primal Teen: What the New Discoveries about the Teenage Brain Tell Us about Our Kids.* New York: Doubleday, 2003.

Chapter 2: Your Body

Madaras, Lynda. *What's Happening to My Body? Book for Boys.* New York: Newmarket Press, 2000.

Madaras, Lynda. *What's Happening to My Body? Book for Girls.* New York: Newmarket Press, 2000.

Richardson, Justin, and Mark A. Schuster. *Everything You Never Wanted Your Kids to Know about Sex, but Were Afraid They'd Ask: The Secrets to Surviving Your Child's Sexual Development from Birth to the Teens.* New York: Crown, 2003.

Chapter 3: Your Psychological Development

Thompson, Marcia. *Who Cares What I Think: American Teens Talk about Their Lives and Their Country.* Boston: Charles River Press, 1994.

Chapter 4: Your Craziness

Nelson, Richard E., Ph.D., and Judith Galas. *The Power to Prevent Suicide: A Guide for Helping Teens.* Minneapolis: Free Spirit Publishing, 1994.

Chapter 5: Your Culture

Burkett, Elinor. *Another Planet: A Year in the Life of a Suburban High School.* New York: Harper, 2002.

Murray, Jill. *But I Love Him: Protecting Your Daughter From Controlling, Abusive Relationships.* New York: Harper Collins, 2000.

Terkel, Susan Neiburg. *Finding Your Way: A Book about Sexual Ethics.* Danbury, CT: Franklin Watts, 1995.

Chapter 6: Your Parents

Bradley, Michael. *Yes, Your Teen is Crazy! Loving Your Kid Without Losing Your Mind.* Gig Harbor, WA: Harbor Press, 2002.

Packer, Alex, Ph.D. *Bringing Up Parents: The Teenager's Handbook.* Minneapolis: Free Spirit Publishing, 1993.

Chapter 7: Your Family

Velasquez, Gloria. *Maya's Divided World.* Houston: Arte Publico Press, 1995.

Chapter 8: Your Peers

Wiseman, Rosalind. *Queen Bees and Wannabes: Helping Your Daughter Survive Cliques, Gossip, Boyfriends, and Other Realities of Adolescence.* New York: Three Rivers Press, 2003.

Chapter 9: Your School

Burkett, Elinor. *Another Planet: A Year in the Life of a Suburban High School.* New York: Harper, 2002.

Riera, Mike. *Surviving High School.* Berkeley, CA: Celestial Arts Publishers, 1997.

Rubin, Nancy. *Ask Me if I Care: Voices from an American High School.* Berkeley: Ten Speed Press, 1994.

Part Three

Death

Digiulio, Robert, Ph.D., and Rachel Kranz. *Straight Talk about Death and Dying.* New York: Facts on File, Inc. 1995.

Krementz, Jill. *How It Feels When a Parent Dies.* New York: Knopf, 1988.

Drugs

Inaba, Darryl S. and William E. Cohen. *Uppers, Downers, All-Arounders: Physical and Mental Effects of Psycho-Active Drugs.* Ashland, OR: CNS Productions, 2000.

Pregnancy

Arthur, Shirley. *Surviving Teen Pregnancy: Your Choices, Dreams, and Decisions.* Buena Park, CA: Morning Glory Press, 1996.

Gravelle, Karen and Caputo, Leslie Peterson. *Teenage Fathers.* iUniverse.com, 2000.

Racism

Duvall, Lynn. *Respecting Our Differences: A Guide to Getting Along in a Changing World.* Minneapolis: Free Spirit Publishing, 1995.

Kukin, Susan. *Speaking Out: Teenagers Take on Sex, Race, and Identity.* New York: Putnam Publishing Group, 1993.

Sexual Differences

Heron, Ann. *Two Teenagers in Twenty: Writing by Gay and Lesbian Youth.* Los Angeles: Alyson Publications, 1995.

McNaught, Brian. *On Being Gay: Thoughts on Family, Faith, and Love.* New York: St. Martin's Press, 1989.

Various Issues

The American Academy of Child and Adolescent Psychiatry publishes "Facts for Families," single-page fact sheets that provide you (and your parents) with up-to-date information on subjects that concern you. You can find them online at www.aacap.org under "Publications," or contact them at

The American Academy of Child and Adolescent Psychiatry
3615 Wisconsin Ave., N.W.
Washington, DC 20016-3007
Phone 202-966-7300; FAX 202-966-2891

Index

About the Author

Dr. Michael Bradley grew up in Philadelphia where, he says, he barely survived his own adolescence. He tried being an officer in the U.S. Army, a disc jockey, and a lawyer before fate landed him in a job working with teenagers. To his amazement, he loved that job so much he went back to school to become a psychologist. In the thirty years since, Dr. Bradley has worked with all kinds of teens in all kinds of places, such as schools, jails, and community programs.

After writing his first book, *Yes, Your Teen Is Crazy!*, Dr Bradley received the Benjamin Franklin Award for *Best New Voice in Nonfiction.*

Dr. Bradley lives in suburban Philadelphia where he worries constantly that his own two kids might turn out like him.